# Liberating Hollywood

# Liberating Hollywood

## WOMEN DIRECTORS AND THE FEMINIST REFORM OF 1970S AMERICAN CINEMA

Maya Montañez Smukler

RUTGERS UNIVERSITY PRESS
*New Brunswick, Camden, and Newark, New Jersey, and London*

Library of Congress Cataloging-in-Publication Data

Names: Smukler, Maya Montanez, author.
Title: Liberating Hollywood : women directors and the feminist reform of 1970s American cinema / Maya Montanez Smukler.
Description: New Brunswick, New Jersey : Rutgers University Press, [2018] | Includes bibliographical references and index.
Identifiers: LCCN 2018018808| ISBN 9780813587486 (cloth) | ISBN 9780813587479 (pbk.)
Subjects: LCSH: Women motion picture producers and directors—United States. Women in the motion picture industry—United States—History—20th century. | Feminist films—United States—History and criticism. | Feminism and motion pictures.
Classification: LCC PN1995.9.W6 S638 2018 | DDC 791.43/6522—dc23
LC record available at https://lccn.loc.gov/2018018808

A British Cataloging-in-Publication record for this book is available from the British Library.



♾ The paper used in this publication meets the requirements of the American National Standard for Information Sciences—Permanence of Paper for Printed Library Materials, ANSI Z39.48-1992.

www.rutgersuniversitypress.org

Manufactured in the United States of America

*Dedicated to all the films that did not get made in the 1970s*

*and to all the women who tried their best to direct them.*

# CONTENTS

# Liberating Hollywood

# Introduction

On March 7, 2010, American filmmaker Kathryn Bigelow became the first woman to win an Academy Award for Best Director.[1] The film she directed, *The Hurt Locker,* also won an Oscar for Best Picture. Accepting the award, Bigelow described to the global audience how "this was the moment of a lifetime." The presentation of this award was a crowning moment with historical roots in Hollywood and American culture that reflected the breakthrough decade of the 1970s.

Hollywood icon Barbra Streisand presented the Oscar for Best Picture to Bigelow, who earned her MFA from the film program of Columbia University School of the Arts in 1981 and directed her first independent commercial picture, *The Loveless*, in 1982. Streisand had begun cultivating her ambition to direct in the 1970s before making her directorial debut with the studio-made film *Yentl* in 1983.[2] *Yentl* won awards for Best Comedy/Musical and Best Director at the 1984 Golden Globes, and in 1992, Streisand's second feature, *Prince of Tides,* was nominated for Best Director at the Directors Guild Awards and for Best Picture at the Academy Awards. Although her output as a director received some of the highest acclaim of any filmmaker working in Hollywood, Streisand was never nominated for Best Director at the Academy Awards.[3] The historical significance of the 2010 Best Director award for both Streisand and Bigelow was emphasized by the enthusiasm with which Streisand announced the award: "Well, the time has come, [pause] Kathryn Bigelow. Whoahoo!"

As the music swelled and Bigelow arrived at the podium, she could be heard saying to Streisand, "I am so honored. I am so honored," while Streisand, as she handed Bigelow the statue, enviously joked, "Can I hold this?"

In this exchange—reflecting Barbra Streisand's obvious disappointment in never having been recognized by the Academy Awards for her work as a director and the respect the two women displayed for each other's place in history—the legacy of American women directors was implicitly acknowledged on stage. As if this symbolism was not enough, as the two directors exited the stage the orchestra played Helen Reddy's 1975 women's liberation anthem, "I Am Woman." A clichéd but resonant soundtrack, the song linked Bigelow's award as a woman director to the feminist movement of the 1970s.

## Women Directors in 1970s Hollywood

The 1970s was a crucial decade for women directors working in Hollywood. The activism of the feminist movement during that decade, in particular the feminist reform efforts taking place within Hollywood's professional guilds—the Directors Guild of America (DGA), the Screen Actors Guild (SAG), and the Writers Guild of America (WGA)—led to an increase in the number of women directors making commercial feature films. *Liberating Hollywood* examines the relationship between the feminist movement and the film industry during the 1970s, specifically how the movement affected the hiring patterns and creative output of women directors working at that time. During the silent era, an estimated fifty-seven women were directing films.[4] In sharp contrast, from the mid-1930s through the mid-1960s, only two women filmmakers had careers as directors in Hollywood: Dorothy Arzner and Ida Lupino; in addition, between 1961 and 1966, two New York-based women, Shirley Clarke and Juleen Compton, were directing independent feature films outside of Hollywood (both are discussed in more detail in the prologue).[5] My research shows that, for the first time in almost forty years, the number of women directors began to increase beginning in 1967: between then and 1980, sixteen women made at least one feature film within the commercial U.S.-based film industry, either as part of the studio system or as independent filmmakers. These directors were Penny Allen, Karen Arthur, Anne

Bancroft (1931–2005), Joan Darling, Lee Grant, Barbara Loden (1932–1980), Elaine May, Barbara Peeters, Joan Rivers (1933–2014), Stephanie Rothman, Beverly Sebastian, Joan Micklin Silver, Joan Tewkesbury, Jane Wagner, Nancy Walker (1922–1992), and Claudia Weill (see the appendix for a list of their films).

*Liberating Hollywood* begins in the late 1960s, when a wide range of social movements and shifting cultural attitudes in the United States began to influence the film industry's approach to audience demographics, the content of its films, and its production practices, all of which affected women directors and their professional experiences throughout the 1970s. The study ends nearly two decades later with an examination of the landmark lawsuit filed in 1983 by the Directors Guild, at the behest of its Women's Steering Committee, on behalf of its female and minority members against Columbia Pictures and Warner Bros. for employment discrimination (*Directors Guild of America, Inc. v. Warner Brothers, Inc. and Columbia Pictures Industries, Inc.*).[6] This lawsuit serves as the symbolic culmination of more than a decade of feminist reform efforts within the film industry that affected women filmmakers, both directly and indirectly.

Within the time span of approximately 1966 to 1985, this study hones in on the years between 1970 and 1980 when each of these sixteen women (with the exception of Rothman and Sebastian who made their first movies in 1966 and 1967, respectively) directed her first feature film. These directors were not part of a cohesive group and in many instances did not know of one another. Rather, they are broadly connected by their gender, historical moment (the impact of second-wave feminism on commercial filmmaking during the 1970s in the United States), location, and a shared ambition to direct feature films. *Liberating Hollywood*'s focus is on the narrative films made by these directors that were intended for a commercial, revenue-generating marketplace and were screened in some form of movie theater for a ticket-buying audience. Although during the 1970s many women directors were working in documentary, experimental, or avant-garde filmmaking, I focus on commercial feature films, which I define as those that adhere to the regulatory standards set by the Motion Picture Association of America's letter rating system, specifically in terms of representations of sex and violence.[7] Pornography thus falls outside of *Liberation Hollywood*'s scope, thereby excluding the films of

Roberta Findlay. In a similar fashion, sexploitation cinema does not fit within this scope, and as a result the prolific, independent low-budget filmmaker Doris Wishman is not part of this study.[8]

Of the sixteen directors featured, some made only one picture during the decade, while others made as many as seven. Some directed television before directing movies; several worked almost exclusively in television *after* directing features. The manner in which their films were made and their career trajectories varied considerably. For example, some movies were produced or distributed by major studios, some were low-budget films made by minor studios, and others were independently produced and distributed by the filmmakers themselves.

The level of box office success achieved by their films also varied greatly. Some movies were successful on release, such as Joan Micklin Silver's directorial debut, the independent feature *Hester Street* (1975)—a period piece about Jewish immigrants coming to New York City in the 1890s. Made for an estimated $400,000, the picture was critically well received, earned approximately $5 million on its theatrical release, and garnered a Best Supporting Actress nomination for its star, newcomer Carol Kane.[9] In contrast, the studio-made *Moment by Moment* (1978, Universal), written and directed by Emmy winner Jane Wagner and starring two of the decade's most prominent performers, Lily Tomlin and John Travolta, in a May–December romance set in contemporary Malibu, was met with tepid reviews that reported audience walkouts.[10]

Not all of the directors profiled in this book began their careers in commercial filmmaking in Hollywood. Several started out in New York City as part of other artistic communities, such as improvisational comedy and documentary filmmaking. Some were performers or writers in film, television, or on stage before moving into the role of feature film director. While directing, many continued to shift between multiple careers, such as actress, writer, and producer. Frequently they combined their skills on individual projects. For example, Anne Bancroft—an Emmy, Oscar, and Tony Award–winning actress—starred in, wrote, and directed the film *Fatso* (1980, 20th Century-Fox); comedian Joan Rivers cowrote and directed *Rabbit Test* (1978), a film that she financed independently; and Stephanie Rothman directed and wrote or cowrote all seven of her feature films for the low-budget independent companies,

New World Pictures and Dimension Pictures. Half of these filmmakers, in spite of their best efforts, were only able to make one feature film during the 1970s: Barbara Loden self-produced and self-distributed *Wanda* (1970), and Joan Tewkesbury directed *Old Boyfriends* (1979, AVCO Embassy Pictures). Some who created bodies of work as directors in the 1970s found it impossible to continue to direct movies. After an acrimonious experience with Paramount Pictures on the film *Mikey & Nicky* (1976) that reinforced her reputation as a "difficult" director, Elaine May worked as a screenwriter and actress before directing her final film, *Ishtar*, in 1987.[11] In 1980 Barbara Peeters directed her fifth low-budget exploitation film, *Humanoids from the Deep*, after which she became an established television director of episodic, one-hour dramas. At the time Peeters had strategized that moving out of low-budget filmmaking and into television would lead to a career directing mainstream movies, but she found that, as a woman director, she was unable to make the transition from independent production to Hollywood and she has not made any additional features.[12]

All of the women who made feature films in the 1970s are white. That this is a white woman's history reflects the institutionalized gendered racism within the film and television industries during the 1960s and 1970s. African American men were able to gradually break through the white male-dominated directing ranks, at first in small numbers; yet they helmed more studio pictures, as well as profitable independent projects, than the white women who would follow them.[13] The first women of color to direct feature films began building their filmmaking careers during this era, but did not release their first features until later. For example, Julie Dash began making short films as a film student in the 1970s at the American Film Institute and UCLA; others, such as Maya Angelou (who is discussed in chapter 1), Kathleen Collins, and Jessie Maple, were then working as screenwriters, editors, and camerawomen. These filmmakers released their first features in the 1980s and 1990s: Jessie Maple, *Will* (1981, independently produced/distributed); Kathleen Collins, *Losing Ground* (1982, independently produced/distributed); Euzahan Palcy, *Dry White Season* (1989, Metro-Goldwyn-Mayer); Julie Dash, *Daughters of the Dust* (1991, American Playhouse/Kino International); and Maya Angelou, *Down on the Delta* (1998, Showtime Networks/Miramax Films).

## The Liberation of 1970s Hollywood

Still suffering from a postwar slump, the film industry in the 1960s and into the early 1970s was forced to reckon with the growth of a diverse and successful independent filmmaking community, the enduring dominance of television, and a changing audience demographic whose tastes were influenced by the many social movements of the era.[14] During these years, film culture in the United States thrived and its diversity increased, as the marketplace for non-studio-made pictures expanded, both inspiring a young generation of filmmakers and cultivating the tastes and purchasing power of a large youth audience. An influx of foreign films, with subject matter frequently contested by American film censors as being too explicit, screened in independent art house theaters; a variety of low-budget, independent exploitation films, or "B-movies," dominated drive-ins and grindhouse theaters, venues located in urban neighborhoods specializing in cheaply made genre pictures for inexpensive admission prices; and independent films, those made with neither studio nor big business financing, experimented with form and narrative conventions while utilizing grassroots modes of production, distribution, and exhibition.

In 1968 a new rating system by the Classification & Rating Administration (CARA) introduced lettered categories (G, PG, R, and X) to classify a film's suitability for certain audiences based on its content.[15] CARA, as an industry-created organization, allowed the studios to stay current with changing cultural tastes by creating a self-regulating classification method that sanctioned adult content in Hollywood films: the rating system enabled a range of "adult" content to be included in movies that ran the gamut of high-culture art cinema, low-budget exploitation pictures, and avant-garde films. The realization—achieved through the success of movies such as *Easy Rider* (1969), an independent production distributed by Columbia Pictures—that young directors might be those most adept at making films targeting the cash cow youth demographic, combined with CARA's evolving guidelines that allowed studio films to broaden their spectrum of "mature" subject matter, created a conducive set of circumstances for a new generation of Hollywood filmmakers.

These industry changes in audience demographics, modes of production, and marketplace regulation and distribution, as well as changing economic conditions, prompted the studios to take more chances on the next generation of directors. Journalist Mel Gussow, writing for the *New York Times*, summarized the status of Hollywood in 1970: "Hollywood—the old studio system—is dead, but movies as a medium have never been more alive. Doors once locked by tradition, unions or inertia are wide open. Film students are directing features. Playwrights are writing original screenplays, and they are not being ground into studio formulas. No subject is taboo. . . . Studios are no longer the only places where movies are made, financed and distributed. The movie industry has fragmented into a million places. Power is decentralized."[16]

These industry and cultural conditions fostered a popular and romantic historicization of 1970s Hollywood as an era of extraordinary potential for young filmmakers. In *Lost Illusions: American Cinema in the Shadow of Watergate and Vietnam 1970–1979*, David A. Cook describes this period as "a time in the history of . . . the [U.S. film] industry [when] almost anyone with talent and the will to do so could become a film director."[17] Yet, even though this period in film history may have been exceptional in the opportunities it provided for a new generation of filmmakers, the open door for "almost anyone" to enter the ranks and direct feature films was entered primarily by white men.

Frustrated by their failure to get hired within the industry, six female members of the Directors Guild—Susan Bay, Nell Cox, Joelle Dobrow, Dolores Ferraro, Victoria Hochberg, and Lynne Littman—formed the Guild's Women's Steering Committee at the end of the decade, in 1979 (see chapter 4 for an in-depth discussion of their activism). Determined to assess the current employment status of women directors, the group spent a year researching who had actually gotten hired in Hollywood during the past few decades. They discovered that, between 1949 and 1979, 7,332 feature films were made and released by major distributors, of which women had only directed 14, or 0.19 percent.[18] Soon after completing the group's initial data sweep, the Women's Steering Committee, with the support of the Directors Guild's executive staff, released these numbers to the media. The activism and persistence of those six women at the close of the 1970s spurred the Guild's late enculturation into the politics of employment justice, of which the national civil rights and women's movements had been at the foreground for years.

Yet in various ways, the feminist movement had been trying to raise Hollywood's political consciousness since the early 1970s. On screen, the women's movement and its objective of female autonomy were represented by characterizations and narrative themes in several kinds of movies, including large-budget studio films directed by men such as *Klute* (1971, Warner Bros., dir. Alan Pakula), *Alice Doesn't Live Here Anymore* (1974, Warner Bros., dir. Martin Scorsese), *Claudine* (1974, 20th Century-Fox, dir. John Berry), and *An Unmarried Woman* (1978, 20th Century-Fox, dir. Paul Mazursky). Off screen, female industry employees had organized networking groups. In 1973, Tichi Wilkerson Kassel, publisher of *The Hollywood Reporter* from 1962–1988, founded Women in Film, a nonprofit, nonpolitical organization, to create opportunities for women who were already established in the field of film and television to connect with one another.[19] In 1974 the American Film Institute, created in 1967 as an organization dedicated to the preservation of American film culture, formed the Directing Workshop for Women, a hands-on program that trained individual women to become film and television directors (see chapter 3).

While the Directors Guild did not make a concerted effort to address the low employment numbers of its female directors until 1979, between 1974 and 1976 both the Screen Actors Guild and the Writers Guild had conducted statistical surveys that explicitly documented the disenfranchisement of its women members. These efforts, spearheaded by the two organizations' individual Women's Committees, were reported on widely by the press: the WGA documented the low number of women writers working in film and television, and SAG called for improved—in both quantity and substance—roles for actresses (see chapter 1 for a discussion of the work of SAG's and WGA's Women's Committees). Although the DGA was slower than SAG and the WGA to organize within its membership ranks around issues of employment discrimination, it was its Women's Steering Committee that pressed the issue in court. On July 25, 1983, the DGA filed a class-action lawsuit with the U.S. District Court for the Central District of California against Warner Bros., and on December 21 a case against Columbia Pictures, for employment discrimination against its women and minority members. (Initially filed separately, eventually the two cases would be joined together as one suit by the judge.) On August 30, 1985, Judge Pamela Rymer ruled in favor of Columbia and

Warner Bros. and effectively against the DGA. The loss in court confirmed that, after a decade of attempts at feminist reform of the industry, there was no reliable legal recourse against discrimination based on sex and race, specifically with regard to the position of director. Yet despite the sexist hiring practices uncovered by the committee's research, more women were directing feature films throughout the 1970s, and that number would continue to grow slowly during the 1980s. Progress was so miniscule it could be perceived as regressive, but the very existence of these sixteen directors of feature films working at different times throughout the 1970s meant some women were able to break through the barriers to advancement. How they were able to do so is *Liberating Hollywood*'s central question.

## Women Directors in Hollywood: Guy Blaché to Bigelow

Kathryn Bigelow's 2010 win for Best Director, the first ever awarded to a woman, suggests that female directors have had a difficult relationship with Hollywood. Historically, however, women directors were not always such pariahs. During the silent film era, although they were by no means on parity with their male peers, a considerable number of women were making films. In 1896 Alice Guy, a twenty-three-year-old Frenchwoman, was one of the first filmmakers to develop techniques in narrative filmmaking while working as a secretary at the Gaumont Film Company in Paris. In 1907, Guy, by then married to Herbert Blaché, moved to the United States, and in 1910 she opened her state-of-the-art film studio Solax in New Jersey. Over the course of her career, Guy Blaché was involved in the making of about 600 short films, and she directed more than 20 feature-length pictures.[20] In early Hollywood, film production frequently took place in individual director units that were not supervised by company executives or a single producer. The "doubling in brass" tradition, borrowed from the theater, where above- and below-the-line employees performed double duty, created fluidity between jobs.[21] The leading lady might be in charge of hair, makeup, and costumes, and the actress might also be the picture's screenwriter. This system discouraged the establishment of labor hierarchies and the gender segregation associated with later stratifications in the studio system; women, as well as men, had opportunities to gain a broad range of experience, which was accepted as the norm. Lois Weber had her own movie studio and in 1916 was hired to direct Universal's biggest feature to date, *The Dumb Girl of Portici*. At the time she was ranked as one of the industry's top ten directors, along with D. W. Griffith and Thomas H. Ince.[22] Frances Marion, head writer for MGM, directed a handful of films, including *The Love Light* (1921), which starred her best friend Mary Pickford. Former actress Dorothy Davenport took up the megaphone after the death of her husband, famed actor Wallace Reid. As a tribute to her deceased spouse, Davenport was listed in her directorial credits as Mrs. Wallace Reid. Lillian Gish directed one feature starring her sister Dorothy; comedian Mabel Normand directed numerous movies, some including Charlie Chaplin; and Nell Shipman made independent action adventure films on location in the wilds of Idaho in which she performed all her own stunts.[23]

The cultural legitimacy that women had given to the film industry in the 1910s was supplanted by the end of the 1920s by financial legitimacy as dictated by masculinized Wall Street.[24] Production eventually became structured around the centralized producer system, which limited the flow of collaboration among crew positions. The establishment of craft unions further diminished women's employment opportunities by containing them within sex-typed jobs, such as secretaries and assistants, which wielded less creative and economic power. During the classic studio period, women were almost entirely locked out of directing films. From the mid-1930s through the late 1960s there was never more than one woman director at a time working in commercial films: Dorothy Arzner was employed as a studio director from 1927–1943, and Ida Lupino directed movies for her own independent production company between 1949 and 1953 before making her last and only studio-produced and distributed film, *The Trouble with Angels* for Columbia Pictures, in 1966.

By the late 1960s, coinciding with the mobilization of the feminist movement on a national level, a few more women were working as directors in the film industry. Stephanie Rothman was pursuing a master's degree from the University of Southern California's (USC) School of Cinematic Arts in 1964 when she met and began working as an assistant to the successful low-budget film director-producer Roger Corman. This was her entrée into writing and directing exploitation films, all of which she made in collaboration with her husband Charles Swartz. Rothman directed her first film, *Blood Bath,* also known as *Track of the Vampire,* in 1966. Director-producer-writer Beverly Sebastian collaborated with her husband, Ferd Sebastian, on several low-budget exploitation films, their first being *I Need* in 1967. Other filmmakers such as Joan Tewkesbury and Barbara Peeters began honing their directorial skills as students of theater and dance before moving into film production. Tewkesbury attended USC's School of Theater in 1958 and directed plays and acted in television commercials before working with director Robert Altman as the screenwriter for his films *Thieves Like Us* (1974) and *Nashville* (1975). She directed the feature film *Old Boyfriends* in 1979 before becoming a successful television writer-director-producer. Peeters attended the theater program at the Pasadena Playhouse in 1964. She began working in low-budget B-movies in the late 1960s and wrote and directed several films, some for Roger Corman's New World Productions, before becoming a prolific television director. She made her first film, *Just the Two of Us,* in 1970.

Crossover between the television and film industries was a significant factor in the careers of many of these women. Karen Arthur directed two independent feature films, *Legacy* (1974) and *Mafu Cage* (1978); in 1976 she began directing television shows as a way to earn a living while developing her film projects. Joan Darling and Nancy Walker were well-known actresses and television directors before they made feature films—Darling's *First Love* (1977) and Walker's *Can't Stop the Music* (1980)—after which they returned to television. Jane Wagner had already won two Emmy Awards for her work as a television writer with her creative and life partner Lily Tomlin before writing and directing her only feature film, *Moment by Moment* (1978). She then returned to television and the theater as a successful writer-producer. Academy and Emmy Award–winning actress Lee Grant made *Tell Me a Riddle* (1980) while continuing to act in film and television; after *Riddle,* she began a productive career as a director of documentaries made for television, in addition to directing scripted content. Joan Rivers was a popular comedian who appeared frequently on television and in successful one-woman comedy shows. In 1978 she cowrote and directed the film *Rabbit Test,* a comedy starring Billy Crystal as the first pregnant man.

Independent filmmakers, working outside of the studio system, came from various backgrounds to make feature films in the 1970s. Joan Micklin

Silver began writing and directing educational movies in the early 1970s. In 1975 she wrote and directed her first feature, *Hester Street*, a period piece about Jewish immigrants in the late 1800s. Her husband, Ray Silver, who worked in real estate, produced and distributed the film. Together, as independent filmmakers, they made several more pictures, eventually securing studio financing and distribution deals. Barbara Loden, a Tony Award–winning theater actress also known for her work in film and television, wrote, directed, produced, and starred in the independent film *Wanda*, which won the International Critic's Prize at the Venice Film Festival in 1970. Claudia Weill began her formative years on the East Coast making documentaries within the feminist filmmaking community. She financed her first feature, *Girlfriends*, through artist grants and grassroots fundraising. The picture was a success on the film festival circuit; its critical acclaim drew the attention of Warner Bros., which distributed the movie in 1978. Weill's second feature, *It's My Turn*, was made for Columbia Pictures in 1980.

As gleaned from this introductory sketch, these women's careers were diverse and, in many instances, different from each other. I describe these directors as a figurative "generation," because although they shared the same era professionally, they were of different ages: Nancy Walker, the oldest, was born in 1922; Claudia Weill was the youngest, born in 1947. I refer to them as a "group," although they did not work together or make films collectively: in fact, as mentioned, several of them did not even know each other. Instead of by age or acquaintance, they are "grouped" together by their mutual historical experience. Although the content of their work and how it might relate to the choices they made and the opportunities they were offered are discussed in my examination of their industry biographies, textual analysis is not the framework for the project as a whole. Instead, *Liberating Hollywood* privileges a comprehensive look at these individuals' biographies and filmographies as a way to investigate a crucial historical juncture during the 1970s when industrial and cultural factors led to the increase in the number of women directors, despite their continued marginalization. This is not a study of feminist filmmakers, although some of the directors profiled may identify as such; nor is it a study of feminist films, although some of the movies may be read as such. Rather, this book is an examination of the relationship between the feminist movement and the commercial film industry as it affected women directors. This is not a study of "women's films"[25]: it is a study of the women who made feature films in the 1970s.

## Straight from the Source's Mouth: Methodology and Materials

Scholarship on Hollywood during the 1960s and 1970s favors male filmmakers and is dominated by the auteur theory as an historical framework.[26] Academic studies of women directors in Hollywood during the 1970s tend to be sweeping histories of these filmmakers with generic scopes.[27] Women working in commercial cinema during this decade occupy an awkward place in feminist scholarship, which emphasizes noncommercial production communities that often rejected Hollywood conventions and production models and instead mobilized experimental, avant-garde, and documentary filmic modes, with a focus on European artists.[28] Somewhere in between these different approaches lie, in limbo, the women who made feature films in and around Hollywood during the 1970s. Their absence from the prevailing scholarship has also meant that these filmmakers are missing from archival collections. *Liberating Hollywood*'s methodological intervention literally gives a voice to its historical subject. The most personally rewarding components of my research are the substantial oral histories that I conducted with women directors and their colleagues during this era. Delving into material omitted for decades from the historical record, these interviews give *Liberating Hollywood* a unique perspective on 1970s American filmmaking. My long-form interviews complement existing oral history and interview collections that have been invaluable in assembling my subjects' biographies, including those in the Academy of Motion Picture Arts and Sciences Visual History Program, the Academy of Television Arts & Sciences Foundation's Archive of American Television, the American Film Institute's Harold Lloyd Master Seminar, the Directors Guild Visual Oral Histories, and UCLA's Center for Oral History Program.

Journalistic sources play a key role in *Liberating Hollywood*. Reporters such as Charles Champlin, Linda Gross, Mary B. Murphy, and Kevin

Thomas writing for the *Los Angeles Times*; Sue Cameron, Arthur Knight, and Will Tusher for the *Hollywood Reporter*; and Gene Moskowitz and David Robb for *Variety* were witnesses to the unfolding of these directors' careers and championed their work by paying special attention to their talents as filmmakers, while acknowledging the struggles they faced as women in often unfriendly territory. Molly Haskell and Marjorie Rosen came of age during these years as two of the most prolific and outspoken feminist film and cultural critics. In 1973 they published two of the first histories of women in Hollywood: Haskell's *From Reverence to Rape: The Treatment of Women in the Movies* and Rosen's *Popcorn Venus: Women, Movies, and the American Dream.* Both writers grappled with the influence of the women's movement, which was unfolding before them, on audiences, filmmakers, Hollywood, and sometimes even themselves.

Contemporary journalist-historians Rachel Abramowitz's *Is That a Gun in Your Pocket? Women's Experience of Power in Hollywood* (2000) and Mollie Gregory's *Women Who Run the Show: How a Brilliant and Creative New Generation of Women Stormed Hollywood: 1973–2000* (2002) are two of the most detailed books on women working in a variety of crafts in the film and television industry from the late 1960s through the early 2000s. Both authors' main source materials are the interviews they conducted with their subjects. And both books have been invaluable to this study for their sheer quantity of information on women working in the contemporary film and television industries—subject matter and individuals who are rarely privileged in academic or commercial film histories.

To understand the feminist activism within the professional unions—the DGA, SAG, and WGA—I relied not only on press coverage of their activities but also on the publications each produced. During these years, each guild published either an internal newsletter available to members only or a magazine for purchase by the public that served as a publicity mechanism for the organization and its members. While in-house documentation was not always easily accessible, the guilds' newsletters provided valuable insight both into their internal dialogues and the way they presented themselves to the public. In 2010, I reconstructed the 1983 DGA lawsuit in part by reviewing the complete court documents located at the National Archives at Riverside, located in Perris, California. In 2011, these five boxes of paper materials were deemed unimportant by the archive administration and destroyed without any electronic copies made. Except for what the attorneys involved in the suit may have retained, my research here is the most complete source material on the case.

To contextualize the historical relevance of this "generation" of filmmakers and the intricacies of their careers, *Liberating Hollywood* situates this group within the industrial, sociopolitical, and legal circumstances that created the momentum for change in the late 1960s and into the early 1980s necessary to boost the number of working women directors. The book is organized chronologically. Chapter 1 establishes the context for the debates over equal employment opportunities for women and minorities in Hollywood, examining first the government intervention by the Justice Department in 1969 and then the feminist activism taking place in the early 1970s by the professional guilds, SAG and the WGA. Chapter 2 profiles directors who were making films during the first part of the decade primarily in two independent film communities: the art house commercial feature and the low-budget exploitation film. Chapter 3 picks up the narrative from 1977 until 1980, examining Hollywood's trend of "New Woman" films and the way women directors during the second part of the decade were relegated, under various circumstances, to making films that perpetuated certain social perceptions of gender. Chapter 4 continues the discussion started in chapter 1 of feminist political action by historicizing the Women's Steering Committee of the Directors Guild and its fight against biased hiring practices that led to the 1983 class-action lawsuit it filed against Columbia Pictures and Warner Bros. for employment discrimination against its women and minority members.

The goal of *Liberating Hollywood* is neither to rewrite the history of American cinema during the 1970s nor to construct a separate history of women directors of commercial films during that period. Instead, this study is an *expansionist* and *integrationist* film history: my objective is to *expand* the existing historical narrative of the 1970s film industry and to then *integrate* within it the contribution of women directors during this period. These women have not yet been lost: many of their films are not widely available, but are accessible; many of these individuals are not privileged in film history, but they are still very much alive, in some cases still working and enthusiastic about contributing to the record of their historical legacy. Paltry numbers, of films and filmmakers, do not exclude subjects from my study, but rather qualify them. The "exception to the rule," the virtually absent, and the parenthetical are the main subjects of this book.

## History Looks toward the Present

The historic moment of Kathryn Bigelow as the first—and still only—woman in eighty-two years of Oscar history to win an Academy Award for Best Director underlines how the struggle for parity for women directors persists to this day. Rigorous discourse regarding Hollywood's lack of meaningful inclusion and representation—in front of and behind the camera—has dominated award shows and headlines over the past few years. The effectiveness of the #OscarsSoWhite campaign in 2015 in pushing the Academy to an almost immediate response—opening up its voting membership to more women and constituencies of color—demonstrates the power of social media as a tool of aggressive activism in infiltrating even the privileged and glamorous hierarchy of Hollywood. Earlier, in 2014, the vulnerability of the film industry was exposed by the Sony hack. It divulged, through illegal means, confidential information describing the company's business practices—including the pay gap between female and male executives and stars—thereby forcing Hollywood into a transparency that it had not prepared for. Incriminating emails revealed a culture of sexism and racism protected by corporate culture elitism; their content was disseminated by the press, social media platforms, and peer-to-peer file-sharing networks. The studio threatened lawsuits, but much of the stolen material had already been absorbed into the vacuum of the Internet. According to Martha Lauzen's annual report, "The Celluloid Ceiling," in 2017 women directed 11 percent of the top 250 films, a proportion that had never been exceeded for the preceding eighteen years.[29] In 2015, the American Civil Liberties Union requested state and federal officials to investigate discrimination against women directors. To date, these claims remain under investigation by the Equal Employment Opportunity Commission. In 2017, massive allegations of sexual harassment against men of power—studio executives, writers, directors, and performers—were made by hundreds of women and some men. The entertainment industry responded quickly by firing and suspending those accused. Against this contemporary landscape, *Liberating*

*Hollywood* provides an historical context for understanding how the continued fight for gender and racial equality in the media industry has its roots in the 1970s.

## Will You Last?

In the early 1980s, Joan Tewkesbury began developing a project she had written called *Saving the Rainbow,* about the period when Atlantic City was being demolished so that Donald Trump could rebuild it. "I loved the way Airstream trailers looked," Tewkesbury remembered. "So I envisioned this woman owned a trailer park of Airstream trailers that was right in the heart of—enough square feet of the mega real estate people who were trying to buy her out. And her thing was all about retired people, but her retired people would be Fred Astaire, Gene Kelly—you know all those good folks." Tewkesbury imagined Katharine Hepburn as the lead in this group cast of luminary Hollywood seniors. She secured a meeting with the legendary actress at her home in New York City to talk to her about her participation in the project. "So we talked and she said, 'I think this is a lovely idea, dear, but I don't do ensemble work,'" Tewkesbury laughed, remembering the conversation. "At the end of the meeting she looked at me and said, 'It's wonderful dear. Do you think you'll last?' and I said, 'What do you mean?' and she replied, 'As a director . . . I've worked with [Dorothy Arzner] and she would have been wonderful and do you think you'll have staying power.' I said, 'Yes, I will.' And then she said, 'Well that's good dear.'"[30]

Tewkesbury found humor in the story as she told it some thirty years later, but at the time she was speechless: "I thought, 'Huh.'" Indeed, how should one answer such a blunt question about one's professional fate, especially when asked by an iconic actress known as the embodiment of female independence? Tewkesbury has since made good on the answer she gave Katharine Hepburn: the challenges she faced as a film director in the 1970s gave way to a prolific career writing, directing, and producing television movies and episodic series for several decades.

Whereas Hepburn wondered in the 1980s about the survival rate of women directors, the question that drives *Liberating Hollywood* is how this generation of women directors emerged during the 1960s and 1970s. What compelled these filmmakers? Who encouraged them or, as the case may be, discouraged them? What makes them representative of the cultural zeitgeist of that era? How did the social and political momentum generated by the feminist movement infiltrate the seemingly impenetrable, sexist, and exclusive culture of the film and television industries? Linked together by their shared moment in history, industrial location, and their professional skills and aspirations, these women, their biographies, and the scope and challenges of their professional lives as directors of feature films reveal a history of filmmaking that deserves to be told.

# Prologue

## *Before There Was 1970s Hollywood, There Was New York City in the 1960s*

Before the women's movement began to infiltrate Hollywood in the 1970s—in the years between Ida Lupino's reign as the film industry's only woman director during the early 1950s and the hiring of Elaine May in 1968—there were two New York City-based, independent filmmakers: Shirley Clarke and Juleen Compton. Clarke, born in 1920 in New York City to a wealthy family, began her artistic work as a dancer. In the 1950s, using a Bolex camera she had been given as a wedding present, she began making short experimental films that explored the relationship between dance and cinema. Clarke and her peers—Willard Van Dyke, D. A. Pennebaker, Richard Leacock, and brothers David and Albert Maysles—were part of the New American Cinema movement that emerged in New York City during the late 1950s and 1960s. This group was influenced by the approach to realism and the tradition of social relevancy in American documentary, cinema verité, and the growing popularity of European cinema, such as Italian neorealism and the French New Wave films. In 1958 Clarke and her male peers established Filmmakers Inc., a co-op that served the production and networking needs of the independent film community in New York. Two years later, she and fellow filmmaker and film activist Jonas Mekas and some twenty other filmmakers founded the New American Cinema Group, an informal collective organized to encourage independent commercial films.[1]

In 1961 Clarke made the transition from short experimental films to feature endeavors when she directed *The Connection*, a screen adaption of a play by Jack Gelber. *The Connection* is a scripted and edited narrative film about a cinema verité crew making a documentary about a group of drug addicts awaiting their "connection." In its dialogue, characterization, and camera and editing work, the movie projects the Beat and jazz aesthetics that permeated popular culture at the time. The film is also provocative in its subject matter, portraying with some degree of realism the squalor of a junkie's tenement apartment filled with cockroaches and syringes. In a 1962 interview, Clarke explained her philosophy on filmmaking: "Right now, I'm revolting against the conventions of movies. Who says a film has to cost a million dollars, and be safe and innocuous enough to satisfy every 12-year-old in America? . . . I just want to pick up a camera and go out and shoot the world as it really is."[2] *The Connection*'s explicit depiction of a drug addict created conflict with the New York State censors, and the ensuing legal battles helped generate publicity for the picture.[3] The movie screened at the Cannes Film Festival in 1961, where it received much praise including the French Society of Film Authors award.[4] Writing for *Variety,* Gene Moskowitz described Clarke as a "tour de force," complimenting her picture as an example of how "America can make its own art films."[5]

Clarke's next project, *The Cool World* (1963), based on the novel by Warren Miller, is the story of an African American teenager faced with challenges associated with living in Harlem in the early 1960s: drugs, violence, and crime. Clarke, now divorced, collaborated on the project with her boyfriend Carl Lee—she as director, he as an actor—and they adapted the story together. Like her previous work, the film was independently produced, financed, and distributed. Praised for its authenticity, Clarke's approach continued to be informed by issues of realism; the film was rooted in a cinema verité tradition, but in a fictional narrative form marketable for a commercial release. The topicality of its subject—the impact of urbanization on race, class, and young people—and its being filmed on location in New York City, with a cast of predominantly nonprofessional actors and accompanied by a jazz soundtrack, continued to place Clarke's cinematic style within contemporary bohemian culture. *The Cool World* had a theatrical release in New York City and showed in some cities around the country; it screened at the Venice Film Festival in 1963.

By the end of the 1960s, the camaraderie experienced during the formative years of the New American Cinema movement had begun to dissipate. An innovator of independent filmmaking that served as an alternative to mainstream cinema, Clarke came to want the greater financial sustainability and access to a broader audience that Hollywood made possible. In the mid-1970s the filmmaker recalled an economic epiphany she had after making *The Cool World*: "I never thought about the money situation until, one day, I realized there *was* a situation: I had made two successful films and wasn't able to get money to do another."[6] In 1968 Clarke came to Los Angeles to play a version of herself in Agnès Varda's *Lion's Love*, a fictional film about a New York independent filmmaker trying to make a movie in Hollywood. By 1975, Clarke was living out that movie, as she actively strove to make films in Hollywood. That year the New Yorker shared her experience of being a woman in Hollywood with an audience of students at the American Film Institute: "People ask me why I haven't made Hollywood films. I reply, 'If I were a man, I might have tried to be Orson Welles.' But, as a woman and an artist, it's impossible. Producers think of us in childlike terms, as cute, or sweet, or cunning. During a meeting it's always 'honey' or 'sweetheart' . . . they don't take us seriously."[7] Lodged between industry sexism and the different value systems underlying Hollywood's (profit-making entertainment) and New York's (the artist as filmmaker) approach to filmmaking, she was frustrated by the experience.

Clarke acknowledged that she was a latecomer to the women's movement and the perspective it might have engendered for women directors—both in their work and their efforts *to* work. After reflecting on her experience of being part of Varda's film, she became involved in the feminist movement. "I became active in women's groups and found out where other women were coming from. Before, I didn't even know other women filmmakers." Although her formative years occurred during a period of radical transformation for cinema, Clarke recalled the detachment she had experienced during that time:

> As I got more into the women's movement, I realized how I had let myself be brainwashed. I never felt my films were as worthy as men's, and I never felt women were as important. For years I'd felt like an outsider so I identified with the problems of minority groups. I used

Fig. 1. Shirley Clarke in *Lions Love (. . . and Lies)* (dir. Agnès Varda, 1969)

> all kinds of standins [*sic*] for me in my films because I didn't think anyone was interested in my personal life, as a woman. I thought it was more important to be some kind of goddamned junkie who felt alienated rather than to say I am an alienated woman who doesn't feel part of the work and who wants in.[8]

Clarke was a pre-liberationist. Her self-critique is harsh, because the feminist movement was still young and inaccessible enough that Clarke was not able to benefit from its ideology, language, and peers to help comprehend, in a cultural context, her experience as a woman. The majority of the directors I interviewed for this project spoke of their admiration for Shirley Clarke, even before I could ask them about her. Her career may not have reached its full potential, but the next generation repeatedly acknowledged the importance of her work. Nell Cox, who began her career working for Leacock, Pennebaker, and the Maysles brothers in the mid-1960s, described Clarke as an "extraordinary woman." "It was so heartbreaking that she could not get anywhere [after moving to Hollywood]," recalled Cox. "She said she would scream and holler and practically faint on the floor and grovel and they wouldn't hire her after all those wonderful features that she made."[9] Barbara Peeters remembered meeting the director in the early 1970s at the Canadian Women's Film Festival, at which Peeters's low-budget biker film, *Bury Me an Angel*, was screening with Clarke's *Portrait of Jason*, her documentary released in 1967. Worried that her exploitation picture might be out of place at such a serious feminist event, Peeters found solace with Clarke and the actress Viva. "We all ended up in the balcony with a pint of gin!" she recalled.[10]

Clarke continued making films, but was never able to do another narrative feature. Instead, she shifted her focus to documentaries. Collaborating with Robert Hughes, together they made *Robert Frost: A Quarrel with the World* (1964), which won the Academy Award for Best Documentary Feature; she followed that with *Portrait of Jason* (1967) and *Ornette: Made in America* (1985). In 1978 she bought the rights to Joan Didion's novel *A Book of Common Prayer*, but claimed that "no studio considered it possible to turn the book into a film."[11] She was never able to produce the project independently. Always an innovator, Clarke had begun to work with video in the early 1970s; in the 1970s and 1980s she taught film and videomaking at UCLA. She died in 1997.[12]

Unlike Shirley Clarke, Juleen Compton did not begin her career in the avant-garde film world of 1950s New York. Instead, she cut her teeth as an actress in the city's equally innovative theater community for a decade before she would write, produce, and direct two independent feature films, one in Greece—*Stranded* (1964)—in which she also starred, and the other in the United States: *The Plastic Dome of Norma Jean* (1966). In 1988 she made her last film, *Buckeye and Blue*.

Compton was born in 1933 in Phoenix, Arizona. Her father left the family when she was a child, and her mother married her stepfather, a lawyer and prominent member of the Mormon community, when she was around eight years old. "I was a real little Mormon girl," recalled Compton affectionately of her childhood in Phoenix. "[I was] taught to be polite—'a penny saved is a penny earned,' 'to be seen and not heard'—real Americana ethics of that period," she laughed. "To *defy* the church, because we went to church three times a week, when I was about fourteen I went to the corner drugstore and had a cup of coffee, because Mormons don't drink coffee."[13]

Compton's mother, Julia, encouraged her daughter from a young age to pursue her interests and to define her self-identity on her own terms. Julia had aspired to be a doctor, but as a woman and a mother of three during the Depression, her personal goals were unrealistic within the expectations of her generation. She became a high school home economics teacher and eventually completed a doctorate in child psychology. Julia was not shocked by her daughter's precociousness, a trait that Compton exhibited at an early age. When Compton, still in grade school, questioned the existence of God, her mother explained, "Well darling, everybody worships in their own way." "She was very philosophical about it," said Compton. "She was a *really* extraordinary and wise woman." Julia's advice to her daughter was to "decide what you want. And if you try hard enough and long enough, you'll get it." Compton smiled while remembering her mother. "And then later in life she said to me, 'I was very, very young when I told you that. I should have said, 'within your limitations.'"[14]

Compton, with her mother's continued encouragement, moved to New York City by herself when she was seventeen to study ballet, but was informed soon after her arrival of her inadequacies. "I got there and I went to a line up for an audition, and they said, 'You can't be a ballet dancer, you're too little,'" remembered Compton of her first weeks in New York City. "I was 5-foot-2. [George] Balanchine liked girls to be at least 5-foot-8 or 5-foot-9."[15] Abandoning her aspirations to be a dancer, she soon settled into the role of a popular ingénue in New York's theater community. During her first year in New York she was cast as Little Red Riding Hood in a Children's World Theatre's production, playing opposite Jason Robards as the Wolf. Other roles followed: in 1955, she played the maid in the Fourth Street Theatre's production of *The Cherry Orchard*; in 1956 she was hired by Margo Jones's theater company in Dallas for its winter stock company; and in 1957 she costarred with Roddy McDowall and Zero Mostel in the short-lived Broadway production of *Good as Gold*.[16]

During the 1950s Compton juggled two careers—one as an ingénue on the stage and the other as an emerging real estate magnate. In the early 1950s, a friend had introduced her to the prominent real estate developer Norman Winston. Winston became an important mentor to the young woman, bringing her into the field of interior and exterior design where she excelled as a colorist (an expert on color design). By 1955 she had established herself in this profession, in part by working on a government contract to redesign military bases in Dayton, Ohio, and Limestone, Maine.[17] Meanwhile, as part of the tight-knit theater community in New York City, she was close friends with playwright Clifford Odets and stud-

Fig. 2. Gary Collins and Juleen Compton in *Stranded* (UCLA Film & Television Archive)

ied acting with Lee Strasberg; her teacher recommended that she take acting classes with Harold Clurman, theater director, critic, and cofounder of The Group Theatre. In 1961 Compton and Clurman were married.[18] Eventually, Compton came to understand her limits as an actress: "I realized, 'I'll never be a leading lady.' I didn't have this big voice. I wasn't tall. So I thought, 'You know what, I want to direct. Forget about acting.'"[19]

In contrast to her acting career, her work in interior design and real estate was expanding. In 1961 Compton purchased a four-story red brick school building in Greenwich Village for $256,000 and invested another $250,000 in transforming it into the Village Centre, a theater multiplex housing four stages and a theater school.[20] Her success in real estate and as a colorist provided her with the financial resources for her next artistic venture: directing movies.

In 1964 Juleen Compton was in production on her first independent feature film, *Stranded*. She wrote, directed, produced, and starred in the picture, which was filmed primarily in Greece. The filmmaker had made her first trip to Paris in 1950 and since then had traveled frequently to Europe, where she would eventually own real estate and live part-time.

*Stranded* is her autobiographical story of a young American woman (played by Compton) traveling through Greece with her American lover (Gary Collins) and her gay, French best friend (Gian Pietro Calasso). Shot in multiple European locations, Compton used a Greek crew and completed postproduction in Paris. The film screened at the Cannes Film Festival in 1965 and had a theatrical run in Paris.[21]

What is surprising about *Stranded* is the freedom that Compton's protagonist, Raina, enjoys throughout the movie. Reporting for *Variety* from Paris two months before the Cannes Film Festival, Gene Moskowitz described Compton's character in the film as a "heroine [that] may get caught up in some spicy and even equivocal goings on in Europe, but has a buoyant morality of her own that keeps her a truly innocent character and gives what she hopes is a zest to her film without pontificating or moralizing."[22] Raina partakes in several love affairs, travels around Europe following her own whims and at her own expense, and rejects marriage offers for no other reason than that she likes her life the way it is. Compton, as writer-director, never makes her onscreen alter ego suffer the punishments often imposed on similar types of female characters in films during this era: Raina's sexual freedom is neither stigmatized as promiscuity nor punished by sexual assault, nor is her female agency contained through marriage. Compton's drive to make her first movie without any formal filmmaking training was similar to Raina's unrestrained curiosity and confidence in pursuing her interests and living life on her own terms. The filmmaker recalled that she made the picture for less than $300,000, investing her own monies into the project. "I acted in my first movie because I thought, 'That's how I'll get into movies. I'll make my own movies and then I'll make movies in Hollywood.'"[23]

In 1966 Compton returned to the United States to make her second feature, *The Plastic Dome of Norma Jean*. Written and directed by Compton and coproduced with Stuart Murphy, the film features a clairvoyant teenage girl, played by Sharon Henesy, who is taken advantage of by a boy band fashioned after the Beatles when they exploit her powers as part of a hoax religious revival. Filmed in the Ozarks, it had a cast of young and unknown actors (twenty-five-year-old Sam Waterston costars in his first film appearance), and included a musical score by the then already accomplished French composer Michel Legrand. The narrative's focus on the struggle of a teenage girl to resist romantic temptation and manipulation and to assert control over her psychic powers presents pre-liberation themes about female agency that were rarely portrayed then on screen. Stylistically accomplished, the movie is an impressive example of independent feature filmmaking during the mid-1960s. Created outside an established production community, such as Shirley Clarke's and Jonas Mekas's New American Cinema Group, Compton worked with a small cast and crew and self-financed the film with funds generated by her lucrative career in real estate, as was the case with *Stranded. The Plastic Dome of Norma Jean* screened at a small number of film festivals, including the San Francisco International Film Festival and at Cannes as part of the "Third International Female Week," where it was given an award for best picture in that series, but like *Stranded*, it did not have a wide theatrical release in the United States.[24]

During these years, Compton continued to thrive in her real estate and interior design endeavors. In addition to the Village Theatre project, by the 1970s she also owned the 72nd Street East [movie] Theatre in Manhattan.[25] In 1970 the *New York Times* profiled her new eight-room "duplex with a two-story-high living room in a fine old building in the Sixties on Lexington Avenue" and described Compton as "an actress who has dabbled successfully in real estate and who has now turned to directing movies." At the time she also owned an apartment in Paris on the Rue de la Sourdiere, and as she explained to the reporter, "I'd found I was spending at least half of my time in Europe. I made my first movie, *Stranded*, in Greece—and so it seemed sensible to buy a place in Paris. . . . But of course I wanted to have a home in New York, too."[26]

Juleen Compton, a successful businesswoman with homes in New York and Paris, was able to self-finance her low-budget independent art house films without funding from Hollywood or support from established independent filmmaking communities. However, the ability to finance her own movies ultimately diminished her legacy. Self-financing meant there were no investors to pay back, and therefore there was no impetus to obtain a wide distribution for her films. Lacking a theatrical release, her work was not widely reviewed in the press or industry trade papers; without a distributor multiple prints of her movies were not made and circulated, greatly limiting both awareness of her work and access to her materials (film prints and paper documents). In 2013, looking back on her years making independent films, Compton felt that what she had needed but lacked was a strong producer to take over once she completed the project. What most excited her and what she was so good at was the making of films, but the next stage, selling them to a distributor and seeking out an audience, did not appeal to her.

Yet Compton did want to make films in Hollywood. She moved to Los Angeles and in 1974 was accepted into the American Film Institute's pilot year of the Directing Workshop for Women (DWW). During that year, Compton and DWW cofounder Jan Haag became friends, and later Compton hosted a networking and fundraising lunch for Haag and the DWW. Haag later recalled her vibrancy and many talents:

> [Compton], a self-made millionaire, had the most delightful house in Bel Air . . . . Before I met her, she had also been invited by Andre Malraux, then Minister of Culture in France, to be his official castle-restorer because she had flawless taste and loved to live around lumber and flying plaster dust. She declined the honor re [*sic*] the castles and had recently moved to the City of the Angels to, again, try her hand at movies. She was brilliant, witty and had infinite energy.[27]

Compton had been advised that the best way to get the opportunity to direct films in Hollywood was to start as a screenwriter. Compton wrote the script for the NBC television movie *The Virginia Hill Story*, which aired in 1974, about gangster Bugsy Siegel's girlfriend, Virginia Hill. Directed by Joel Schumacher, the broadcast was praised by Kevin Thomas of the *Los Angeles Times*, who called it a "good punchy melodrama."[28] In 1975 Mary Murphy's *Los Angeles Times* column, "Movie Call Sheet," which reported on scheduled productions and film releases, noted, "Juleen Compton's story of a real estate saleswoman torn between romantic fantasy and personal independence in Southern California, called 'Open House', will be made by AIP in association with Spangler, Spangler & Sons Pictures. Compton is executive producer."[29] According to Compton, the film was made into a television movie, but she ultimately had nothing to do with it.

Coming of age in the 1950s, Compton found herself in a unique position. Often the only young woman in a group of established older men, they looked at her in a paternal way, acting as guardians and mentors. Contributing to the way she was received, Compton is petite, a physical attribute that served her well during her early career in theater. "Because I was so little—I weighed 103—and I looked so young—when I was seventeen I was playing Little Red Riding Hood so I looked like a child. . . . I didn't know anything about women's lib, because women's lib hadn't happened yet and I was just treated like this little, strange creature." As the ingénue playing younger characters, she would get a call backstage from the army base in Dayton, Ohio, to discuss the color design she was overseeing. "It was a paradox," laughed Compton.[30]

These circumstances coalesced with Compton's already profound, at a young age, understanding of business and her drive for creative expression, which had begun being nurtured in her childhood. But where being an oddity had been a positive experience during the 1950s, when Compton arrived in Hollywood, against the backdrop of second-wave feminism, with a body of work in theater, film, and business, she found herself as the odd woman out. Compton was a friend of studio executive John Calley. The two had known each other in New York. By the time she moved to Los Angeles in the early 1970s, Calley was an executive at Warner Bros. When Compton went to her old friend looking for work, she found that her credentials added up to nothing. Calley told her, "Look, I'll just level with you, I've got guys working here that have been directing shit for ten years waiting until they got a chance to direct. A small film comes up. I can't suddenly bring in a total stranger, somebody who has never stood in line," said the studio executive, defending himself. "I run a studio. I couldn't run it if I ran it like that." Remembering the conversation forty years later, Compton was still unconvinced by his defense. "Well, that was *his* story."[31]

Calley's advice to Compton was to "make yourself as a hot writer, and when you become a hot writer then you demand directing it." For many years during the 1970s she was successful in selling her scripts, but the experience did not yield the professional results she had hoped for, and creatively Compton found the process repellent. She was pigeonholed in a manner that would become common for many women directors in the 1970s discussed in this book. She later recalled that television and studio executives would advise her, "'Oh you're a woman writer. Write a women's piece of trash. I wrote some *wonderful* things, but they would never do them. I once said to the executives: 'Why do you buy them if you're never going to do them?' They said, 'We don't want anyone else to do them. Keep them off the market.'"[32]

Similar to the way Compton found that her professional background served as an obstacle in her pursuit of a career in 1970s Hollywood, feminists found her achievements during the 1950s and early 1960s off-putting as well. After moving to Los Angeles, she recalled, "when I would go to these women's lib meetings they would say, 'yes, but you're the loophole case. [You are] the one who got through.'" Feminists saw Compton, and her accomplishments of the previous decades, as an exception to the struggle that women were facing in Hollywood then. When she made *Stranded* and *The Plastic Dome of Norma Jean*, "it was a time [during the 1950s and early 1960s] before women were a threat, before women were an army," she explained in 2013. "I was just someone wandering out in the battlefield, but the army [second-wave feminism] hadn't been organized." Laughing at how having made two feature films before arriving in Hollywood's hostile territory alienated her from "women's libbers," "Once the army had been organized, I was a deserter and that was a totally different story."[33]

Feminists may not have known where to place Compton as a "loophole" case in their fight for equality in Hollywood, but the men running the film industry were clear: they did not see her accomplishments as assets worthy of investment. Before second-wave feminism established itself as a powerful movement that protested the ways in which women were disenfranchised by longstanding social beliefs regarding gender and the political systems designed to reinforce those attitudes, Compton as a talented and ambitious young woman was an oddity worth nurturing. But in the 1970s for John Calley or any other studio executive or established producer working in the male-dominated film industry, to cultivate a female talent would have seemed disloyal to the other men in line. For Compton, Clarke, and the women featured in this study, *how* to get into that line would be one of their biggest challenges.

In 1988 Compton made one last feature film, *Buckeye and Blue*, an action-filled Western about a young woman outlaw, which she wrote and directed under the name J. C. Compton because she wanted to maintain gender ambiguity. It was independently produced, but this time the filmmaker had a distributor, Academy Entertainment. The experience became a negative one when the distributor made her change the ending to make it less feminist. Buckeye, the film's female protagonist, undergoes a process of profound self-discovery throughout the narrative, as she gains autonomy and power both as the leader of a gang of bank robbers and with regard to her idol and love interest, the outlaw Blue Duck Harris. Compton had initially intended her script to end with Buckeye choosing to continue the "quest" of self-discovery rather than forgoing her independence in order to become part of a romantic couple. Instead the distributor forced the filmmaker to alter the ending: in the final cut, Buckeye wakes up from sleep during which she had dreamt all her adventures and accomplishments.

Following this disappointing experience, Compton decided to leave Hollywood after close to twenty years of trying to make a career for herself within the film industry. She cited profound self-preservation as the reason for the move:

> I didn't want to be tough. I didn't want to sell my soul to the devil for an armor. I liked my soul and if I had to forfeit it for an armor, no reward would have been great enough. A reward to me was to *realize* yourself, not sell yourself. How can you realize yourself to sell yourself? It's a contradiction in terms. That's why I say to win is to lose and I left Hollywood. I just couldn't see myself as a bitter old woman living in a Bel Air mansion.[34]

Compton returned to New York City where she opened the off-Broadway theater company, Century Center for the Performing Arts, and served as its artistic director for the next decade. In the early 2000s she and her husband, Nicholas Wentworth, established a private foundation, the Century Arts Foundation, which provides financial support to a variety of arts organizations.

In 2017, newly restored prints of both *Stranded* and *The Plastic Dome of Norma Jean* premiered at the UCLA Film and Television Archive's Festival of Preservation. Compton and Wentworth had worked with the Archive to preserve all three of her feature films, which are now part of the institution's permanent collection.

A transnational professional in several fields, Juleen Compton spent her formative years as an artist in New York City during the 1950s and early 1960s. Her work in theater and her success in real estate and design informed her filmmaking that took place outside of Hollywood's stylistic conventions and modes of production. In this way, Compton can be compared to Shirley Clarke. Both women belonged to burgeoning New York artistic communities that valued the exploration of realism in films through performances, visual style, and production methods that were made more versatile by the use of portable equipment and smaller budgets. Compton fared better in Hollywood than Clarke, writing two television movies and writing-directing an independent feature. However, her inability to continue her career in the entertainment industry in a way that met her expectations as an artist might suggest that the two women who shared a New York—and for Compton, a European—independent filmmaking sensibility could not embrace nor be embraced by Hollywood. The bodies of work that Clarke and Compton produced demonstrate what was possible for women directors to create, independently and thousands of miles away from Hollywood, before there was a social movement in which to contextualize their experience as filmmakers in terms of gender. These two women are the precursors to the next generation of filmmakers who arrived ambitious and ready to work in a film industry that was unwilling to admit them, but that in the face of feminism would be forced to defend itself.

# 1

# Feminist Reform Comes to Hollywood

## *New Hollywood, Old Sexism*

Writing for *Ms.* in 1977, film critic and historian Marjorie Rosen reflected on the status of women directors at the time: "A couple of years ago women filmmakers were closet movie directors. Their energy and numbers were in the East, their focus was on documentaries and personal revelations. For them, 'film' meant an alternative vision to the drivel about earthquakes, sharks, and homoerotic gangbusters passing for what we commonly call 'movies' . . . but [the film industry] seems to be the ironic center for women who want to be, yes—directors."[1] By identifying this new crop of directors as bound for Hollywood, Rosen recognized their interest and potential to be part of the creative and economic power that defined Hollywood. To acknowledge these women was to confront their absence in male-centric Hollywood and to challenge the popular notion held by many in the film industry that women were not cut out for the job of director. Rosen drew an important distinction between the "personal-revelation" filmmakers from the "East" [Coast]—code for the feminist, counter-cinema filmmaking that flourished during the era—and the commercial aspirations of women coming out of the Hollywood director "closet." By differentiating between the two kinds of filmmakers, the author made a significant point that not all women directors are the same, nor should it be assumed that they are. Also significant was Rosen's assertion that not only were there women skilled and ambitious enough to thrive in Hollywood but also that they wanted a part in profit-making cinema.

The years 1977 and 1978 were pivotal for women directors in Hollywood. For the first time since the 1910s, they appeared as a critical mass—if but a small one. The number of women directors did not rival that of their male peers by any means, but collectively the handful of women filmmakers indicated a measure of progress while simultaneously drawing attention to the continued and significant gender gap within the industry. By 1976, Karen Arthur, Barbara Loden, and Joan Micklin Silver had each made one film; Elaine May and Barbara Peeters, three; Stephanie Rothman, seven (two completed in 1966 and in 1967); and Beverly Sebastian, five (one completed in 1967). In 1977, Micklin Silver completed her second feature and Joan Darling her first. In 1978, Penny Allen, Joan Rivers, Jane Wagner, and Claudia Weill released their first films, and Peeters completed her fourth. Between 1970 and 1978, twenty-five films were made by a total of twelve female directors. These twenty-five films made up 0.6 percent of the 4,149 films released between 1970 and 1978 in the United States that were rated by the Motion Picture Association of America (MPAA).[2]

As the number of women directors increased for the first time in four decades, debates regarding power, authority, and gender, both behind the camera and on-screen, circulated in the entertainment industry. In 1978, Verna Fields, an Academy Award-winning film editor who was then the vice president of production at Universal, predicted, "The worst thing that could happen to a woman director, even at this point, is that she should have trouble on the set, go over budget, over schedule, that kind of nonsense. I think it would be very easy for a lot of people to blame it on the fact that she had no control—that she didn't shoot well that day because she had her period."[3] Field was quick to identify a myth that many resisting the inevitable change taking place in Hollywood often raised: the belief that women's physiology made them ill-suited for the job of film director. Estrogen made women too docile to command a movie and too irrational to handle the responsibility. Such detractors believed that women were innately conditioned to nurture, based on their biological ability to have children. This "female" quality was considered contrary to the "masculine" competitive drive essential to making it in Hollywood.

According to this idea, if women were controlled by their biology, ultimately it would take over and derail their ambition, taking down along with it a movie's budget and production schedule. Male directors, critically but affectionately described as "movie brats," would make famous the 1970s film era with their excessive behavior that on numerous occasions resulted in productions that notoriously went over budget—in many ways, that conduct was condoned by the studio executives who oversaw those budgets.[4] For the rising number of women directors attempting to enter the motion picture workforce during this time, a double standard was firmly in place.

Speaking candidly in the *Los Angeles Times* in 1978, director Nell Cox attested to the reality of gender-focused hostility: "I've had studio executives look me right in the eye and say there are no women directors because there are no women qualified—and I've been directing films for 18 years and done a feature."[5] In the 1960s, Cox began her career as a prolific documentarian as part of the New York City cinema verité movement before making the transition to narrative filmmaking as writer-director of the feature film *Liza's Pioneer Diary* (1976) for the PBS broadcast series *Visions*. In the mid-1970s, she relocated to Hollywood and started writing and directing episodic television, working on network shows such as *The Waltons* and *M*A*S*H*. The studio executives' deliberate disregard of Cox and the ease with which they made statements similar to the one cited by her typified the industry's belief system that kept women—in spite of and, more often, because of their experience and qualifications—from positions with creative and economic power.

Long-standing cultural perceptions of how women and men act when in positions of power—women are nurturing and subservient, and therefore unqualified, men are domineering and confident—shaped attitudes in the film industry, providing another layer of resistance that women directors would need to trudge through. "The director is a papa figure," observed Fay Kanin, the award-winning screenwriter-producer for film and television, who was president of the Academy of Motion Picture Arts and Sciences from 1979–1983. "We were always told women couldn't exercise authority over a bunch of men. It's nonsense, of course. Some women are lousy at authority. But then, so are some men."[6]

In a 1979 interview conducted before an audience at the American Film Institute, filmmaker Joan Micklin Silver refuted the assumption that women lacked the necessary gumption to succeed in Hollywood. By this point in her career Micklin Silver had made two films in collaboration with her husband-producer, Ray Silver: *Hester Street* (1975) and *Between the Lines* (1977); both were independently financed and distributed by the couple. At the time of the interview, her third feature and first studio project, *Chilly Scenes of Winter* (United Artists, 1979), had just been released. "I'm sure lots of people quit because it is just too damn hard," she offered, describing her personal experience in making films as something common to both women and men. "It is. It's terrible," confessed Micklin Silver. "You have to lean into it all the time. . . . You have to push at it and push at it. It's incredibly hard. But it's such a thrill to do it. I mean, to make a movie is so worth it. It's so worth every bit of it."[7] As the mother of three daughters and collaborator with her husband on her professional endeavors, Micklin Silver devoted herself to both family and filmmaking: meeting the "terrible" challenge of making movies was the motivation that helped her stay the course.

Joanna Lee (1931–2003) echoed Micklin Silver's work ethic with equal gusto. Interviews with Lee, a successful television writer-producer-director, almost always described her striking looks. In 1978, she joked how, early in her career, she used assumptions about her appearance to gain access for her work. "I used to write simple, mindless sitcom [*sic*]. I was very 'cute.' So they said, 'Let's hire her, I hear she's got a great pair of legs.' What did I care? I would've worn a G-string as long as I had four good ideas in my briefcase and I'd sell one before I left the office."[8] Quick to make light of the industry's notorious reputation for demanding sex from women as collateral for employment, Lee did not sacrifice her professionalism or her personal integrity. "I was always very prepared. I always dressed terrific, looking fancy but acting *very* straight. And I worked six days a week for ten years. I see people waiting for things to be given to them; well, I broke my ass."[9] Perseverance and hard work were required for anyone—female or male—determined to succeed in the industry.

Lee won an Emmy in 1974 for Best Writing in Drama for the *Waltons* episode "The Thanksgiving Story." In addition to her success with episodic series, in the 1970s and 1980s she excelled in the television movie format, where she frequently created programming focused on social issues such as divorce and teen pregnancy. In her 1999 autobiography,

*A Difficult Woman in Hollywood*, she offers the reader her mantra for achieving success in the entertainment business: "So, how do you become a producer in Hollywood? Simple. Have a vision. Have guts. And be willing to risk everything."[10] Lee was cognizant of what was required to compete in the exclusive, cutthroat media industry. Her success and preparedness to "risk everything" belied sexist attitudes about women not having the innate tenacity to thrive in Hollywood. She was also aware that her gender could function as both an asset, in the most superficial way ("femaleness" as employment currency), and as a detriment (a limited and mostly false currency), suggesting a complexity to being a woman in Hollywood.

Lee wrote, directed and starred, with her young son, Christopher Ciampa, in *A Pocket Filled with Dreams* (1976), the only feature film she directed; it was independently financed and filmed in Greece. There is little material on Lee's film, other than a short chapter in her memoir.[11] *A Pocket Filled with Dreams* was invited to be screened at the Cannes Film Festival in 1975, but does not appear to have received any kind of theatrical release in the United States.

Monique James, vice president of new talent at MCA-Universal, shared Lee's assessment that women during these years were constantly forced to negotiate Hollywood's double standard: to maintain "feminine," nonthreatening qualities in an industry that was predicated on assertive and aggressive behavior. "Women who are in responsible positions are often called tough and mean and loud and castrating," explained James. "Unless you take a position and really feel strongly about something and are willing to stand on your two feet, nobody is going to do it for you."[12]

In 1975, Maya Angelou (1928–2014) became the first African American woman to join the Directors Guild in the director's category.[13] Angelou had participated in the American Film Institute's first Directing Workshop for Women in 1974; in 1977 she directed *The Tapestry*, an hour-long episode for PBS's *Visions* series. Angelou would direct her only feature film, *Down on the Delta*, featuring Alfre Woodard, Wesley Snipes, Esther Rolle, and Loretta Devine, for Showtime Networks, with a limited theatrical release, in 1998. Yet she first tried to break into directing feature films in 1971 when she started writing a screenplay adaptation of her award-winning autobiography, *I Know Why the Caged Bird Sings*, which Angelou was slated to direct for Kelly-Jordon Enterprises Inc., an independent black-owned and operated production company where she was primed to be the first African American woman to helm a feature.[14] That was not to come to pass: the script eventually was produced as a television movie that aired on CBS in 1979, starring Diahann Carroll and helmed by veteran television director Fielder Cook. "Hollywood never before trusted a budget of $1.5 million to a black woman," Angelou told the *Los Angeles Times* in 1978, alluding to her struggle in bringing her book and herself to the big screen. "Suddenly, I'm in the business where everybody and his dog can say something about your work. In television, they treat me well, according to their likes."[15]

During these years, Angelou, a multifaceted artist-intellectual, accomplished not only as a writer of prose and poetry but also a singer-songwriter, dancer, theater director, and activist whose work resonated with the era's social justice movements, had all the promise of a Hollywood talent. In addition to her work on *I Know Why the Caged Bird Sings*, in 1972 Angelou wrote the screenplay for the feature film *Georgia, Georgia*, also produced by Kelly-Jordon Enterprises Inc., distributed by Cinerama Releasing Corp., and starring Diana Sands as an American Jazz singer in Sweden. The film received mixed reviews, but critics recognized the significance of a film centered around a black female protagonist, with a screenplay by a leading black female writer during a time when such roles were rare and such writers nonexistent. Charles Champlin, writing for the *Los Angeles Times*, admitted that the "plot is honest but overcontrived and mounts to an unconvincing bit of melodrama. But what matters and what gives 'Georgia, Georgia' its special strength and pleasure are its insights to the black experience . . . it is a valuable and interesting look at at least a part of the black experience in our time by a remarkable writer."[16] The film was directed by the Swede Stig Bjorkman, and Angelou felt that he misinterpreted her material because of his gender, national identity, and race. She said, "[I] think the essence of my work was lost. He had no understanding of Black Americans, so he had no understanding of the romance in my script."[17] An article in *Variety* made a similar observation: Bjorkman "appears a bit mystified as to how to handle an American story and a basically American black-and-white cast, and this uncertainty has been passed on to his actors to the point where it affects their interpretations."[18] For Angelou, the film reflected her repeated struggle to retain a measurable amount of control over her original material throughout the development and production process.

In 1979, Angelou wrote and coproduced the television movie *Sister, Sister* for NBC featuring a cast of prominent black actors, including Diahann Carroll, Rosalind Cash, Paul Winfield, and Irene Cara. The show was shelved until it was eventually broadcast in 1982. Howard Rosenberg of the *Los Angeles Times* speculated that the two-hour television feature about the complex relationships among a trio of sisters was put in limbo because the network was concerned about the popular appeal of a contemporary drama featuring black performers. "Here we are 30 years past 'Amos 'n' Andy,'" mused Rosenberg, "and still without an all-black weekly dramatic series on the small screen."[19]

Angelou's status—outside of Hollywood—as an esteemed, eloquent, and outspoken black woman artist (and one who was six feet tall) appealed to the film and television industries as they looked for new, innovative talent to work with—yet it was exactly these qualities that alienated the industries and prevented them from truly investing in a talent so prominent but different from the white status quo. Describing the frustrations of making *Sister, Sister*, in 1982 Angelou mapped out the ease in which her market appeal could rise and fall during the course of production:

> One of the first things I noticed while working on the project was that on a day when my stock was obviously up—that is when somebody had probably said, "That Maya Angelou is brilliant."—the next morning the executive of the studio would come to my office and say, "Darling, Maya, how are you?" Now if somebody had said at another gathering, "Well, you know, Maya Angelou, she's a tough lady, she holds to her vision"—the executive would come back into my office the next morning and say, "Hey, how are you? Watch it, you're putting on weight." You see, if you stick to your guns as a man, you're persistent. *And* if you're black and female and six feet tall—phew![20]

As the first "generation" of female directors to have a presence in the film industry since the silent era, women filmmakers during the 1970s not only challenged the industry's gender caste system in which women traditionally dominated clerical and assistant positions but also, as skilled and ambitious newcomers, posed a threat to its patriarchal structure. Regardless of whether they acted in a feminine manner or aggressively, these directors, as well as aspiring ones, faced the reality that they were seeking work in a male-dominated industry unaccustomed to recognizing a potential female peer and collaborator: a type of colleague they had never seen nor imagined. In 1978, Martha Coolidge shared, "I've had executives say I was one of the few women directors they'd met who they felt was not intimidated by them. That means they assume that women directors are intimidated by men." Coolidge, a graduate of New York University's cinema studies program and known in the 1970s for her documentaries, crossed over to feature films in the 1980s; in 2002 she became the first and, thus far, the only female president of the Directors Guild of America. "On the other hand," Coolidge explained, "I've had a couple of meetings with [male] producers who wouldn't look at me, where literally they didn't know what to do. A woman director was just incomprehensible to them."[21]

Dan Melnick, vice president of production at MGM during the early and mid-1970s, understood that sexism was ingrained in the male-centric culture of Hollywood, admitting in a 1973 interview, "We don't have many women in management positions. Here you have what is symptomatic of the whole industry, which is a tradition that takes a long time to overcome. To be honest about it, there are many of us in this business who have unconscious areas of being threatened by women executives." Making sure to align himself on the right side of progress, Melnick added, "I think I am fairly comfortable with them."[22] At the time of that interview, MGM had not hired a female director since 1937 when Dorothy Arzner directed *The Bride Wore Red.* Indeed the studio would not work with a woman director until 1984 when it produced Australian filmmaker Gillian Armstrong's film *Mrs. Soffel.*

In what Alice Kessler-Harris describes as a society's *gendered imagination*—based on gender-associated roles that are "historically thought of as appropriate" in the way they define normative behavior until such expectations are challenged when their unjustness is revealed—male executives resisted the decade's gradual influx of women directors because those women threatened the patriarchal norm these men perpetuated as a way to ensure their power.[23] None of them had ever seen a woman direct a film. With the exception of the singular examples of Arzner and Lupino, directing for generations had been an exclusively white male domain. Women directors had been edged out of their jobs when early Hollywood made the transition to sound and both the masculinized culture of Wall Street and the paternalistic familial structure of craft unions helped shape the gendered employment hierarchy of the studio system. As Erin Hill shows in her book on feminized labor during the studio era, the organization of classic Hollywood, from the geographic mapping of the studio lot to the day-to-day execution of its business model, adapted systems of efficiency that were wholly dependent on "women serving as a cheap, exploitable workforce to facilitate and subsidize [company] growth."[24] Beginning in the late 1920s women in Hollywood dominated service jobs from food preparation and wait staff in the commissary to housekeeping and studio nurses; they had a significant impact by holding clerical positions as secretaries and assistants working in all departments. An integral characteristic of this female workforce was the way in which it performed "*both* explicit labor they were assigned on the basis of gender—typing, sewing, inking and painting—*and* the implicit 'shadow' labor—the interpersonal competencies, gender performativity, and emotion work their jobs required."[25] The female secretary to the powerful male director or studio executive—his "girl Friday"—not only fulfilled her official job description as support staff but also handled the unnamed "service" duties in her assumed biological ability as a woman to console, comfort, and protect her boss in a nonthreatening, feminine manner. Here the gendered imagination of women working in Hollywood was solidified as the helpmate who was highly competent, but not competitive. Her lack of ambition never impaired her ability to be an effective employee; as a female, she was not expected to see herself, nor did she, as an individual in pursuit of career goals. She was always present, but never aggressive; reliable, but not indispensable in that there were many more just like her ready to go.

A core tenet of this book's argument is that women directors during the 1970s were entangled in a paradox of progress.[26] The historical circumstances of the time period and their intersection—the impact of social justice movements as they altered the perception of gendered equity, shifting industry trends, and the production, consumption, and reception of film and television as mass media—suggested that, in many ways, women—in particular white middle-class women—were in a position to gain access, for the first time in generations, to creative and economic power in the motion picture business. Pushing against this possibility of progress was the legacy of institutionalized discrimination in Hollywood, which was not going to succumb easily without strong resistance and some casualties.

While studio executives gawked at the "incomprehensibility" of Angelou, Coolidge, Cox, and Lee, the film industry was grappling with a dire financial situation. Toward the end of the 1960s, the industry faced serious profit losses and released fewer films each successive year.[27] Those pictures the studios did produce were made for very large budgets and were anticipated to recoup equally large profits at the box office. Audiences, now dominated by a younger demographic, did not respond to the lavish musicals that were once Hollywood's most reliable genre.[28] High-cost titles such as *Hello, Dolly!* (1969, 20th Century-Fox) and *Sweet Charity* (1969, Universal) were failing at the box office, while smaller-budget movies like *Alice's Restaurant* (1969, United Artists), *Medium Cool* (1969, Paramount Pictures), and *Midnight Cowboy* (1969, United Artist), about topical social and political themes, were succeeding. In particular, the success of *Easy Rider* in 1969, independently produced and distributed by Columbia Pictures, had become the new standard of a film's box office achievements. "Increasingly these days, the Easy Riders are riding high at the box office, while the Doctor Dolittles are in ill health indeed," reported Stanley Penn for the *Wall Street Journal*. "The hits of 1969 are a new breed of movie—most often low-budget, carefully crafted films that bear the distinct stamp of an individual director or producer and that are explicitly tailored to a youth audience."[29]

Hollywood struggled to understand and appropriate this new filmmaking paradigm of independent productions made for and by the "youth." A popular notion began circulating in the press that the ideal candidate to direct motion pictures was anyone young, especially someone just starting out. "Novelists, playwrights, critics, film editors, cameramen, photographers and actors are being given opportunities to direct—and so are film students," wrote Mel Gussow for the *New York Times* in 1970. "Many are graduates of film departments at the University of Southern California and University of California in Los Angeles, which are 'raided' every year as if they were basketball teams. Some of the new filmmakers just come in off the street."[30]

Surely it was hyperbole that filmmakers were being hired "off the street," but the focus on film students was real: indeed Francis Ford Coppola and George Lucas were hired while they were still studying at UCLA and USC, respectively. In the United States, the number of film programs at universities and colleges increased during the 1960s. In 1968 it was reported that "60,000 graduate and undergraduate students [were] enrolled in 1,500 film courses at 120 colleges. All three figures are double those of last year and expected to double again in the fall semester."[31] The New Wave directors, the French Jean-Luc Godard and the American Mike Nichols, were touted as the inspiration for the surge of interest in film studies.

In the face of reduced profitability, studio executives considered all possible options of finding the next hit and its maker, and targeting college campuses was seriously pursued. In 1967 executives from 20th Century-Fox organized a "college-weekend" at the Yale Club as a promotional opportunity for the studio, enabling old guard Hollywood to reach out to the youth contingent as both a powerful film-going demographic and the next generation of filmmakers. At this event several new releases were screened for an audience of forty-three student representatives from twenty-nine East Coast colleges. There were also panel discussions; in one, long-time studio president Darryl F. Zanuck, who was in his late sixties, attempted to appeal to the crowd by painting himself and his company as open-minded and forward thinking. He claimed, "In this industry today, certainly we must explore. We must move on. I've seen it from the silent days go into talk [*sic*], and I've had them tell me that talkies were a three-picture deal and then they'd be out. I've gone through all those stages of it and I want to keep working. Not because of financial reasons particularly, because I want to be a part of creating, a part of whatever is new."[32] Zanuck might have had personal reasons for the pledge to keep his studio current, but financial concerns were also a serious consideration. The failure of *Doctor Doolittle* that year would set an unfortunate precedent for the company. In 1969 Fox would release two big-budget flops: *Star!* and *Hello, Dolly!*[33]

Well-publicized success stories of student-to-studio filmmakers fueled the young director mythology: Steven Spielberg (California State, Long Beach) and Martin Scorsese (NYU) were hired soon after graduation. However, film school proved an unwelcoming place for female students. In 1970, only 20 of 350 film majors at USC were women; the comparable statistics at UCLA were 30 of 500 film majors.[34] In describing the frustrated aspirations of his female students, USC professor Bernie Kantor highlighted Hollywood's chauvinism. "A burning, passionate desire to do film leads girls into film school," Kantor explained, an advocate who was still a man of the times in referring to grown women as "girls." "The girls are well aware that there are no places—beds but no places—for a girl in the profession. Most are placed in jobs, USC sees to that, but not in the places the girls want. The typical offer is as secretary."[35]

While old Hollywood, prompted by financial necessity, reimagined itself as open to hiring new, young directors who had not come up through the meritocracy of the previous generation, the industry was closed-minded with regard to gender parity and remained invested in the traditions of a female service-only workforce. Women directors encountered the paradox: the industry was in need of young talent that could connect with the valuable youth demographic, but instead of exploiting or nurturing talented filmmakers of all genders and race/ethnicities for maximum benefit, it maintained the status quo of only hiring Caucasian male (or "ethnic" Caucasian in the case of Italian American filmmakers such as Coppola and Scorsese) directors. Thus, as the older generation of studio moguls aged out of the business, the only palatable exchange of power, resources, and access was one from father to son. This transition was both literal and figurative. For example, Darryl F. Zanuck's son Richard Zanuck succeeded him at 20th Century-Fox; Stanley Schneider served as studio president and Bert Schneider had a six-picture deal with Columbia Pictures while their father Abe Schneider served as chairman of its board; and Leo Jaffe, who became president of Columbia Pictures in 1969, served as a role model for his son Stanley, who was named president of Paramount in 1970. The rise of a young generation of studio executives, many younger than forty years old, over the course of the 1970s represented the changing of the guard: they included David Picker at Columbia, Peter Bart, Robert Evans, Barry Diller, and Michael Eisner at Paramount, and Mike Medavoy at United Artists. The few veteran females who wielded influence mentored those young men; for instance, the editor Verna Fields, whose pool-house editing suite was a legendary meeting place for up-and-coming male directors, edited the films of Peter Bogdanovich,

George Lucas, and Steven Spielberg because these young directors were considered a valuable investment for the major studios.

Although several women in this study began their careers working with an established male filmmaker or producer (e.g., Joan Darling with Norman Lear, Joan Tewkesbury with Robert Altman, and Barbara Peeters and Stephanie Rothman with Roger Corman in collaborations that are detailed in subsequent chapters), rarely did they feel as if those professional relationships created the stepping-stones for career progression that for their male peers were typical and, in many cases, expected. In an industry dependent on connections and networking, these kinds of contacts for access and validation were vital. Yet, the mentorship of women—nurturing their careers with the direct intention of assisting less experienced individuals' upward professional mobility—was antithetical to Hollywood's belief that women were dispensable service employees. "I think what happens is that in the 1960s and 1970s the young men were the first ones to invade the bastion of older white men who directed movies," explained Tewkesbury, in 2011. "So because of Lucas, Coppola, Spielberg the girls were able to think—'OK, they kinda let the new guys into the club.'" Thirty years later, the gender double standard was no less striking: "The women could sort of filter in, but only if you didn't make too much noise and if you were in the same paradigm with movies that had gone before you. If you were going to work in the industry what you followed was the schedule of the feature film that had gone on before you. And in that your scripts were also tailored to fit a certain mold."[36]

Women in the 1970s found themselves constantly challenged by industry stereotypes of what a female director should be. They needed to act aggressively in working toward their professional goals and be confident in asserting and defending their creative visions—not only because those were the accepted behaviors of a Hollywood director but also because as women they had to disprove stereotypes that they were too shy or insecure to command a crew, too physically weak to sustain the stamina required for a twelve-hour day on set, and too sensitive to withstand the constant barrage of decisions and demands. On the other hand, as Tewkesbury pointed out, women could not "make too much noise," lest someone notice that they had gotten into the fraternity. To speak up was to threaten Hollywood's male-dominated community, but being a director meant you were ambitious and driven and that you believed—based on your experience, skill, hard work, and desires—that you were entitled to the opportunity to direct, a conviction shared by each of these women.

While women directors found themselves up against a hostile institutionalized mindset that resisted their presence, on a national level, the feminist movement—represented by elected officials in different branches of government and federal agencies, in nonprofit organizations ranging from the mainstream National Organization for Women (NOW) to the radical Redstockings, and by individual women who challenged discrimination in a variety of ways in their daily lives—gave momentum to the struggles and accomplishments of these filmmakers. During the 1970s, women's rights were being elevated to the status of *human* rights. Social and public policies were becoming gender specific, and laws were passed that addressed inequality based on sex. In 1972 the ratification of Title IX legally enforced equal opportunity between women and men in education and school sports. Both houses of Congress passed the Equal Rights Amendment in 1972, although its ratification effort would fail in 1982. The landmark case *Roe v. Wade*, decided by the Supreme Court on January 22, 1973, legalized abortion and increased women's reproductive rights.[37] In 1974 Congress passed the Equal Credit Opportunity Act, which protected credit applicants from discrimination on the basis of age, race, religion, sex, or marital status, allowing married women to obtain credit in their own name. Congresswoman Barbara Jordan became the first African American and the first woman to give a keynote speech at the Democratic National Convention in 1976. On October 31, 1978, Congress passed the Pregnancy Discrimination Act, which prohibited discrimination against pregnant women in their place of employment.[38] In the face of such fierce and persistent social and political discourse regarding women's civil rights, the film industry would be forced to respond to its most demanding critics, its employees.

## Hollywood's Civil Rights

In the 1960s no formal civil rights mechanism existed in Hollywood to regulate gender and racial discrimination at any level of industry employment. As Eithne Quinn details in her research on race politics in Hollywood during the 1960s civil rights era, there is considerable scholarship on representations of race in film during this period; however, the intersection of industry labor policies, production culture, and race has been left unmined.[39] Similarly, very little has been written about how in the early 1970s, building on the momentum of the African American civil rights movement during the 1950s and 1960s, the feminist movement's advocacy of employment equity—across a variety of industries and business sectors—began to find its way into the film and television industries. Activists working both outside the industry, in organizations such as NOW, and those inside—specifically feminist members (predominantly female, but joined by several male peers) of the professional guilds (the Directors Guild, the Screen Actors Guild, and the Writers Guild)—initiated reform efforts that set in motion critiques of Hollywood's sexist hiring practices. These groups proposed various remedies—in particular, affirmative action programs—in an attempt to overhaul the system. At the core of each of these groups' efforts was the gathering of statistical evidence to prove the employment discrimination experienced by women working in above-the-line positions: those who held both economic and/or creative power (sometimes at the same time), including studio executives, producers, directors, writers, cinematographers, and actresses. In addition, below-the-line jobs, such as the technical crafts—editors, camera operators, hair, makeup and wardrobe, set decorators, grips, and gaffers—were represented in the antidiscrimination agendas of these activists. Key to reformers' influence was their use of the media to create awareness of gender inequality in the entertainment business. Accusations of prejudice were supported by statistical data that were circulated in the press, frequently in the *Los Angeles Times* and *New York Times*, as well as in the *Hollywood Reporter* and *Variety*, the industry trade papers. Protestors released the statistics as a way of outing studios, production companies, networks, and individuals as perpetrators of sexism and racism. Such reportage introduced into industry vernacular the reality of feminist protest of and within Hollywood and in doing so helped legitimize this opposition by recognizing in a public forum the frustrations of the female workforce.

As argued repeatedly by activists, female employees, and journalists, women's low employment numbers were not due to a lack of qualified applicants. During this time many women with the experience and skills needed for below-and above-the-line positions were eager to work. It was the systematic exclusion based on their gender, which was the norm within Hollywood's patriarchal hegemony, that prevented them from getting hired. In the early 1970s women in the industry began enlisting federal agencies and their guilds to play a role in negotiating with broadcast and film companies for more and better employment opportunities. Government agencies such as the Federal Communications Commission (FCC), which regulated broadcasting, and the Equal Employment Opportunity Commission (EEOC), established in 1965 to protect employee civil rights, served as legal watchdogs *external* to the industry; unions like the DGA, SAG, and WGA were *internal* industry organizations that were meant to protect their members' creative and economic rights. Yet, even though activists' fervor in calling out the chauvinism that was impeding their career potential became increasingly strong, systematic change continued to be elusive throughout the 1970s and into the 1980s. What these activists did accomplish was the subtle and gradual introduction of a feminist consciousness into the media industries that sparked a dialogue around the disenfranchisement of female workers and changed, ever so slightly, the treatment of these employees. A concentrated advocacy effort on behalf of women directors led by the DGA Women's Steering Committee would not take place until the end of the decade (see chapter 4). However, the feminist campaigns in the early 1970s, inclusive to a range of female workers in film and television, set an example for future activists, and, in small steps, began to break ground for women directing films during this era.

## 1969: The EEOC Comes to Hollywood

In 1948 the Supreme Court ruled against the studio system in the antitrust case *United States vs. Paramount Pictures*, signaling the demise of Hollywood's system of vertical integration that had allowed the major film studios to control the production, distribution, and exhibition of their motion pictures, to the disadvantage of theater owners and independents.[40] This legal decision dismantled the core of Hollywood's power structure, making the studios careful to avoid any risk of government intervention in the future. In this setting, with the potential threat of coming under federal control, on March 13, 1969, the EEOC conducted a one-day hearing in Los Angeles on job discrimination in the film industry.

The EEOC was established in 1965 by President Lyndon Johnson to enforce Title VII of the Civil Rights Act of 1964, which stipulated that it was illegal for employers to discriminate against workers on the grounds of race, color, religion, sex, or national origin. However, it did not have the power to make court-level, legally binding decisions to settle conflicts; its jurisdiction only allowed it to conduct federal investigations of discriminatory employment disputes, with the authority to recommend to the Justice Department the filing of a lawsuit. Led in 1969 by Chairman Clifford L. Alexander Jr., an appointee from the Johnson administration, the EEOC conducted the Los Angeles meeting as part of its investigation of employment patterns in the major business sectors in the country. Since 1967, it had evaluated the textile industry's employment of African American workers in North and South Carolina, held hearings in New York City concerning the white-collar job sector's hiring of women and minorities, and looked at Los Angeles' aerospace and media industries.[41] Representing the film studios at the 1969 hearing were executives from Universal Studios, Warner Bros./Seven Arts, 20th Century-Fox, and Walt Disney; the television networks ABC, CBS, and NBC; and union spokesmen from the Association of Motion Picture and Television Producers (AMPTP), Motion Picture Machine Operators, and IATSE (Local 790, Illustrators and Matte Artists; Local 847, Set Designers and Model Makers; and Local 854, Story Analysts).

The EEOC believed that the motion picture and television companies could and should have a written affirmative action plan as evidence of their commitment to being equal opportunity employers, particularly in the era of the Civil Rights Act. Ten years later, the women of the DGA would push for a similar plan of action, calling on the entire film and television industry to implement quotas and timetables as a way to hire more qualified female directors. Meeting such demands of the industry, whether by federal agencies in 1969 or by employees supported by their union in 1979, would require surmounting enormous challenges. Implementing affirmative action measures would call for the studios and networks to actively recruit, hire, and train minority groups as a way to counteract what the hearing testimony was revealing: Hollywood was dominated by a white male labor force fortified by union seniority lists and the culture of studio networking, often in what seemed to be in collusion with one another. Walt Disney, Warner Bros., and 20th Century-Fox each admitted that it did not have any affirmative action policies in place. Throughout the hearing, the commissioners appeared unable to hide their incredulousness at the respondents' answers, which confirmed their companies' lack of diversity and lack of incentive to make any changes. In many instances these companies refused to even acknowledge that there was a problem that needed to be addressed.

The companies put the blame for their hiring practices on factors outside their control. According to James Riddle, vice president of ABC's Western Division, "it was a geographical problem."[42] The network was located in Hollywood, which made transportation difficult for minority clerical recruits traveling from other parts of the city. For Arthur Schaefer, industrial relations manager for Warner Bros./Seven Arts, the size of his staff was to blame: his small staff of four lacked the resources necessary to actively recruit prospective minority hires. In answer to Commissioner Luther Holcomb's inquiry about the company's future expansion plans, Schaefer deferred any responsibility in his defiant response: "Sir, I haven't the slightest idea. We are now being acquired by Kinney National Services, which is another company, and I wouldn't have the slightest idea what our plans are for next year."[43] Schaefer thus defended his unit's lack of diversity by stating that his was just one small department in a very big corporation, then in the throes of a conglomerate takeover. Achieving workplace equity was beyond his control.

Schaefer's answer voiced a sentiment found in other testimonies in the 1969 hearing: studio hiring was not organized in a centralized manner, and as a result the industry's workforce was not aggregated in a way that lent itself to the rigid structure of an affirmative action plan. As Frank H. Ferguson, resident counsel for 20th Century-Fox, detailed in a written statement to the panel, employment in the craft and technical areas was subject to change from week to week depending on fluctuating feature film production schedules and, in the case of broadcasting, when network programming aired or a television series went on hiatus. As he explained,

> The nature of the motion picture industry, that is, its labor pool on one hand, and the peculiarity of its labor demands on the other, make long range planning and programming difficult. Due to the illness of a principal player or another matter beyond the producer's control an immediate alteration of the schedule becomes necessary,

> and the set must be started and completed at an earlier date. This calls, on a day or 2 day's notice, for the employing of the craftsmen necessary to commence and complete the set. They must immediately be recruited from available sources.[44]

This line of reasoning enabled the studios to use the unpredictability of a decentralized production system as an excuse requiring their reliance on word-of-mouth hiring from a familiar labor pool—the only kind that could be "available" on short notice. To make a concerted effort to diversify the studio's labor force through hiring quotas was not just impractical and inefficient but also close to impossible in the face of constant industry demands and deadlines. Fifteen years later, Columbia and Warner Bros. would fall back on similar reasoning against the Directors Guild in its suit regarding racial and gender discrimination, when the companies argued that they were not in charge of hiring crews, but that each production was a unique combination of professionals who worked well together based on previous productions and word-of-mouth recommendations. According to the studios—in 1969 and again in the early 1980s—the highly creative environment of making films depended on organic, well-matched relationships that could not coalesce within the calculated confines of affirmative action's quotas and timetables.

Concluding the day of testimonies, Daniel Steiner, general counsel for the EEOC, made the panel's closing remarks. He declared that the hearing had provided "clear evidence of a pattern or practice of discrimination in violation of the Title VII of the Civil Rights Act of 1964" within the motion picture industry.[45] The commission was critical of the studios' lack of official affirmative action and recruitment plans. Faced with company representatives tripping over claims that their studio was committed to diversity, the panel was unconditional in its final judgment that it had "seen, in sum, no concrete evidence of a willingness to change the employment pattern in this industry" and would recommend that the EEOC follow up with the Department of Justice regarding a possible legal suit against the AMPTP, television networks, films studios, and the different craft unions.[46] Most importantly, the EEOC identified the main culprits as the craft unions and their roster lists.

Historically, the unionization of the film business had been part of Hollywood's transition into a masculinized industry in the 1920s, and in 1969, industry unions—for both below-the-line and above-the-line positions—were dominated by a white male membership. Many applications to craft unions included racial/ethnic profiling questions such as whether a prospective member was "foreign-born."[47] Given that these craft unions were made up of predominantly white men, the nationality question signaled to the EEOC that they were actively controlling the makeup of their constituencies. Nationality had no bearing on whether a prospective union member could do his or her job, but racial and ethnic profiling was a means of enabling what the panel felt were patterns of discrimination.[48] Similarly problematic to the EEOC was the unions' reinforcement of family lineage as a means to gain union membership, as suggested in the application question, "What type of vocation did your father and/or guardian pursue for a livelihood?"[49] Embedded in this question was an automatic vetting based on paternity: if one's father had worked in the industry and been part of the union, then, regardless of his qualifications, the son was an assumed member of that community with access to its perks. Father–son hiring maintained the white-patriarchal hierarchy of the union by favoring familial legacy over individual skill and aspiration—affecting both women and men outside of these bloodlines. Furthermore, passing down a trade between only male generations coded such jobs as "male," thus creating for women—both white and of color—a double obstacle: they were neither male (and so could not do men's work) nor the male descendant of a male union member (and so would not be accepted into the union).

Studio productions hired union crews, and the crews were chosen from lists based on a craftsperson's seniority within his or her respective union. Those with the most experience (i.e., number of hours worked) were at the top of the list and therefore hired before others with less experience. To join a union the applicant was required to have worked a certain amount of hours, but to get steady work on a film or television production an individual had to be a member of the union.[50] In this context, it is thus not surprising that, at the end of the 1960s, the majority of men of color and women of any race/ethnicity existed outside the union culture, and membership applications reinforced their marginalized status.

In October 1969, the *Los Angeles Times* reported that the Justice Department had named Columbia, MGM, Paramount, 20th Century-Fox, and Warner Bros; television networks ABC and CBS; and the unions AMPTP and IATSE in a "secret" memo regarding alleged racial discrimination.[51] (Universal Studios was excluded based on the company's comparatively better hiring record.) By the early spring of 1970, in agreement with the EEOC, the Justice Department had decided it would not take the issue to court and instead negotiated a settlement with the entertainment industry focused on affirmative action. In April 1970, the *New York Times* reported, "Seventy-two movie and television production companies agreed to an equal-employment plan that includes hiring, training and upgrading of minorities and sets racial quotas." Although the companies denied "the existence of discrimination, [they] agreed in the document to the need for remedial training and for affirmative action to insure equal employment."[52] Those named in the settlement included the three television networks and their four primary craft unions; seventy-three film producers and their nine local film craft unions; and the AMPTP, IATSE, and the Moving Picture Machine Operators (MPMO).[53] The major film studios that signed the agreement were Columbia Pictures, MGM, Paramount Pictures, 20th Century-Fox, Walt Disney Productions, and Warner Bros.[54]

The settlement accounted for non-acting-related, below-the-line positions such as camera and sound technicians, costume and set design, grip and electric, editors, and hair and makeup. Writers, directors, and producers—working in both film and television—were not included. The agreement spelled out ways to integrate the unions' rosters. Emphasized in the plan were instructional programs that would guarantee placing "at least one Negro and one Spanish-American" from trainee groups onto union referral lists, as well as eliminating discriminatory job testing such as questions about origin of birth. These measures were intended to ensure that in some jobs "two of every five new employees would be members of a minority group and to establish a job-training program with participation made up of two-fifths Negroes and two-fifths Mexican-Americans."[55] The EEOC and Justice Department defined their goals numerically, hoping to ensure that 20 to 24 percent of media industry craft jobs were staffed by minorities and that, after a certain amount of years, the separate minority pool created by this fair hiring plan would merge into the main union roster—thus finally racially integrating those labor organizations and, as a result, the film and television industries as a whole.

The agreement focused solely on race, specifically African Americans and Latinos, because they were the two largest nonwhite demographics in the Los Angeles workforce.[56] It also focused exclusively on male employees, because, according to an attorney with the Justice Department who was part of the investigation, women did not constitute a large enough portion of the workforce to be considered their own labor pool worthy of factoring into the plan.[57] Yet, according to the numbers submitted by the five major studios attending the hearings, the film industry's workforce totaled 16,046 employees, of whom 3,663–22.8 percent—were women.[58] Ignoring women in this way was contrary to the EEOC's purpose of enforcing Title VII of the Civil Rights Act, which protected workers against discrimination based on race, color, religion, *sex,* or national origin. The Standard Form 100/Employer Information Report (EEO-1 form) filled out by the studios in preparation for the hearing accounted for the number of all permanent and part-time employees, which was broken down by the total number of men *and* women and then into subcategories of male *and* female minorities identified as "Negro, Oriental, American Indian, Spanish Surnamed American." Thus, in 1969 the EEOC had data on both race *and* gender, but chose not to foreground sex along with race as a class of discrimination in its analysis of Hollywood—nor did the Justice Department in its subsequent settlement in 1970.

During the hearing, the members of the EEOC, Chairmen Alexander and Commissioners William H. Brown, Luther Holcomb, Elizabeth J. Kuck, and Vincent T. Ximenes, consistently focused their lines of questioning on the status of male employees of color. Not until midway through the hearing did Commissioner Kuck—the only woman on the panel—ask during IATSE's testimony if sex was included along with race, creed, color, and national origin in the union contract's nondiscriminatory clause. Once confirmed by union representative Josef Bernay that in fact sex was *not* included in the clause, Kuck requested that it be incorporated.[59] Chairman Alexander immediately upheld her comment, adding, "This Commission feels that sex discrimination, and its pervasiveness in this society, is important business. We are not interested in the mere addition of the word 'sex'; we are interested in the inclusion of women at every level without the prior biases that we, as males, may have, and it should be based upon their talents."[60] However adamant Alexander was about the inclusion of sex in this one instance, gender was not mentioned again during the rest of the hearing. Only two journalists included the topic of women in their coverage of the hearings and then only in the briefest of mentions. Both the *Los Angeles Sentinel* and *Chicago Daily Defender*, each an African American newspaper, noted in their one-page articles that "while women held a higher percentage of white collar jobs [compared to blue collar jobs], only one fifth of them had jobs above clerical level."[61]

For a federal labor investigation of this magnitude to fail to prominently address sex as a category of discrimination was to discount close to one-quarter of the workforce in one of the country's largest business sectors. Ignoring women as an employment demographic devalued the feminized jobs that were a crucial component of Hollywood's workforce, in which they were overrepresented: doing so ignored the fact that women were disproportionately represented in low-wage positions with little authority. Women were not, in significant numbers, being hired as executives or managers of departments. Nor did many hold positions of power, such as associate and assistant directors, stage managers, or unit production managers, in below-the-line production jobs on film and television crews. Grip, electric, and camera departments were historically off-limits to women. Those professions were controlled by male-dominated trade unions that justified their exclusion of women by claiming that operating the necessary equipment was too dangerous or demanded too much strength for females. Furthermore, within Hollywood's patriarchal power structure, employees were discriminated against for reasons of gender *and* race; gender and race, as general categories, were not mutually exclusive of each other.

Gender and the Civil Rights Act of 1964 had a tenuous relationship from the start. Originally conceived as a law designed to combat racial discrimination in the workplace, "sex" was only included when Howard Smith, a conservative Democrat from Virginia and staunch segregationist, who was chair of the House Rules Committee, believed that adding the category to the law would derail its passing altogether. The act was nevertheless passed, and for the remainder of the decade, feminists—public activists and elected officials alike—in addition to the EEOC, debated how to define sexual discrimination within the parameters of Title VII. What would take place during these years was a major and painstaking shift from the belief that women—given their historical place within the heteronormative family in which their rights, such as their earning power and ability to work, were subordinate to those of their husband and assumed reproductive roles—should be understood within the workplace as individuals whose "economic citizenship" would be protected under the law as such. Yet, drawing parallels between race and sex were complicated. Some advocates drew an analogy with how Title VII had succeeded in defining racial discrimination and argued, in similar terms, that women and men should be measured as equals when being considered for a job. Others argued that if sex as a protected category was not strictly enforced, then white women were without legal recourse under the Civil Rights Act or that women of color would be vulnerable in the face of gender discrimination. Further impeding the effectiveness of the law during its early years was the EEOC's difficulty in defining sexual discrimination; in many instances individual members of the commission even failed to take sex as a protected category seriously.[62]

In contrast to these differences of opinion and uncertainty among lawmakers and enforcement officials, American women were clear about the discrimination they were experiencing at work and vocal about their need for legal recourse. According to the EEOC's first annual report published in 1966, 37 percent of the complaints filed that year were with regard to sex discrimination.[63] In that same year, NOW was established in direct response to what its founding members, who included employees of the EEOC, felt was the ineffectiveness of the commission in doing its job and the resulting need for an outside, grassroots advocacy group to lobby for its mandate.[64] Pressured by its critics, the commission began to take gender discrimination seriously toward the end of the decade. However, in 1969, while the EEOC's hearings in Hollywood revealed that both gender *and* race should have been areas of legitimate concern for the agency, any enforcement of Title VII, for either protected category, would prove impossible in the entertainment industry.

## Good Will Civil Rights

Before the Justice Department devised a voluntary, "good will" affirmative action plan for the industry to "agree" to, a vicious bipartisan battle took place. Shortly after the March 14, 1969, hearing concluded, Commissioner Alexander, a Democrat and African American, came under attack from the cantankerous white Republican senator, Everett McKinley Dirksen of Illinois. As a vocal opponent of civil rights legislation, Dirksen accused the EEOC chairman of "harassing business men over job discrimination" in "carnival-like hearings," threatening Alexander that he would "go to the highest authority in this Government and get somebody fired."[65] A *New York Times* article on March 29 reported that President Nixon, inaugurated just two months earlier, planned to replace Alexander; faced with his looming dismissal, Alexander voiced his dismay that the Nixon administration was altering the tenor of the EEOC, declaring, "Superficial statements about hard-core unemployed or about plans for progress or other volunteer actions are nice, but not sufficient."[66] Before he could be dismissed, Alexander resigned his post on April 9 as the head of the EEOC, though his term was not scheduled to expire until 1972. While it was not uncommon for an incoming president to appoint his own picks for federal commissions and departments, Alexander's resignation was symptomatic of the Republicans' lack of support of the EEOC. Yet, just a week prior to when the chairman stepped down, the president affirmed his commitment to the Civil Rights Act in what could be perceived as an effort to neutralize himself in the wake of Dirksen's outburst: "I wanted to emphasize my own official and personal endorsement of a strong policy of equal opportunity within the Federal Government."[67]

In response to the EEOC chair's resignation, there was an outcry from several members of the House of Representatives, as well as from Senator Edward Kennedy, a Democrat from Massachusetts, who expressed doubts about the president's commitment to job equity. Kennedy criticized the administration's multimillion-dollar contracts with textile companies and highway developers that required only informal assurance regarding fair employment policies, even though these industries were notorious for their discriminatory hiring practices. The government's internal conflict about enforcing civil rights, exacerbated by the hearing in Hollywood, did not exist in a vacuum. The U.S. recession during 1969 and 1970 had a significant impact on the motion picture industry: higher interest rates combined with a reduced production schedule that depended on a few large-budget films, which did not appeal to the changing youth demographic, had resulted in about $200 million in losses to the industry. The country's economic downturn ended in 1971, but not before Hollywood lost an additional $300–400 million.[68] President Nixon was instrumental in rescuing the film industry from pending financial disaster by creating tax shelters and investment tax credits that allowed studios to take advantage of significant tax breaks on production costs. Such provisions were the primary source of financing in Hollywood until 1976, when tax code reform prohibited such business deals.[69]

The EEOC's confrontation with Hollywood and the Justice Department's subsequent negotiations demonstrate the complexities of enforcing federally mandated civil rights in the film industry during these years. Without the backing of a court order, the agreement—and the disempowered employees it was meant to protect—had no legal recourse if the plan was not followed. One government lawyer described the situation as "another gentlemen's agreement . . . which sound good but are loaded with loop-holes even a racist could crawl through."[70] Indeed, the responsibility to see that this pledge of workplace reform would be implemented rested on the accused, in this case, those with power: the network, the film studio, the producer, and the labor union. These entities found support broadly throughout the industry for their opposition to the plan. In an editorial titled "Sock it to 'Em" that appeared in the *Hollywood Reporter* soon after the hearings, Tichi Wilkerson Miles, publisher of the trade paper, lambasted the EEOC's presence in Hollywood, describing Alexander as a "prosecuting attorney, judge and hangman for these sessions." Wilkerson Miles admitted that "there is no question the film industry could do better in finding jobs for Mexican Americans and for Negroes and, for that matter, for Orientals and American Indians;" yet she was enraged that "some of the hardest-working and most distinguished men in the film industry were subjected to a kind of courtroom procedure rarely seen in this country, although legal historians might find precedents in the Moscow system of jurisprudence." Indignant at the exposure and the threat of intervention, the publisher turned the tables and wanted to know, "How many Negroes or Mexican Americans are there in policy-making, executive positions with the US government?"[71]

Taking a similar position of defensive anti-interventionism was Jack Valenti, president of the Motion Picture Association of America and industry spokesman and diplomat extraordinaire. Valenti, who had worked as a media specialist for President Johnson and was therefore associated with that administration's civil rights agenda, was cautious in how he described the reality of racial discrimination in Hollywood. Shortly after the EEOC hearing, Valenti hosted a lunch in April 1969 honoring Roy Wilkins, president of the NAACP, who had publically criticized the Nixon administration and Senator Dirksen for their treatment of Commissioner Alexander. Valenti, in what Eithne Quinn identifies as his "metaphoric refrain," acknowledged the need for better opportunities for blacks in Hollywood without acknowledging the reason for this need—the industry's legacy of institutionalized racism—or permitting any outside criticism. According to Valenti, "We have the desire to open the door for new Negro talent rather than have someone force it open."[72] As Quinn argues, Valenti, who had strong relationships in government, in particular with Dirksen, introduced the early rhetoric of "racial neoconservatism" in which "the roles of victim and perpetrator—those opening and those obstructing doors—[were] reversed."[73] Wilkerson Miles and Valenti, in harmony with many of the responses given during the hearing by studio and union representatives, resisted any interference from the government that challenged the industry's long-standing history of self-regulation. For these industry stalwarts, opportunities existed for everyone to succeed—without "special treatment"—if they were ambitious, hardworking, and demonstrated their individual talent, thus perpetuating the belief that the dynamic of Hollywood's workforce existed outside of patterns of discrimination influenced by America's legacy of racism and sexism.[74] In 1969 gender, as with the EEOC, was not on Valenti's radar. Yet in the early 1980s, as discussed in chapter 4, when the discrimination experienced by female directors was regularly in the headlines, he would respond with a similar disregard for the role of institutionalized sexism and would be quoted in the press as wondering whether there were in fact women capable of directing a multimillion-dollar movie.[75] Nor at the time was gender a concern for Wilkerson Miles, although in 1973 she would be a founding member of the nonprofit organization Women in Film established to "promot[e] equal opportunities for women" in the motion picture industry.[76]

The 1970 negotiations allowed both the industry and government to appear amicable to the demands for fair hiring without having any legal obligation to implement or enforce systems of real change. If it was a priority for the government to facilitate financial deals with the industry to help it avert an economic crisis, then it was no doubt willing to work with those same companies on an antidiscrimination plan that avoided court

TABLE 1. Universal City Studios

| *Report year* | *Total number of employees* | *Total number (percentage) of female employees* | *Total number (percentage) of employees of color* | *Total number (percentage) of female employees of color* | *Total number (percentage) of male employees of color* |
|---|---|---|---|---|---|
| 1969 | 3,716 | 731<br>(19.67) | 500<br>(13.46) | 147<br>(3.96) | 353<br>(9.50) |
| 1976 | 3,547 | 1,038<br>(29.26) | 581<br>(16.38) | 162<br>(4.57) | 419<br>(11.81) |

intervention and public criticism. It is no surprise, then, that the Justice Department kept its negotiations regarding job discrimination "secret" from the press. Similarly, the effectiveness of Hollywood's efforts to meet the plan's goals went unreported; for example, the industry's failure to meet established numerical goals for hiring minority men through special roster lists and employment training programs was never made publicly known. This lack of transparency allowed the relationship between Hollywood and the government to go undebated in the media, keeping the public and those affected employees uninformed about the government's unique treatment of the industry, both financially and with regard to workplace ethics.

In 1976 the California Advisory Committee to the Commission on Civil Rights conducted a follow-up investigation of the 1969 EEOC hearings and the subsequent agreement of 1970; its findings were published in a 1978 report titled "Behind the Scenes: Equal Employment Opportunity in the Motion Picture Industry." According to the Advisory Committee, the major motion picture studios, IATSE, and the MPMO had not diversified their workforce (in the case of the unions, their membership) in a meaningful way over the last eight years. Although the numbers of women and minorities had doubled since the last investigation, those statistics were very low to start with, and most of the new hires were craft, laborers, and service workers (dominated by men of color) and clerical workers (dominated by white women).

For example, in its 1969 report to the EEOC, Universal indicated that female employees of all races or ethnicities made up just 19.67 percent of its workforce; 9.50 percent of the total workforce were men of color; and 3.96 percent were women of color (see table 1). Each of those percent-

TABLE 2. 20th Century-Fox

| Report year | Total number of employees | Total number (percentage) of female employees | Total number (percentage) of female employees of color | Total number (percentage) of male employees of color |
|---|---|---|---|---|
| 1969 | 3,136 | 493 (15.72) | 21 (0.67) | 126 (4.02) |
| 1976 | 1858 | 689 (37.08) | 93 (5.01) | 116 (6.24) |

ages increased slightly by 1976. However, most of that progress came in the form of jobs for white women, the majority of whom worked in clerical positions. Though the percentage of women overall increased to 29.26 percent, the number of minority women at Universal increased by only fifteen, accounting for 4.57 percent of its total workforce; these women were employed predominantly in clerical and service worker positions. Universal's percentage of employees of color had increased from 13.46 to 16.38 percent, but in both 1969 and 1976, only eight minority men were in managerial roles, less than 7 percent of those given positions. In neither report did women of color hold a single managerial role.[77]

In another example, at the time of the EEOC hearing, 20th Century-Fox Film Corporation had an abysmal representation of women and minorities even compared to the low standards of its competitors (see table 2). Of their 3,136 total reported employees, only 15.72 percent were women of any race/ethnicity; 4.02 percent were men of color; and 21 employees—or 0.67 percent of its workforce—were women of color. By 1976, Fox's total number of employees had dropped, but there was an increase in the number of women and minorities: of 1,858 total employees, the percentage of women had jumped to 37.08 percent. However, segregation by gender and race was apparent in the kind of jobs held by these female employees. While in 1969, 65 percent of Fox's female employees worked as service workers or in clerical positions, in 1976, 87.8 percent—or 605 of the company's 689 female employees—worked in the same roles. Similarly, in managerial positions, there was little progress. In 1969, 4.07 percent of women held managerial roles; that increased marginally in 1976 to 5.53 percent. In neither report, did women of color hold any managerial roles.[78]

Based on this statistical evidence, the Advisory Committee cited the industry's culpability for the lack of progress since 1969. It found that the major studios did not have official, written affirmative action plans as part of their hiring policies, as urged by the EEOC in 1969, and that the limited ones that did exist were not strictly enforced.

As they did in 1969 and 1970, the unions and studios took turns blaming each other. In defense of the unions, the number of films produced had decreased and the studios and production companies were hiring fewer people, so there was less opportunity to rotate names from the bottom of qualification lists to the top. More damaging was that the studios continued to maintain their own roster lists, ensuring an insular hiring pool that was yet another obstacle for minorities not historically part of union culture. Studios countered that the unions' strict roster system prohibited companies from hiring minorities—guild members who presumably had lower seniority ranking because they were newer to the organization. In actuality, the craft unions and the film studios were equally complicit in the use of seniority lists: the two systematically negotiated collective bargaining agreements that reinforced this hiring structure. The Advisory Committee also cited the federal government as part of the problem. Following the 1970 agreement, the EEOC, as empowered by the Justice Department, had failed to monitor how well the film studios were implementing the plan. This was partially due to the drastic downsizing of the EEOC staff, who were required to enforce the details of the agreement. Furthermore, the 1970 agreement expired in 1974, and neither the EEOC nor the Justice Department made an effort to renegotiate the terms.[79] It was apparent that these government agencies had made a conscious decision not to pursue job discrimination based on race and gender in Hollywood.

Despite their poor results, the 1969 EEOC hearing and the subsequent Justice Department agreement with Hollywood were significant in several ways. Democratic Commissioner Alexander's conflict with the incoming Nixon administration inspired a bipartisan battle, suggesting that interpretation of federal law was at the discretion of the political party in power at the time. The 1970 agreement exposed the backdoor allegiance between the film industry and the Nixon administration that not only functioned as a financial safety net for the studios but also maintained the patriarchal power structure that defined both the government and the entertainment business. The events of 1969 and 1970 also set a precedent for *good faith* agreements with regard to discriminatory hiring in the media industry. These agreements were predicated on the belief that those with hiring power would, to the best of their ability, demonstrate an honest intention to employ those who were traditionally underrepresented. However, because there were no specific standards or metric by which to measure what constituted a "good faith" effort, much was left up to the discretion of those in charge. Such agreements would be a constant in Hollywood throughout the 1970s, resulting in compromises in conflicts between female employees and the companies they accused of inequitable hiring. Initially, these industry concessions appeared to provide hope for women workers that their attempts to be considered for jobs made inaccessible by sexist employment patterns would succeed. Ultimately, however, good faith concessions revealed the one-sided power wielded by the industry, of which women had no part.

Although these proceedings were essentially a failure in that they did not create a reliable system of employer accountability for increased hiring of women and minorities, they did create an awareness at the start of the 1970s of labor injustice within Hollywood. Throughout the decade, below- and above-the-line employees responded by organizing to change Hollywood's culture of sexism and racism. During these years, female members of trade and technical unions filed several lawsuits on the grounds of discrimination, and unions admitted their first female members.[80] For the first time feminist activism took place within the professional guilds. Women members of the Screen Actors Guild and the Writers Guild organized committees within their respective unions and led high-profile critiques of industry hiring practices. These protests were conducted within the context of civil rights legislation, but did not rely on federal intervention and instead attempted change through internal-industry grassroots organizing.

## Guild Women: The Rise of the Women's Committee

In November 1972, Steve Toy, writing for *Daily Variety*, announced, "A campaign to press for the demands of women in showbiz has become industry-wide." In what the reporter described as "an attempt to revamp both employment practices towards the hiring of women and their image as presented in films and on tv [*sic*]," female employees were collectively advocating for each other, across guild memberships, creating a sense of camaraderie and power in numbers and professions that nudged studio and network heads to meet with representatives.[81] During the early 1970s, feminist community building had begun in and among SAG, WGA, DGA, the Inter-Studio Alliance of Women, Rights of Women Playwrights (New York), the National Organization of Women Image Committee, and Actors Equity and Publicists Guild Local 818.[82] In 1972, in an uncustomary move, SAG and the WGA met together with television networks to discuss how companies could improve their hiring track records with regard to women. Kathleen Nolan, founder of SAG's Women's Committee and later the Guild's first female president, was particularly driven by a vision of collaborative activism among all industry women. "SAG-WGA joint women's committee will enlarge and grow to encompass all the creative women in America—a pretty lofty objective," claimed Nolan.[83] The organizing efforts across professions demonstrated both the passion with which women were responding to the discrimination they faced and their collective understanding of how to use feminism as a tool of political action and reform.

The Writers Guild Women's Committee was founded in 1971 by member Diana Gould, who in the next year described her fellow comrades-in-arms, including Joyce Perry, Jean Rouverol, and Noreen Stone, as "a strong, closely-knit group of women writers. . . . We wanted to find out if we really were being discriminated against. We learned from each other immediately: *We were*."[84] When the Women's Committee was formed, the Writers Guild had an estimated 3,000 members, of whom 337 (11 percent) were women.[85] Gould and her peers represented a new generation of forward-thinking writers who were received with some wariness by the Guild. Maggie Weisberg, interviewer for the *WGAw Newsletter* (Writers Guild of America, West), the publication that circulated to WGA members only, conveyed the hesitancy that a portion of the membership felt about moving into the feminist age. Weisberg admitted, in the first paragraph of her cheerful profile of Gould, that "in this discomfiting era of pressure and demands for change at a pace faster than we are willing to accommodate, we sometimes feel that the words *revolutionary* and *undesirable* are synonymous. And if that sounds like Personal True Confessions, so be it. Most of us are somewhat guilty of dragging our heels."[86]

The Women's Committee members were not shy about naming their political influences and affiliations even at the risk of professional marginalization in an industry where sometimes "*revolutionary* and *undesirable* are synonymous." As Gould wrote in the *WGAw Newsletter* about the formation of the group, "Others of us came for the chance to meet other women writers. Others of us came from the Women's Liberation Movement—yes, still the Women's Liberation Movement."[87] Gould described how the impact of the group gave its participants "the courage to become more aggressive." Faced with similar career obstacles these women were empowered by the rhetoric of second-wave feminism, which they cultivated within their committee meetings. "The word aggressive is only pejorative when applied to a woman daring to go beyond the role assigned to her," explained Gould to the WGA's broader membership, confronting head-on the stigma associated with "aggressive" women. "A professional writer who wants to work has to be tenacious, persistent, determined—and AGGRESSIVE. Damn it."[88]

Gould, in 1967, had found early success in Hollywood: while still an undergraduate studying film at UCLA she was hired by Columbia as a screenwriter on *Short Ends*, a movie about film students. The film ultimately did not get produced, but Gould, who had a ten-week guarantee, was all of a sudden making $450 a week compared to the 75 cents an hour she had been earning as a college student working in the library. "By the time I had graduated from college I was a member of the [WGA], I had an agent, and I had job. It was ridiculous. It was unheard of."[89] In 1969 she sold her script, *Did You Hear about Jenny Shapiro*, to ABC's newly formed Palamor, where it was slated to be the company's first feature film. It was an expansion of the script for the short film *I Lost It at the Movies* (1968), which Gould had made while still a student at UCLA.[90] The feature tells a feminist-themed story about a young Jewish woman who is an impassioned cinephile—obsessed and inspired by the actresses of classic Hollywood—and then becomes pregnant. Jenny is single and facing social disgrace, especially from her overbearing mother, when she meets a young filmmaker who has just been drafted. Together they strike a deal to get married to keep her from being shamed and to keep him out of the war. Marlo Thomas, who was looking for material that would expand the independent but wholesome brand cultivated in her popular television series *That Girl*, was attracted to the material's feminist subject matter and was signed to play the lead character, with Alan Alda as the male costar. Thomas had initially wanted a prestigious director, imagining the project to be like a foreign independent film. French New Wave filmmaker Agnès Varda was brought in for a meeting, but in the end, Thomas decided on George Bloomfield, a first-time director from Canada.

Gould's original script was from the female protagonist's point of view, but during rewrites, Bloomfield began to refashion the narrative to favor the male character's perspective. Concerned about the redirection of her story, Gould had a revelation of how to explain what was at the core of her character's conflict and transformation. It was the weekend that the Beatles' "White Album" was released, and she had read a review about how the song "Julia" "was all the more resonate when you realized that Julia was John Lennon's mother. I showed [Bloomfield] the review and told him: 'this is what this movie is about. It's about this girl and her mother,'" remembered Gould. "The next day I got fired. He said, 'you're too close to the material' and he brought in a friend of his and they rewrote it." The exact qualities that made the novice screenwriter stand out—a distinct young female voice broaching topics of empowerment and emancipation, at a time when feminist themes, driven by a female protagonist, in Hollywood scripts were not commonplace—was precisely what ostracized Gould on her first produced feature. "I was young and I wasn't that skilled a writer, yet, and he was asking me to do things I didn't know how to do and so, of course, I thought it was my fault."[91]

The film, renamed *Jenny*, was released to mixed reviews. Understandably, Gould's reaction was of dismay. "When I saw the movie, I just ran out. I couldn't watch it. It was *unbearable*."[92] Deeply disappointed by the experience, Gould found herself in New York City at the moment when feminist agitation was igniting. She joined the radical feminist group Red Stockings and then Media Women, where she was part of the 1970 *Ladies Home Journal* protest, when a group of feminists staged a sit-in in the magazine's offices demanding better treatment of its female staff and female-focused content, and she attended her first consciousness-raising group. Encouraged by these encounters with women coming together and speaking about their personal and professional experiences, Gould returned to Los Angeles with the idea to talk with the women of the WGA about their work as writers. "It was very exciting," recalled Gould in 2016 of the early meetings. "Everybody who came came because *they knew* that the women's movement was starting to happen and people knew that it meant them. People talked about what they had experienced as women writers. . . . We didn't have any idea—I certainly didn't—of what we'd become. We decided we'd become a committee."[93] In a 1978 interview with the Guild History Committee, Betty Ulius was equally emphatic about the need for and impact of the WGA's Women's Committee, of which she was one of its original members. She recalled that in 1971, "We had a nucleus of about 35 women and we sat down in a circle and we started to talk to each other and it was the most incredible consciousness-raising session that I can conceive of, because these were people who had been absolutely invisible in the Guild and when we started to talk to each other about the problems of going in and telling a story to producers or to story editors we found that we all had exactly the same problems."[94] The problem was that women were not being hired to the same extent as their male peers.

In 1973, angered by women writers' inability to secure jobs, committee member Joyce Perry came up with the idea of gathering hiring data and creating a statistical analysis that would serve as evidence for how few female writers were being employed by television network shows.[95] In this effort the Women's Committee found an ally in board member Howard Rodman, who was initially the only male committee member. Rodman—whose wife, actress Norma Connolly, was an active member of the Screen Actors Guild's Women's Committee—was influential in getting the WGA board's approval for the collecting of statistics from confidential WGA records.[96] According to Jean Butler, who was one of the chairpersons during the committee's early years, the statistics committee (a subcommittee within the Women's Committee), headed by Perry, "went down the employment figures for every production company—every show that year. How many men. How many women. What percent. And it was so shocking and without realizing that we were breaking rules," she laughed, "we released it to the trades. You're not supposed to release anything" without approval."[97] As Sue Cameron, feminist columnist at the *Hollywood Reporter* during the 1970s, told Mollie Gregory, "In November 1973, Joyce Perry slipped me a copy of the WGA Committee's survey of the '72 to '73 shows. I was truly amazed. That survey shocked me. I printed it word for word without anyone's permission, just slapped it in there and sent it off."[98] The data broke down by gender the writers hired on sixty-two shows whose credits had been posted by the time Cameron's column went to press in November 1973. "That survey was an explosion," recalled Cameron, thirty years later. The day her column ran, the phones at the *Hollywood Reporter* rang nonstop. Women and men called horrified at the numbers, and some producers, implicated by the evidence, phoned up trying to defend themselves. "It woke up the city," marveled Cameron.[99]

*The Mary Tyler Moore Show*, the era's groundbreaking "working-woman" sitcom created by James L. Brooks and Allan Burns, had that season's best record for hiring women: of the staff of 75 writers, 25 (33 percent) were female. Norman Lear's Tandem production company, heralded for producing shows with progressive political themes involving class, gender, and race, did not fare as well. Tandem's *Maude*, one of the most explicitly feminist series on television during the 1970s, had a staff of 37 writers, of whom 7 (19 percent) were women. Tandem's *All in the Family* tallied much worse numbers with a staff of 73 writers; only 4 (6 percent) were women. Any assumptions that women were best suited for humorous topics related to personal relationships and parenting driven by female characters were quickly disproven by the low number of female writers hired on family-themed comedy series. The *Brady Bunch* had a staff of 133 writers, 15 (11 percent) of whom were women; the *Partridge Family* had a staff of 76 writers, only 7 (9 percent) of whom were women. The *Carol Burnett Show* had a staff of 9 writers, with only one woman among them (11 percent). Reinforcing attitudes common in the industry that women could not write for male characters or genres associated with men, action-oriented, male-centric dramas reported the lowest numbers of female hires: *M*A*S*H* had a staff of 38 writers, with only one woman (3 percent); *Hawaii Five-O* had a staff of 133 writers, of which one woman cowrote a script, giving the show half of a female writer. Some programs did even worse than half of a woman: *Barnaby Jones* (staff of twenty-seven writers), *Columbo* (staff of twenty writers), and *Kojak* (staff of seven writers) did not hire a single woman writer that season.[100]

Reporting on the numbers for *Variety*, Bill Greeley addressed the industry's mood while on the precipice of a revolutionary shift: "In the light of a lot of talk about opening up the field to more women writers, the women's committee of the Writers Guild of America (West) has made a survey which is likely to surprise more than the hardline women's rights advocates."[101] This numerical data analysis was the first of its kind to be conducted by members of a Hollywood union. The women of the WGA produced indisputable evidence of sexist hiring practices that publicly shamed networks and production companies, establishing a template that would be used by other industry professionals, particularly those organizing within their guilds, for generations to come.

Necessary to validating the women's argument that they were being shut out of employment due to gender was enlisting the support of WGA's board of directors. In addition, Michael H. Franklin, WGA's executive director, provided strong support to the Women's Committee. Franklin would become one of the era's most influential and ardent advocates for guild women, first at the Writers Guild and from 1978–1988 as the national executive secretary of the Directors Guild (see chapter 4).

In June 1974, Franklin followed up the release of the incriminating data from the 1973 television season with a letter to all 850 WGA signatories. In this letter, Franklin situated the union as a promoter of equal opportunity based on talent and not quotas, explaining that "we do want all of our members to have an *equal chance* at employment. . . . We want you to employ our members solely on the basis of merit, not because of sex, color, age or any other reason not related to talent."[102] Accompanying the letter was an analysis of the 1973 statistics detailing the number of women and men writers hired on each show. Franklin presented the information as an opportunity for producers to "analyze these findings with a view to examining your own hiring practices." However, the executive director's intention was not merely to encourage superficial reflection. This introductory material was followed by questions that asked explicitly about company attitudes toward hiring women: "Have you done anything subtly or directly to discourage women from seeking writing employment on your projects? Do you believe that men write better than women? If so, do you have solid evidence to support that belief? Have you ever employed a woman as a writer? If not, why?"[103] Although it is unclear how the signatories responded to Franklin, what is certain is that a letter such as this one, written by the executive director and reprinted in the union's newsletter, sent a strong message to the WGA membership, studio heads, and television executives. It indicated that the Writers Guild was not only interested in exposing patterns of discrimination within the industry but was also resolute about supporting its female members' fight against sexism. Furthermore, the Women's Committee instilled, through its example of advocacy and fearlessness, a sense of empowerment that proved to be of benefit for all the union's members. "I feel that the whole Guild structure has been loosened for the good because of what the Women's Committee has done," said Betty Ulius, proudly, in 1978. "Male writers are also feeling much more comfortable with the structure of the Guild. They also feel more comfortable about getting up and screaming, which I don't think they did for a long time."[104]

In the Screen Actors Guild, the initiative to create a Women's Conference Committee in 1972 and, later in that same year, a Minority Committee came from the board and not an individual member, as in the WGA. Dennis Weaver, then president of SAG, later described how he convinced the board to create a Women's Committee: he had heard a powerful speech made by an unnamed woman member at a general Guild meeting that detailed the "overt discrimination" taking place within the film and television industries and the "distorted image" it was creating of women in the media. "So disquieting was her description . . . so telling was her candid analysis . . . [that] the Board moved quickly and forcefully to initiate a program [the Women's Committee] which hopefully would result in a proper balance of employment for members of *both* sexes."[105] The Women's Committee's mission statement was explicit: "to work in all areas for equal opportunity for employment, regardless of sex, age or race." The Women's Committee and the Minority Committee frequently teamed together on outreach and advocacy efforts, and many of SAG's women of color members were members of both.[106]

Kathleen Nolan, one of the Women's Committee's founding members, who at the time was the first vice president of SAG, became the committee's first chair. Other SAG members who were active in the Women's Committee and the Minority Committee were Norma Connolly, Janet MacLachlan, and Sumi Haru, all of whom, along with Nolan, had formed a "Women's Bloc" on the Guild's board of directors.[107] During the early and mid-1970s an unprecedented surge of female leadership took place within SAG, a union with a conservative past. Nolan was chairwoman of the Women's Committee from its inception in 1972 until 1975 when she was elected as the Guild's first female president by a landslide; she was reelected for a second term in 1977. At the time of her first election, SAG's total membership was an estimated 28,000, of whom 30 percent were women.[108]

Described by historian David F. Prindle as a "positive dynamo," Nolan "embarked on a personal crusade to reshape the Screen Actors Guild into an activist, politically liberal labor union."[109] On winning her first presidential election she praised her fellow actors, celebrating their potential power within the industry: "We are really something to be reckoned with," Nolan beamed. Quoted in a *Variety* article headlined "First Femme to Hold Top Post Vows Militant Action," Nolan explained, "The actors are not going to play anybody's game anymore. We're going to make changes in this community and country. We're going to have the economic justice and creative dignity that we all deserve."[110] Yet Nolan was careful not to appear as too much of a militant feminist, in spite of the sensationalized headline: as the leader of one of the largest guilds in the film and television industry, Nolan recognized the importance of being responsive to a membership that included both women *and* men. However, while "community" was a consistent part of her rhetoric as a SAG leader, she was a fierce spokesperson who never shied away from the truth, which demanded a new and what some would consider a revolutionary approach. "Ours is a male-oriented business, just as ours is a male-oriented society," said Nolan to the *Los Angeles Times* in 1972. "It's time that some of that changed."[111]

Following the example of the Writers Guild, SAG's Women's Committee began gathering data to provide hard evidence of the discrimination actresses were experiencing. It organized a research team of forty-two members, including both women and men, and monitored for a month the three networks' primetime programming to measure how often and in what capacity their female members were employed. The data sweeps focused on network television, presumably because there was more programming produced than film, particularly in terms of commercials, and thus more roles to be cast. Researchers measured the screen time, as well as the kinds of characters women played and in what kind of formats (e.g., drama, comedy, variety shows, game shows, commercials). In the surveyed month in 1974, the researchers found the following: ABC programming featured 75.6 percent men and 24.4 percent women, CBS programming featured 66 percent men and 34 percent women, and NBC programming featured 73 percent men and 27 percent women.

Racial and ethnic minority representation on all three networks totaled 12.7 percent: African Americans, 5.8 percent; Asians, 1.6 percent; Mexican Americans, 0.83 percent, Native Americans, 0.29 percent, and "other minorities," 4.2 percent.[112]

An area of concern was women's employment in television commercials. According to data gathered by SAG's New York branch of the Women's Conference Committee, television commercials produced the most income, of any screen time, for SAG members. In 1973, commercials generated 53.6 percent of the income for Guild members, for a total of $73.5 million. These earnings were almost $50 million more than what performers were paid in theatrical films and $36 million more than what they made in television.[113] Using television commercial reels submitted to the Clio Awards by the top ten advertisers, which represented a range of consumer products, the volunteer committee members calculated screen time by gender. Men outnumbered women on-screen by an average of 2 to 1. Men were hired for off-camera speaking parts (voice-over) in 93 percent of commercials and for 71 percent of off-camera singing parts. Men even dominated commercials selling goods that targeted women, such as cleaning products and cosmetics. Seventy percent of women in commercials were cast in nonspeaking roles.[114]

Like the statistics calculated by the Writers Guild, SAG's data provided indisputable evidence that women and minority performers were excluded from leading roles and from screen time altogether. Less work meant less pay and so lower contributions to these members' pension plans: employment discrimination thus affected not only their present standard of living but also their future financial security. Discrimination also affected the quality of their careers. Women and actors of color were consistently being cast in minor parts and were playing unrealistic characters that perpetuated stereotypes. How could they build a meaningful body of work based on these small and demeaning roles? Furthermore, what impact were these portrayals—or lack thereof—having on audiences? In 1973, at what *Variety* described as an "historic meeting" between representatives of the Guild's Minority and Women's Committees and about twenty network executives, SAG member Karen Welch challenged the television industry's contention that it did not have the power to correct the imbalance. "Don't lie to the viewers. Show them the truth. The truth is variety. . . . Share some of your strengths by giving us all a chance to show our talents," implored Welch. "All we ask is to be given a chance to be treated on an equal basis."[115]

To support their pleas for better roles and their warnings regarding the ramifications of withholding the "truth" from audiences, the committee researchers distributed an "attitude survey" to twenty-two daily newspapers across the country asking reader-viewers what they wanted to see on television. The 10,000 questionnaires yielded 8,700 responses; 83.6 percent were from women, 15 percent were from men, and 1.5 percent did not specify gender. Although fewer men responded to the survey, those who did participate were overwhelmingly in support of seeing women on television in positions of authority: 62.6 percent of men and 67.2 percent of women respondents were in favor of these changes. An overwhelming majority of those polled said they would like to see female characters, and the actresses who played them, in roles of authority such as spokeswomen for national products, as hosts of talk shows and children's programs, and as newscasters reporting on national headlines.[116] More than 63 percent of viewers responded that the portrayal of women on television was unrealistic and not believable, and 66.2 percent felt that the media representation of women did not present good role models for girls. Feedback from viewers supported the committees' claims that representations of women on television did influence the way in which women were perceived in contemporary society. Furthermore, viewers, specifically women viewers, *were* paying attention to the networks and production companies' casting decisions and the kinds of women characters being presented to them. For these audiences there was room for improvement.

Throughout the early and mid-1970s, SAG's Women's and Minority Committees would continue this approach of aggregating detailed statistical research that they then presented to executives from the networks, leading production companies, and film studios, as well as casting and talent agents, with the press on hand to report. In 1973, the two committees held what the press called the "first of its kind" meeting between women and minority leaders of the Screen Actors Guild and industry reps. In attendance was Thomas Sarnoff, NBC West Coast vice president, who was optimistic about the gathering. "The very fact that we're all here is proof that progress is being made," he said encouragingly.[117] Still, Sarnoff was cautious, acknowledging the committees' findings without making any definitive promises. "No matter what we try to do, there's no way that we can do it fast enough to satisfy all of you," the executive warned. "That doesn't mean that we're not trying, or that we don't care. If when we don't do things that we should do or that you think we should do, you don't get mad at us, but help us to learn . . . then I think we will all succeed in this effort."[118] Sarnoff's comments were to become a familiar refrain during these years in exchanges between industry representatives and activists. Confronted with the numbers, executives could not avoid acknowledging that a gender and racial imbalance existed, but without a court order forcing them to adhere to antidiscrimination policies, such as company hiring quotas, those in power had no reason to make any definitive promises.

The Screen Actors Guild rarely threatened recourse to Title VII during these years when it exposed industry discrimination. In 1975, SAG targeted the appalling employment record of Universal Studios, disclosing how from 1973–1975 it hired men for 7,082 days of work compared to 1,834 days for women. During these three years women were hired for 650 parts versus the 2,221 roles men received. In response to these findings, the Guild's board of directors passed a resolution to pursue meetings with Universal, and if dissatisfied with the outcome, the union would consider filing a complaint with the EEOC.[119] Federal intervention was avoided as talks between the Women's Committee and Lew Wasserman, chairman of MCA Universal's parent company, and Sid Sheinberg, president of Universal, and an estimated dozen Universal executives—including Frank Price, president of Universal Television, casting chief Monique James, and labor relations director Gareth Hughes—continued over the next year. Eventually, and under what seemed to be amicable conditions, Universal agreed on a strategy to increase the casting of women and minorities by setting up meetings with individual producers.[120] But without a formal contract or official system in place to monitor and enforce the studio's supposed efforts to adjust the casting process, any hope for a significant change was unrealistic.

Even though the members of SAG and the WGA created the first model of intraindustry feminist activism at the start of the 1970s, by the middle of the decade no systematic change in the employment status of women in above-the-line professions had taken place. As previously described, the government again became involved in Hollywood in

1976 in the form of the California Advisory Committee to the U.S. Commission on Civil Rights. The commission's purpose was to report on the effectiveness of the "good faith" affirmative action agreements resulting from the 1969 EEOC hearing and agreed to in 1970 in increasing the hiring of women and minorities, primarily in below-the-line professions. In 1976, the studios and trade unions were far less willing to cooperate with the General Services Administration, a federal agency reporting for the commission, than they had been with the EEOC seven years earlier. Craft unions resisted providing employment records, and subpoenas had to be requested for Warner Bros., Paramount, and 20th Century-Fox, which did not send representatives to attend the proceedings. Universal was the only studio willing to have its files audited. The effort in 1976 seemed less about finding an effective strategy for achieving job equity and more of an empty presentation of unimpressive numbers.[121]

By 1976, industry feminists, representing a range of employees, had met several times with network and studio representatives. The issues at stake had been clearly defined by comprehensive research and outlined in the press, and yet the number of women employed were still very low. A sense of fatigue settled in, making seem futile what felt promising and possible just a few years earlier at the beginning of the decade. In place of all the "firsts"—first released statistics, first meetings between union representatives and executives to "change" industry attitudes—guilds and federal agencies were hounding companies for annual employment reports that illustrated how little progress was being made. Even the government's involvement was suspect. In 1979, after close to a decade of vigilant advocacy, Sumi Haru, a representative for SAG's Minority and Women's Committees, expressed a profound sense of frustration: "These nice little meetings (with producers and studio heads) are not accomplishing it. The testimony before the U.S. Commission on Civil Rights [in 1976] isn't changing things."[122] Eventually, contractual provisions in guilds' basic agreements would become the new "good faith effort" recommending, rather than mandating, that companies try harder to end gender and racial discrimination. As discussed in chapter 4, this strategy would be used to increase the hiring of women directors, whose fierce activism at the end of the decade within their union, the Directors Guild, would be recognized, but also controlled in the "Non-Discrimination" Article 15 of its 1981 Basic Agreement.

During the first part of the 1970s, female employees, particularly those in above-the-line jobs who had engaged in high-profile activism, found themselves locked in a paradox: the industry leaders acknowledged the inequities faced by women working throughout the film and television industries, but did not admit to having any official policy of sexual and racial discrimination, nor were they willing to participate in any aggressive solutions for change, specifically court-ordered enforcement and affirmative action timetables and quotas. Government-mandated mediations and affirmative action solutions, as well as nondiscrimination policy clauses in guild contracts, created loopholes at every turn, making clear that the film and television business would not follow through on any lasting policy changes. While these flaws derailed reformists' strategies of confrontation and rectification, the dialogues, in particular those initiated by the Women and Minority Committees of the Screen Actors Guild and the Writers Guild throughout the decade, did result in some measure of increased opportunities for women and minorities—few as they were. This push and pull between the implementation of some small change while the system stayed in place would characterize the struggle experienced by women directors during these years, individually in their careers and collectively as a group.

# 2

# 1970s Cultures of Production

## *Studio, Art House, and Exploitation*

In 1968, Robert Evans, the young, brash vice president in charge of production for Paramount Pictures, announced in the press that the studio would be focusing on story development, a key component of which would be promoting the writer to "star status."[1] Paramount's shift to an emphasis on the writer as "star"—several of whom would also write and direct—was engineered by its new management, who was trying to make the studio's offerings more appealing to the younger and then powerful generation of moviegoers. Two years earlier, the studio had been bought by Gulf & Western (G&W), a conglomerate that manufactured a wide array of industrial materials. Charles Bluhdorn, who founded G&W, became president of the studio after the takeover. New to filmmaking, he hired Evans, a former actor and up-and-coming producer, along with entertainment reporter Peter Bart, to head production. Bart and Evans, both under the age of forty and themselves new to studio executive leadership, recognized that, for the company to stay competitive, it needed to produce innovative content that resonated with contemporary audiences.

In 1967 the company was promising its most ambitious production slate in twenty years. "It's Happening [*sic*] at Paramount," boasted Evans. "There is literally no limit to the activity that is planned or already in progress at the Paramount Studio to 'make it happen.'"[2] For these executives the source material would come from literary agents, books still in galley form, and writers. The studio had contracts with forty-one screenwriters, many of whom were slated to double as writer-producers or writer-directors. The roster was a mix of industry veterans, including Walter Bernstein and Alan Jay Lerner, and newcomers, such as Elaine May.[3]

## Elaine May

Clint Eastwood could do anything because he's tall and they respect him and in that way it is better to be Clint Eastwood than a woman in Hollywood.

—Elaine May[4]

In the late 1960s Elaine May was in the midst of a transition from a successful career performing live sketch comedy to film, initially as an actress and screenwriter, when she signed with Paramount in 1968 to write, direct, and costar in her directorial debut, *A New Leaf*.[5] Born in 1932 in Philadelphia, May was raised in a theatrical family. Her father, Jack Berlin, was a well-known actor in the Yiddish Theater and would often bring May on stage with him. After her father died when she was eleven, May and her mother, Ida Berlin, moved to Los Angeles. At fourteen, already self-assured and showing signs of defiance—qualities that would define her career in Hollywood—May "stopped going to school. . . . I really didn't like it," she told the *New York Times* in 1959. "The truancy people came around and threatened to take me to court, but I called their bluff. I sat around the house reading—mostly fairy tales and mythology."[6] At sixteen years old, she married Marvin May and at eighteen had her daughter, Jeannie Berlin. Never having graduated high school, May, then divorced from Marvin, decided to attend college and hitchhiked to the University of Chicago because that school did not require a high school diploma.[7] She met Mike Nichols in Chicago in 1954 when the two became part of the Compass Players, the landmark theater group that revolutionized the technique of improvisational comedy. As members of Compass, May and Nichols began to cultivate a unique brand of humor: social satire that teased the pretentiousness of highbrow intellectualism as much as it poked fun at the ordinary, everyday banter between coworkers at the office cooler, often making these two—seemingly separate worlds—collide. In 1957, after the Compass Players disbanded, the duo took their act to New York City where they experienced sudden and phenomenal success performing live comedy on television and in their 1961 Broadway show *An Evening with Mike Nichols and Elaine May*, which was later released as an album. By 1962 the team had split up. "She told me she was tired of what we had been doing of so many years," explained Nichols in 1967. "It was always a rule between us that we would respect each other's wishes."[8] Nichols was equally fatigued by the repetitive nature of the Broadway show and how fame required them to replay material that played favorably, "The longer you go, the harder it is. . . . It got so dehumanized and so unreal by the time we'd played [Broadway] for a year."[9] Nichols went on to immediate success as a theater and film director. May appeared to take her time deciding in which direction to aim her career, spending the 1960s as a playwright-director; a screenwriter contributing to *The Loved One* (1965); and an actress appearing in 1967 in Carl Reiner's film *Enter Laughing* and costarring with Peter Falk and Jack Lemmon in the screen adaptation of *Luv*—all before she embarked on directing her first film.

*A New Leaf*, based on the short story "The Green Heart" by Jack Ritchie, is a dark comedy starring May as Henrietta, an earnest but oblivious botanist-heiress, who is married to Henry, played by Walter Matthau, a bankrupted millionaire plotting the murder of his bride for her fortune. May had recruited Matthau, who at the time could guarantee ticket sales, to the project early, but she still could not secure studio interest in the film. Producer and talent manager Hillard Elkins recalled that it was Arthur Penn, who had directed May and Nichols's Broadway show, who introduced him to May, and together they successfully pitched the film to Paramount.[10] Eventually the project was packaged by Elkins and Howard Koch: Koch was Paramount's former vice president of production who had recently stepped down from his post (to be replaced by Evans) to accept an exclusive independent producer deal with the studio. But it was Koch and Matthau who were named in the initial deal memos as guaranteeing the delivery of the picture for $2.5 million to Paramount.[11] The two men were not only close friends but also co-owned a number of racehorses together and had collaborated previously at Paramount. In 1966 Koch had produced for the studio the successful film adaptation of Neil Simon's 1965 Tony-nominated play *The Odd Couple* (directed on Broadway by Mike Nichols, for which

Matthau had won a Tony Award for Best Actor); Matthau repeated his role in the film, which also starred Jack Lemmon. In spite of her well-recognized talent, it was imperative for May, as a novice filmmaker and as a woman, to have the production associated with experienced and successful male collaborators, and Matthau and Koch's track record with the studio provided the weight she needed.

Elaine May was the first woman director Paramount had hired since Dorothy Arzner directed *Merrily We Go to Hell* for the company in 1931. And the last studio feature to have been directed by a woman was *Trouble with Angels* (Columbia Pictures, 1966), helmed by Ida Lupino. Initially television director Norman Lloyd, who was then preparing to work with Matthau on another project for ABC, was slated to direct *A New Leaf*.[12] In Elkins's account, he had suggested to Bluhdorn that May would be willing to be paid less for writing and acting in the film if she could also direct it.[13] May, who throughout her entire career has given very few interviews, all of which teem with her quick wit and sarcasm, has always been quick to whittle down the politics of her hiring to economics. "I never wanted to be a director," she claimed in 1975. "Never . . . I wrote this script, and I wanted to sell it for a lot of money so I could be richer. . . . They were offering me an enormous amount of money. $200,000, I think. And [Elkins] . . . he had been my manager for two days, said, 'I've set a wonderful deal. I produce. You direct and write. And you get $50,000.'"[14] In 2006, May explained these negotiations in more detail: "Elkins said they won't give you director approval but they will allow you to direct it. . . . And then they wanted to have Carol Channing play the woman, and I said, 'No it has to be someone who really disappears. It's the guy's movie.' I said, 'Can I pick the person?' And they said, 'No, but you can play it. And all for the same money.'"[15]

May was paid $50,000 for her three roles; in contrast, costar Walter Matthau's salary was $375,000, in addition to various participation bonuses, and Elkins and Koch each received $50,000. After Matthau received his grosses, May shared 35 percent of the film's earnings with Matthau, Elkins, and Koch.[16]

Elkins had also argued that May, as the first woman to direct for Paramount, could boost the company's reputation, making it the only motion picture studio at the time to have hired a female director. Evans and Frank Yablans, Paramount executives at the time, resisted his offer,

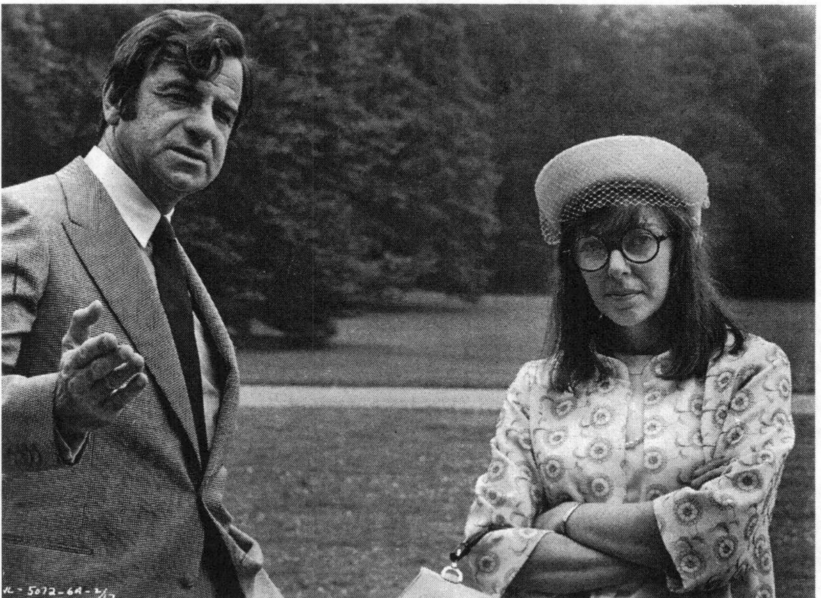

Fig. 3. Walter Matthau and Elaine May on the set of *A New Leaf* (Margaret Herrick Library, Academy of Motion Picture Arts and Sciences)

but Bluhdorn agreed to it.[17] In 1968, the studio seemed hardly interested in breaking gender barriers. While the picture's press release briefly mentions that May's multiple roles "mark[ed] the first time in film history a woman has handled the three assignments," pressure to hire women directors from the government and feminists, in or outside of the industry, had not yet begun to mobilize.[18] What was clear in Paramount's hiring of May as a triple threat—writer, director, actor—was that it enabled the studio not only to economize on paying for talent but also to exploit her skills and her position in the industry because she was a first-time director and a woman.

By May 1969, while the film would not begin production until June, the original budget of $1,875,00 was projected to increase by $325,000, partially due to the script revisions that were taking place, on top of which Bernard Donnenfeld, Paramount's production executive, anticipated another $300,000 could be added in the event that May, as a first time director, might require more time.[19] According to internal studio memos, in February Peter Bart had voiced his concerns about the screenplay to

Robert Evans. Bart was critical of what he saw as a disjointed story with moments of long-winded and unnecessary dialogue. "What we have here are two movies, not one," he complained. "The first is comedy-satire. The second is bald farce. The first has characterizations. The second has only shtick. I like the first. I dislike the second."[20] When the script revisions pushed the production schedule back, Donnenfeld expressed anxiety over May's ability to keep her film on track. Writing to Bluhdorn and Martin Davis, he explained how he and Evans agreed that the slight upward bump in the budget was a "good buy" to ensure that "without any experience with Elaine May—this being her first picture—we feel that we should add at least fifteen to twenty days to the schedule, which should cover delays, retakes or script revisions." Yet Donnenfeld was anticipating a larger conflict than what Bart and May had presumably encountered over script differences: as he reminded his colleagues, "We certainly have the right to step in and take over the completion of the picture; but, as we all know, this is a highly volatile procedure [taking a film away from its director] and usually does not work."[21]

Production began on June 2, 1969, and was completed in October 1969, but by then the budget had ballooned to $3,010,000, and animosity among the various studio executives and their star filmmaker had continued to grow. Howard Koch had departed the production during filming to oversee *On a Clear Day You Can See Forever* (1970), another Paramount project, and in July had expressed his doubts about *A New Leaf* in a bittersweet letter to May: "I look forward to seeing the final result, and I hope that any reservations I had as far as the quality of the picture is concerned are all dissipated at that time."[22] In a 2015 interview with Mae Woods for the Visual History program of the Academy of Motion Picture Arts and Sciences, Stanley Jaffe, who would become president of the studio in 1970 and who took over for Koch as a producer on the picture, recalled how Bluhdorn had summoned him when the film "finished shooting its 32nd day on a 33 day original schedule, and they were 40 percent into the movie. So the picture was clearly going runaway."[23] Even after principal photography was completed in the fall of 1970, Jaffe wrote to the studio brass that he anticipated more delays, expenditures, and difficulties in postproduction: he predicted that "Elaine May, being one of the more indecisive people, will probably require more editing time than is presently estimated."[24]

Editing on the film did go over schedule, and eventually the studio stepped in and took the picture away from May. According to the contract, the director was allowed to make the first and second cuts of the film, each with a public preview, permitting she adhered to the agreed-on schedule; however, the final cut was in the studio's hands.[25] Evans, Jaffe, and Koch supervised the re-editing of the film, changing May's original ending, in which Henry succeeds in murdering two characters while preparing to kill Henrietta, before having a change of heart and sparing his bride because of his newfound feelings of affection.[26] In response, May sued the studio in January 1971, claiming in the complaint filed by her attorneys "that the script was drastically changed and there has been a distortion and truncation of plaintiff's work. . . . The film has been changed from a comedy suspense story to a cliché-ridden, banal story. Totally new scenes have been constructed, large parts of the story have been omitted. Nearly every line of dialogue is out of context with the result that the film being released is in no way plaintiff's [*sic*]."[27] May claimed that "the film is more the work of Par v.p. Robert Evans . . . and she wants an injunction against its release and any publicity about it."[28] Paramount countered with a breach-of-contract defense, appealing to the judge directly by showing him Paramount's version of the film. According to Koch, "The lights went down and the judge sat there and he screamed and laughed, and the lights go up and he says, 'It's the funniest picture in years. You guys win.'"[29] Jaffe remembered a similar reaction from the judge after he saw Paramount's cut: "Ms. May, I have to tell you, if my wife saw this she would think it was fantastic. It's a terrific movie you've made." The case was heard in the New York Supreme Court, where the judge denied May's request for an injunction and Paramount went ahead with the release of the film as planned.[30] "I understand [that she was] upset," empathized Jaffe, "but it was the same movie except for this one thing which for her was material, and for the audience was not."[31]

In spite of the conflict between May and Paramount, and the director's attempt to separate herself from the picture, the film did well at the box office, after opening around Easter of 1971. *Variety* reported, "Paramount's solid-gold 'New Leaf' at Radio City Music hall [was] continuing to crowd them in with a holiday take of something near $250,000. Despite her objections, the success of the film will almost certainly establish Elaine May as an important director."[32] Critics and the public, as indicated by the initial box office returns, were eager to see an Elaine May film. Gene Siskel of the *Chicago Tribune* described how "Miss May writes and directs with uncommon grace. . . . Her comedy—both visual and aural—is reminiscent of such classic films as 'It Happened One Night' and 'Bringing Up Baby.' Tender zaniness and all that. . . . [*A New Leaf*] deserves your attention."[33] The *Hollywood Reporter* found some of the comedy uneven, but admitted, "One forgives the indulgences, one genuinely wonders what the picture was like before it was cut." Endorsing the film, the review continued: "For those who lack enthusiasm for slickly manufactured comedies, 'A New Leaf' is a lovely alternate way of seeing the world, and there will be a lot of people who will welcome the change."[34] Critics openly sided with May, and their praise of the film vindicated her talent as a filmmaker, while inadvertently validating Paramount's decision to interfere with her creative process. Vincent Canby, film critic for the *New York Times*, whose acerbic style rarely swayed toward the sentimental, offered unconditional praise for May. "Miss May may be right," Canby pronounced. "Her version may be better than Paramount's, and, theoretically anyway (not having seen the other version), I'm on her side. Still, the movie . . . is so nutty and so funny, so happily reminiscent of the screwball comedies people aren't supposed to be able to make any more, I'm quite satisfied to let things stand."[35]

By the end of the year, despite the delays and disputes, the film had grossed $5 million, making back its budget and overruns.[36] It is conceivable that the movie could have earned more if there had not been so much discord between the executives and May, if May had been willing to promote the film, and if Paramount was not then dedicating a good deal of its resources to its first blockbuster success of the 1970s, *Love Story* (starring Evans's wife at the time, Ali MacGraw). However, considering the circumstances, breaking even on such a small picture may have been the best conclusion to an unpleasant situation. During a rare interview in 1975, May described the fallout from *A New Leaf* in humorous terms. "I went way over budget, and I went over schedule and became a very hot director as a result," she joked. "I think it has only to do with going over schedule, that had I come in on time, no one would have wanted me."[37] In fact, May embarked on her next project soon thereafter: in January 1972 she started production on *The Heartbreak Kid*, directing Neil Simon's script for 20th Century-Fox.[38] The film is a classic 1970s romantic comedy: hilarious at the expense of great heartbreak (as the title aptly suggests). Charles Grodin stars as Lenny, a Jewish New York newlywed obsessed with appearances, who is on his honeymoon with his bride Lila, played by Jeannie Berlin, May's twenty-three-year-old daughter; she is less self-conscious than her husband, eating candy bars in bed and talking incessantly during sex. Lenny leaves Lila for Kelly, an idealized, bikini-clad blonde WASP played by Cybil Shepherd. In contrast to *A New Leaf*, *The Heartbreak Kid* was completed without any studio interference or delays due to May's creative process, occurrences that would plague each of the subsequent two films she would go on to write and direct. Anthea Sylbert, who was the costume designer on *A New Leaf* and *The Heartbreak Kid* and knew May well, thought that she was more successful as a "director for hire," because the script was not hers. "It divorces you slightly," explained Sylbert. "You can look at the material a little more objectively than your own material."[39]

Again, Canby was in May's corner, describing the movie as "a first-class American comedy" and giving credit for that to the talents of May, rather than the veteran playwright Simon: "'The Heartbreak Kid' occasionally goes for laughs without shame (which is what has always bothered me about Simon's brand of New York comedy), but behind the laughs there is, for a change, a real understanding of character—which is something that, I suspect, can be attributed to Miss May. The film is an unequivocal hit."[40] The dark satire that May had attempted to pull off in the original murderous plot of *A New Leaf* was achieved in *The Heartbreak Kid*, with its devastating interpretation of romantic love in the 1970s. Stephen Farber, writing for the *New York Times* was dazzled by May's ability to cut through what he considered the pretense of matrimony and the way Hollywood packaged the fantasy. "The movies have defined 'love' for us—in impossibly exalted terms," the critic bemoaned, "and 'The Heartbreak Kid' sets out to redefine it." For Farber, much of the film's pleasure stemmed from how relatable he found the characters and their circumstances. "At first the film seems to be a slight, narrow satire about people to who [*sic*] we can feel comfortably superior," he admitted. "Gradually that sense of superiority disintegrates, as we recognize the delusions we share with the characters." The critic proclaimed that, "with her second feature, Elaine May becomes a major American director."[41]

Where Farber found gratification in the ease with which he could identify with *The Heartbreak Kid*'s central themes, feminist critics bristled both at the depiction of Lila and at May's casting of her daughter in a role many felt was degrading. Joan Mellon was incensed: the portrayal of "Lila is so gross that her body and its carriage are used by May to revolt us all. It is a conception born of a considerable self-hatred—of women, Jews, and, at some level, her own daughter."[42] Molly Haskell was equally concerned with how May seemed to be "punishing" her daughter in the film.[43] Marjorie Rosen, who acknowledged that "it's a tricky movie, because a lot of it *is* funny," was ultimately disappointed in how the only woman making films for the studios was behaving "like an Uncle Tom whose feminine sensibilities are demonstrably nil." These critics, who would emerge as some of the most ardent watchdogs of Hollywood sexism, were especially tough on female artists who, because there were so few of them, automatically carried the burden of representing all women directors. Rosen, who felt "May enjoys broad caricatures, especially of her women characters," and that Lila received "special buffoon treatment," was sure that the filmmaker, based on her skill and experience, knew what was at risk by working with characterizations that were funny on the one hand, but to many perpetuated negative stereotypes of Jewish women. She speculated that, after the team of Nichols and May disbanded, May must have felt some disappointment in watching Nichols's immediate ascension as Broadway and Hollywood's "Golden Boy," while she was given fewer opportunities. "*She's been there*, as they say," exclaimed Rosen, "she knows what's at stake."[44]

Yet the mother-and-daughter team prevailed. This first collaboration would be the first of many, although later the two would work together in theater more often than in film. "This girl I was playing was so naïve, she was kind of standing there with her paws out, listening to whatever he said and understanding it and thinking it was all her fault," reflected Berlin in an interview conducted soon after the release of the movie. "I knew I had to keep it real."[45] In a *New York Times* article, Berlin described working with her mother as "a dream. A pleasure. Terrific. No scenes. No trauma. . . . There was nothing about mother-daughter relationships. She directed me the way she directed everyone else, which was allowing you to 'go'—to do what your impulses told you to do."[46]

Simon was possessive of his dialogue and had it in his contract that no lines could be changed unless discussed with him. "I'm not wedded to the words, in that you have to do my words," he explained. "I just want to be in on the conversation. . . . I don't want coauthors unless I am there to coauthor it with them." When asked if she would "polish up Simon's script a bit," May snapped back, "Why should I? I think 'Doc' can do this stuff without my help."[47] Yet Simon did allow May to improvise as a part of her rehearsal process: "For a number of days during shooting Elaine threw the [script] out and said to the actors, 'Just play those attitudes, make up your own words.' . . . Then when they put these words back in, it seemed as though they were still improvising." After so much strife and conflict on *A New Leaf*, the way in which Simon exerted his artistic control while leaving some room for May's practice did seem to elicit a conducive creative experience. "It's her style of directing," praised Simon, "and I found it wonderful."[48] The broader industry response echoed Simon's admiration: Berlin and costar Eddie Albert were both nominated for Best Supporting Actress and Best Supporting Actor Oscars.

May was beginning to accumulate hits as she started production on her next film, *Mikey & Nicky*, which she would both write and direct. *Mikey & Nicky* stars John Cassavetes and Peter Falk in a gangster-buddy melodrama that takes place during the course of one night: it is centered on two mobster best friends, one of whom (Falk) has been hired to kill the other (Cassavetes). May had sold *Mikey & Nicky* to United Artists in 1969 while she was in production on *A New Leaf*. At that time, Cassavetes and Falk were already attached to the project, and the film was set to start shooting during the spring of 1970.[49] Surprisingly, based on her recent history with the studio, May ended up back at Paramount, but this time under the protection of studio chief Frank Yablans, who had become a champion of the filmmaker. *Mikey & Nicky* was reportedly budgeted at close to $2.2 million, and Paramount was extremely cautious working with May a second time.[50] The studio produced a thirty-three-page, single-spaced contract that stipulated that, if the film went over budget, the costs would come out of May's salary. Furthermore, if the film went 15 percent over budget, Paramount would be allowed to take it away from the filmmaker. In return, May was given final cut—complete control over the picture's final version—and the guarantee that the only executive she would have to work with would be Yablans, thus avoiding contact with

Robert Evans, her adversary from *A New Leaf*. The film was to be finished and delivered to the studio by June 1, 1974.[51]

Even with the built-in protection and warning system, the film's progress soon slowed. The production lasted for 120 days, all of which were night shoots, and accumulated enough footage "to stretch, if not halfway to the moon, at least from New York to Washington and on over Key Bridge into Virginia."[52] May was notorious for reshooting scenes numerous times and requiring the crew to dismantle and rebuild sets, including repaving the street because she wanted the characters to be walking in a different direction.[53] Her demands pushed the logistical limits of a film production—even those of a major studio with ample resources. But May's talent was also acknowledged and revered by those around her. During his visit to the set in 1973, journalist Dan Rottenberg observed, "She may be shy, insecure, nervous, gawky, and female in a field dominated by men. But she is also a perfectionist in an age of schlock. For that reason everyone on the crew, from [her producer Michael] Hausman on down, worships her."[54]

Paramount agreed to rent out several rooms in the Sunset Marquis Hotel in West Hollywood for May to oversee the editing of the film—a process that suffered prolonged chaos similar to that afflicting the production. In Andrew Tobias's exposé of the film's debacle in *New West*, published around the time of its theatrical release, he described May during the editing as "obsessed. . . . You could walk by her rooms at two or three in the morning and there she would be with an editor, cutting." May rarely left the hotel suites, which "were hopelessly strewn with candy wrappers, half-eaten sandwiches, and, seemingly, months of accumulated cigarette butts." The joke was that the only way for the studio to get a copy of the film was to call in the health department.[55] The flipside to such obsessive behavior was May's acute understanding of the movie she wanted to make. Sheldon Kahn, one of the film's editors, described her as the "brightest person I ever worked with. . . . Elaine has a photographic memory. If we cut a scene thirteen ways, she'd go, 'The third way was the best.' Then she'd recall it frame by frame."[56]

In September 1975, after May had been editing the film for more than a year, Paramount finally refused to advance the production any more money. According to different accounts in the press, she then sold the movie—legally Paramount's property—to Alyce Film Inc., a company owned by Peter Falk, for $90,000. Paramount sued the filmmaker, and a judge ordered her to return the film. May gave back all but two reels of the movie, keeping them hostage in the hopes that Paramount's new vice chairman, Barry Diller (who had replaced Yablans), would agree to release additional funds. In a phone call between the two, Diller told May, "If you return it, I give you my word that things will go right for you. But I won't be blackmailed." Within minutes, the missing reels were delivered to Diller's office.[57] May remembered the story differently. During a retrospective of her work at the Harvard Film Archives in 2011, she told archive director Haden Guest that her conflict with Paramount over the film stemmed from the fact that Yablans and Diller did not get along. Diller had replaced Yablans, May's strongest advocate at the studio, under contentious circumstances in November 1974. During the changeover, "I think Diller said to Yablans, 'Why have you let her make this movie,'" laughed May. "And Yablans said to Diller, as was his wont, 'Fuck You.' And then they had a big fight. I mean they were *really*, *really* at each other's throats."[58] When pressed to explain why the studio filed charges against her, May was as incredulous as she was coy: "I never knew why. And I once asked [Diller], because we became, of course, friends: 'I said why did you sue me?' And he said: 'I don't know.'"

May also offered another account of the missing reels. Confirming that the negative had in fact been stolen, although the circumstances of its disappearance and the identity of the thief she continued to elude in a playful way, when the legal team at Paramount decided to file criminal charges, "because the negative may have crossed state lines," Diller was adamant in his opposition to such a move. "'Are you *crazy*?'" May quoted the studio chairman as saying. "'You want us to be the only studio that *jails* a director for going over budget?! Are you *crazy*?'" According to May, "They actually dropped the suit because of that . . . they just let the subpoena ride . . . and they said 'OK, just have the negative show up, although I didn't know where it was, but I put the word out, and it came back," and the studio finished editing the film." Addressing the Harvard audience, May added, "But I want to tell you." That no matter how you re-cut this, it wasn't going to be a comedy, anyway."[59]

Paramount gave the film a limited release at the end of 1976. Including legal fees, the picture ended up costing the studio close to $5 million. Those critics who wrote about the picture were bewildered. Charles

Champlin was remorseful in his poor review of the film: "In a long lifetime you are not apt to find more intelligence and good acting expended on a lost cause than in Elaine May's 'Mikey and Nicky' [*sic*]."[60] For the *Independent Film Journal*, the months spent working with her two actors had paid off, but not for the benefit of the overall movie: "Cassavetes, in fact, has rarely been better. Unfortunately, the story is slight and the reverberations from what transpires, intended as shock waves, emerge more like ripples. Downbeat in subject and commercial prospects. Elaine May loses her story, her characters and most of her audience."[61] Similar to the critics, the studio executives were also disappointed as they had been expecting an "Elaine May" comedy and were instead faced with a visually and thematically dark film about two neurotic gangsters battling their paranoia and guilt over the course of a rainy night. "It was odd to them because it was about guys," recalled May. "It was a gangster movie that was funny only for a limited amount of time. And I wanted it to look streety [*sic*], rainy; it was shot at night, sort of like it was captured. And they didn't like that. . . . They weren't prepared for it." In 2011 May was still dumbfounded by their expectations: "Thinking this was a comedy really killed me. It was a cheap little movie. I don't know why they let me do it. . . . I think because *The Heartbreak Kid* was so successful. But they were also horrified to see it."[62]

In 1967, years before her conflicts with the studios, Mike Nichols had predicted, "Elaine is going to suffer in Hollywood. She must have complete control of a given situation. Out there she will be at the mercy of many people."[63] Perhaps the difficulty she experienced as a writer-director was adapting her creative process to fit within the strictures of a production schedule that was controlled by deadlines, the budgetary bottom line, and upper management. During the late 1960s, May had thrived doing improvisation where she could practice the technique over and over again, but where the content and audience were different every time. She once described improvisation as "nothing more than quickly creating a situation between two people and throwing up some kind of problem for one of them."[64] Mark Gordon, one of her collaborators in the Compass Players, described her this way: "She had a commitment to improvisation, and she was not going to let it go. . . . She was truly remarkable."[65] Even when she and Nichols became famous and developed set skits and routines, their ability to workshop the material together drew on the kind of spontaneity discouraged and impractical on a multimillion-dollar film set.

Looking back on her experience making studio-produced films, May put the blame for her difficulties on company politics: "Every movie I made except for *The Heartbreak Kid,* the studio changed regimes in the middle of the movie. It's not a great thing because whoever is coming in doesn't like you a) because you have been chosen by someone else and they don't really know whether they want to take responsibility for it." In a moment of self-reflection, she did consider her role in creating the difficulties repeated in each film: "And it could just be me because I've had trouble with every movie I've done. I had trouble with *A New Leaf.* I had trouble with *Mikey & Nicky.* I didn't have trouble with *The Heartbreak Kid* because I was hired for it. But with every movie that I have done, I may just be a pain in the ass."[66]

That May's approach to directing was often impractical and indecisive was a common refrain of those who worked with her. Stanley Jaffe made the observation that "she was the kind of person who would say, 'Set this theater up.' The theater would be all set up. We'd walk in and she'd say, 'No, I meant the other theater.' And everybody was set up. She did it a lot." But Jaffe offered some context to the difficulties he experienced overseeing *A New Leaf.* "Holy mackerel. She has some talent," he emphasized. Remembering advice he was given when he became COO at Paramount, "I think it was John [Golan] . . . he called us in and he said, look, 'We're not making the movies, the filmmakers are. We're here to support them and to distribute them. And as long as they know the rules going in, we will totally support them. If they are not respectful of our rule, then I want you to come down on them.'"[67] Jaffe's recollection reflected, in some part, Evans's philosophy in the late 1960s when Paramount's cohort of young, male executives worked to refashion and upgrade the failing studio with young, new talent that brought fresh and original ideas. However, the risk was that these neophyte filmmakers had not yet been groomed to navigate large union sets or boardroom and budget protocol. "It was her first movie. I think she was frightened, as any first-time director would be," speculated Jaffe. "She was a woman director, which at that time was really almost pioneering. And she felt strongly about her script." Her inexperience, and yet her confidence she had despite it, was part of May's innovation and appeal.

It also was part of what created problems for her. "There's no way to know unless someone teaches you or you screw up," said May in 2006, recalling how inexperienced she was in the logistics of directing a film when hired on *A New Leaf*. "And when you start a movie by someone saying, 'You can't pick a director, but you can direct it,' you really start knowing nothing. And that was the story of [*A New Leaf*]. Everyday became about trying to remember just what it was about and not screwing up too badly."[68]

Film critic and historian Todd McCarthy, who was May's assistant on *Mikey & Nicky*, suggested that May's difficult and unruly behavior as the only female director then making films for a studio impeded the prospects for other women during the 1970s:

> I really do believe that [May] set back the cause of women directors in Hollywood by ten years. The isolated moments when she could really put all else out of her mind and concentrate on the work, she was great. But every negative notion that any male executive might want to have about how difficult it might be to work with a woman director was confirmed by her: "She was irresponsible. She didn't know what she was doing. She couldn't be controlled." . . . All those things that people with conventional minds wanted to believe—she confirmed them in spades.[69]

What is likely is that May's behavior and reputation for being difficult resulted in the end of *her* career as a director. After *Mikey & Nicky* she did not direct another film until regaining legitimacy within Hollywood by earning an Oscar nomination, in 1978, for her coauthored screenplay with Warren Beatty on his film *Heaven Can Wait*.[70] Nearly ten years later, with the Oscar nod and the clout of her stars Beatty (who also served as a producer) and Dustin Hoffman, May was given the opportunity to direct *Ishtar* for Columbia Pictures in 1987. However, she had similar feuds with the studio to those that occurred on her earlier productions, and the film suffered a buried release and damning reviews. She has not directed a film since *Ishtar* went over budget by a supposed $40 million.[71] In 1998, May was nominated for her screenplay for *Primary Colors* directed by her longtime friend and collaborator, Mike Nichols. She continued to serve as a noncredited "script doctor" on films; write for the theater, and occasionally act, most recently in Woody Allen's limited Amazon series, *Crisis in Six Scenes* (2016).

It is difficult to believe McCarthy's notion that May's behavior as a filmmaker—her disputes with studio executives, her indecisiveness, her legal battles—alone set back her female peers by confirming male executives' sexist fantasies as to why Hollywood should not hire women directors. Male executives in Hollywood had those delusions before, during, *and* after Elaine May. As to the "woman question," May explained how at the start of her directing career she "didn't want to frighten anyone, and people would leave me saying, 'she's a nice girl' . . . the thing is, of course, I wasn't a nice girl. And when they found this out, they hated me all the more. . . . And in the end, when it comes down to it, you're just as rotten as any guy. You'll fight just as hard to get your way."[72] In 1977, one year after the company's dispute with May over *Mikey & Nicky*, Paramount hired Joan Darling to direct *First Love*. Darling would become the second woman, following May, to direct for a major studio since 1966 (see chapter 3).

## From Art House to Drive-In: 1970s Independent Production

In 1968, Robert Evans was singing the praises of new writers and directors, calling them Paramount's star investment. Yet only a few years later, in 1971, he asserted studio authority over filmmakers who took issue with executive power. In an article titled "Cut Directors down to Size," Evans told *Variety*'s Gene Arneel, "I want to be close to the script development the casting and the final cuts." Evans saw the production executive as part of the "'creative force' rather than just the bankroller"; if the "'creators' don't like it that way they should stay away." According to Arneel this "trend would end the day of the director as superstar."[73]

Yet the director as superstar trend continued well into the 1970s (some would cite Michael Cimino and the *Heaven's Gate* [1980] debacle at United Artists as the final death knell for the director as star), but such status was elusive for women directors, especially those working for major motion picture companies. Before 1978, the majority of women directors made films independently.

American independent cinema during the 1970s was defined in two ways. First, it was described as *exploitation*, *B-films*, and *low-budget independent films*, terms that were used interchangeably for movies that were made cheaply for budgets around $500,000 or less, were produced in large quantities, and targeted a youth audience.[74] These films were characterized by their excessive portrayal of sex; nudity, with an emphasis on female nudity; violence; and action sequences. They were recognizable by the frequent use of genre conventions, including, but not limited to, horror, science fiction, biker, nurse, and teacher films. B-films tended to exploit topical subjects. In the 1960s and 1970s that meant depictions of an antiestablishment, youth-focused counterculture typified by drug use, rock 'n' roll, and casual sex, as well as storylines about issues inherent in the era's social movements such as racial inequality, antiwar protest, sexuality, and feminism. Exploitation films had marketing campaigns that capitalized on the films' content by using flashy images and sensationalized taglines in movie trailers, posters, and advertisements for trade publications and newspapers. Because these films were made on the cheap and often contained explicit or salacious material, they tended to feature lesser-known performers.[75] These films also relied on and exploited lesser-known directors. Thus, the sensationalized marketing campaigns compensated for a lack of star power. Exploitation films had their own distribution networks and dedicated exhibition sites, such as grindhouse theaters and drive-ins that targeted specific audiences, which tended to be a younger demographic of both women and men.

The second kind of independent cinema was described as *art house films*, *smaller commercial films*, or *independent commercial films*.[76] These films were made cheaply, but because they did not all follow a standardized production and economic model as did exploitation films, their budgets could range from under $100,000 to more than $1 million. Directors making art house films faced obstacles unique to these kinds of projects. B-films were supported by a uniform production, distribution, and exhibition network designed to produce and sell similar pictures to a specific market on a regular schedule. In contrast, independent art house films were not homogeneous in terms of genre or stylistic choices; therefore they did not have a single target audience. Their budgets were small not because they were adhering to a production model of churning out titles quickly for mass consumption, but because financing was provided either by a private investor, piecemeal donations from friends and family, or cobbled-together funding from nonprofit, grant-making institutions. Art house cinema depended on the domestic and international film festival circuit to generate exposure in the press that might then build a domestic audience and attract the attention of a distributor. Filmmakers also relied on museums and nonprofit arts organizations as sites for exhibition and to build cultural cachet that would help draw audience and critical attention. In contrast to exploitation films, these independent films were frequently in competition with studio productions whose access to financing and distribution budgets gave them significant advantages.

Both art house and exploitation films existed on the margins of Hollywood and were differentiated from the mainstream industry by a disparity in economic resources—which affected production values and creative opportunities for the films and their makers—as well as in distribution and marketing prospects. At the same time, these three production communities were closely linked. Audiences in the 1970s moved regularly between art house, exploitation, and dominant cinema, as did above-the-line workers; both independent communities served as launching pad for some writers, producers, directors, and actors to move into mainstream films and television.

Considering the resistance that women experienced throughout the 1970s within Hollywood, the inclination of many directors to begin their careers on the margins does not seem surprising. How else could they make their films—particularly their first film—if they lacked financing or distribution from an established film company? Although this argument holds true in some respects, making independent features had its own set of challenges. The creative autonomy of those working on exploitation films was often restricted by the demands of the B-film market. Art house directors did not have the financial clout or the industry connections to match the studio films they competed with, nor did they have exploitation films' infrastructure. For the production cultures of both exploitation and art house films, restrictive budgets frequently prevented these directors from realizing their full talents. The number of women making studio films would increase in small increments by 1978, but it was within the varied independent film communities that women, during the early part of the decade—in spite of these challenges but sometimes because of them—would make their first films and begin building bodies of work.

## Barbara Loden

> It all comes down to this: if you don't want to be a part of what exists you've got to create your own reason for existence.
>
> —Barbara Loden[77]

In her 1971 article, "Lights! Camera! Women!," Marion Meade of the *New York Times* noted that "a rather remarkable development has taken place" in that year: two films were released that starred the women who wrote and directed them—Barbara Loden's *Wanda* and Elaine May's *A New Leaf*. Yet, the two filmmakers and their films could not have been more different from one another. The former film, independently produced and distributed, was an atmospheric, melancholic character study, while the latter was a studio-made screwball comedy with slapstick undertones. For Meade what the two films and their makers shared was this: "Barbara Loden, of 'Wanda,' and Elaine May, of 'A New Leaf,' give us an unusual slant on the realities of women's existence and feelings. Their heroines—Wanda and Henrietta Lowell—reveal facets of womankind not ordinarily seen on the screen."[78]

Barbara Loden died in 1980 at age forty-eight after a three-year struggle with cancer. A *Los Angeles Times* obituary ran with this headline—"'Dumb Blonde' Made One Brilliant Film"—a tasteless title for the death notice of the late actress turned award-winning writer-director.[79] It seemed that the reporter was attempting to play on the apparent incongruity between her critically acclaimed film *Wanda* and the characters Loden was best known for early in her acting career, when she was singled out for her conventional beauty and was often typecast as the "dumb blonde." She detested these roles, and during the press attention she received on the release of *Wanda*, she was frequently candid in interviews about how they had affected her sense of self. "I didn't think anything of myself," she revealed in 1971. "So I succumbed to the whole role. I never knew who I was, or what I was supposed to do."[80] Loden's awareness of the limited range she was locked into as a performer in mainstream film, theater, and television informed her turn toward making independent films. "I slowly began to realize that if I was going to be any kind of artist in that sense as an actress," Loden explained to an audience at the American Film Institute in 1971, "I [would] have to create my own corner to work from; no matter how small it might be, it would be better than being in everybody else's big things that I didn't really feel at home in." Loden was trapped as an actress and became a filmmaker to avoid the roles she saw as degrading and narrow; by creating her own parts she was able to explore the experience of a character's tendency—and presumably an artist's as well—to be submissive in relationships and roles, to appear passive and directionless. In that interview, she also described the inspiration for her fictional character: "I think . . . I created [the role of Wanda] out of myself. It was based on my own personality, more or less—passive, wandering around—passing from one person to another not having any direction. . . . I think a lot of people are that way . . . not just women, but men too. They don't know why they exist and they have no direction in their lives, they have no reason to exist."[81]

Born in 1932, in rural Marion, North Carolina, Loden managed to break away from a tough family life, where, as she described in a 1964 interview with Dick Kleiner, "I spent most of my childhood hiding behind the stove."[82] At sixteen she moved to New York City with $100 and eventually got work as a model for detective and romance magazines and as a dancer in the chorus at the Copacabana Club. Ernie Kovacs saw her working at the club and in 1956 hired her as his comedic and sexy sidekick on *The Ernie Kovacs Show*. By 1957 she was appearing on Broadway in small roles. It was also around this time that Loden began a turbulent personal and professional relationship with successful film and theater director Elia Kazan, twenty-three years her senior, which lasted until her death. She was cast in supporting roles in the films *Wild River* (1960) and *Splendor in the Grass* (1961), both directed by Kazan. In 1964 Loden won a Tony Award for her performance as Maggie, a character closely resembling Marilyn Monroe, in Arthur Miller's autobiographical play *After the Fall*, also directed by Kazan. Following *After the Fall*, Loden continued to perform on stage while also raising her two young children: Leo, whom she had with Kazan while he was married to his first wife, Mary Day Thacher, was born in 1962, and Marco, whom she had with her first husband Larry Joachim, was born in 1964.

Loden got the idea for *Wanda* from a newspaper article about a woman who had been convicted for being an accomplice to a bank robber and, when sentenced to twenty years in prison, thanked the judge. Loden was fascinated by what she perceived as the woman's sense of relief: "She wanted an institution to supervise her and regulate her. But why did she get into that state where she thought it would be a good thing to be sent to jail? That was the beginning of my ideas for 'Wanda.'"[83] As a young woman, Loden turned to acting classes "to get over being withdrawn and inhibited. It was like group therapy."[84] For many years she was a student of acting coach Paul Mann, who trained her in the method approach that draws on an actor's personal experience and memory. In this sense, the character of Wanda was one that Loden had been cultivating for years.

*Wanda* takes place in an industrial working-class setting: a coal-mining town in Pennsylvania. It is the story of a poor, unemployed, and aimless young woman who does not have access to opportunities and also lacks the awareness to look for them. The film follows Wanda as she meanders from divorce court, to dive bars, and to a motel room with a sleazy traveling salesman, until she meets up with a small-time bank robber, Mr. Dennis, played by Michael Higgins. He is belligerent and controlling, but he is also the only person who shows her any kindness: Mr. Dennis buys her a new dress and high heels, in which she delights, and encourages her to improve her reading skills. In return, Wanda does not fight back, displaying a passive and blank, but almost amenable, manner.

Loden's primary investor for the film was Harry Shuster, whom she had met in 1966 when she and Kazan were on safari in Africa. Shuster was the president of National Leisure, Inc., a Los Angeles-based company affiliated with Lion Country Safari, an African wildlife preserve. With no prior experience in filmmaking, he took on the title of producer and financed the film for an estimated $115,000.[85] Through a mutual friend, Loden and Kazan were introduced to Nicholas T. Proferes, who became the film's cinematographer and editor. Proferes had worked as an apprentice editor for cinema-verité filmmakers Robert Drew, Richard Leacock, Albert and David Maysles, and D. A. Pennebaker. Through that experience he had learned the handheld, documentary-style camera techniques that gave *Wanda* its naturalistic look.[86]

Production took place in 1969 with a crew of four people: Loden, Proferes, lighting and sound technician Lars Hedman, and Christopher Cromin, an assistant. The small cast was made up of inexperienced actors with the exception of Loden and Higgins. Loden's wardrobe, which consisted of two outfits, cost $7 dollars and was purchased from Woolworth's, and Higgins wore some of Kazan's old suits. Sometimes the director would cook for the crew, and when her babysitter quit, she took her two children to the set.[87] Even so, she admitted after the film was completed, "I wasted money because I didn't know what I was doing," but promised that "my next film will be made much cheaper."[88] In the press, Loden was forthright in her disdain for Hollywood: "I really hate slick pictures. They're too perfect to be believable. . . . The slicker the technique is, the slicker the content becomes, until everything turns into Formica, including the people."[89] Screening her film in Dallas at the USA Film Festival, Loden told a reporter that "she deplored the demands of film unions to load down production crews with what she described as 'all that deadwood' or unnecessary technicians."[90] The New York "underground" filmmakers inspired her. "I thought movies had to be so technical and had to have big crews," explained the new director, "[b]ut Warhol's movies were out of focus sometimes and had poor sound."[91]

Loden as director and Proferes for his technical skill were praised for the unpolished look of the film that critics felt effectively revealed an honesty in mood, setting, and character. Roger Greenspun of the *New York Times* enjoyed the film "because it seems at home with its idioms, close to its action, opening up only rarely and to moments of genuine insight and not admiration-begging cinematic claptrap. *Wanda* is a small movie, fully aware of its limits, and within those limits lovely."[92] Gene Moskowitz, reporting from the Venice Film Festival where the movie won the International Critics Prize, heralded Loden as a new filmmaker with much potential, specifically for her ability to realize characters and her skill in cultivating performances: "Miss Loden may lack polish in her direction as yet, but she makes up for it by a knowing feeling for her milieu and characters and does not condescend or try to make them exemplary or pitiable in any way. This is in a U.S. film tradition but without the pat social blames and castigations and moralizing."[93] Reviewers thus forgave Loden and *Wanda* for its novice qualities, instead finding in her beginner's touch an original and moving cinematic style.

As expected, reporters asked Loden about her Oscar-winning director-husband's involvement in the project. She credited Kazan with being the one to encourage her to make the film: "It was his idea, actually that I should direct it. He gave me courage, sort of set me up an organization. . . . He was a great questioner, he made me think. But he wouldn't tell me anything. He left me alone and finally disappeared."[94] *Variety* reported,

Fig. 4. Barbara Loden in *Wanda*

"Visiting his wife on the local set, Kazan said that he had no connection with the film, ('I'm just around and run errands. It's Barbara's project.')."[95] Critics saw past her Hollywood connections and evaluated the film on its own. In his glowing review, Vincent Canby dismissed the nepotism question: "I suppose it's impossible not to wonder about any aid she might have received from her husband, but 'Wanda' does not have the look of a Kazan film. It looks like an original."[96]

Loden began writing the script for *Wanda* in 1961 when she was "hanging around the house" pregnant with her first son—a "love child" with Kazan.[97] Although she and Kazan would marry and live together years later, at the time of her pregnancy the two had decided to end their romantic relationship: Kazan was not only still married to his first wife, Molly Day Thacher, but was also involved in a number of other extramarital affairs; he was an absentee father to Leo for many years.[98] The most detailed account of Loden and Kazan's relationship and of much of Loden's life is found in Kazan's autobiography and is therefore from his perspective, which was frequently critical and vicious. Although it is unknown how Loden felt about having a child with Kazan under these circumstances, her film was influenced by the complexities of their relationship. In the AFI interview in 1971, she described how Wanda and Higgins were based on her early interactions with Kazan. Kazan "is a very forceful, very authoritative person," she explained to the audience; "that's why I was first attracted to him because I was one of those floaters floating around and I met a dynamic force that was able to give me some kind of direction. It just happened to Wanda, but with the wrong person."[99]

Shuster established Bardene International Films to self-distribute the movie, and after showing at festivals, *Wanda* played for a short time at both Cinema II in New York City and in Los Angeles at the Plaza in Westwood.[100] Loden was buoyed by the attention and acclaim the movie received, specifically the prize awarded by the Venice Film Festival. In a 1995 interview, Proferes described how receiving that recognition "completely changed [Loden]. She became a director in her own mind. She had a vision."[101]

Determined to make more films, she and Proferes continued to develop projects. In 1971 it was reported that Loden's next film would be *Love Means Always Having to Say You're Sorry,* the story of a housewife who gets involved with three men at the same time. The costars were to be Michael Higgins, Joe Dallesandro, and Steve Billings; Loden was said to be writing, directing, and starring in the picture.[102] That same year, riding the industry buzz of *Wanda*'s success, Army Archerd reported that legendary Hollywood producer Ray Stark was interested in making films with Loden.[103] In 1974 she was listed in *Variety* as being part of writer-director Henry Jaglom's and producer Bert Schneider's newly formed HHH Rainbow Productions. The company's goal was to make low-budget features for around $1 million that were "freed from traditional economic pressures and studio restraints." Other members of the company were Jack Nicholson, James Frawley, Carole Eastman, Penelope Gilliatt, Paul Williams, Dennis Hopper, and Martin Scorsese.[104]

However, none of these projects materialized for her. In the years after *Wanda* was produced, Loden directed off-Broadway productions and taught acting classes.[105] She and Proferes remained creative collaborators until her death, making in 1975 two short films—*The Boy Who Liked Deer* and *The Frontier Experience*—for the Learning Corporation of America, an educational media company. However, they never made another feature together. In a 1971 interview with Rex Reed, Loden proclaimed, "I've got more movies in me, but they will have to be done my way. I'm not interested in entertaining people. I only want to do things that mean something to me, that I can say about a human being on film and then communicate that feeling to others."[106] By the close of the 1970s Loden was consumed with battling the cancer that would eventually take her life. She was dedicated to her work until the very end: in March 1980, just five months before her death, she codirected an off-Broadway production of *Come Back to the 5 and Dime, Jimmy Dean, Jimmy Dean* at the Hudson Guild Theatre.[107]

At the time of her death at age forty-eight, Barbara Loden had been trying for almost ten years after the release of her first and only feature to make another one. In 1971 *Wanda* was acknowledged by reviewers not only on its own merits but also as a women-directed film—a breed that was so rare early in the decade it could not go unnoticed. Where at the start of her directing career Loden's determination to do things *her way* and her dislike for the commercial aspect of filmmaking were qualities that resulted in a unique film and a self-realization of who she truly was as an artist, later, in addition to her declining health, these traits were key deterrents to her ever making another film.

## Karen Arthur

> I'll kiss my way through anything before I fight. I'm not a run-in person. I deal with conflicts differently: I manipulate. I think direct confrontation is a male space and that doesn't suit me. The point is that I get my way.
>
> —Karen Arthur[108]

Foreign film festivals were the lifeblood of independent feature films being made in the United States during the early 1970s. During these years, the U.S. festival circuit was smaller than it would grow to be in the 1980s and did not yet have a strong marketing component; that business mechanism would begin to evolve toward the end of the decade and flourish into the 1980s with the establishment of what would become the Sundance Film Festival and the Independent Film Market. In the meantime, prominent, long-standing international festivals—Berlin, Cannes, and Venice—would serve as an important platform for directors who made films on their own. For example, *Wanda*'s success at the Venice Film Festival was instrumental in introducing the film and its maker to the press, enabling Loden to then leverage the critical acclaim in her attempt to find foreign, but more importantly, domestic distribution and exhibition options. For many of these directors, making an independent feature was a difficult option, but was their only chance to break into the industry.

Karen Arthur made two independent feature films in the 1970s: *Legacy*, which she began production on in 1973 and took to the festival circuit in 1974 and 1975; and *The Mafu Cage* that finished production in 1977 and premiered at Cannes in 1978. "Oh guys, use the film festivals!" Arthur urged a crowd of AFI students in 1978. "Make a film, and see the world . . . there's a real community of critics, of filmmakers, that you get to share your energy with. . . . I didn't have any money for public relations [on *Legacy*] . . . the festivals did the public relations."[109]

Born in Nebraska in 1943, Karen Arthur was raised by a single mother who moved the family to Palm Beach, Florida, when Arthur was a child. As a teenager, Arthur was a member of the ballet company sponsored by Frank Hale's Palm Beach Playhouse. It was there that she was introduced to choreography, which she later credited with providing her with a foundation for directing. "That's where I really learned the skills," explained Arthur in a 2011 interview. "I realized at one point, everything I knew about choreography in terms of right, left, the stage, if I turned the stage upright it was a frame. It was a motion picture frame."[110] Around age eighteen, Arthur understood that she was not going to succeed as a ballerina. Moving to New York, where she worked steadily as a "triple threat" theater actress—singing, dancing, and acting—she decided to leave for the West Coast because "I never got the brass ring on Broadway. . . . I figured, while I still have a face and body, I should go to Hollywood!"[111] Starting off in Hollywood as an actress, Arthur was hired in minor roles for television and film. She joined the Melrose Theater, where she realized that she no longer wanted to act, but instead wanted to pursue directing, and in Hollywood that meant movies.

With no prior experience in production, Arthur began to strategize how to build her skill set by tapping into the resources available in Los Angeles's wider film community. With money from an income tax refund, she took a summer production class at UCLA where she made her first film, shot on 16mm, called *Hers*, an autobiographical short that provided Arthur the opportunity to familiarize herself with both the technical and creative aspects of production. On the strength of that short, she was accepted to the American Film Institute's internship program that paired new filmmakers with Hollywood veterans. Arthur was assigned to Arthur

Fig. 5. Left to right: Ross Martin, Britt Nilsson, Laurie Burton (back), and Karen Arthur in the television show *The Wild Wild West*, episode "The Night of Running Death" (CBS Enterprises, Inc., 1967) (Margaret Herrick Library, Academy of Motion Picture Arts and Sciences)

Penn's feature *Night Moves* (1975). It was on this film that she met John Bailey, then an assistant cameraman, and his wife Carol Littleton, a film editor just getting her start. Bailey and Littleton would collaborate with Arthur on her first two feature films as cinematographer and editor, respectively. Arthur never had a formal mentor, but saw her friendship with Bailey and Littleton, who brought a strong visual knowledge of film, photography, and art that complemented Arthur's experience with performance and choreography, as the most influential relationship during her formative years: "To grow up with the two of them—each of them are *wicked, wicked* intelligent—to have that intelligence in my ear for those early years—and they say my audacity and daring is what allowed them to be fearless, because I was so fearless, so we complemented each other."[112]

During this time, Arthur saw writer-actress Joan Hotchkis perform her one-woman show *Legacy*. She was captivated by Hotchkis's portrayal of Bissie Hapgood, a self-involved, upper-middle-class woman experiencing an emotional breakdown under the pressures of a vapid and materialistic society consumed with dinner-plate settings and domestic help. Arthur convinced the actress that the play was meant for the big screen, and Hotchkis agreed not only to reprise her role on film but also to write the screenplay. Securing funds for the independent production proved challenging. Arthur raised money in fits and starts, receiving donations from Hotchkis's wealthy family and, after many applications, was awarded $10,000 from the AFI Independent Filmmakers Grant.[113] "I think I applied to AFI like ten times," said Arthur joked decades later. "I said, 'I either get a gold watch or I get a grant. Now, give me a break!'"[114]

In 1975 *Legacy* toured the international festival circuit, including Cannes. Through the efforts of a French film agent, Jeannine Seawell, the picture was shown in theaters and on television in some parts of Europe, where it was well received. However, landing a domestic distribution deal proved to be difficult.[115] U.S. critics' response to the movie was mixed. Several felt there was something off-putting about the format: the monologue did not translate well to the narrative structure of a feature film. Vincent Canby of the *New York Times* described it as "a most peculiar sort of movie but not a very good one." Wishing that the film had some humor in its treatment of this rich woman's problems, as a way to humanize her, he wrote, "Nothing that either Miss Hotchkis or Miss Arthur does can disguise the awkwardness and artificiality of this monologue

Fig. 6. Joan Hotchkis in *Legacy*

form, which finally destroys any serious thoughts the filmmakers might have about women, the bourgeoisie, sex, America and the difficulty of getting good domestic help in Southern California."[116]

Like Canby, Marjorie Rosen was unsettled by the film's overwrought seriousness. Writing for *Ms.* magazine, she pondered the category of "women's films" in her review of movies made by women about women that were screened at the Cannes Film Festival in 1975. Whereas the end of the 1970s would see the emergence of the New Woman film from Hollywood—both dramatic and funny—Rosen observed that, in 1975, "Nobody seems to be laughing at films these days, and especially not at women's films."[117] She did not fault *Legacy* for taking on the "grievances" of its female protagonist, but instead criticized it for leaving "no feminist cliché unturned. There's boredom, booze, pills, a disinterested shrink, a loveless marriage, a withholding mother; there's the obligatory masturbation scene (in a sunken bath, in the midst of a telephone chat with a friend), the discussion of menstruation, the allusions to menopause." Rosen ended her review with this pleading question: "I mean you *do* know the Women's Movement has a sense of humor, don't you?"[118]

In contrast, reviewing the film from the Locarno Film Festival in Switzerland, Gene Moskowitz of *Variety* championed it and drew attention to how Arthur, "who was a legit dancer, singer and actress, and made some shorts, does well with her first feature. She does not intrude and allows Hotchkis to grow through her actions and words."[119] Moskowitz felt Arthur did right by Hotchkis in both her capacities as the film's screenwriter and actor. His praise can also be read as a strategy to prop up the first-time director. By cataloging her background in the arts, Moskowitz validated the new expression of her talent as a director and introduced Arthur to Hollywood.

While critics debated the role of humor in the dramatic film's close read of a woman experiencing the unraveling of her sense of self, what stands out in the reviews of *Legacy* are the expectations some had of a woman director in relation to her female subject. Some critics projected onto Arthur a gendered obligation. For example, Canby worried that *Legacy* was "uncommonly cruel for a film about a woman made by a woman."[120] Women filmmakers were oddities. With so few of them pushing to enter an industry designed to keep them out, they often bore the burden of representation, in front of and behind the camera. Did they then have a special obligation to pick particular stories and characters? If so, how would they avoid being pigeonholed? It was rare during this decade, especially in the early 1970s, for a female protagonist to break out from cinematic expectations of *femaleness* contained within certain standards of beauty and sexuality: Hollywood still clung to these social attitudes and expectations about women's relationships, biology, careers, and personal identity, even as the women's movement was outing them as increasingly retrograde. On arriving in Hollywood in the 1960s, Arthur claims she was not political. "[I was] *the most non-political person on the planet*," she emphasized in a 2017 interview. "Now that's not true today [in 2017]. But back then it was very true. I could not see anything outside of my own asshole, as it were. It was *strictly* what was going on about me. I wouldn't have known a feminist if I fell over on one. I burned my bra along with other people, but just because I hated wearing a bra, it had nothing to do with the feminist movement. I didn't know the name—my God—Gloria Steinem, or any of those ladies. Forget about, I had no idea. I [just] wanted to keep working."[121] Yet Arthur's interest in *Legacy* and her dedication to bringing Hotchkis's confrontational rendition of the middle-class, Anglo American woman to the screen were laced with feminism.

Another reason for the harsh critical response is that, in addition to Arthur's and Hotchkis's possible missteps in adapting the stage monologue to the screen, the character of Bissie Hapgood deviated from the traditional portrayal of women in film. She is sexually explicit without being sexy, and vulnerable without being sentimentalized; she is critical of her social strata, while benefiting from her privileged status; she is unlikeable because she is not relatable; and she is unique in how the filmmaker took a familiar image and had her strip down, physically and psychologically. Did women filmmakers, in 1974, have a responsibility to not force much more change than they already generated by their mere existence? Rosen attempted to get at this issue of gendered standards by asking, "How generous should we be to 'women's films'? Do we defer to sisterhood and apply a different set of criteria?"[122] She did not answer those questions, but in asking them, Rosen pointed to the demands being made of these filmmakers and the challenges they faced in being able to interpret any material with the artistic freedom entitled to a director, in addition to being judged as a woman and, because of her gender, denied the chance to express herself as an individual.

For Arthur and her collaborators—Hotchkis, Bailey, and Littleton—the benefits of introducing a different kind of female lead and exploring the formal elements of cinema were worth the risks:

> We were learning with each other, but we had the freedom because there was no studio saying, "Oh, you can't do this and you can't do that." There were no big stars saying, "Oh, I wouldn't do this and I wouldn't say that." Nobody looking over our shoulders. It was us. . . . And sure we made mistakes and they're in the film for all to see. But it was *so* challenging and *so* invigorating it was *so* exciting to be out there on our own doing our own thing. In something we *believed* in.[123]

After screening at fourteen festivals around the globe, *Legacy* was set for its theatrical release in New York at the Cinema Studio Theater in April 1976 until Canby's sour review killed it.[124] In those days, a review by Vincent Canby of the *New York Times* could determine a film's shelf life in its initial and most important theatrical releases, and the reviewer knew the level of anticipation and pressure the first-time filmmaker was facing with her New York premiere. Arthur had been introduced to Canby at a dinner party shortly before he reviewed the film. Shocked and disappointed by his review, the filmmaker telephoned Canby in anger: "Well I got my balls in my hand and I called him and said, 'What the fuck did you do?' He said, 'Oh my God, Karen, I didn't realize that was your film. You should have called me. I would have seen it, but if I hated it, I would have recused myself and asked another critic look at it. That's what a relationship is for.'" Looking back, Arthur recalled, "Oh my God. I had no idea," noting the steep first-timer's learning curve.[125] After the review came out, the theater first offered her a week's run, but then decided to cancel the film. Whether Canby was telling her the truth or trying to appease an angry filmmaker, Arthur did not know, but what was clear were the endless politics and pitfalls of making an independent film and how the smallest misstep may have mattered the most.

After *Legacy*, Arthur began work on her second feature, *Mafu Cage*. It was based on the play "You and Your Clouds" written by Eric Wesfall, which Arthur had seen in 1971 in Europe. It tells the story of two sisters entrenched in a dysfunctional, highly dependent relationship with each other. The project appealed to Arthur as a strategic career move. She soon came to understand that *Legacy* was not a good calling card for getting work in Hollywood. In 1975 she admitted to the *Washington Post*, "It was written as a tour de force for one woman. As director, I was not sophisticated enough to open the piece visually."[126] "It wasn't a traditional story," Arthur reflected in 2017. "The woman was talking to the camera for Christ's sake. Are you crazy? You're not supposed to do movies like that. You're supposed to do a close-up and a two-shot of people talking to each other."[127] Arthur's ability to recognize her limitations as a new filmmaker demonstrated the commitment she had to learning her craft and her ambition to succeed at it. She considered *Legacy* to be an art film, and not mainstream enough, and thought that making a movie like *Mafu Cage*, with its horror and thriller qualities, would give her an opportunity to attract a larger audience and in doing so expand her range and marketability as a filmmaker.[128] "I had things I wanted to say," she remarked in 1978, "but I wanted to say them on a larger scale than I was being allowed, because of where my limits were. So I made up my mind. I changed my trip in the process of *Legacy*, to decide that I wanted to work in the industry."[129]

While Arthur underwent the slow and arduous process of finding investors for her next independent film, she worked at honing her craft as a filmmaker. In 1974 she was accepted to the pilot program of the American Film Institute's Directing Workshop for Women (DWW), and in 1976 she directed her first episodic television show. Michael Gleason, a friend from her theater days, had become a successful television writer and was developing the series *Rich Man, Poor Man* for Universal. He was impressed with *Legacy* and went to the Universal executives with the intention of giving her a job as a director on his new show. Their reaction was, "Oh for God sakes, Michael, fuck her, don't hire her." Gleason's response was, "You don't understand. I don't want to fuck her, I want to hire her. She's going to be a really good director."[130] Gleason succeeded in getting Arthur hired. The new television director was an oddity on the Universal lot. "'You're the first woman director we've seen on this [sound] stage since Ida Lupino,'" male technicians would tell her while visiting the set to be eyewitnesses to history.[131]

Familiar with the challenges of independent financing, Arthur attempted to interest a studio in *Mafu Cage*. "They don't know what to do with me," she told Marjorie Worcester of the *Hollywood Reporter*. "First of all they wanted to make a $4 million picture and cast it with people who are just a joke. Then they offered to pay me off, to buy the screenplay, the whole route. Once they had the rights they could have dumped me and I would have had no control anyway, so I pulled out and raised the money myself," she said defiantly.[132] Arthur was diligent in putting together her plan to break into the film industry as a director. While raising money for *Mafu Cage* she taught dance and acting; she also worked as a script supervisor on commercials and porno films, because the fledging director "wanted to be next to a director, at least someone who was saying 'action.'"[133] Eager to fill in her knowledge gap about camera work, she then went to the camera department at Universal and told them she wanted to hone her skills. She worked in the changing room prepping the camera magazines and cleaning slates for the next day shoots: "My shift was at 2 A.M. and I would get out at 8 or 10 A.M. I would be locked in the [film] changing room all night. I would get the film ready, put film in the magazines, clean all of the slates. I would get everything ready for the day's shoot. And then I'd go home. Take a shower. Put on my clothes and go out and play the shell game of trying to raise money on the movie." When asked if she ever slept in the 1970s, Arthur gave a long, hard laugh. "Not much! And this girl had to have fun too! I was a busy girl!"[134] After four months implementing her plan to rise through the ranks of camera assistants and then break into directing, she obtained the financing for *Mafu Cage*.

Arthur was able to secure a private investor for *Mafu Cage*—a businessman from Arizona who had no ties to the film industry, but was interested in the "Hollywood experience." He contributed $250,000 to begin production. She teamed up again with Bailey and Littleton, who, since *Legacy*, had embarked on successful careers as a cinematographer and editor, respectively, and she cast the veteran, Oscar-winning actress Lee Grant as the lead. The two women had met at AFI when both were participants in the DWW. Joan Micklin Silver introduced Arthur to Carol Kane, with whom Micklin Silver had recently worked on the film *Hester Street*, who would play the second protagonist in the picture.

*Mafu Cage* toured the festival circuit in 1978, screening as part of the Director's Fortnight at the Cannes Film Festival. However, the film received mediocre reviews. Charles Champlin of the *Los Angeles Times* found that Grant and Kane's performances were "excellent," but the plot was lacking: "The story . . . is absurd without being absurdist, Grand Guignol melodrama without a saving sense of the preposterous, a two-penny shocker tricked out as if it were a serious study of schizophrenia."[135] Reviewing the film at the Dallas USA Film Festival, film critic Arthur Knight was more generous, appreciating the filmmaker's skill in making such an unusual film—a stylized horror-melodrama about sisters, starring a well-known, working actress—independently: "Absolutely nothing about this movie betrays the fact that it was made on a very low budget. But it is heartening to know that a film of this quality can be produced independently of the major studios—and that because of this independence, the film makers can depart so widely from conventional stories and themes."[136]

As did *Legacy*, *Mafu Cage* found some distribution outlets in Europe, secured by Arthur's foreign sales agent Jeannine Seawell, but was unable to obtain a formal release in the United States. There was a place for small, art house films like *Legacy* and *Mafu Cage* on the festival circuit, where screenings would showcase these projects to audiences and generate press. However, for independent filmmakers, theater distribution was the lynchpin in securing a successful life for their movies. A contract with a distribution company provided a budget for marketing, sales, and developing relationships with exhibitors—costs that most filmmakers could not afford on their own. In the 1970s, wide-release distribution was controlled by the major studios, competitors that Arthur did not have the resources or the connections to match.[137]

In 1978, while struggling to sell her independent film, Arthur signed a four-picture development deal with Universal. The experience of trying to get projects made within the system, however, proved to be very frustrating. For four years she supported herself this way, but none of her projects came to fruition. In a 1986 interview, Arthur explained the development deal conundrum: "You earn enough to live on, but you're not saying 'Action!' Eventually I threw my hands up and said, 'No more.' I called my agent and said, 'Let's do TV.'"[138] Arthur's career in television gained traction by the end of the 1970s when she started directing the one-hour action drama series *Hart to Hart*; in the 1980s she directed prime-time shows such as *Cagney and Lacy* and *Remington Steel*. In 1985 she won an Emmy for Outstanding Directing in a Drama Series for her work on *Cagney and Lacy*. Her career continued to flourish, especially in television movies and miniseries, for more than forty years.

In 1987 Arthur directed her last feature film to date: *Lady Beware*, a psychological thriller starring Diane Lane. She had begun development on the movie in 1978 as part of her Universal deal. Nearly a decade later a new production company, Scotti Bros. Entertainment, agreed to finance and distribute the movie.[139] The producers felt her version needed more explicit material, and so, without the director's consent, they added outtakes of footage with actress Diane Lane naked to the finished film. Arthur was adamant in the press that the film had been recut without her permission and that the final version's handling of Lane's character and on-screen performance was exploitative.[140] This loss of creative control is not unique to women directors, but is experienced by both male and female filmmakers who do not have the clout to negotiate deals that give them the power of the final cut. However, women are disproportionately represented among directors who wield less authority and are therefore vulnerable to losing creative control over their work.

In 1978, on her way to *Mafu Cage*'s premiere at Cannes, Arthur spoke about her directing career to an audience at AFI with her trademark charm and honesty:

> I remember in the beginning, I used to think that the world was waiting for a Karen Arthur film. I suddenly realized one day, 'There's nobody out there waiting for a Karen Arthur film." That Vincent Canby didn't give a rat's butt if I never made a movie. He wouldn't care! . . . There isn't anybody out there that gives a shit about your movie, but you. As soon as I realized that, then I thought, "Well then it's up to me. Then I have to make it happen." They may help, but they aren't going to make it happen.[141]

Karen Arthur's determination to direct films in the early 1970s led her to the few resources in the broader Hollywood community that were designated for women directors, the DWW, and for independent filmmakers—the AFI's Independent Filmmakers Grant—from which she received financial support and gained industry credibility for her first two feature films. As an independent filmmaker who was directing films whose content challenged the conventions of the commercial film marketplace, she found it difficult to compete with larger films and as a result was unable to secure distribution for her work. In spite of these odds and the limited theatrical life of her films, it was her ability to successfully produce and direct two feature films outside of Hollywood that helped her build her skills and reputation. For her, independent film production was the necessary means to an unexpected end, directing television.

## Joan Micklin Silver

> Frankly, what distinguished me from other independent filmmakers—men and women—who were just as talented was that I had a husband who was able—and willing to help me. I wish I could clone him and give one to each of my filmmaker friends.
>
> —Joan Micklin Silver[142]

Joan Micklin Silver was one of the few directors during the 1970s not only to make independent films a decade before there was a viable marketplace for such films but also to make a successful transition into the studio system by the end of the decade, with her creative vision mostly intact. While distribution was a difficult problem for most independent filmmakers, Micklin Silver, in partnership with her husband, Raphael (Ray) Silver (1930–2013)—she as the writer-director and he as the producer-distributor—produced and self-distributed her two first films with much success.

Joan Micklin Silver was born in Omaha, Nebraska, in 1936. She attended Sarah Lawrence College in the early 1950s during which time she met Ray, a graduate of Harvard Business School and five years her senior. The couple married in 1956 and moved back to Ray's hometown of Cleveland. In 1967, then with three small daughters, the family relocated to New York: there, Ray opened a branch of his real estate business, Midwestern Land Development Corp., while Joan began to explore a career in filmmaking. In New York at a fundraiser for the future mayor of Cleveland Carl Stokes, Micklin Silver met Joan Ganz Cooney, soon to be cofounder of the Children's Television Workshop and cocreator of *Sesame Street*, who introduced her to Linda Gottlieb, vice president of the Learning Corporation of America, which produced educational films.[143] She and Gottlieb began collaborating on projects, Joan as screenwriter and Linda as producer; one project, *Limbo*, was made by Universal in 1972 and directed by Mark Robson. Dismayed by the final product and struck by the powerlessness of the writer in the filmmaking process, Micklin Silver was determined to protect her future work by becoming a director. Emboldened by her newfound focus, she and Gottlieb teamed up to make three short films for the Learning Corporation—*The Immigrant Experience* (1972), *The Fur Coat Club* (1973), and *The Case of the Elevator Duck* (1974)—this time with Micklin Silver as writer *and* director. With her screenwriting credit on a Hollywood feature and the shorts that had done well on the educational media market, Micklin Silver was certain that her resume showed potential. At that time, however, it was almost impossible for a woman to get hired by a studio to direct. "Those were the years of very flagrant sexism; women were absolutely not working at all in television," she said in a 1988 interview. "Women were only making feature films if they—like Shirley Clarke and Barbara Loden, my immediate predecessors—managed somehow to find backdoor ways to money. I got screenwriting offers, but not directing offers. . . . My husband saw my frustration and said, 'I don't know if you're talented or not, but you certainly have the right to find out.'"[144]

With no prior experience in the film business, Ray Silver used his financial skills and business contacts from a successful twenty-five-year career in real estate to start another career with his wife. "I didn't feel that I was doing her a favor," Ray said of stepping up to produce for his wife. "I think it's a lot different for a woman in the creative world than it is for a man. Men have got this whole support system—the old boys."[145] He and Joan decided that the best and possibly only option to sidestep the sexist obstacles facing her was to create for themselves a different way of filmmaking.

The couple independently produced and self-distributed their first feature film *Hester Street* (1975), she as writer-director, he as producer: it is a period piece about Jewish immigrants living in New York City in the early years of the twentieth century. Born to Russian Jewish parents who had immigrated to the United States as children, Micklin Silver had grown up hearing stories about the experience of assimilating between cultures. She had explored the topic cinematically in her short film *The Immigrant Story*, which was about Polish immigrants coming to the United States at the turn of the century, and then decided to adapt the short story "Yekl," by Abraham Cahan as her first feature. The picture began production in the fall of 1973. To create a convincing New York immigrant community in the early twentieth century, the movie was filmed in black and white on location in Greenwich Village, and large parts of the dialogue were in Yiddish. Because it was a period piece, much of the small budget was spent on costumes, sets, and a dialect coach to work with actors on learning the necessary Yiddish. After being convinced by the Teamsters that the picture needed to be a union film, the cast and crew were paid union scale, and shooting was completed within thirty-four days. The couple contributed their own money to supplement funds from investors outside of the film industry whom Ray had access to, and they completed the film for under $400,000.[146]

In November 1974, Joan and Ray had a finished version of the film and began sending it around to studios in hopes of finding a distributor. Although they had an agent, Howard Housman, at William Morris in Los Angeles, getting access to the people with power proved to be difficult. For new filmmakers with no industry standing, Hollywood's pecking order was a deterrent. "You always want the top person," explained Ray. "But this is excruciatingly difficult since, as he's the most important person, he's also the least available."[147] There was interest from some independent domestic distributors, but none had the financial stability to assure the filmmakers that they would get a return on their investments. A small period piece film about Jewish immigrants, with no well-known stars and made by first-time filmmakers, proved to be a challenge to sell to companies, large and small. According to Ray, distributors rejected the picture because they thought it was "a totally ethnic, Jewish film and only old Jews would see it because younger people could not relate to the story."[148] Joan remembers this as an extremely difficult time: "I went through one of the worst winters of my life. The only offer was to release it on 16mm to the synagogue market."[149]

So the couple began showing the film at festivals. When it received positive reviews from a predominantly non-Jewish audience at the USA Film Festival held on the campus of Southern Methodist University in Dallas, this response strengthened Joan and Ray's belief that their movie was not limited to a niche audience.[150] The film screened at Cannes, where it also received good reviews. Gene Moskowitz, covering the festival for *Variety*, predicted that the film would be a "sleeper" hit. He also singled out Micklin Silver as a new talent who "should be a filmmaker to be reckoned with after this effective and touching film."[151] Ray was able to sell distribution rights to some European markets, making a profit that he could invest back into a wider release effort.

In this effort Ray received help from John Cassavetes, who had self-distributed his own film *Woman Under the Influence* in 1974. The veteran director encouraged Ray to do the same. Key to the Silvers' future success was generating positive critical attention in New York and then building box office earnings on the basis of those favorable reviews. Once the film was established as reputable in New York City, there was a better chance that the rest of the domestic market would be receptive.[152] Ray hired Cassavetes's booking agents, Blaine Novak and Jeff Lipsky, to assist with the marketing; their publicity campaign was so successful that Carol Kane was nominated for an Oscar. The film grossed an estimated $5 million.

The couple's second film, *Between the Lines* (1977), was directed by Joan, produced-distributed by Ray, and financed using their earnings from *Hester Street*. The story of a young and ambitious staff of an independent newspaper in Boston in the midst of a corporate takeover, the

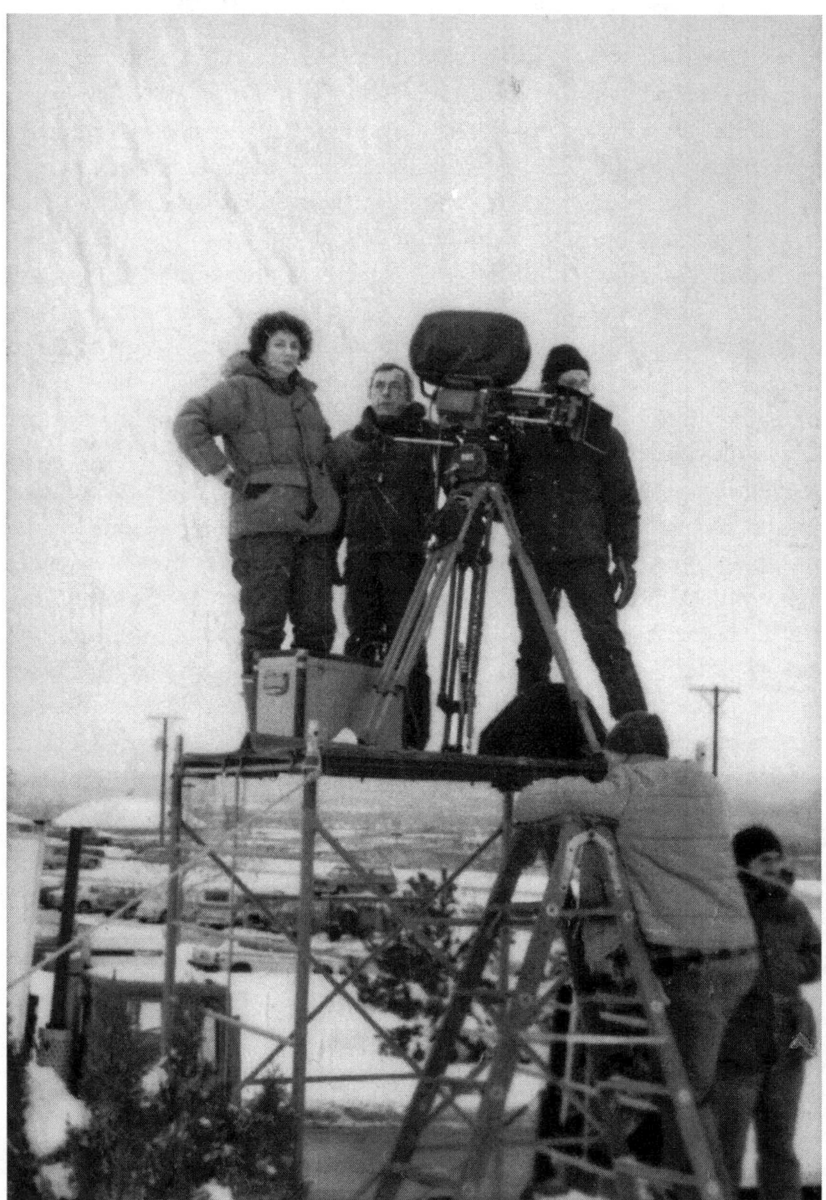

Fig. 7. Joan Micklin Silver with the crew on the set of *Head Over Heels/Chilly Scenes of Winter* (Margaret Herrick Library, Academy of Motion Picture Arts and Sciences)

film features an ensemble cast that included Lindsay Crouse, Jill Eikenberry, Jeff Goldblum, John Heard, Marilu Henner, and Gwen Welles in some of their first starring roles. Written by Fred Barron, a journalist who based the script on his experience working for the independent Boston paper, *The Real Paper*, the movie is set in 1977 and captures the complex dynamics of a group of friends and coworkers grappling with their fading social and political idealism of the 1960s.

The Silvers self-distributed *Between the Lines* through their company Midwest Film Productions, but found the experience more difficult than with *Hester Street*. In 1975, studio films opened nationally at about eighty theaters and the couple was able to find exhibition options for their small, independent picture. But that same year, *Jaws* was released and introduced the saturation booking model—a movie opening on hundreds of screens in multiple cities simultaneously, the use of television promotion, marketing research, pre-sold property (a film based on a book or a Broadway play), and tie-in products such as toys and soundtracks. Moving forward the studios began to restore their market dominance with the discovery of this blockbuster formula; *Jaws* opened in 409 theaters, *Saturday Night Fever* (1977) opened in 726 theaters, and *Grease* (1978) opened in 902 theaters.[153] Ray Silver held the studios' move to an even wider release schedule responsible for the change in distribution patterns since 1975 and the detrimental affect it had on smaller films that were then pushed out of the market. "By 1978, when we were distributing *Between the Lines*, we found it difficult to get either the theaters we wanted or the numbers we wanted," said the indie producer-distributor. "We'd ask for twelve theaters in Atlanta, and we'd get six."[154] In this industry landscape, a human interest story, with no special effects or chart-breaking soundtrack and headlined by a cast of young unknowns, had a difficult time reaching audiences.

Critics found *Between the Lines*'s overarching theme of journalistic integrity in the face of media corporatization to be the least interesting part of the film. What did stand out to reviewers was the cast. The *New York Times* thought the film was "at its best when it ambles in and out of [the characters'] lives, overhearing lovers' quarrels, professional conflicts, office politics . . . the performances, which are uniformly first-rate, the kind of ensemble work in which no actor is more or less important than another."[155] *Variety* was impressed with the film's estimated budget of $800,000: "Every cent of the budget shows on the screen and it should be received, with open arms, [by] the class of customers for which it has apparently been made—the young." The reviewer praised the script, the performances, and "Joan Micklin Silver's firm director's touch." This reviewer's only criticism was that "the overall handsomeness of the cast is one of the [film's] unbelievable aspects."[156] For a small film created outside of the star-package deal that was beginning to dominate Hollywood, this light jab at irony was a compliment the filmmakers might welcome.

Having made two successful commercial films outside the studio system, in 1979 Micklin Silver made her first studio picture, *Head Over Heels* (which was later re-released as *Chilly Scenes of Winter* in 1982), with United Artists. Set in Salt Lake City, *Head Over Heels* is a romantic dramedy starring John Heard, in his second film with the director, as Charles, a thirty-year-old civil servant who falls in love with a married coworker Laura, played by Mary Beth Hurt. The narrative follows the ups and downs of Charles's heartache and is supported by an eclectic cast of characters, including Charles's neurotic mother played by Hollywood veteran Gloria Grahame, and his best friend Sam, in an early role for Peter Riegert, who would star in Micklin Silver's next film, *Crossing Delancey*.

The film was based on Ann Beattie's novel, *Chilly Scenes of Winter*. Actors Griffin Dunne, Mark Metcalf, and Amy Robinson and their newly formed company, Triple Play Productions, had optioned the rights to the story and were looking for a writer to adapt it when Micklin Silver, who had always been interested in the book, contacted them. At the time, Micklin Silver had a two-picture development deal with 20th Century-Fox. Robinson knew Claire Townsend, a creative executive who was working at Fox. Townsend supported the project, and Micklin Silver was signed to write and direct with Triple Play producing. Eventually, Fox lost interest in the film, and Townsend took the deal with her when she left the studio to work for United Artists as the vice president of production, where the picture was ultimately made for $2.2 million. Salary deferrals kept the budget low: most of the cast deferred a portion of their pay, and Micklin Silver deferred three-quarters of her income.[157]

*Head Over Heels* was derailed as soon as it got to United Artists, which was then going through a turbulent time. Prompted by a major dispute

Fig. 8. Hannah Scheel (front), Joan Micklin Silver, and Gloria Grahame (in bath) in *Head Over Heels/Chilly Scenes of Winter* (Margaret Herrick Library, Academy of Motion Picture Arts and Sciences)

with its parent corporation, Trans America, the long-standing and successful UA leadership team had quit the company in 1978. This management turnover, in combination with the studio's losses suffered in the production of *Heaven's Gate*, a film that went $30 million over budget and led to the downfall of the company, had a big impact on Micklin Silver's small picture.[158] "They felt the need to push somebody around and there was my little movie!" Micklin Silver said in defense of her film years later to an audience of students at the AFI.[159] The studio changed the name of the film to *Head Over Heels* because it felt that the title of Beattie's novel, *Chilly Scenes of Winter*, was too dark and that audiences would think it was a melancholy Ingmar Bergman film, rather than an American-styled bittersweet romantic comedy.[160] Yet the new title misrepresented the film's depth of feeling concerning romantic relationships. Beattie, who was supportive of the producers' and director's vision of her book, joked that *Head Over Heels* "sounded as if Fred Astaire should be dancing across the credits."[161]

UA's marketing department felt that the film was peculiar and therefore difficult to sell. They rushed the release, skipping preview screenings that Micklin Silver felt would have been worthwhile in gauging audience response and thereby fine-tuning the movie's final version. The film received mediocre reviews. Vincent Canby was unsure about what was wrong with this "tantalizing movie, seeming to be on the verge of some revelation of profound feeling that, at long last, never comes."[162]

In an unlikely but *lucky* turn of events, in 1982, UA Classics decided to re-release the film under the condition that Micklin Silver edit the ending that leaves Charles and Laura happily together. "When they said that to me," explained Micklin Silver. "I said, 'Look, I've been dying to do this, this is wonderful.'"[163] No reshoots were necessary. The director cut the final scene, and the film—retitled *Chilly Scenes of Winter*—closes on Charles alone, but ready to start over. The small re-release of an already small film generated positive reviews. Sheila Benson of the *Los Angeles Times* saw the film as a triumph: "'Chilly Scenes of Winter' [is] an impeccably performed comedy frosted with sadness. . . . Silver has assembled a splendid cast and achieved performances which are vivid and haunting. Her writing is almost equally successful." As for the title that United Artists had originally balked at, Benson forgave its gloominess. "For all its bleak title," she wrote, "'Chilly Scenes' is a warm, lovable, enormously appealing film."[164]

Although her first studio picture had been an arduous experience, Micklin Silver preferred working with an established company. In 1979, soon after making *Head Over Heels*, the filmmaker who had accomplished the near-impossible feat of making two commercial features independently, was adamant in her preference for studio work: "Oh, I would much rather work with the studios. Everything costs so much—all the costs are up, up, up, up—and it's just enormously hard. If you've never made films before—as far as I'm concerned, make any kind of film you can. I mean, make it any way. But having got this far along, I hope that I can get studio backing for the films I want to do."[165]

Micklin Silver would go on to direct three studio-made feature films—*Crossing Delancey* (1988, Warner Bros.), *Loverboy* (1989, TriStar Pictures) and *Big Girls Don't Cry . . . They Get Even* (1992, New Line Cinema)—as well as an independent film, *A Fish in the Bathtub* (1999), produced by Ray and Silverfilm Productions and released by independent distributor Curb Entertainment. She directed many television movies for PBS, HBO, and Lifetime Television in the early years of the twenty-first century. In contrast to her earlier films that she wrote and directed, much of Micklin Silver's work after the late 1980s did not originate with her as the writer, but instead she served as a "director for hire." This was a position that she embraced. Her 1988 film, *Crossing Delancey*, serves as a bookend to the body of work that she, in collaboration with her husband, created during the 1970s. The film starred Amy Irving as Isabelle Grossman, a single, thirty-year-old New Yorker who goes back and forth between the Lower East Side, where her lovable and meddlesome Jewish grandmother hires a matchmaker for her, and the Upper West Side, where she lives as a 1980s "independent" single woman. Based on the play by Susan Sandler, who also wrote the screenplay, the film was produced by Michael Nozik with Ray Silver as executive producer. Steven Spielberg, then married to Amy Irving, helped get the film to Warner Bros. *Crossing Delancey*'s narrative about the experiences of a New York Jewish woman balancing cultural traditions with contemporary gender roles connected to the themes that Micklin Silver explored in *Hester Street* a decade earlier. *Crossing Delancey* also resonated with her interest in the complex and evolving emotional terrain of the transition into adulthood, subject matter the director approached in *Between the Lines* and *Chilly Scenes of Winter*. In these four films, she is playful in her approach to romantic themes, while never using humor to undermine the seriousness of falling in love or of heartbreak.

Joan Micklin Silver is a singular example, not only alongside her peers in independent film but also within this complete history of women directors. She was the only woman who was able to build a body of work during the 1970s and then into the 1980s that was hers, without any studio or producer interference. (In the re-issuing of her earlier film as *Chilly Scenes of Winter*, she was able to realize her ideal version.) She acknowledged her husband's role in her success: "What distinguished me from other independent filmmakers—men and women—who were just as talented was that I had a husband who was able—and willing to help me."[166] As will be discussed later, other women directors worked with their husbands and partners in different ways and to a variety of outcomes. For Micklin Silver, her personal relationship meant she was able to *control* her creative vision and means of production and distribution because she had a dedicated *producer-distributor*. This, combined with her material that was distinctive *and* had commercial appeal, led to her success.

## Penny Allen

That was my first awareness—going to Sundance [in 1978]—that there were other indie films that had come out of all these corners of the United States.

—Penny Allen[167]

Most independent filmmakers during the 1970s worked out of Los Angeles and/or New York City and focused on selling their films to the moviegoing marketplace of those urban and cultural centers. One exception was Penny Allen, a regional filmmaker who in the late 1970s began making independent feature films—*Property* (1979) and *Paydirt* (1981)—in and around Portland, Oregon. Allen was born in Portland in 1942, and both of her parents were from Oregon. Her father was a structural engineer, and her mother was a high school chemistry teacher before she started a family and became a stay-at-home mother. In her junior year at the University of Oregon in the early 1960s, Allen traveled to Paris as part of a school program. That trip introduced her to theater and laid the groundwork for her connection to France, where she has lived since the 1990s.

In the early 1970s, Allen taught at Portland State University, where she created the Paris Theater Seminar, in which students visited the city for six weeks and saw live performances almost every night. "It was exciting and it was a great time for theater in France, during the early 1970s," recalled Allen in 2017. "We saw early Robert Wilson; we saw the first performances of *Deafman Glance* in Paris. It was *incredible*; so influential."[168] By the mid-1970s, Allen had left teaching to pursue her artistic interests. She began directing theater, working with a troupe of actors developing agitprop, Brechtian-inspired productions, which focused on contemporary politics, including feminist subjects.

Allen's transition to film began with her work with local television. She and Eric Edwards, who had recently graduated from the Rhode Island School of Design and was later to be her cinematographer and collaborator on *Property* and *Paydirt*, began to work—for free—on a weekly, neighborhood cable TV series called *Urban Free Delivery*. For that show, they made short pieces, shot on video, most of which were in a documentary style about local issues. After becoming frustrated with the low-quality equipment, they took their experience making the videos for cable and

Allen's access to actors she had already worked with and moved to a better-quality medium: film.

*Property* was shot on 16mm; Edwards borrowed a camera from his next-door neighbor who was the cameraman for the local network television affiliates. As regional filmmakers in the Pacific Northwest, hours away from the concentration of competitors in Hollywood whom Karen Arthur had to contend with in her repeated applications for the AFI Independent Filmmaker Grant, Allen and her collaborators had access to different resources, including an unlikely investor: the U.S. government. They applied to the Comprehensive Employment Training Application (CETA), a federally funded program administered by the Department of Labor and established by President Nixon in 1974 to address the high unemployment rate during the recession. The grant paid a small sum for cast and crew salaries, and a private donation of $25,000 helped her meet *Property's* budget of roughly $120,000.

*Property* is a topical and local film: it dramatizes what would later become known as gentrification in the neighborhood where Allen then lived. At the time, Corbett-Terwiliger-Lair Hill was a low-income, bohemian community in Portland whose residents were being displaced by bank buyouts and real estate development. The film is driven by a quirky and charismatic ensemble cast of local talent, including comedian Corky Hubbert, poet Walt Curtis, and Lola Desmond, the dynamic leading lady who would later star in *Paydirt*. Similar to Joan Micklin Silver's *Between the Lines*, which addresses the encroachment of corporate power on community-based values, *Property* captures the vibrant idealism and pluck of the 1970s, as seen through the microcosm of this motley crew of neighbors, standing up to the Goliath of big business by attempting to buy back their neighborhood.

The film's crew was minimal, made up of Allen, Edwards, a production assistant, and their soundman, Gus Van Sant—earning one of his first production credits before embarking on his own successful career as a writer-director with roots in regional Northwest filmmaking. (His first film, *Mala Noche*, is the screen adaptation of Walt Curtis's novel by the same name. Edwards would go on to work with Van Sant as cinematographer for several of his movies.) On *Property*, Allen combined improvisational techniques with scripted material. Speaking to *Filmmaker Magazine* in 2017, she explained to Steve Macfarlane, "I like very much working with people to arrive at something, and that's how we were doing it in the theater troupe: arriving at what we wanted to do, and doing things over and over and over until we arrived at what we wanted. That's how it went with some of the scenes in the movie, but there's no live improvisation onscreen."[169]

Bob Sitton, the director of the Northwest Film Center, encouraged Allen to apply for *Property* to be screened at the Telluride Film Festival and to the newly established Utah-U.S. Film Festival, which would eventually become the Sundance Film Festival. Her film was accepted by the latter festival, screening in 1978 during its debut year and winning a $1,000 prize. That same year at the festival, Claudia Weill's *Girlfriends* won the $5,000 prize for "best picture."[170] In January 1979, *Property* made its New York City premiere at the first American Mavericks Festival, a newly established showcase for "America's 'hidden cinema.'"[171] The critical response to the work captured not only the uniqueness of the film—its unpolished qualities full of conviction and imagination—but also its place in the American independent film scene that would begin to gather momentum at the end of the decade. Reviewing the film as part of the Mavericks' series, Vincent Canby displayed some appreciation for *Property*, describing it as a "folksy sort of movie" that is "a fond improvisation, competently photographed and adequately mimed." Canby, however, appeared lost without a more conventional structure to engage him: "Experiencing it is like thumbing through somebody else's photograph album. The pictures are clear but the important associations are missing."[172] On the other end of the spectrum, both in perspective and publication, David Harris, writing for *New Age*, understood the film as a sign of what was taking place in domestic independent cinema: "Films like *Property* simply let the strange state of American life speak for itself, leaving us to watch and respond on our own. And the sense of freedom and discovery is tremendous." For Harris, the film's rough edges, its mix of quiet moments and frenetic energy dared to show the "breaking down of the barriers between 'life' and 'art,' 'fiction' and 'reality' that lets in the implicit violence, vitality, and indigenous surrealism of American life."[173]

Allen started production on her next feature, *Paydirt*, in 1979, soon after completing *Property*. She worked again with Edwards, a small crew, and Lola Desmond as the lead, costarring with Eric Silverstein, Allen described the new film as the second in her land-use trilogy: whereas

*Property* introduces the story of an urban community in conflict with structures of power, *Paydirt* moves those themes to a rural setting. It tells the story of a group of hardworking vintners whose vineyard depends on the profits from the secret marijuana crop of one of the farmers, played by Desmond. Desmond and her partner must fight, with violence and through business negotiations, the encroachment of a more powerful narcotics businessman who attempts to stronghold the smaller entrepreneurs by stealing their drug crops. *Paydirt* repeats the loose and poetic visual style of *Property*, which is made even more vibrant by the rural landscape setting. This time, however, Allen adheres more closely to a script and a narrative structure that invoke the genre conventions of a thriller-heist, made especially compelling by Desmond's rendition of a countercultural farmer as the outlaw heroine. As she did with *Property*, Allen took *Paydirt* on the festival circuit, making appearances at stateside programs, including the Utah-U.S. and Telluride Film Festivals; she was unable to secure funds for travel to international festivals to which she was invited and instead just sent the prints to the screenings without any cast or crew representatives.

Allen did not map out a distribution strategy for either of her films. "I didn't know anything about it, truly," the filmmaker admitted in retrospect, laughing at her naiveté. "I didn't know anything. I didn't know anything about it as a business. I did meet the distributor who brought out John Sayles's first movie—*The Secaucus Seven*—at Telluride, in the sauna!" She laughed again. "He asked me some questions—I didn't know who he was or anything about distribution or what I suppose to say—I didn't follow up on it."[174] Even though she did not set her sights on a wide distribution deal for the movie, *Property* did circulate broadly, supported by the festival buzz and generating special interest among Portland audiences. "*Property* was written about in a lot local publications. It was sort of like the first movie there in Portland," remembered Allen. "It was very popular. We four-walled it [rented a commercial movie theater for the exclusive screening of her film and kept all of the box office returns] in a cinema for a couple of weeks and it was sold out all the time."[175] Around 1981, Sandra Schulberg, who founded the Independent Filmmaker Project in 1979, made available funds for Allen to travel to New York to talk about the film with other filmmakers; Shulberg provided a contact with Ray Fischer, an independent distributor who was the exclusive booking agent for the American Mavericks Festival's national tour, for a limited release;[176] and the film aired on WNET, New York's public television station.

Allen was wary of Hollywood. Speaking at the Utah-U.S. Film Festival in 1978 on the distribution challenges faced by independent films made outside of the film industry, she warned that "if the goal is going to Hollywood, there won't be any more regional cinema."[177] Pursuing Hollywood "was never something I was going to do," recalled Allen in our interview. However, after touring with *Paydirt* on the U.S. festival circuit, she got a meeting with a studio executive in Los Angeles. "I told him my idea for my following movie and he seemed interested. And he said, 'Write it and come back,'" she laughed. "That whole setup didn't interest me much, so I didn't follow up."[178]

After *Paydirt*, Allen moved away from filmmaking. "It was exciting, but it was also exhausting. *Paydirt* didn't have this wide circulation that *Property* did and it felt kind of like a dead end and that was why I was willing to move to the country on a horse ranch." The final part of her land-use trilogy was not in the form of a film but of a memoir published in 2001: *A Geography of Saints* chronicles her years living on a ranch following the rush of making her first films. Allen returned to filmmaking in the early years of the twenty-first century after moving to Paris in 1991 and working on environmental issues. Her documentary *Soldier's Tale* (2007) is the story of a U.S. soldier's experience in the Iraq War; it was followed by the feature *Late for My Mother's Funeral* (2013) about a Moroccan family in Algeria after the death of their mother.

The first wave of independent art house films made by women directors in the early and mid-1970s shared the woes of obtaining financing and the limited distribution typical of the time; for a regional filmmaker working during the latter part of the decade, Hollywood itself was alien and uninteresting. The narrative content of these films encompassed a range of themes and genres. Some, as in the case of *Legacy*, risked their box office appeal, perhaps unknowingly, in favor of innovation. Others, like *Wanda*, found admiration among critics for openly disregarding the conventions of popular appeal in their presentation of an abject protagonist. *Hester Street* took a niche subject and engaged a contemporary audience with the novelty of a period piece made relevant through characters and performance. And *Property* celebrated the idiosyncratic values of a neighborhood without worrying about whether the rest of the world, or Hollywood, knew where it was located. Independently made films that were intended to *entertain* audiences in the most unadulterated ways—using sex, politics, violence, action, and humor—would come from the margins of Hollywood too, but across a different set of tracks.

## Stephanie Rothman

> Many people are surprised and don't believe that women can assume positions of leadership and decision-making, that they can come to grips with the various technical aspects of film-making—which, of course, is nonsense.
>
> —Stephanie Rothman[179]

Roger Corman, a prolific independent producer-director of B-films, culled his development staff and production crews from the ranks of inexperienced young people eager to break into the film business. In 1964, when he was looking for an assistant, he mined local Los Angeles universities looking for someone—male or female—who was at the top of their class, with classroom training in the technical and creative aspects of filmmaking, and, most importantly, was eager and ambitious to make movies. On the recommendation of Bernard Kantor, chair of the University of Southern California's Cinema Department, Stephanie Rothman obtained an interview with Corman. Rothman, then a twenty-eight-year-old graduate student in the film program, had recently won the Directors Guild Student Director Award and $1,500 cash for her proposed documentary on Alice Ehlers, a world-renowned harpsichordist who taught at USC. Rothman was the first woman to receive this prize. The assistant job entailed reading scripts for potential projects and working in production on low-budget independent films already in development. Rothman abandoned her student film project and the fellowship money and accepted Corman's offer enthusiastically: "He asked me if I would be interested, and I said, 'Yes! I would love to!'"[180]

In his 1990 autobiography, Corman remembered that he also interviewed Julie Halloran from UCLA for the position. "Stephanie Rothman was Phi Beta Kappa in English Lit from Berkeley, top of her class with a master's degree in film from USC," wrote the veteran producer. "She had just won the Director's Guild Award as the outstanding student director at an American university. There was no way I could not hire Stephanie. So I offered her the job and I asked Julie for a date. Both said yes."[181] Corman and Halloran would marry in 1970 and become producing partners during the 1970s, a collaboration that continues through the present.

Born in New Jersey in 1936, Rothman moved to Los Angeles with her parents in 1945. She was an only child in a middle-class, secular Jewish home: her father was a neuropsychiatrist, and her mother was a public health nurse and medical social worker before Rothman was born, who then became a stay-at-home mother. Socially conservative and politically liberal, Rothman's parents were committed to exposing their child to a progressive worldview while placing a high value on education. In a 2001 interview conducted by Jane Collings for UCLA's Center for the Study of Oral History, Rothman explained her mother and father's approach to parenting: "They wanted me to be educated and pursue a career that would feed me rather than a career that would make me starve."[182] Growing up with this kind of encouragement, Rothman excelled as a student, graduating high school at sixteen and going on to UCLA for two years before transferring to University of California, Berkeley, where she majored in sociology.

Since she was a girl, Rothman had always been interested in film. She would go to the movies weekly, enthralled by pictures such as *The Bad and the Beautiful*, *Meet Me in St. Louis*, and *The Razor's Edge*. "I *adored* films," she remembered of her cinephilic awakening. "It didn't matter whether it was a good one or a bad one, I was just entranced by the images, and just by the opportunity to escape into a world of strange images."[183] While at UC Berkeley she saw Ingmar Bergman's *The Seventh Seal*. "That [film] absolutely astounded me, because it said everything I wanted to say about the human condition as I understood it. . . . I was absolutely awestruck by it."[184]

After completing her bachelor's degree, Rothman abandoned her studies for a master's degree in sociology at UC Berkeley because of the rampant sexism she encountered in academia. Anxious and unsure about what to do next, in 1959, Rothman returned to Los Angeles, where she started work as a technical writer at Systems Development Corporation (SDC), an early software company. "It sort of occurred to me that it would be wonderful to be able to make films at that time," she said, as she recalled her curiosity about filmmaking. "But I did not think of that as a career goal because I had no idea how one could go about doing this."[185]

While working at SDC, Rothman met Jeb Gholson, a cinematographer in his thirties who specialized in underwater and action photography. Gholson explained the nuts and bolts of filmmaking to Rothman, even taking her to a television studio where she saw for the first time a production in process. This exposure began to demystify for Rothman the craft of filmmaking and to make real its possibility as a feasible career. Gholson had trained by apprenticing to a cinematographer and thought she might do something similar, although he had "never seen a girl apprentice to anybody."[186] As an alternative, he recommended she go to film school. The late 1960s would be a time when the younger generation would gain access to Hollywood without the help of nepotism and through a system of meritocracy (in particular, through advancement in the unions) and in many cases through film school; however, in 1960 access to a career in filmmaking was still elusive. With Gholson's encouragement Rothman began to look at film schools. William W. Melnitz, the founding dean of UCLA's College of Fine Arts (later the School of Theater, Film and Television) who was a family friend, nevertheless advised her to apply to USC rather than UCLA because the latter was primarily a theater program and USC had more hands-on film production courses.[187]

When she visited the school before starting her studies there, she saw that all the students were male. Rothman described her first impression: "They were lugging all this equipment around and they were doing things with pieces of equipment that I had never seen before. It was an alien world to me." Faced with the reality of being the sole female in film school—a microcosm of the film industry—Rothman was worried that the program was not the right choice for her. She consulted with department chair Bernard Kantor for advice. Kantor was enthusiastic about Rothman's abilities, reassuring her that based on her academic record and her self-determination she would do fine. "Of course you will, don't worry about it," he told her. "You'll master it if you want to." Bolstered by his encouragement, in 1962 she enrolled in the program. Two years later, she left school to take the job as Roger Corman's assistant, having completed her course work, but had not yet completed her thesis film or graduated.

As his assistant, Rothman had what would be characterized as an experience typical to working with Corman. She was quickly promoted because of her skills, talent, and drive, all of which she needed to deal with the low-budget productions' fast-paced schedule and her boss's frugal nature. Rothman initially provided notes on screenplays that Corman was considering producing and conducted set visits to his various productions, keeping her boss informed of any problems. Soon her responsibilities increased to directing the second unit on films like *Beach Ball* (1965, dir. Curtis Harrington); in 1966, Corman asked her to take over the troubled production of director Jack Hill's *Blood Bath* (also known as *Track of the Vampire*), having her rewrite scenes and shoot new footage for the picture. For this project, Rothman received her first screen credit for cowriter and codirector, which she shared with Hill.

In 1967 Corman hired Rothman to direct the teen beach comedy *It's a Bikini World*. Working with Rothman on this film as cowriter and producer was her husband, Charles S. Swartz. The couple had met in 1962 on the first day of film school while in line to register for classes.[188] *It's a Bikini World* was significant both because it was the first feature film she directed on her own and it marked the beginning of a creative and business collaboration with her husband that would span her entire career in filmmaking. In 1969 Corman hired the pair to serve as production executives (positions that included but were not limited to location scouting, production management, production design, and storyboard artistry) on his film *Gas—s-s-s!* . . . (also known as *It Became Necessary to Destroy the World in Order to Save It*). And in 1970, when Corman started his own production and distribution business, New World Pictures, he hired Rothman and Swartz to make the company's first film, *Student Nurses*: she served as director and he as producer, and together they came up with the story idea.

At USC, once exposed to the reality of filmmaking as a profession, Rothman knew that she wanted to be a writer-director. She was grateful to Corman for the chance to begin sharpening those skills and decades later was generous in her appreciation: "Roger gave a lot of young people the opportunity to work as filmmaking professionals. He gave them a degree of responsibility and freedom that nobody in Hollywood would do, ever."[189] But, after working on *It's a Bikini World*, she realized that low-budget exploitation films were not where she wanted to make her career.

Rothman had hopes of breaking out of sensationalist independent film production and into the mainstream industry. However, she found this extremely difficult and eventually impossible to do. To get a job in Hollywood required access to certain networking circles, gained through family, personal, or guild connections, none of which Rothman or Swartz had. The young director also experienced the limitations imposed on her gender. "I couldn't get an agent to represent me," explained Rothman of her professional standing in the late 1960s. "I had no access, for example, to anyone producing television shows who might be looking for young directors. They sometimes gave people a chance, but they certainly didn't give women a chance. Nobody I knew was hiring women, and the few times I inquired I was told, they don't hire women."[190] In 1970, when Corman offered the couple *The Student Nurses*, the director came to understand her predicament. "At that point I realized two things," remembered Rothman. "First of all, that I was not going to get an opportunity to make films anywhere else. Only Roger was giving me that chance, and I really appreciated it because I saw that my chances anywhere else were nonexistent."[191]

On *The Student Nurses*, Rothman made a compromise that she would struggle with for the rest of her years as a film director. While she was still working within the constraints of an exploitation film—a small budget, a short production schedule, and the company's requirement of scenes with violence, action, and female nudity—she was able to integrate her personal politics into the project because she was at the helm of her own film and was able to collaborate with Swartz. Corman did not require the film to reflect the progressive views of the day, but he was not opposed to its doing so, as long as the message was packaged in typical exploitation excess. In a 2015 interview with the Academy of Motion Picture Arts and Sciences, Visual History program, Rothman remembered that, in addition to the film's being about nurses, the veteran producer's only other requirement was that "we had to make an R rated film that was at the very edge of the R rating, in other words . . . [it] had to be just before an X. . . . It had to have considerable nudity in it. . . . And it had to have some violence. And aside from that we were on our own."[192]

From the beginning of her career as a filmmaker, Rothman was outspoken about being a feminist. Writing for the *Hollywood Reporter* in

1972, Will Tusher described the filmmaker in no uncertain terms as "Stephanie Rothman—a 35-year-old distaff director who is not coy about her age or her Women's Lib viewpoint."[193] In *The Student Nurses*, as well as her later films, Rothman invokes feminist themes and characterizations, such as female friendship and the value of women working in a variety of careers, including, but not limited to, those traditionally associated with men. Her films celebrate female agency and individuality, and while women are the protagonists of her movies, male characters are given the same opportunity for growth and potential. Her fair treatment of both genders was described by one interviewer in 1970 as rooted in the fact that as a "dedicated feminist, Miss Rothman feels women's lib ought to be followed by a men's liberation movement. 'Men have to realize it's all right to be what they want, even if the role is traditionally female.'"[194] *The Student Nurses*, the story of four student nurses emphasizes camaraderie among the cohort and professionalism while never sacrificing each character's distinctiveness. The friends are a diverse group: Pricilla (Barbara Leigh) is the 1960s flower child open to experimentation; Sharon (Elaine Giftos) considers the philosophical side of nursing when faced with the challenges of a terminal patient; the political consciousness of Lynn (Brioni Farrell) is awakened after she provides medical attention to a radical Chicano protest group; and Phred (Karen Carlson) is a steadfast careerist unwilling to bend any rules on her path to secure employment.

Many critics understood the constraints dictating these movies and celebrated the film in spite of and sometimes because of those limitations. *Variety* described *The Student Nurses* as "a good contemporary dual-bill. . . . The acting level is fair at best, which drags down what otherwise is a well-crafted film. . . . Rothman's physical direction is excellent. . . . Don Spencer's script is good. . . . Pic is an exploitation item to be sure, but beyond those angles, general audiences will find a surprising depth."[195] Other reviewers were unforgiving, unable to make any concessions to the limitations of exploitation films. One such critic described the story as what "appears to be a first draft and goes off in as many directions as a strung out octopus in attempting to keep up with four nurses." Yet the review was somewhat sympathetic: it did not hold Rothman entirely responsible for the film's flaws, admitting that while "Miss Rothman's direction is of little help in keeping all the trails the story takes in focus, though, in all fairness, it is doubtful anyone could have or would have done much better."[196] With the aid of good reviews and in spite of the bad ones, *The Student Nurses* was a success, earning more than $1 million in rentals.[197]

Rothman declined Corman's offer to write and direct the next installment of the nurse series. Instead they agreed to make a vampire film together. "I've always wanted to make every kind of film I could, at least once," she told an interviewer in 1981. "To see what the demands of the particular genre were and whether I could make it."[198] *The Velvet Vampire* provided her with the chance to momentarily escape the sexy girl-group genre that was taking hold while also transforming the traditional vampire narrative. Rothman's version is set in contemporary Los Angeles and the surrounding desert areas: vampire Diane LeFanu (Celeste Yarnall) rides her dune buggy in the sunlight, inviting her victims to her elegant desert ranch house, where, as a genial host, she seduces them. In contrast to the traditional vampire, this blood-sucking predator is an assertive, tantalizing, modern-day female. "The only way that I could see to make this kind of film and to make it interesting was to reverse expectations," justified Rothman. "The obvious passivity of women in vampire films was both disturbing to me and rather boring." As dictated by the marketplace, originality was a necessity for the filmmaker, who with her limited budget felt she could not go up against well-known horror producers: "I couldn't compete with the [vampire films] made by Hammer Films. I didn't have the money, I didn't have the facilities . . . all you can do is hope that you have presented it in a way that people will laugh in recognition at the fresh twist you have given it."[199] Despite these efforts, box office returns for the film were low. Rothman speculated that the picture's failure may have also been due to how it "fell between two schools. [It was] not a traditional horror film nor a hard-core exploitation movie."[200]

By 1971 Rothman and Swartz had left New World Pictures because of money. As much as Corman was credited for giving new filmmakers opportunities to work, he was equally as notorious for not paying them enough. When, for their next project, he offered the couple even less than the low rate he was already paying them, the trio amicably parted ways. New World's former head of distribution, Lawrence Woolner, had started his own independent production-distribution company, Dimension Pictures, which also specialized in a variety of exploitation films, and asked Rothman and Swartz if they would join as partners. The couple agreed, and instead of investing money, they committed their "labor and imagination" to the business.[201] Rothman was named vice president of creative development in charge of seeking out potential projects and overseeing script development, as well as directing (and cowriting) features with Swartz, who became vice president of production.[202] Together the wife-and-husband team made three feature films during their tenure at Dimension: *Group Marriage* (1972), *Terminal Island* (1973), and *The Working Girls* (1974). Still desperate to get out of exploitation films, they joined Dimension in the hopes of gaining more creative control and an opportunity to build their body of work to serve as a bridge into mainstream filmmaking or television.

At Dimension, the couple continued to incorporate their personal politics into the work they wrote, directed, and produced for the company. Like Corman, Woolner was open to the addition of social politics as long as it did not come at the expense of the exploitation films' copious sex, nudity, and action. Rothman and Swartz's three films maintained focus on the dynamics of a group of characters. *Group Marriage*—a marriage farce with a swinging 1970s twist—follows three heterosexual couples in Los Angeles who participate in the shenanigans of polyamorous wedlock. In *The Working Girls*, with a similar design to that of *The Student Nurses*, three women become roommates and their separate storylines intersect, leading to three times as many opportunities for sexual escapades and occasional fisticuffs with gangsters. Finally, *Terminal Island*, a dramatic action film, is centered on the struggle for power among the exiled inmates of an interracial, coed prison colony located on an island somewhere off the coast of Los Angeles.

Rothman's identifiable style conveys her feminist sensibility in each of these films. Her protagonists are female and are marked by a sense of empowerment that is individually defined and yet always serves the community of characters. Key to the protagonists' ambition and identity is a focus on career and vocation; every character has a unique skill set that in each film's narrative plays the role of explaining individual motivation, and scenes showing them at work are used to move the plot along. "I'm interested in how their careers mold their identity," explained Rothman of how she approached her characters. "And how the identity they have at the beginning of the story molds their careers. It's a two way influence."[203] In *Group Marriage*, Chris (Aimée Eccles) has a day job working at a car rental business, but her real talent is as an auto mechanic. Her ability to fix cars is used as a narrative device to introduce new characters. In *The Working Girls*, Honey (Sarah Kennedy) is an innovative and unemployed entrepreneur. Unable to find work, she places an ad in the paper: "I will do anything for money. Young woman. MA in math. Phi Beta Kappa. Can solve your problems. Will work cheap." In its suggestion of sex for money, the first line of the ad was titillating enough for a drive-in audience without sacrificing any of the film's feminist message conveyed by a woman with an advanced degree in a masculine-dominated field determined to create her own career path. Honey's search for work functions as a narrative device to introduce the movie's other "working girls." Jobless and homeless, Honey meets Denise (Laurie Rose), an aspiring artist/billboard painter, who offers her a place to stay with her and her roommate Jill (Lynne Guthrie), a cocktail waitress by night and law student by day. In *Terminal Island* the female convicts band together to fight the most abusive male prisoners. Pooling their collective talents and building on their female solidarity, they form an unstoppable army: Carmen's (Ena Hartman) grandmother taught her about poisonous plants, knowledge she then uses to make lethal darts; Lee (Marta Kristen), who is incarcerated for blowing up banks as a means of political protest and was working on a PhD before getting arrested, is an ingenious chemist who configures makeshift bombs from minerals she finds on the island.[204]

For Rothman, these depictions of female friendship, frequently through acts related to work, was both appealing and feasible: they enabled her to strike a balance between feminism and exploitation while employed by Corman and Woolner: "I could show a relationship amongst women that at that time just wasn't shown that much, which was that they were only friends, but their concerns were quite adult. They were not frivolous. They were not looking for husbands. They were not obsessed with clothing, or their looks."[205] Mainstream movies in the 1970s disproportionately featured male protagonists, and low-budget filmmaking's mandate to exploit femaleness, most prominently through sexual objectification and acts of sexual violence, as a service to male protagonists, made it particularly challenging to feature female camaraderie. Rothman's women were team players as much as they were leaders.

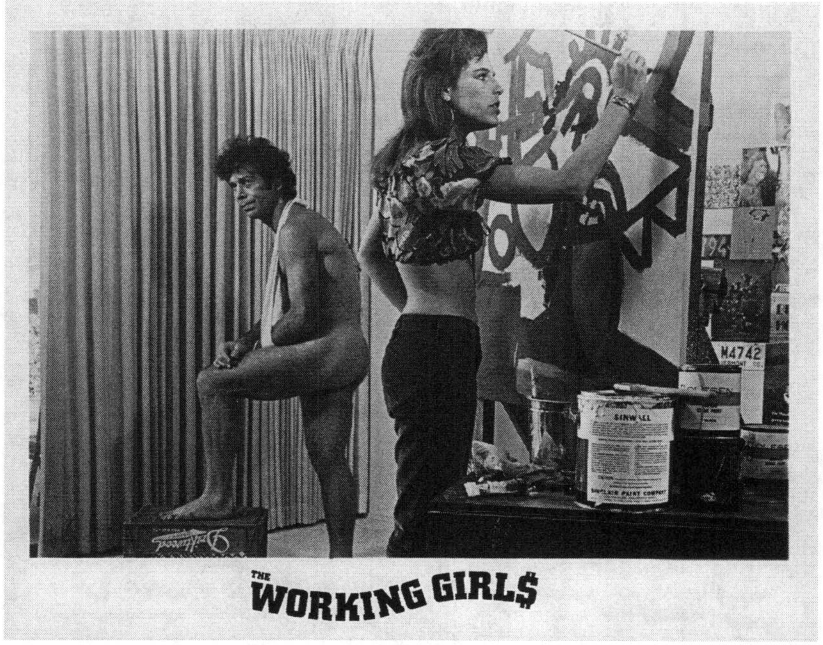


Fig. 9. Ken Del Conte and Laurie Rose in *The Working Girls* (Margaret Herrick Library, Academy of Motion Picture Arts and Sciences)

*The Working Girls* was the last film Rothman directed for Dimension. Sometime in 1974, Woolner elected not to renew Rothman and Swartz's annual contract with the company. The exact reason for his decision is not known. Perhaps Woolner felt that the couple's taste was becoming out of synch with his company's products; he most likely knew that they were unwilling to make even more sensationalized content. For their part, Rothman and Swartz were not only dissatisfied with making exploitation films but also thought that Woolner's business plan was not sound. Looking back, in 2007 Rothman reflected, "We could see that the way [Woolner] was managing the company, it wasn't likely to be very successful. . . . While he would ask our opinion [on] projects, he wouldn't necessarily agree with it, and he tended, in our opinion, to pick projects that were not as promising and were not as likely to be commercial.[206]

*The Working Girls* was also the last movie Stephanie Rothman ever directed. After leaving Dimension, she did everything possible to move out of exploitation pictures and into more mainstream media production. She and Swartz, who was also looking for work, optioned the rights to Philip K. Dick's novel *The Man in the High Castle*, and although the couple's screenplay adaptation was well received by several literary agents at Creative Artists Agency, the two could not garner real interest in it: the project never came to fruition.[207] She reached out to friends employed in television and got new agents who showed her films around, but to no avail. While several men graduated from the "Roger Corman School of filmmaking"—some with fewer credits than she had—and went on to have illustrious careers making studio pictures, such a crossover for Rothman proved to be impossible. She heard more than once that companies were not willing to work with a woman, even one as experienced as she was.[208] At a 2008 screening of *The Velvet Vampire*, Rothman recalled Hollywood's reaction to her film:

> I was called in to meet an executive at MGM after I'd made *The Velvet Vampire*, in fact it was perhaps three or four years later. And this person said to me "Oh, you know, we were talking about you the other day in a meeting, because we've hired the younger brother of Ridley Scott to make a film, and we think we'd like it to be a vampire film, and we were talking about how we would like it to sort of be like *The Velvet Vampire*." And my response was, "Well, if you want a film like *The Velvet Vampire*, why don't you get Stephanie Rothman to make it?"[209]

MGM did make a vampire film in 1983, with British filmmaker Tony Scott directing his first Hollywood picture, *The Hunger*, starring Catherine Deneuve as a vampire, David Bowie as her vampire lover, and Susan Sarandon as the mortal caught in a dangerous triangle with the couple.

Rothman had always aspired to make films in Hollywood: "It was my fervent wish that I would be able to make mainstream films. I wanted to, I never got the opportunity. I tried for about 10 years [after making *The Working Girls*] and then I gave up and just decided to continue living my life, not making films anymore."[210] In the process, however, because she had no other option, Rothman built a significant and distinct body of work that made a unique feminist contribution to low-budget independent filmmaking.

## For Better or Worse: Director-Wife and Producer-Husband

The premature end of Rothman's career also terminated the director's extremely productive filmmaking partnership with her husband, but not their marriage: the couple remained together until his death in 2007. Although Swartz would go on to be the CEO of Entertainment Technology Center, a research unit in the School of Cinema and Television at USC, and to head his own media industry firm, Charles S. Swartz Consulting, *The Working Girls* would be their final film and their last cinematic collaboration.[211] Articles and reviews of Rothman's work almost always acknowledged Swartz as the producer of her films and most mentioned that the two were married, but they rarely paid any consideration to the specialness of a director-wife and producer-husband team. What was rare about this combination was not that they were married—spousal collaborations have a long history in Hollywood—but that in the 1960s and 1970s there were so few women directors at all.[212] On the infrequent occasion that a reporter would draw attention to this personal-professional combination, it was to emphasize the progressive, egalitarian nature of the duo. In 1970 Kit Snedaker wrote in the *Los Angeles Herald Examiner*, "The Swartzes work together daily on their pictures—'He's my favorite colleague and best friend,' Miss Rothman said—and share housekeeping chores when they can't find a maid."[213]

During this period, there were five director-wife/producer-husband couples. Two are discussed in chapter 3: Anne Bancroft and Mel Brooks, and Joan Rivers and Edgar Rosenberg; and the other three—Stephanie Rothman and Charles Swartz, Beverly and Ferd Sebastian, and Joan Micklin Silver and Ray Silver—are discussed in this chapter. In chapter 3, I also examine the career of Jane Wagner: she and Lily Tomlin were domestic partners when they made *Moment by Moment*, and Tomlin used her star power to help Wagner get her first directing job. (The two were legally married in 2013.) Their situation differs from the spousal director-producer teams in that they were a star-director/writer team. From an objective point of view, these couples (with the exception of Rivers and Rosenberg, who were separating at the time of his death) appeared to have strong relationships: they are either still together or were together at the death of their spouse and have conveyed in the press, over multiple decades, a positive relationship. However, the reality of these couples' relationships is, of course, impossible for the historian to truly know. Furthermore, regardless of how mutually supportive and professionally in synch a couple might be, making films in Hollywood was a challenging and unpredictable occupation even for the most loving producer-husband and director-wife team.

According to the sexist assumption that, within the male-centric culture of Hollywood a woman director would benefit from the "protection" of a male producer, the wife-husband model should be a successful one. In this worldview, male executives who were resistant to the idea of a woman overseeing a multimillion-dollar budget would feel comfortable making the deal with her husband as producer. This line of reasoning fails in two respects: it relies on the belief that not only does a woman director need the protection of a man but also that a male producer could defend a woman director from industry sexism or from the demands any director or producer—regardless of gender—faces from studio executives, stars, crew, publicists, distributors, and so on. It is also problematic in its romanticization of marriage—within a heterosexist context—in assuming that wives need or look to their husbands as a guardian and that husbands would assume such a role and be successful at it. To some degree, each of these five pairs had a different experience. For Rothman and Swartz, even though they were best friends and successful collaborators, no combination of director-producer, husband-wife could enable them to break through the impasse created by Stephanie Rothman being a woman director of exploitation films.

## Beverly and Ferd Sebastian

> We learned a long time ago to keep peace in our family. We've been married fifty-eight years, you learn little tricks along the way—we share a mutual credit—produced, directed, and written by Beverly and Ferd Sebastian—on everything we do.
>
> —Beverly Sebastian[214]

Like Rothman and Swartz, spouses Beverly and Ferd Sebastian worked in independent, low-budget exploitation films. However, unlike Rothman and Swartz, who were hired to make films for a company that was able to finance and distribute their work, the Sebastians produced and self-distributed many of their films. They also shared credits as writer, director, and producer on the majority of their movies. To date the Sebastians have made fourteen films together: their first feature-length film was *I Need* (sometimes listed as *I Need a Man*) made in 1967, and their most recent one, *Running Cool*, was released in 1993.

In 1953, when Beverly was eighteen years old, she met nineteen-year-old Ferd at a skating rink; she was from Georgia, and he was from Texas. The pair was married ten days later. From early on the couple were collaborators. When Ferd quit his job as a pipe fitter to begin work as a photographer, Beverly ran the darkroom. While living in Houston, the couple first made the transition from still photography into producing television commercials and educational films. A feature film was the logical next step.[215] *I Need*, sometimes retitled as *I Need a Man*, was made for $7,500 in 1967 and initially self-distributed by the Sebastians out of necessity because no distributor would pick up the title. With the profits earned they were able to cover their living expenses and finance their second film, *The Love Clinic* (1968).[216] Little is known about the couples' early films—the prints were stored in and then disappeared from a lab that went bankrupt—except that they featured strong sexual themes and explicit depictions. According to the American Film Institute Catalog's description, *I Need* is about a woman who was raped at ten years old and as an adult becomes a sex addict who eventually goes insane because of her past trauma's impact on her life.[217] In a 2017 interview, Ferd described this movie as "very arty," laughing in remembrance as he categorized the low-budget, black and white sexploitation film as a "European, [Federico] Fellini film."[218] The film toured drive-ins and grindhouse movie theaters around the Southern exhibition circuit, but audiences were not interested. Finally, the Sebastians found a distributor in California who rented the film to a San Jose drive-in where the owner, an "old showman who had been around forever," refashioned the promotional material to feature the female lead with her head thrown back in ecstasy screaming, "I need a man!"—and from there the film was renamed *I Need a Man*. Where previously the movie had made $1,000 in a week, an amount the Sebastians considered substantial, after its makeover in San Jose, the picture's box office returns skyrocketed to $12,500 a week.

*The Love Clinic* is another example of how the shaping of marketing materials, to accentuate the sensational qualities of these independent films, was so crucial to their success. The tagline on the film's poster read, "She submitted to the most intimate of physiological tests . . . at THE LOVE CLINIC." Following exploitation films' protocol of provocative themes, the words are printed over an image of a young woman, whose face is obscured by shadows: bare shouldered, she is photographed from the cleavage up. The warning in small print at the bottom of the poster reads, "Suggested for Mature Audience."[219] "It was a kick-off on Masters and Johnson, comedic—it's a comedy," explained Beverly in 2017. As the couple broke out in laughter, delighting in the premise of their film made fifty years ago, Ferd added, "[The characters] have to tell all their problems to a computer, and the computer talks, and [the female lead] falls in love with the computer. . . ."[220]

In the early 1970s, the Sebastians made films that fit into the genre that *Variety* called a "new rash of sex education marriage manual documentaries." Their 1970 release, *Marital Fulfillment*, was one such cinematic "how-to-do manual." Distributed by All-Film Enterprises, a company that specialized in sexploitation films, the picture was shot on 16mm and then blown up to a 35mm theatrical release print for a budget of $15,000.[221] At the time of its release, *Marital Fulfillment*'s box office returns, based on similar films distributed by All-Film Enterprises, were projected to be more than $1 million.[222] In its review, *Variety* noticed how the movie purposefully toed the line between soft-core pornography and an educational film in an effort to appeal to a broader audience and attract reviews from critics who might otherwise write it off as a "sex house" picture. Instead, *Marital Fulfillment* was "a technically adroit cinema handbook which manages to be both instructional and arousing—graphic indeed without showing the two remaining screen no-nos (penetration and erection) but still enough to elicit gasps from maiden aunts everywhere."[223] Noting that while this genre was sure to be short-lived for its inherent lack of depth and repetitiveness, this particular picture stood out for Ferd's high-quality camera work that helped the film avoid "the dirty-motel-room look of some other sex pix."[224]

Continuing to work in the genre of nonfiction "sexpics," in 1971, the Sebastians made the documentary *Red, White, & Blue!* about the pornography industry and the debate about obscenity taking place at that time

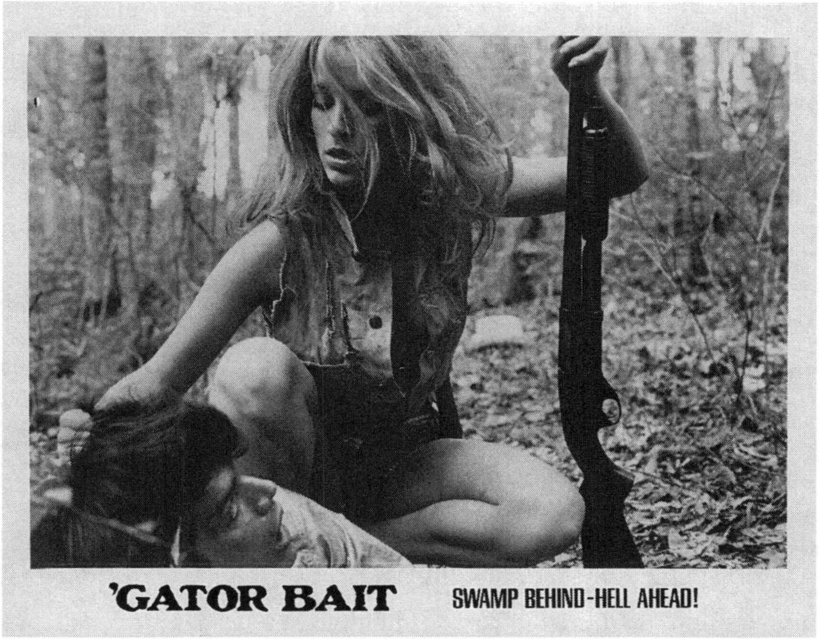


Fig. 10. Claudia Jennings in *'Gator Bait* (Margaret Herrick Library, Academy of Motion Picture Arts and Sciences)

within the Supreme Court. Again, reviewers were quick to point out the way in which the filmmakers showed explicit material under the rubric of a "pseudo-journalistic format," which allowed access to a range of ticket buyers and venues. *Variety* picked up on how the movie featured clips from upcoming films made by the documentary's own distributor Entertainment Ventures, Inc. "'Red, White & Blue' is touted as 'an in-depth study of censorship and obscenity in America.' What it really is is a 90-minute trailer for the distrib [*sic*] Entertainment Ventures Inc. feature nudie 'Trader Hornee.'"[225] Although the film was unenthusiastically received, the filmmakers, credited as both Ferd and Beverly, were again commended for "work that is straight forward, ungimmicky and professional."[226]

In 1972 the couple moved out of the "educational" format and into nonpornographic exploitation films where they continued to employ sexually themed narratives. Tapping into cultural trends, *The Hitchhikers*, produced by their production company, Sebastian Films, Ltd., and distributed by Entertainment Ventures, is about a coed group of hippies—reminiscent of the Manson family but without the brutal violence—who pose as hitchhikers to rob unsuspecting male motorists.[227] Their next film, *Bloody Friday* (1973, also known as *Single Girls*), capitalized on the era's singles culture and the popularity of the slasher genre, with a storyline about an island retreat called "Liberated Living" whose sexual encounter group is threatened by a serial killer. The film was produced by the Sebastians and distributed by Dimension Pictures.

Beverly and Ferd excelled in movies that hinged on elaborate action sequences, particularly those with chase scenes, explosions, shootouts, and female sexuality and nudity, the defining characteristics of 1970s B-films. In *'Gator Bait* (1974), a fierce, scantily clad Cajun woman (Claudia Jennings), must defend herself and her family in the swamplands, a feat that often requires her to flee lecherous men in her speedboat. *Flash and the Firecat* (1975) reprises a Bonnie and Clyde narrative in a contemporary setting that has the outlaws (Roger Davis and Tricia Sembera) racing the law in dune buggies. Their 1977 release, *Delta Fox*, follows a hit man (Richard Lynch) who finds himself a target and must track his enemies using fast automobiles and gunplay. The film's opening sequence is an expertly executed car chase worthy of a big-budget Hollywood picture.

Absent in the Sebastians' work were the overt progressive cultural attitudes seen in Rothman's and Barbara Peeters's films (to be discussed in the following section).[228] This was not unusual for the exploitation films made in the 1970s, but highlights that low-budget independent film communities were diverse in their subject matter and approach.

The couple credited much of their success to knowing who their target viewers were. Of *Flash and the Firecat*, made for $300,000 and produced and distributed by Sebastian Films, Ferd admitted, "We [make] the picture with the 14-year-olds in mind because they like vehicles. . . . You've gotta remember there's L.A. and the movies that do well in L.A. and then there's the rest of the world."[229] The Sebastians were frequently painted in the press as down-home, "folksy" Southerners, unpretentious and unlikely to put on Hollywood airs. However, Beverly was worried that, as wealthy filmmakers living in Los Angeles, they would lose touch with "common-folk." As the primary screenwriter for the majority of their films, she described her technique as "listening to people talk. I put it down on paper just the way they say it."[230] Added Ferd, "We make our movies for the Sears-Roebuck audiences. Our audience is a blue-collar audience from 12 to 50 years old."[231]

The Sebastians did not achieve success through the apprenticeship model of Roger Corman and his young filmmakers. Instead they gained entrée to the film industry by becoming independent producers and distributors of films in the marginalized sexploitation genre—ones that were more sexually explicit than the majority of exploitation films but were not pornographic. Early in their career, they did produce films for smaller independent companies; for example, *Marital Fulfillment* (All-Film Enterprises), *The Hitchhikers* (Entertainment Ventures, Inc.), and *Bloody Friday* (Dimension Pictures). By the mid-1970s, however, all their films were self-distributed through Sebastian Films Ltd. And Sebastian International Pictures Distribution Co. (SIP). Filmmaking was a family business: their two sons, Ben and Tracy, appeared in several of their parents' films and were listed as contacts for SIP. The way in which the couple's positions were listed within the distribution arm of their company suggests their sharing of responsibility and the fluidity between job descriptions. For example, an advertisement in *Variety* for SIP titles lists Ferd as the "Production" representative and Beverly and son Ben as "World Sales" representatives.[232] In contrast, *Boxoffice*'s list of theatrical feature film distributors names Beverly as president of SIP and Ferd as vice president.[233] The low-cost, self-sufficient, do-it-yourself approach to filmmaking, in combination with self-distribution, was a lucrative business model for the Sebastians. For example, *'Gator Bait*'s script was written in a weekend, preproduction took no more than four weeks, and the film was shot in ten days. The Sebastians, in addition to producing, directing, and writing, also handled the film's sound, lighting, camera, wardrobe, and makeup.[234] According to calculations made in 1975, the film, which cost $90,000 to make, grossed $4 million, with $1 million net profits for the filmmakers.[235]

Unlike other wife-director and husband-producer couples that worked together, but in clearly demarcated roles always reflected in the film's credits, the Sebastians collaborated so closely they sometimes shared job titles. "We learned a long time ago to keep peace in our family," explained Beverly. "We've been married fifty-eight years, you learn little tricks along the way—we share a mutual credit—produced, directed, and written by

Beverly and Ferd Sebastian—on everything we do."[236] (Though the two shared the main creative credits for their work, Ferd always took a sole credit for cinematographer.) Reviews of their work acknowledged both Beverly and Ferd as they were listed in their film credits. Kevin Thomas in his review for the *Los Angeles Times* of *The Hitchhikers* praised the pair: "Producers-writers-directors Ferd and Beverly Sebastian are able, imaginative (and even graceful) film-makers who may have what it takes to go on to bigger things."[237] "The team of Ferd and Beverly Sebastian has the ingenuity to make much out of little," wrote Marjorie Bilbow, for *Screen International*, describing the couple's work on *Flash and the Firecat*. "They have taken the No. 1 basic plot of countless exploitation B-movies—a crime followed by a chase—and made a highspirited [*sic*] lark with splendidly exciting stunts but no real violence."[238] Reviews of the Sebastians' films paid no attention to the unusual fact that a husband and wife were codirecting. Again, this was unusual not only because there were so few women directors during that time but also because codirecting, in general, was equally rare. As independent filmmakers who successfully self-distributed their films, the couple not only controlled their work but also used their autonomy to create a production community of their own design—with codirectors, producers, and writers.

Fulfilling Kevin Thomas's prediction that the Sebastians "have what it takes to go on to bigger things," the couple signed a three-picture home video distribution deal in the late 1980s with Paramount Pictures: *Gatorbait II: Cajun Justice* (1988), a sequel to *'Gator Bait*; *American Angels: Baptism of Blood* (1989), an action film about female wrestlers; and *Running Cool* (1993), a story set in the South about a biker community featuring real bikers fighting for land rights. As with the "sex education" films they made in the early 1970s, which crossed over between soft porn, sexploitation, and mainstream audiences, the couple continued to maintain their connection both to the dominant motion picture industry and low-budget, independent filmmaking.

During the mid- to late 1990s the Sebastians retired from making movies and began their next career in religious-based charity work. In 1993, while shooting *Running Cool*, Ferd was diagnosed with a heart condition that required immediate bypass surgery. Six months after the procedure, he had a dire prognosis. "I was down for the count," he explained. "The doctors said my best chance would be if they blocked off or killed half of my heart. I would be severely restricted in my activity but that if I didn't do it I was sure to have a massive heart attack which would probably kill me."[239] Never a devout person, it was then that Ferd had what he would later describe as a religious transformation. On the way back from the doctor to the Paramount lot, he heard a voice "as clear as day as if he was sitting next to me: Jesus is the answer."[240] In 1999 Ferd was ordained as a minister in the Mt. Zion Church of Jesus Christ and established his online ministry, 2Jesus.org.[241] A few years earlier, in 1994, Beverly had established the National Greyhound Foundation, a nonprofit that rescues retired greyhound racing dogs.[242]

Using prints of their films preserved in the Paramount archives, Beverly, Ferd, and their son Ben founded Panama Films Distribution, LLC in 2012 and began to reissue several of the family's titles.[243] Ever resourceful, the couple has used the re-release of their films not only to make a profit, once again, but also as a platform to promote their charity work. Each DVD contains a variety of extra features, such as videos of Beverly discussing her charity efforts with greyhounds and working with prisoners to train these dogs as service animals; Ferd's testimony about his spiritual conversion is also included. Recognizing the incongruity between evangelical Christianity and the explicit sexuality and violence of their films, Ferd uses the films to entice—and market to—potential believers: "Maybe the audience would never come into a church, they would never see a TV evangelist, but they would look at this movie and might find out that Ferd Sebastian—he made all these movies. He did all these things and yet Jesus saved him. You can't do anything too bad that Jesus won't save you if you would just ask him."[244]

## Barbara Peeters

> The argument that women are too emotional to direct is a very bad holdout. It takes a very emotional person to direct.
>
> —Barbara Peeters[245]

Between 1970 and 1979, Barbara Peeters wrote and directed five low-budget, independent films. Like Stephanie Rothman, she made movies with explicit feminist themes, and she worked for Roger Corman, mastering her craft in the fast-paced, industrious community of exploitation

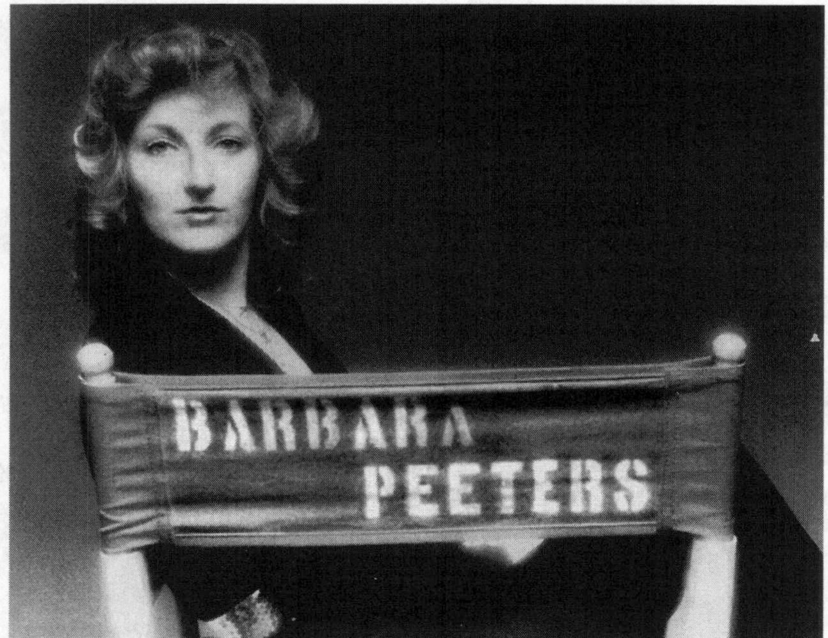


Fig. 11. Barbara Peeters (Courtesy of Barbara Peeters)

film. Also like Rothman, Peeters had aspirations to direct mainstream films, but encountered sexist obstacles that prevented her from doing so. As with Beverly and Ferd Sebastian, Peeters's first foray into filmmaking was through marginal sexploitation films, as an actress and writer. Peeters, however, differed, from both of her contemporaries in two important ways. First, she did not make films with a life partner, but instead directed (and frequently wrote) on her own, often working with different producers and production companies. Second, during the 1980s she made the transition from low-budget filmmaking to a prolific career as a television director of network one-hour dramas.

Barbara Peeters was born in 1943 in Davenport, Iowa. When she was nine years old, her family moved to a farm in Tipton, also in Iowa. As a child she always wanted to "make movies," without knowing what that meant or could mean. Each week, she would go to the local movie theater—the Heartgrove in Tipton—and watch films. The owner, an old man who was going blind and changed the reels without seeing them, would let her come back and watch for free in the projection booth. Later, when she was working at Paramount and driving through the studio gates, and the guard gave her a pass and said, "Hello Miss Peeters," she was amazed that she had arrived at such a level of success. "I grew up on a farm in Iowa," she remembered some thirty years later with great enthusiasm and joy. "I was a girl!"[246]

Peeters attended the State University of Iowa in Iowa City, where she majored in theater arts. At twenty years old, she was young, ambitious, and road hungry. Working for a summer in Cripple Creek, Colorado, she earned $12,000 in cash playing poker and panning for gold. Describing her choice to go to California, Peeters framed the decision as a classic fork-in-the-road, life-changing moment: "I was down at the train station and I flipped a quarter. Heads would have been New York City, tails, California."[247] Landing on tails, she traveled west. With a recommendation from one of her professors, Peeters attended a training program at the Pasadena Playhouse, which she graduated from in 1964.

Peeters soon moved from theater into independent filmmaking, working on a variety of low-budget sexploitation and exploitation genre films. She was a costume designer on Walnut International's *The Fabulous Bastard from Chicago* (1969), a period piece about a 1920s bootlegger-gangster that was "aimed strictly at the skin trade . . . [playing] up frank Lesbian (sic) scenes as well as sadism, fisticuffs and murders."[248] The following year was significant for Peeters. Richard (Dick) Compton, the screenwriter for *The Fabulous Bastard from Chicago*, hired her as a script supervisor on his biker revenge film *Angels Die Hard* (1970), which he wrote and directed. Less sexually explicit than *The Fabulous Bastard*, the movie was distributed by Roger Corman's New World Pictures. Also in 1970, she wrote and costarred in the sexploitation women-in-prison film *Caged Desires*, directed by Donald A. Davis and made for Hollywood Cinema Associates, a distributor of sexploitation films. As if this were not enough work, that year she also wrote and directed her first feature film, *Dark Side of Tomorrow* (also released as *Just the Two of Us*), the story of two Los Angeles housewives who have an affair with each other. The producer of the film David Novik had wanted Dick Compton to direct the picture, but Compton was busy on another project. In his place, the director recommended Peeters for the job. "Dick calls me and says, 'Ok, you want to direct, here it is. This guy's got $5,000 for a director. Tell him you want $10,000 for the script and when he says he can't afford it, tell him you'll direct it for the same price,'" remembered Peeters of her crash course in deal negotiations. "I said, 'OK!'"[249] Novik agreed to hire Peeters for both script and director duties at a rate far less than the originally sought $10,000. Hesitant about hiring a woman director, Novik teamed his cinematographer, Jaque Beerson, with Peeters as codirectors (they share a credit).

Revived today as a lesbian cult classic, at the time of its release *The Dark Side of Tomorrow* (1970) received poor reviews. It seemed critics were less forgiving than usual of low-budget filmmaking's limitations. The *Hollywood Reporter* bemoaned "the tendency among exploitationers to take a first draft and say, in effect, 'This is good enough for the money we have. Next time it'll be better.'"[250] *Variety* was more generous in its assessment of the film's aspirations, describing the film as a "low-budget indie melodrama about loneliness and lesbianism, in that order . . . that tries hard to be sensitive and in good taste, not successfully enough to make it commercially as art but just enough to take it out of the sexploitation class."[251] As was the norm—exploitation films' success was not dependent on reviews—Peeters was undeterred by the poor critical response and immediately started work on her next project, writing and directing *Bury Me an Angel.*

*Bury Me an Angel*, a revenge biker film about a sister who takes to the road to find her brother's killer, stars not an actor but a six-foot-tall biker, Dixie Peabody, who is French and Native American. Peeters and Peabody had become good friends on *Angels Die Hard*, for which Peabody and several other nonactor/real bikers were hired as extras. Peeters got the idea for *Bury Me an Angel* one night on location for *Angels Die Hard* while hanging out in a bar with the cast and crew. Rita Murray, who had a role in the film, was interested in financing a motorcycle movie about women riders. Peeters, already primed for the independent filmmaker hustle, jumped at the chance and pitched Murray an idea right on the spot. "I have one!" she told her. "You do? What's it about?" asked Murray. Peeters looked over and saw Peabody shooting pool with some of the other bikers and launched into a tale she made up on the spot "about a six-foot-tall woman." She then hurried back to her hotel room and quickly wrote the treatment, giving it to Murray the next day, whose response was enthusiastic.[252] Rita Murray and her father John Meier were inexperienced producers eager to get into the film business: they financed the picture, which Peeters eventually wrote the screenplay for, and each received an executive producer credit. New World Pictures distributed the movie, marking Peeters's and Corman's first project together.

*Bury Me an Angel* stands out in the biker genre—which had by 1971 become clichéd and formulaic—because of its female protagonist, Dag. Peabody convincingly portrays this loner, using her inexperience as an actor to create a naturalistic portrait of an aloof individual hell-bent on the mission to avenge her brother's murder.[253] The performer, so comfortable on her motorcycle, offers a new take on the traditional biker style of leather jacket and heavy boots: Peabody sports a two-toned 1960s hairstyle, leather riding pants with slits on the side, and soft-shoed moccasins; her character often rides with her feet on the handlebars. What makes this film distinct from other exploitation films is the way in which Peeters refrains from excessively sexualizing Peabody on screen and is conscientious in making sure that the character of Dag is never brutalized as part of the narrative. This was a unique detail during a time in film—and in exploitation biker films in particular—when sexual violence against women characters was a common and casual occurrence.

Representing the community effort inherent in independent filmmaking, the filmmaker enlisted her friends to work on the picture, some of which was filmed in her home in the San Fernando Valley. Peeters later described her work experience during these years as collaborative and fun: "It was very communal. It wasn't so much competitive as it is now. In the independents it was like do wardrobe for me and I'll do masks for you. Do my lighting and I'll do your gripping. We all just liked working together. So we took whatever job was needed."[254] *Bury Me an Angel* was her favorite film. "I do like sagas," she explained. "I do like people going on adventures and discovering themselves on the road. In my most naïve state I did everything in *Bury Me an Angel* that I wanted to do. Since I had no restrictions. We were on the road," she said through a big smile.[255]

Following *Bury Me an Angel*, Peeters began steady work for Corman's New World Pictures. In this environment, where so many films were being made and so quickly, everyone had the opportunity to learn all aspects of production. Peeters was a working writer-director, but she was also the production manager on *Night Call Nurses* (1972), the second-unit director on *Student Teachers* (1973), the art director on *Young Nurses* (1973), and the location manager on *I Never Promised You a Rose Garden*

(1977)—just to name a few credits. Her proficiency in overseeing the action sequences as a second-unit director on several New World films garnered her glowing reviews in the trade papers. For her work on *Eat My Dust* (1976), *Variety* credited her directorial skills: "On the lowest-common-denominator level of cheap thrills, the film is very effective, with lots of wrecks and stunts well coordinated by Ronald Clark Ross, and slapdash but gaudy action direction by [director Charles B.] Griffith and second-unit director Barbara Peeters."[256] In a review of *Moving Violation* (1976), directed by Charles S. Dubin, she was praised for having a familiarity that not only made her seem like a household name but also elevated the below-the-line position of second-unit director: "Demolition derby . . . [where] the filmmakers are occupied with engineering virtually non-stop auto wreckage . . . Barbara Peeters did her typically good job of second unit direction."[257]

In 1975, Peeters wrote and directed *Summer School Teachers*, another installment in New World's trio of female teachers and nurses franchise. Roger Corman's approach to these films was a "three girls in a dilemma formula," as described by Peeters, "[w]hich broke down [the ninety-minute narrative] into about thirty minutes per woman." Echoing Stephanie Rothman's experience making *The Student Nurses*, Peeters explained that "every fifteen minutes there had to be tits and ass, an action sequence, or a car chase. [Roger] didn't care what you did as long as you got those basic elements that he felt sold these B-movies. The rest of it, great, as long as it moved *quickly*."[258]

The story of three Midwestern young women who travel to Los Angeles for summer teaching jobs, *Summer School Teachers* is a comedic romp that includes the requisite female nudity and action scenes while also introducing a feminist storyline: one of the teachers (Candice Rialson) takes on the sexist school administration and starts an all-woman football team that demands equal rights. *Boxoffice* applauded the film's representation of women, declaring, "It is refreshing to see women portray strong, aggressive and believable characters in this picture, instead of the passive, part-of-the furniture type roles now generally available to women."[259] In her review, *Los Angeles Times* reporter Linda Gross, accepting the constraints of the genre, found room to appreciate the film: "Despite the obvious limitations of parlaying sex, football and the Equal Rights Amendment, 'Summer School Teachers' is an entertaining and

Fig. 12. Barbara Peeters on the set of *Starhops* (Courtesy of Barbara Peeters)

breezy exploitation film."[260] Gross acknowledged Peeters's skill in a film limited to the "three girls in a dilemma formula": "Even though she operates on a very superficial level, screenwriter Peeters deals with real issues like the danger of labeling people or the trauma of a teacher-student romance. As a director, Peeters excels in zany slapstick."[261]

Peeters's next directorial effort was *Starhops* (1978) released by First American Films.[262] Although this movie was not made with Corman and New World Pictures, it follows the "three girl formula." The story of three women who take over a burger stand, the actresses spend the majority of the film on roller skates wearing red, white, and blue string bikinis. But the film's pro-small business, anticorporation theme cuts through the portrayal of the female characters as being just "burger bunnies." The women use their feminine wiles to flirt their way into obtaining a bank loan and growing their business while fighting an oil tycoon who is trying to take over their property. Like most of the "three girl" films this is a working-girl movie. Again, Linda Gross admired Peeters's work: "Director Barbara Peeters makes you care about these no-nonsense working women.

Peeter's [*sic*] direction exudes energy and displays style and skill in the handling of actors and action."[263] Contemplating the feminist themes in these two films more than thirty years later, Peeters considered how the political rhetoric embedded in the pictures was a reflection of "the way we lived our lives." Likening her good friends and frequent collaborators during the 1970s—Terri Swartz, a coproducer on *Starhops*, and Josh ZanZera Willow—to the women in the film, she said, "[*Starhops*] is camp. Just these girls running amok. It was stuff we would have done, just crazy kind of stuff."[264] *Variety* complimented the "girls running amok," attributing the success of the movie, with an otherwise "threadbare plot," to how it was "directed in [an] upbeat fashion by Peeters, who employs rapid cutting and lotsa [*sic*] visual humor to keep the mixture bubbling away."[265]

Although Peeters found making movies in the 1970s enjoyable, *Starhops* marked an extremely difficult time for the filmmaker in her personal life. Peeters had been diagnosed with end-stage melanoma. During the film's production she was undergoing experimental treatment at UCLA. "We'd call wrap for lunch and I'd get into the car and go over to UCLA," remembered Peeters. "I'd be back and in about ten to fifteen minutes I'd start throwing up and sweating."[266] Trained in the efficiency of low-budget filmmaking, Peeters storyboarded every shot of her film the night before, so the next day on set, there were no surprises or moments of indecision. "The faster you have to go and the less money you have to deal with the more you have to prep."[267] Lying on the floor of the women's bathroom after returning to the set from the hospital, Peeters would hand her shot list to producer Swartz, who would go out to the crew and relay the director's instructions until she was well enough to return to work.

One day the key gaffer innocently approached the director (who had concealed her cancer diagnosis from the crew). He told Peeters that he had sent some of the guys off to buy watermelon, because when his wife was pregnant and had morning sickness that was the only thing she could keep down. "I looked at him and thought, 'He thinks I'm pregnant,'" she remembered incredulously. "I thought that was really cute because he was so concerned and thought it was too hot for the pregnant woman to be out here." Laughed Peeters, "'Well, if you think that's bad, I have cancer and really shouldn't be out here!'"[268] Despite her ill health, Peeters finished *Starhops* on time and on budget. She credited the familiarity generated among crew members in low-budget filmmaking where people worked together repeatedly with limited resources and became so practiced in the art of making a deadline "so the director should be able to fall over the cliff and the crew continues on."[269]

After finishing the film, Peeters was worried about getting work while rebuilding her health. So she accepted Corman's offer of a directing job on what would become *Humanoids from the Deep* (1980), a science fiction film set in the present day about genetically altered sea monsters that wreak havoc on the mainland, especially on young attractive women. She took on the job even though it was a non-union production, as was typical of a Corman film, and she had been a member of the Directors Guild since 1978.[270] Although it was not necessary for her to be a member while working on non-union independent films, Peeters saw joining the Guild as part of a larger strategy to reach her goal of directing studio films. In accordance with the DGA Basic Agreement, Guild members can only work for companies that were signatories of the union, and New World Pictures and *Humanoids from the Deep* were not. Peeters was sure it was her assistant director, who was after her job, who turned her in to the DGA. She was fined $15,000, more than what she was getting paid for the job. Corman promised to pay the fine, but in the end did not. Making the situation worse, after completing principal photography, Peeters was told by the film's producer, Martin Cohen, that some additional scenes would be shot. According to Peeters and one of the movie's lead actors Ann Turkel, what was added to the final film was footage of gratuitous female nudity (even for a low-budget film) and rape scenes that added no value to the narrative. "It was a good quality film and the footage was beautiful," said Turkel at the time of the film's release. "The [added] stuff is like out of a bad porn movie."[271]

With this altered final cut, Peeters experienced something similar to what Karen Arthur went through on *Lady Beware*, and like her colleague, she took to the press and made public her anger about what happened to *Humanoids*. In an article on the film's conflict in the *Los Angeles Times* she is quoted as saying, "I may sound lame standing around with my hands in my pockets saying, 'I didn't shoot it.' And it may sound like sour grapes now, but I'm really goddamned mad. . . . I'm worried that feminists will see this movie and say 'How can she do this? How can she justify it?'"[272] *Variety*'s review of the film was aware of the troubled production, stating, "Given . . . the fact that considerable footage was added to director

Barbara Peeters' original footage, editor Mark Goldblatt did a good job in making disparate elements at least hang together."[273] Even though the reviewer acknowledged the power grab that took place, the critic zeroed in on the fact that Peeters as a woman director would be seen as responsible for the added footage: "Irony of the entire production, which will confound feminist-minded critics, is that a female helmer was behind one of the more woman-degrading pix to come down the pike in some seasons."[274] This infuriated Peeters, who in the *Los Angeles Times* article called out an industry double standard. "It seems to be built into the business," said Peeters, "that a woman director is reviewed, criticized and looked at as a *woman* director. I don't remember seeing anywhere where a man is criticized for putting male sexuality back 50 years."[275]

In a letter to the editor of the *Los Angeles Times*, Corman refuted the accusations his former employee made in the press that he was antifeminist by stressing, "As for my being a male chauvinist, I can only point to my record of employing more qualified women in responsible positions than any other producer in Hollywood. Barbara Boyle [executive vice president of New World Pictures] is a past president of Women in Film and an Honored Worker for the feminist movement, both in films and in the community."[276] Would not a person with such an esteemed feminist track record make different choices about adding salacious footage and handling conflict with one of his longtime employees? Yet, Corman had always prioritized financial profits over relationships with any of his employees, female or male, and over his political positions. By the time the *Humanoid*'s debacle occurred, Peeters and Corman had been working together for eight years. In 2010, considering why Corman behaved the way he did in 1980, Peeters, through laughter, was frank: "Because the dollar in fine art means a lot to Roger, [and] the future of his children, and the size of his house, and the quality of his furniture means more than his word."[277] Her comment was borne out by Stephanie Rothman's experience as well: although Rothman has made clear that she did not end her working relationship with Corman on bad terms, she and her husband's decision to leave New World Pictures was predicated on the famed producer's unwillingness to share profits with his filmmakers.

The irony was not that a woman made what the *Variety* reviewer predicted to be one of the most anti-woman films of the season, but that

Peeters's public outrage got her a job in television. Agents Richard Lewis and Ronny Leaf approached Peeters after reading the *Los Angeles Times* article and the filmmaker signed with their agency. They liked her "spunk" and felt that her experience in directing cheap, quickly made feature films would translate perfectly to the equally fast-paced schedule of one-hour episodic television. There was also a nervous buzz circulating within the industry that the government might start enforcing affirmative action policies (see chapter 4). As a result, television networks were hiring a very few "token" women to present an antidiscrimination face. Peeters remembered, "They were using Karen Arthur and myself—'Oh, affirmative action, we've got a girl on ours. We hired a woman director.' But it was the same two women directors on everything. And then Gabrielle Beaumont started directing. . . . So [the three of us] were basically being used. They wanted a couple of women who could cut the mustard and use them on everybody's set."[278]

Before beginning to work in television Peeters had never had an agent: having one was not necessary for those working in the exploitation community with its tight-knit network of employees. Furthermore, because in exploitation both above- and below-the-line labor was cheap, and writers and directors typically made no profits from the box office earnings of a film, there were no hefty deals for agents to negotiate or to earn a percentage of. Leaf and Lewis were correct in their prediction that Peeters would excel in network television and make herself and her agents a lot of money. She was hired regularly to direct one-hour dramatic episodes on series such as *Falcon Crest*, *Matt Houston*, *Cagney and Lacey*, and *Remington Steel.* In her first year, Peeters directed seven episodes, a number that was considered typical for a veteran director. Soon she was preparing one program while completing postproduction on another; in another production season, she directed eleven shows. Working at such breakneck speed, Peeters began to burn out by the end of the decade. She also found that a television director had little creative control. Drained by the lack of autonomy and the relentless schedule, she moved to Oregon in the early years of the twenty-first century, where she began producing commercials for local businesses and making documentaries. When interviewed in 2010 Peeters reflected on the intricate career plan that she had devised for herself "when I was young and foolish," she said, with a smile:

> I was going to go from independents into television and get some movies of the week and then I was going to move up to features—*DGA features*. There were *no* women getting to move up. I was told: "Are you kidding? You're lucky to be working. Don't even think about a feature." On my days off I would be looking in *Variety* at the production pages calling my agent saying, "Hey so and so is doing a teen movie over at Paramount. Get me up for it." He'd say, "Are you kidding? They won't consider you." "Well, why not? I've done teen movies. I've done B-movies. I'm doing television. I can work a short schedule." And he goes, "Honey, John Hughes is going to direct that."

Laughing she said, "It was always the boys."[279]

# 3

# New Women

## *Women Directors and the 1970s New Woman Film*

In the heady climate of American cinema at the intersection of the cultural upheavals taking place in the late 1960s and 1970s, not all women directors were outspoken feminists: some did not identify themselves as such, while others talked openly about their political affiliations and discussed the feminist themes in their work. What *was* true for all women directors during the 1970s was that their lives were a feminist experience whether they aligned themselves with the movement or not, whether they were aware of its influence on them, professionally and creatively, or not. Stephanie Rothman was comfortable being identified in the press as a "dedicated feminist" as early as 1970, whereas Karen Arthur claimed that at the time, "I wouldn't have known a feminist if I fell over on one"—yet Arthur's early work put on screen a never before seen female protagonist who challenged cinematic expectations of women. For these women the increase in the number of opportunities, as limited and challenging as they may have been, was part of the ripple effect created by the larger sociopolitical movement that was very much intertwined with popular culture. By the end of the decade, the women's movement had begun to make an impression on Hollywood: industry leaders came to see how feminism could turn a profit.

During 1977 and 1978 the film industry added more women directors than ever before (six) to its payroll, and the studios seemed to embrace representations of women on screen. In her *New York Times* article, "Hollywood Flirts with the New Woman," Jane Wilson took note of these changes: "Credible female life has hardly been a noticeable feature of American movies in recent years, nor have human relationships been a dominate theme, but now, all of a sudden, there is a rush of movies in varying stages of preparation in which women are presented as real people involved in a gamut of relationships."[1] A slew of studio releases centered on female protagonists had recently earned box office and critical acclaim; they included *Annie Hall* and *Looking for Mr. Goodbar* (Diane Keaton, 1977), *The Goodbye Girl* (Marsha Mason, 1977), *Julia* (Jane Fonda and Vanessa Redgrave, 1977), *The Turning Point* (Shirley MacLaine and Anne Bancroft, 1977), and *An Unmarried Woman* (Jill Clayburgh, 1978). Richard Brooks, director of *Looking for Mr. Goodbar*, credited the feminist movement with Hollywood's sudden interest in female-driven narratives: "It was women's organizations and the general outcry for realistic women figures on the screen that resulted in these new films."[2]

Some studios began publicly admitting what the feminist movement had spent years campaigning for: women warranted screen representation as complex, multifaceted characters who would appeal to a complex, multifaceted, ticket-buying female demographic. Gareth Wiggan, 20th Century-Fox's vice president of production, acknowledged, "It has emerged in a general way, that there is now a marked preference for movies about relationships between people. And if you want to do movies about relationships between people, you can't just have men. Women are people too."[3] While coming to this realization considerably late, at the very least some Hollywood executives were catching up to the fact that women could influence the box office.

Throughout the 1970s, feminist film critics had criticized the way in which Hollywood maligned women's roles and actresses' careers. In her 1973 iconic book, *From Reverence to Rape*, Molly Haskell expressed strong disgust with Hollywood's treatment of women: "From a woman's point of view, the ten years from, say, 1962 or 1963 to 1973 have been the most disheartening in screen history. In the roles and prominence accorded women, the decade began unpromisingly, grew steadily worse, and at present shows no signs of improving." Citing the explicit and commonplace sexual violence against women in movies like *Clockwork Orange* (1971) and *Straw Dogs* (1971), Haskell echoed the view held by many women in Hollywood: the industry had responded to the feminist movement by becoming even more misogynistic. The film critic keenly observed that the popularity of "Godfather-like machismo" and the "escape into the all-male world of the buddy films from *Easy Rider* to *Scarecrow*" were symptoms of Hollywood's backlash against "the growing strength and demands of women in real life, spearheaded by women's liberation."[4] In her book *Women and Their Sexuality in the New Film*, Joan Mellen expressed similar disappointment in studio films that had female leads and costars, such as *Diary of a Mad Housewife* (1970), *Carnal Knowledge* (1971), and *Klute* (1971), for what she felt were degrading characterizations of women: "Despite the vociferousness of the Women's Liberation Movement and its campaign to awaken in the media, particularly in advertising and television, a sense of the sexual identity and dignity of the independent woman, the contemporary cinema persists in spitefully portraying the sexuality of its women as infantile and dependent."[5] For these critics, who were bearing witness to both revolutions—1970s Hollywood and 1970s feminism—the film industry had co-opted women's liberation at the expense of actresses, female characters, and the movement's objectives, for the sake of the bottom line.

This critique of Hollywood, in the face of the tremendous feminist-inspired changes taking place in the United States, appeared regularly in the press. Writing for *Daily Variety*, in 1974, Jane Ross reported on a survey of female characters in the major studio films of that year. Of a total of 127 films and 2,437 roles, 1,757 roles, or 72.10 percent, went to men versus 680, or 27.90 percent, to women.[6] In 1975, successful screenwriter and vocal feminist Eleanor Perry wrote an article for *Variety* titled "If You Wanna Make a Film about Women, Better Forget It." Perry detailed the sexist obstacles she faced in attempting to sell her screenplay adaptation of the acclaimed feminist novel, *Memoirs of an Ex Prom Queen*, by Alix Kates Shulman. "The word was that 1975 was going to be a terrific year for women on the screen," wrote Perry, ironically. "The word was that there was a desperate need for scripts with strong roles for women." However, the response she received while shopping her script around was less than enthusiastic: "Not right for Streisand or Minnelli so there's no bankable star to play the girl. Too risky to go with an unknown. You can't make a picture without a male star. I'd be interested if you'd make the sex explicit—don't cut away from all those scenes in bed. I could sell it as an erotic picture."[7] Hollywood was in the business of exploiting the entertainment value of topical issues, such as women's liberation, if it could turn a dime. However, studio executives were careful to control who had access to creative and economic power. "Men write for men, not women," asserted Robert Evans. The Paramount executive defended the industry's abhorrent track record in producing substantial roles for actresses by noting that the majority of working writers were men, who were not concerned with women characters or audiences. Interviewed in 1973, Evans appeared to fit the profile of the resistant producer in Perry's experience when he proclaimed, "There are no female stars except Barbra Streisand who could hold up a film."[8]

Those actresses, in addition to Streisand and Minnelli, who were fortunate enough to get past the industry gatekeepers and star in a female-centric film were suspicious of whether the industry had undergone a genuine shift in consciousness or was only motivated, in the short term, by profit. Shirley MacLaine—whose role in *The Turning Point* opposite Anne Bancroft garnered the seasoned actresses many feminist accolades, as well as box office revenue—was not impressed by Hollywood's new approach to female-driven films. In 1978 she told Janet Maslin of the *New York Times*, "They're starring the women together now, just like they starred the men together for five years but they still can't figure out what to do with adult men and adult women on the screen. And starting a serious discussion about feminism in Hollywood is still the quickest way to empty a room out there."[9] Paul Mazursky, the writer-director of *An Unmarried Woman*, a film that became one of Hollywood's most-lauded depictions of 1970s feminism, framed his movie's success in the most cynical of terms: "Only when you see many women in the Senate and Congress will the image of women in films truly change. You can't expect movies to reflect a fantasy."[10]

In a similar reaction to the increase in the number of women directors by the end of the decade, the perceptions of the few substantial roles for actresses were complicated by a sense that the industry's efforts were superficial at best. In 1979 Claudia Weill attributed the success of her independently produced, feminist-themed *Girlfriends*, which was picked up for distribution by Warner Bros., to the popularity of New Woman films. "I think I made a good film and it came at exactly the right time," said Weill. She continued,

> If *An Unmarried Woman*, *Julia* and *The Turning Point* hadn't come out before mine, no studio looking at my film would even have understood that there was a market for such material. But when I went to Hollywood a year ago, they were really looking for women. If one came along, they took her seriously. If enough of us women get our feet in the door during this period, within a year or two we'll be professionals like everybody else, not just the company freaks.[11]

Weill's optimism, in 1979, was well founded. The number of women directors was at its peak: an estimated four films produced by major studios and five features produced by independent companies, all directed by women, were either released or going into production that year. The New Woman film was experiencing a jump at the box office too. However, the majority of the best-known "women's films" were written by male screenwriters, and all but *Girlfriends* were directed by them.

Several women during this time directed films centered on female protagonists and even spoke openly about a desire to see richer, more complex representations of such characters, but it should not be assumed that the "woman's film," in its 1970s incarnation, was the preferred genre and primary narrative interest for these filmmakers. While Hollywood seemed occasionally willing to appropriate feminism to boost its revenues and reputation, its *un*willingness to hire women—both in front of and behind the camera—illustrated how the film business was determined to contain its female employees' success—and with it their power—even if doing so meant losing money that these directors and actresses could have made for the studios.

## Joan Darling

> What I think happened with me was everybody was looking
> for a woman director. I was lucky that I caught that wheel.
> Anyone who hired me got a lot of press.
> —Joan Darling[12]

Joan Darling was born Joan Kugell in 1935 in Newton, Massachusetts, and grew up in Brookline. Her father, a lawyer, died when she was eleven, and her mother, formerly a housewife, opened an antique store to support Darling, her two brothers, and sister. Since she was a child, Darling had been interested in acting. "As a very little girl, I saw my first movie and I was instantly cursed with a passion to be an actress," she told *TV Guide* in a 1973 interview. "Women's lib wasn't even a gleam in Betty Friedan's eye back then, but I knew I didn't want to be just a traditional wife and mother. Being an actress, I felt, was one of the ways a woman could control her own life."[13]

In 1956 she attended Carnegie Institute of Technology; during the summers, she studied at the Oregon Shakespeare Festival in Ashland, Oregon. In 1958 Darling moved to New York City, where she worked nights at a bank photographing checks so she could keep her days free to sit on the floor by the pay phone in her apartment building, waiting for an audition callback. In 1960 she became the only female member of Ted Flicker's successful improvisational group, the Premise. It took eleven years until she was cast in her "breakthrough" television role as Owen Marshall's secretary, Frieda Krause, on ABC's *Owen Marshall: Counselor at Law*. She played the character for three years (1971–1974), and when that gig was over, she wrote a treatment for a ninety-minute television movie on the life of Israeli prime minister Golda Meir, imagining herself in the lead role.[14]

Darling pitched the Meir idea to Norman Lear, a social acquaintance for whom she had done some writing on a film that was never produced. After hearing the pitch, Lear asked Darling, "Do you want to be a director?" She looked at him and said, "I don't know anything about directing." His response: "I think that's what you really are."[15] This story seems incredible in how easy it was for Darling, who had never directed film or television nor imagined herself in the role, to receive an unsolicited job offer from one of the most powerful producers in television. During an interview in 2012, she swore this is what happened: "It's absolutely word for word!"[16] The job Lear had in mind for Darling was to shoot the pilot for the new series, *Mary Hartman, Mary Hartman*, he was preparing. The two spent eight weeks developing the show, after which he went on vacation and left Darling to direct the pilot. Pleased with her work on the pilot, Lear hired her to direct a significant portion of *Mary Hartman*'s first season.

Before offering her the position, Lear was aware of Darling's extensive experience in acting, her work in improvisational comedy, and her reputation as a sought-after acting coach: her Hollywood acting workshop had a waitlist of 250.[17] According to Darling, at that time Lear was also making a concerted effort to hire a woman director. "The thing about Norman that is so important in this story is he was *absolutely* committed to breaking the barriers for women."[18] In 1974 and 1975, the attention being paid to gender discrimination within the film and television industries was growing so intense that a few production companies and networks were beginning to feel pressured to change their hiring practices. However, as Barbara Peeters (see chapter 2) would observe of her experience getting hired to direct television in the early 1980s, employing a few "token" women was the industry's self-serving way to make it seem to their critics as if they were committed to creating gender equality. Studio executives did not seem to take the need to diversify their workforce all that seriously. Darling recounted an exchange she had when driving off the Universal Studios lot after a day spent directing an episode of the miniseries *Rich Man, Poor Man* in 1976; she passed the studio chiefs Lew Wasserman and Sid Sheinberg, whom she knew from her years on the Universal series *Owen Marshall*. "When I got to the gate, Sid Sheinberg yelled to me, 'Hey Joan, what are you doing on the lot?' 'I'm directing *Rich Man, Poor Man*.' He said, 'Oh God, if only you were black!'"[19]

Darling's agent was also aware that the industry was looking to hire women directors. They sent her a copy of her pilot of *Mary Hartman* to Grant Tinker, producer of the *Mary Tyler Moore Show* (*MTM*). Based on her work, Tinker hired Darling to direct an entire season of *MTM*. One of her *MTM* episodes, "Chuckles Bites the Dust," was nominated for a Primetime Emmy and Directors Guild Award in 1976. That same year *Mary Hartman, Mary Hartman* became a national phenomenon; its star Louise Lasser graced the covers of *Rolling Stone*, *Newsweek*, and *TV Guide*. Darling was the first woman to direct an episode of *M*A*S*H*, "Nurses," for which she was nominated for a second Primetime Emmy in 1977. Between 1975 and 1979, Darling was one of the most prolific female television directors. In addition to directing *MTM*, *Mary Hartman, Mary Hartman*, and *M*A*S*H*, Darling directed episodes of the sitcoms *Rhoda*, *Doc*, *Fay*,

Fig. 13. Joan Darling directing *First Love* (Margaret Herrick Library, Academy of Motion Picture Arts and Sciences)

and *Phyllis*; the pilot to what would become *One Day at a Time*; and the miniseries *Rich Man, Poor Man*.

Having been kept so busy directing sitcoms, Darling had not seriously considered directing features until 1976, when Lawrence Turman, who had produced *The Graduate*, approached her with the script for *First Love*. The movie was to be made at Paramount and to star William Katt, an up-and-coming heartthrob in his first leading role, opposite Susan Dey, who at the time was best known for her role on the television show *The Partridge Family*. The young actors played coeds: Katt as Elgin who has been holding out for a romantic ideal and falls hard for Dey's Caroline, who is more experienced in love and sex. The film was meant to capture the depth of first love—its joy and pain—and the nostalgia that the experience leaves once it ends.

Darling was a good candidate for the project. She was an Emmy-nominated television director well versed in single and multiple camera setups, had extensive experience with actors, and knew how to run a set. She could get the job done, and Paramount would get the publicity for hiring a woman director. "The brass at Paramount were a very nice group of people: David Picker, Dick [Richard] Sylbert," recalled Darling. "They felt that if there was such a thing as a 'woman director' sensibility, this script would be much better in a woman's hands."[20] What Darling did not know was that Turman thought Darling, as a first-time film director, would also be easy for him to control.

Trouble with Turman started early in the production. At six in the morning on the third day of shooting, the producer called her: "Joan, I think we're making a terrible movie."[21] She was so upset that she could not even get in the van to go to the set. Turman's attempt to plant doubt in his director's mind was his way of creating a power dynamic: he as a veteran producer and she as an insecure, first-time feature director. Despite his attempts to disable her, Darling, as was her style, established a good rapport on the set, where cast, crew, and director bantered and joked with each other.[22]

After the shoot ended, Darling left the editor alone—as was customary—to assemble a rough cut of the footage. She returned to discover that Turman had interceded and edited his own version of the film. "I came back and saw two hours and thirty-five minutes of the worst movie I'd ever seen," Darling confided to an audience at the AFI in 1977 around the time of the film's release. "I remember sitting on the floor the night I saw that rough cut in my house, by myself, scared to death. I mean, I was going under the bed and never coming out."[23]

Darling called two of her more experienced friends, veteran film editor and studio executive Verna Field and director Steven Spielberg, for advice. They told her that Turman was "being a bad boy" and that she should fire the editor. She then called her friends from her improvisational comedy days, Buck Henry and Mike Nichols, who had made *The Graduate* with Turman. Both men confirmed that he had similarly interfered in that picture. In the process, she discovered that her contract had been negotiated poorly and that it lacked provisions such as the right to a preview, which Darling felt would have helped her fine-tune the film. As a first-time director, she did not know what she was entitled to or what her rights were. By the time she found this out, it was too late to override Turman or the studio's final word, or ultimately the final cut of the film.[24]

When the film came out Darling openly expressed her disappointment in it, confessing, "I will not look at that film ever again, as long as I live. That's how I feel about that film right now."[25] Twenty-five years later she still remembered the experience as a difficult one. As for the meddling of her producer and the studio executives, "I'm not going to say they butchered the movie," stated Darling, "but they pulled a lot of the subtlety out of it. They diminished it."[26]

Critical response to the film was mixed. Arthur Murphy of *Variety* felt the script was weak and that "the never-ending pall of doom that hangs over everything" weighed down the story. But he was impressed with how the film refused to exploit the topic of young love and sexuality, citing the cast's excellent performances.[27] Molly Haskell felt that there were moments when the movie was uneven. She commented that Elgin and Caroline's relationship left "too many questions unanswered, and the film seems more elliptical than it is meant to be." Perhaps intuiting Darling's disagreements with the studio over editing choices—conflicts that did not seem to have appeared in the press beforehand—Haskell noted this in parentheses: "(As a footnote, in the plot synopsis given critics at the screening there were some four scenes clarifying the relationship that do not appear in the final cut.)"[28] Writing for the *Hollywood Reporter*, Arthur Knight found that "despite its occasionally raunchy dialogue and frequent bed scenes [the film] is as sweet and touching an inquiry into the nature of youthful romance as anyone could wish for." Knight drew attention to Darling's accomplishment as a first-time director: "making an impressive screen debut . . . she manages not only the atmospherics with conviction, but has elicited sustained, complex performances from her largely youthful cast.[29] The majority of reviewers addressed the fact that a woman directed the film. Attention to this point was not unusual: as many of the examples throughout this study show, critics were aware of the small number of women directors and sometimes even advocated for them in the pages of their reviews.

Paramount certainly exploited Darling's gender in the promotional materials for the film. In an interview done by the studio's publicity department, Darling put a friendly face on feminism. She admitted to not being an ardent feminist, explaining that she'd "never been a political person in terms of my professional life."[30] She was also candid about the responsibility she felt to her female peers: "Once I began directing, I realized how unusual it was for me as a woman to be doing such a job . . . if I succeed then it will make it easier for other women to be given the responsibility by male studio executives to become directors."[31]

Fig. 14. John Heard and Joan Darling on the set of *First Love* (Margaret Herrick Library, Academy of Motion Picture Arts and Sciences)

The studio capitalized on Darling's gracious disposition and good nature: she could make feminism funny and friendly. The first press release described the director as "a small, cheerful woman, who in the midst of the total confusion known as moviemaking, never loses her cool or her sense of humor."[32] Darling is quoted as highlighting the contributions of the crew while touching on the historical significance of being a woman director: "Being a woman has been a great help . . . the entire crew has been helpful and I think part of their helpfulness has come from the fact that they realize this film stands for more than most films." A happy female director supported by a male crew demonstrated that Paramount was a progressive company. A follow-up press release gave a detailed history of Dorothy Arzner as the pioneer who made Darling's success possible.[33] As presented in the publicity materials, Paramount was not only in line with contemporary social issues (women's equality), but was also on the right side of *history* (by hiring *a woman*). The studio showcased Darling's importance in 1977 and in doing so was able to take all the credit for this historic moment.

Paramount's PR department had conducted the interview and structured the themes for the press release, but Darling was speaking genuinely about how she saw her responsibility as a woman director. In her

1977 interview at the AFI and in an interview in 2012, she reiterated that she was aware of being one of the few regularly employed women directors and that she felt a responsibility to do well so that her peers would have similar opportunities. Darling had always felt that her poor treatment on *First Love* was not due to her gender, but had more to do with her being a first-time director. Complicating the situation was that, because so few women were directing during these years, their minority status reinforced the long-standing belief—and reality—that men were entitled to exert their power over them, as Turman did with Darling. The thinking went that if women were indeed powerful, there would be more of them in positions of authority. For as "progressive" as Paramount had suggested itself to be in the film's publicity, it was still a patriarchy maintaining its status.

Between 1979 and 1980, Darling tried to make a film based on *The Boys of Summer*, a book about Jackie Robinson and the Brooklyn Dodgers, but the project met a dead end at Universal Artists during its period of transition and turmoil. While she was hired to direct one more feature in 1986, the family comedy *The Check Is in the Mail . . .* , starring Brian Dennehy and Anne Archer, by 1979, after *First Love*, Darling had returned to a busy career directing television that continued well into the 1990s. "I never paid attention to gender," said Darling in 2012. "I had two older brothers who tried to beat me up. That sends you out into the world pretty tough. . . . The job is hard enough. If you focus on the job and that's where your focus is no one can really bait you. I wasn't available for that. I also surprised myself at how tough I could be."[34]

Darling's outlook and how it informed her approach to working as a director served her well: her career has been long and successful. During the making of *First Love* she was operating under one code of conduct, while Paramount and Turman were following their own: Turman's was based on working with a director over whom he could exert power, and the studio was exploiting the cultural capital of hiring a woman. Darling was highly qualified to direct her first film. What seems suspect is why, as a consummate director—and performer—of adult-themed comedy, she was chosen to make a romantic dramedy about college students. The executives' opinion that a female director would be best suited for a sentimental love story shows their fallback on biological essentialism. Women's forced association with motherhood and assumptions of nurturing meant that Darling would be innately attuned to themes of love and tenderness. This was a flawed belief, which made possible a way to control the creative output and success of women by pigeonholing them into genres and storylines that they may not have picked if given the choice.

## Jane Wagner

> One should accept passion as short-lived, though I don't pretend to know the answer to loving. Should we go moment by moment, or should we require the long view?
>
> —Jane Wagner[35]

In 1978 Jane Wagner became the third woman to direct a movie for a major studio during the decade and Universal the third studio to hire one. In contrast to Paramount's handling of Darling, Wagner was not touted as the poster girl for women directors nor the studio as a feminist patron for the film, *Moment by Moment*, which Wagner both wrote and directed. This project had other big selling points for the publicity to exploit: it featured two top stars of 1978, Lily Tomlin and John Travolta.

Wagner was born in 1935 in Morristown, Tennessee. Her two uncles who were involved in local theater introduced her as a teenager to acting. With their encouragement she auditioned and was accepted to the Barter Theater Company in Abingdon, Virginia. At seventeen years old, Wagner left Barter with the $300 she had earned as part of the company and moved on her own to New York City. She got a room at the YWCA for $10 a week and began to pursue an acting career, but grew discouraged after so many rejections. Wagner then became an entrepreneurial artist: she played the piano, wrote music, and eventually established a career as a successful textile designer for Kimberly-Clarke, the manufacturer of Kleenex, and for Fieldcrest linens, for which she developed the Teach-Me-Read line of children's bedding.[36]

By the early 1960s, Wagner's peers were a group of successful and creative women. They included columnist Liz Smith, advertiser Jane Trahey, and author and publicist Pattie Goldstein, who had worked for CBS and NBC and introduced Wagner to Gloria Safire, who became her agent. In 1969 Wagner submitted the script *J. T.*, about an African American boy living in Harlem, to the CBS series the *Children's Hour*, which was produced by Jacqueline Babbin and Barbara Schultz. CBS accepted the work; it starred an eleven-year-old Kevin Hooks and won Wagner a Peabody Award. Lily Tomlin, who in 1969 was well known for her appearances on the television show *Laugh-In*, saw *J. T.* and contacted Wagner in hopes that the writer would help her develop an album for her precocious child character "Edith Ann." The album, which they ended up writing in one weekend, was their first creative collaboration and the start of their personal relationship.

Feminism had a difficult time in 1970s Hollywood, but there were those rare instances when ideology and industry meshed, and Lily Tomlin was one such example. Tomlin was comfortable publicly identifying as a feminist, the press celebrated her as one just as readily, and the networks that made her television specials did so knowing of her and Wagner's creative interests. Between 1973 and 1976, Tomlin and Wagner created several Emmy-nominated television specials for ABC and CBS: Wagner as writer and frequently producer, and Tomlin as the star. In 1974 and in 1976, the television specials *Lily* (CBS) and *Lily Tomlin* (ABC) won Emmys for Best Writing in which Wagner was included. In 1977 the couple collaborated on Tomlin's one-woman show, *Appearing Nightly*, which won a Tony Award. These works featured Tomlin performing a catalog of characters who used comedy as a platform to talk about social issues such as feminism, race, class, sexuality, and contemporary politics. In 1975 Tomlin appeared in her first feature film, *Nashville*, in which she received an Academy Award nomination for Best Supporting Actress.

After seeing a performance of *Appearing Nightly*, John Travolta, who admired Tomlin immensely, was determined to work with her on his next project. In 1977 Travolta was known for his character Vinnie Barbarino on the sitcom *Welcome Back, Kotter*, and he would achieve mega-stardom with his performance as Tony Manero in *Saturday Night Fever* released that same year. The actor had a three-picture contract with producer Robert Stigwood: *Saturday Night Fever* was their first film followed by *Grease* in 1978, and *Moment by Moment* would be the third project.

Stigwood was the manager of the disco-rock band the Bee Gees. He had produced both the stage and film versions of the rock musical *Jesus Christ Superstar* (1973) and The Who's rock opera film *Tommy* (1975). From the onset, the veteran producer was not convinced that a Travolta-

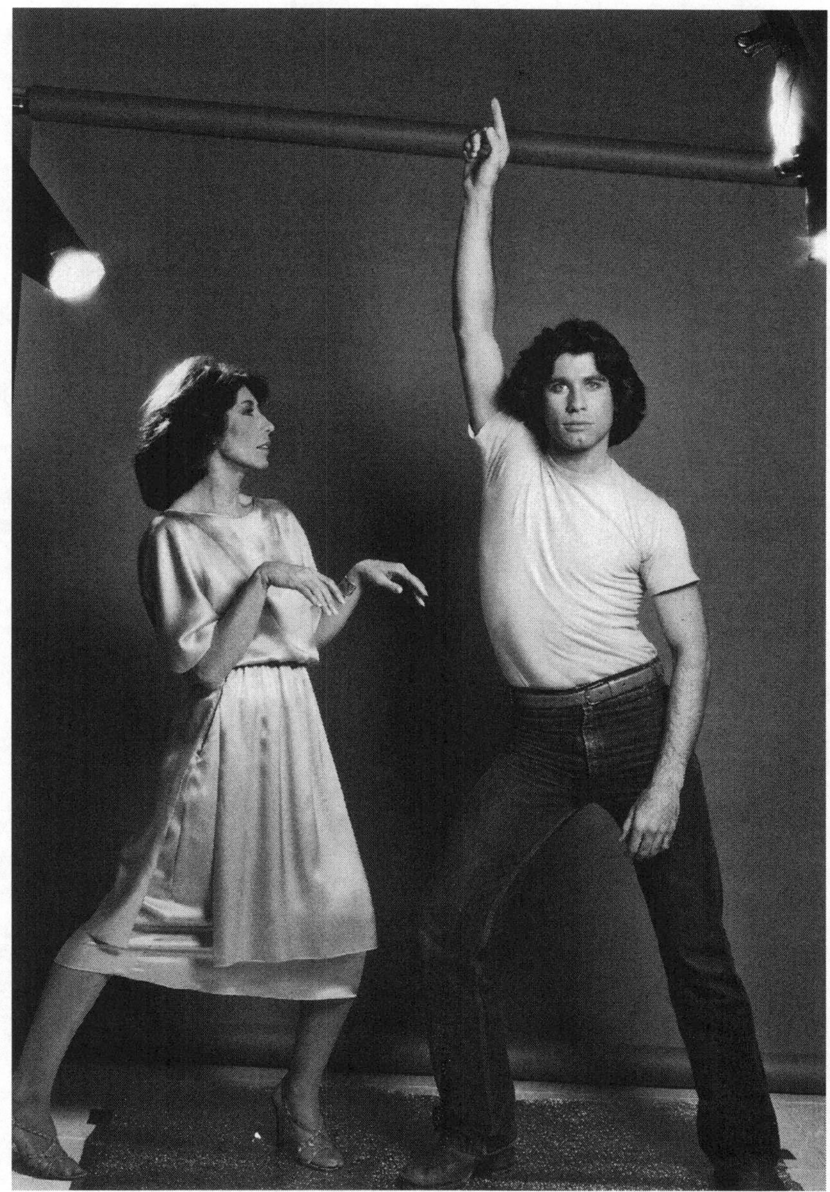

Fig. 15. Lily Tomlin and John Travolta during *Moment by Moment* (Margaret Herrick Library, Academy of Motion Picture Arts and Sciences)

Tomlin venture—a nonmusical comedy—would be the most advantageous follow-up to his first two films with the actor. However, Travolta's current level of stardom gave him leverage in choosing the third project, and after Stigwood screened some of *Saturday Night Fever*'s footage for Tomlin and Wagner, who were impressed, the deal was made. "Lily and John decided they wanted to do a drama," explained Stigwood. "Well, the whole world was bidding for this third project, all the distributors. I didn't like the story that Jane came up with, but everyone wore me down."[37] While on a press junket for *Saturday Night Fever*, Travolta gushed about how much he was looking forward to his next film: "I was so excited about it I called at 2:30 A.M. and woke Lily and Jane up to talk about it."[38] Despite Stigwood's misgivings, the producer succumbed to Travolta's enthusiasm for the project: "If John doesn't want to commit to another musical, then fuck it, let's do it."[39]

Earlier in 1977 Tomlin had signed a three-year contract with Universal to star, write, produce, and possibly even direct two films.[40] *Moment by Moment* became one of the two projects. Stigwood's company, Robert Stigwood Organization (RSO), agreed to produce the film for Universal for an estimated $7 million, and Wagner was hired to direct. Having written and produced for the stage and television, she felt that directing was the natural next step.[41] Yet, even with her extensive accomplishments as a writer-producer, the filmmaker was aware that her affiliation with megastar Tomlin helped her get the coveted job of director. As she explained in the press in 1978, "I haven't had bad experiences for being a woman but I think it's harder for women to develop a power base and experience you need. I've been very lucky. Lily has been a platform for me and we've been so offbeat that no one in the past thought to stop us."[42] Tomlin and Wagner, who were married in 2013, did not publicly define their personal relationship during the 1970s. "There never seemed to be a need," said Tomlin in a 2009 interview with *The Advocate*, a magazine focused on the LGBT community. "We never hid anything and we never denied anything, but we never said anything specific. I referred to Jane a million times as my partner, and people interpreted that as they would."[43] In 1975 *Time* magazine offered Tomlin the cover story if she would come out of the closet: the performer declined. "I never did *not* come out. I wanted to be acknowledged for my work. I didn't want to be that gay person who does comedy."[44] In 1977 the pair's creative success was indisputable, as evidenced by their long list of top industry accolades; augmenting their individual accomplishments were the power and influence of Tomlin's star status that opened the door to Wagner to obtain what otherwise would be a nearly impossible opportunity for a woman: directing and writing her first feature, and this film in particular, for a major motion picture studio.

Wagner had been thinking for a while about the storyline of *Moment by Moment*: a serious and sexy romantic drama between an older woman and younger man (at the time Tomlin was thirty-nine and Travolta twenty-four). Tricia, a rich Beverly Hills housewife, is going through a divorce when she meets Strip, a young street hustler from Hollywood. The two embark on a love affair at her Malibu beach house where they struggle over differences in age, economic class, social upbringing, and relationship expectations: Tricia, the "good wife," is looking forward to having casual sex for the first time, while Strip, who has only ever been sexually objectified, is searching for real love.

Response to the film was brutal. Critics had many reasons for disliking *Moment by Moment*: Tomlin and Travolta had similar hairstyles and therefore looked like lovers who were sister and brother; the film was a concentrated study of romance that dedicated the majority of its screen time to just the two protagonists, an unconventional portrayal for a Hollywood film; and audiences expected comedy, dancing, and music based on both actors' previous work.

Doug Edwards for *The Advocate* was vicious in his response to the movie, declaring it "a disaster of such magnitude that it virtually defies comprehension" and that "its outcome should be bypassed for theatrical release altogether and, rather, should immediately be sold to the nation's university and college film schools as the definitive text for instruction in how *not* to make a movie."[45] Frank Rich at *Time* was horrified, calling the film "downright perverse," and bemoaned the misuse of its actors: "For a couple of hours, two of the screen's best actors, John Travolta and Lily Tomlin, walk around overdecorated rooms and whisper sweet nothings to each other."[46] But Wagner took the brunt of the blame. "Not helping matters is Wagner's banal script," accused the writer for *Variety*, "which has cliché piled atop cliché, and dialog that evokes embarrassing laughter."[47] Edwards blamed Wagner for being an "inept" director with a "disregard for staging, pacing emotional rhythm, or for any of the other basics of dramatic film structure and language."[48] Kevin Thomas was one of the

Fig. 16. Left to right: John Travolta, Jane Wagner, and Lily Tomlin on *Moment by Moment* (Margaret Herrick Library, Academy of Motion Picture Arts and Sciences)

few reviewers who liked the film. In his attempt to rescue it from slaughter he mentioned how badly the movie had been brutalized. "'Moment by Moment' . . . a tender romance, has incurred some of the worst preview reactions within recent memory. It's said that at one showing, 77 walkouts were clocked."[49]

The movie, which earned $7,161,00 at the box office—essentially breaking even—was never released on home video.[50] The reasons why it was disliked had much to do with the actual film, but even more to do with the public's expectations of John Travolta in 1978. Different accounts of the production suggested pressures common to filmmaking such as creative difference, but they do not paint an overly chaotic situation that would typically result in extreme budget overages, which the film did not appear to accrue. Wagner was forced to cut a storyline that she felt might have helped develop more of Travolta's character. She had filmed a scene that focused on the context of drug dealing and street hustling surrounding Strip when he and Tricia meet, but the first cut of the film was forty-five minutes too long and Stigwood told her to trim it. In 2011, Wagner wondered whether the length of the movie was the real reason why the studio ordered her to cut the scene. "It occurs to me now," she ruminated, "that maybe that whole drug scene, that that whole thing came from the studio, they didn't want to deal with the drugs."[51] At this time Travolta's star brand was based on the performer's ability to project what one journalist described as "the punk macho attitude"[52] in such characters as Vinnie Barbarino in *Welcome Back, Kotter*, Tony Manero in *Saturday Night Fever*, and Danny Zucko in the soon-to-be released *Grease*. On the outside these characters were charming, smart alecky tough guys, but on the inside they had layers of sensitivity and vulnerability that, once exposed, made their sexually assertive surface appealing. Strip's character was written as being all sensitivity and sensuality (he spends the majority of the film in bikini briefs), which was a practical strategy to use to expand the star's range and a reason why Travolta had pursued the collaboration with Tomlin and Wagner in the first place. The gentle parts of Strip's character would endear many fans, female and male, to Travolta's character and its romantic and sexual characterizations; in contrast, the seedy underground of drug dealers and the insinuation of bisexual prostitution were edgy, and his producers (and possibly Travolta as well) may have felt they would alienate the mass audience that flocked to this performer.

Stigwood also recalled tensions between the stars, who started fighting over small, inconsequential matters such as whether Tricia would wear gold bracelets when they first sleep together.[53] In an interview before the film's release, Travolta was adamant in refuting rumors that Stigwood was considering replacing Wagner or that he and Tomlin partook in "emotional confrontations" on set.[54] Yet Stigwood closed the production down for a three-week "cooling off" period and later regretted not ending production of the film at that point: "I have to take full responsibility. I could have shut the film down completely."[55] It is unknown how seriously he had considered such a drastic option for a film that was not running over budget or over schedule. Travolta later regretted not fighting harder to have his character's name changed. "Strip" became a joke among audiences and reviewers. When Tomlin's character would call out Strip's name in a dramatic or romantic scene it played as a command for him to actually strip. "I begged them [Wagner and Stigwood]," Travolta told Gene Siskel in an interview a year and half after the film's release, "but I didn't push hard enough. I had too much respect for them, which sometimes can get in the way."[56]

Wagner, as the film's writer and director, experienced the most anguish. In retrospect, Wagner felt that it was not in her "nature" to direct: "I have a vision for something. Maybe the work should be reflective of that vision, but the actual making it happen, drives me crazy." The majority of the film took place on the beach, and more than thirty years later, Wagner found the humor in the practical difficulties of shooting there. "Shooting at the ocean. Having to match waves coming, to wait for the sun coming in—ooh!," she laughed. "It was so much more than I ever wanted to deal with, technically."[57] As a first-time director perhaps she was not prepared enough or she lacked the authority or experience to correct, on set, what was not working in a scene. In 2011 the filmmaker reflected on what went wrong: "You watch the dailies and you know it wasn't right, but you have to go and shoot the next day, but a whole new, different scene and you're haunted by what you missed the last day, but you have to go on to the next scene and it's really painful, but I didn't have the power to just stop everything and say 'It didn't work.'"[58] The "criticism really hurt," said Wagner in 1979. "I wanted to show that two people who feel there is no romance left anymore can suddenly find it. . . . Nobody, nobody, would accept that."[59]

Even given Wagner's insecurities about her ability to do the job and the tensions on the set, what stands out as more of a detriment to the film was Travolta's stardom. *Saturday Night Fever* and *Grease*, which was released in June 1978 while *Moment by Moment* was in postproduction, were two of the top-grossing films of the decade. In 1978 Travolta was a phenomenon. Any film that he made then would have been scrutinized sharply.

The rage that the film invoked appeared to be disproportionate to its flaws. In 1980 Travolta, then able to joke about the experience, remarked, "You would have thought that Lily and I had committed murder," he laughed. "I thought, migod [*sic*], don't ever do a movie people don't like; they'll kill you. . . . I never saw such force directed toward something," reflected Travolta. "I must have made a pretty big impression with my first two films for there to be that kind of disappointment."[60] Travolta suffered through many more poorly received films, particularly during the 1980s, which suggests that the expectations for the young star were a bigger obstacle than the work itself.

Tomlin had a similar reaction when talking about the experience in the 1980s. The failure of the film had a "very deep effect. But you live through it," said the actress with resolve.[61] However, "they treated you as if you'd murdered someone, when all you did was make a bad movie—and not even a costly one."[62]

Neither Tomlin's nor Wagner's careers were irrevocably harmed by *Moment by Moment*. Eight years later on the eve of a huge success, Wagner had a renewed perspective: "You can either wither and die at a time like that or find ways to survive it. It was a good time for me to grow. And Lily was so totally supportive."[63] The growth enabled Wagner to write and produce another one-woman Broadway show starring Tomlin. In 1985 *The Search for Intelligent Signs of Life in the Universe* was met with an ecstatic response from critics and audiences, and Tomlin won her second Tony Award. The production was adapted into a movie for Showtime in 1991 and received an Emmy nomination for Outstanding Variety, Music, or Comedy Special. The couple continued to collaborate with each other, with Wagner as a writer and producer, but never again as a director. Perhaps she was correct in knowing where as an artist she could do her best work.

"Do you see [*Moment by Moment*] as a woman's film, if there is such a thing?" an interviewer asked Travolta before the movie's release. "Isn't the subject matter controversial, dealing with the love affair between a younger man and an older woman?" Travolta, at the time, appeared sensitive to feminist issues, as he speculated about the impact of the movie: "This may be a turning point in *film*, because you're seeing a man for the first time go through as much emotional change and coloration as women have in the past . . . these are two totally different characters that you've never seen before on screen."[64] He was correct. In 1978, *Moment by Moment* was an anomaly in the annals of Hollywood cinema. It was a studio production featuring two of the most popular actors at the time playing not only against their brands but also against industry standards: the film is a conventional drama that celebrates a romance between an older woman and younger man; and the rare instance where the thirty-nine-year-old actress gets top billing over her male costar, a young heartthrob on the rise. As was revealed in the film's apocalyptic reception, Travolta had much at stake in taking this role. For Tomlin and Wagner, a romantic drama was a departure from what they were known for, but its underlying theme of exploring female identity and challenging social expectations was a mainstay in the couple's work. *Moment by Moment* may have not succeeded in its initial goal of telling Trisha and Strip's love story, but the degree to which Wagner, Tomlin, and Travolta—three powerful people in Hollywood who because of their status had the support of Stigwood and Universal—could make a "woman's film" on their own terms was unprecedented at the time. In contrast to Joan Darling's experience in which she was offered work based more on assumptions about how gender could serve the studio than on what project could be best suited to her talents and interests, Wagner and Tomlin, with the support of Travolta's star power, were able to initiate their own vision and one that retained some of its originality even as it failed.

## Joan Tewkesbury

> It was not quite the same for women at that time. If you ever stopped to look at it, it would stop you cold. So I never stopped to look.
>
> —Joan Tewkesbury[65]

Joan Tewkesbury had written two films for Robert Altman, *Thieves Like Us* (1974), in which she shared screen credit with Altman and Calder Willingham, and *Nashville* (1975), which would be an enormous success on its release. By then the screenwriter already had aspirations to direct.

Tewkesbury had met Lily Tomlin and Jane Wagner on *Nashville*'s set in 1974. Two years earlier, Tomlin had optioned the rights to Cynthia Buchanan's novel *The Maiden*, and *Variety* had announced Wagner would write the screenplay and Tomlin would star.[66] Around this time the three women began collaborating on the project, with Tewkesbury as director and Altman signed on to produce. Altman then "punched somebody from the studio (Columbia Pictures) in the nose on the set of *Nashville* and ruined that relationship as he did a lot of times," remembered Wagner, laughing. "Altman was notorious at that point for being very difficult so that project quickly got killed."[67] Four years later, Wagner and Tomlin would make *Moment by Moment*, and in 1979, Tewkesbury would direct her first film, *Old Boyfriends*. Altman did not work on either movie.

Joan Tewkesbury was born in Redlands, California, in 1936.[68] An only child, she was encouraged by her mother, a frustrated dancer who worked as a nurse, to study dancing from an early age. When she was ten, she was cast with thirty-six other girls in the Maureen O'Brien-MGM film *The Unfinished Dance*. At eighteen, Tewkesbury was the understudy for Mary Martin in Jerome Robbins's Broadway production of *Peter Pan*. When she eventually realized that she was not interested in pursuing a career as a dancer, Robbins recommended that she go back to school. In 1958 she enrolled in the theater program at the University of Southern California, where she honed her skills as a choreographer and theater director. She married Southern California land developer Robert Maguire. The couple lived in the San Fernando Valley, and their children were born in 1963 and 1965. Around 1970, frustrated with her role as a suburban housewife, Tewkesbury separated from her husband. She was then directing a play in which actor Michael Murphy appeared. Murphy had worked with Altman and invited him to come see Tewkesbury's production. Awed by his movie *M*A*S*H* (1970) and eager to work in film, she followed up their introduction by calling the director's office to set up a meeting, during which she told him, "I don't know exactly what I can do here. I have danced, acted. I've sold coffee in commercials. I want to work in film."[69]

Altman was preparing to make *McCabe & Mrs. Miller* (1971) in Canada and Tewkesbury asked if she could travel with the production and observe the filmmaking process. The veteran filmmaker balked at this request, telling her, "Nobody can observe, a person can't go on a movie set and observe. You'll observe nothing. And you'll be in the way and you'll get nothing out of it. The only way is to have to work."[70] And with that, Altman hired Tewkesbury as the film's script supervisor. This experience was her film school. Altman was the "king" of his set, but his productions fostered a family dynamic that made a strong impression on Tewkesbury and would inform her creative approach throughout her career. When the picture was finished, he advised her, "If you really want to direct a movie, nobody will let you unless you write a script."[71] She then spent the next year writing *After Ever After*, a dark comedy about the end of her thirteen-year marriage. Geraldine Chaplin was set to play the female lead character, who was based on Tewkesbury; Altman signed on as producer. "One of the most amazing phone calls I ever got, [Altman] called and said 'I will produce your movie,'" remembered Tewkesbury in 2006. "I almost dropped the phone. What I realized was Bob was in a position to see what worked for him and worked for you too. He had to keep making movies too. I think he also thought I could be funny."[72]

Altman asked Tewkesbury to write the screenplay for *Thieves Like Us* and then *Nashville*; the latter film received Oscar nominations for Best Director, Best Picture, and two for Best Supporting Actresses, and it won for Best Song. At this moment of *Nashville*'s success, Altman said to her that they should try and get her own film *After Ever After* made. "We couldn't raise ten cents on Geraldine Chaplin. And we couldn't raise ten cents on me. At the end of *Nashville* no studios were interested in a dark comedy about the end of my marriage," laughed Tewkesbury in 2010.[73] "I had gotten a great deal from [the *Nashville* experience] and I truly wanted to direct a film by that point [1975], but *it—was—just—hard* for the girls. And I hate to say it, but it was a difficult time. Alan Rudolph could get his movie financed [and produced by Altman]. We couldn't make the arrangement for me."[74]

Alan Rudolph had been part of Altman's filmmaking family since *The Long Goodbye* (1973), where he served as Altman's second assistant director. He worked again in the same capacity on *California Split* (1974) and *Nashville* (1975), and wrote the script for Altman's *Buffalo Bill and the Indians* (1976). In 1976 he wrote and then was given the opportunity to direct the feature film *Welcome to L.A.*, which Altman produced. The film was derivative of his mentor's work in style and narrative, so much so that Rudolph used two actors from Altman's stable, Keith Carradine and Geraldine Chaplin. Tewkesbury had introduced Geraldine Chaplin to Altman when she was interested in the actress for her film *After Ever After*, and the actress then secured a featured role in *Nashville* before starring in Rudolph's film. Rudolph went on to a career as a writer-director of nearly twenty independent features.

During *Thieves Like Us*, Tewkesbury had become friends with writer, producer, and production designer Polly Platt, who had worked on the film in an uncredited capacity, and Platt introduced Tewkesbury to her agent, Jeff Berg, who signed the aspiring director. Berg also represented Paul Schrader, who at the time was known as a screenwriter for movies such as *Taxi Driver* (1976); in 1977, he wrote and directed his first film *Blue Collar*. In 1979 Tewkesbury was offered *Old Boyfriends* to direct, a script written by Paul and his brother Leonard with whom he collaborated often; Paul acted as executive producer on the picture.

*Old Boyfriends* stars Talia Shire, known at the time for her work in *The Godfather* and *Rocky* series. She plays Dianne Cruise, a recently divorced psychiatrist in the midst of an identity crisis. Faced with an emotional breakdown, Cruise sets out on a road trip in search of her old boyfriends played by Richard Jordon, John Belushi, and Keith Carradine. The film resembles something of a road movie that invokes themes of revenge and romance, highlighted by a suspenseful score created by David Shire, the actress's husband. Independent producer Edward Pressman made the movie for an estimated $2.5 million and distributed it through his company Avco Embassy Pictures.[75] Tewkesbury recalled the politics that brought her to the project: "Jeff Berg blackmailed Pressman into letting me direct my first movie, because [Pressman] had wanted to be in business with Paul Schrader."[76] The original screenplay, titled *Old Girlfriends*, was about a man going back to revisit his past relationships, "and then suddenly 'women's movies' were hot," Tewkesbury said sarcastically, "and so [Schrader] changed it to a girl going back on this journey."[77]

Both Schrader and Tewkesbury were frustrated during the making of the movie, as Schrader describes in his book *Schrader on Schrader*:

> I mistakenly thought at the time that I shouldn't direct it because I, as a man, couldn't really penetrate the female psyche sufficiently and so on. There weren't many opportunities for women directors at the time and I saw myself as being able to alleviate the situation, so I supported Joan. I would have [as director] pushed things more and made them more edgy, more spooky, more scary, with characters that are more mesmerizing and more obsessive.[78]

Tewkesbury has a different recollection: "Schrader was backed up directing movies and couldn't direct *Old Boyfriends.* He turned it over in one way and didn't turn it over in another way."[79] She rewrote some of the script to soften the darker elements, which upset Schrader, who "would have been more comfortable if we had directed it like a horror film."[80] In this story about a woman's journey, both literally as she travels around seeking out her former lovers, and figuratively as she searches for something in herself in the process, Tewkesbury struggled to portray the narrative's central female perspective. Two Hollywood veterans worked on the film: cinematographer William A. Fraker and editor William Reynolds. Tewkesbury described both as "elegant [men] with all sorts of credits," but each lacked an understanding of the story's main point of view. "There was no reinforcement for the female view of the movie," she explained, "and every time it got to an opening sequence, I'd have Talia Shire looking—she pasted all these pictures of women in her [character's] room, because she was looking for an identity, and Billy, the editor said 'You can't do that, people will think you're a lesbian.'"[81] Michelle Rappaport, Schrader's girlfriend at the time, was one of the movie's producers. Tewkesbury felt she had somewhat of an ally in Rappaport, who was looking out for the picture that otherwise might have been taken over by its cowriter-executive producer. "He wanted a revenge film," said Tewkesbury. "We wanted a revenge film, *but* with some psychological preparation."[82]

The critics had moderate praise for *Old Boyfriends*. What stood out to the majority of reviewers was Tewkesbury's potential as a director; most were also curious about why, as an accomplished screenwriter, she chose as her directorial debut to work with the Schrader brothers' flawed script. David Denby of the *New Yorker* was candid in his surprise: "I can't imagine what the witty, loose-tongued Tewkesbury thought she was saying in this glum, undernourished movie. The screenplay, written by the ubiquitous writer-director-menace Paul Schrader and his brother Leonard, is completely lacking in common sense and ordinary definition. . . . *Old Boyfriends* feels like a workshop production; now I want to see a real movie from Tewkesbury."[83] Like Denby, Robert Osborne, writing for the *Hollywood Reporter*, was disappointed in the film, but still rooting for Tewkesbury's future. "Despite the fact that it was obviously made with good intentions and good breeding, 'Old Boyfriends' doesn't really add up to much more than a rather disjointed odyssey," wrote Osborne. "Tewkesbury, in her debut as director, has moments—only moments—but still shows a potential for interesting work to come."[84]

The film screened at the Director's Fortnight at the Cannes Film Festival, and after a follow-up press conference there, a young French female filmmaker raised her hand and asked Tewkesbury, "I think this movie is shit. You wrote *Nashville*. Did you do this movie simply to make your first movie?" Unapologetically, the director replied, "Yes." Telling the story

Fig. 17. Joan Tewkesbury with camera crew (cinematographer Charles Rosher Jr. in striped shirt near camera) on *The Tenth Month* (Margaret Herrick Library, Academy of Motion Picture Arts and Sciences)

thirty years later, Tewkesbury laughed, remembering how "Schrader was kicking me under the table" when she answered.[85]

"Women's films" and the women making them continued to be derailed. *Old Boyfriends* introduced a twist on this genre by showing the female protagonist's history of lovers, and it was written-produced by Schrader, a star on the rise already known for introducing a new kind of (sociopathic) male character to the screen. However, although Tewkesbury was offered the opportunity to direct the film, she was not able to make it her own, continuing the trend in which women filmmakers' creative agency was trapped in assumptions about gender that were counterproductive to all involved.

After *Old Boyfriends*, Tewkesbury made the turn toward television and never directed another feature film. "My agent said, 'If you do a television show right away [after *Old Boyfriends*], you'll strictly be known as a television director.' And I could see the handwriting on the wall—I was not going to be able to get my movies done as quickly as you could do a film on television, you could wait 4 to 5 years."[86]

Tewkesbury would go on to a successful career as a television writer, director, and producer of movies of the week. "They were cheap to make and women watched them," said Tewkesbury in 2011, understanding the niche that would provide a better path to telling the stories she found interesting. "And so a lot more stories were geared toward a female audience on television, very specifically too. The men watched sports and the women watched these TV movies."[87]

In 1979, the same year *Old Boyfriends* was released, Tewkesbury wrote and directed *The Tenth Month*, a television movie starring Carol Burnett and produced by her husband Joe Hamilton. She followed with more television movies, including *The Acorn People* (1981), *Cold Sassy Tree* (1989), and *Sudie and Simpson* (1990); a director of one-hour episodic programs for series including *Northern Exposure*, *Picket Fences*, and *Doogie Howser, M.D.*; and a producer and director of the series *The Guardian*. She enjoyed the actual making of *Old Boyfriends*—working with the actors and her crew. But the long process of seeking the opportunity to direct a film, and then being given one that did not originate with her as a writer, was difficult. She felt fortunate that she had an agent who advocated for her, but the insidiousness of sexism was powerful. "It was not quite the same for women at that time," she said reflecting on the double standard decades later. "If you ever stopped to look at it, it would stop you cold. So I never stopped to look at it. And you were never quite sure why. There was always an underlying frustration that you could never quite address because it was never overt, but there was this Chinese Wall."[88]

Joan Tewkesbury's vivid description of the nebulousness of sexism that nevertheless stalled women directors' careers in the 1970s is especially poignant, because, with the success of *Nashville* in 1975, she was so primed for the job so early in her career. She had followed Robert Altman's advice to first write a script and then seek directing jobs. Tewkesbury had written one for a film that received several Academy Award nominations, including Best Picture. Following this achievement she had written her own script to direct. While her male peers, such as John Milius, Alan Rudolph, and Paul Schrader, made the transition from the position of screenwriter to director—of their own screenplays—she was unable to do so. Even though Altman was, as Jane Wagner put it, "notorious" for fighting with studio executives, he had made several successful films during the 1970s and was one of the most notable directors of the decade. Alan

Rudolph was able to benefit from having the veteran filmmaker as the producer on his first film, and Tewkesbury should have been able to be helped similarly. Evidently, Tewkesbury's ties to Altman, both as a screenwriter who worked with the accomplished director or his serving as her potential producer, were not strong enough to break through the film industry's gender barrier.

## Joan Rivers

I've learned that by being nice and deferring, you can only hurt yourself. You must be a Barbra Streisand. You have to have the guts to say no.

—Joan Rivers[89]

In 1978 when comedian Joan Rivers made her first and only feature film, *Rabbit Test,* a satire starring Billy Crystal as the first pregnant man, she was already a household name. She had written jokes for Ed Sullivan; made countless television appearances, including on Johnny Carson's *The Tonight Show* and *Hollywood Squares*; and had hosted her own TV talk show. She was a headliner on the Las Vegas circuit for $55,000 per week—at the time the highest-paid opening act.[90] Yet her success was hard-won: "My whole career has been one rejection after another, and then going back and back and pushing against everything and everybody," explained Rivers as she summarized her professional path in 1978. "Getting ahead by small, ugly steps."[91]

Rivers established her self-deprecating brand of humor at the start of her career as a comedian. Born Joan Molinsky in 1933, Rivers grew up in Larchmont, New York. She attended Connecticut College and graduated from Barnard College in 1954. In 1958 Rivers began the arduous climb through the ranks of the comedy world, from the Catskills circuit to Second City in Chicago. Always working a joke into every interview, she described those years this way in 1978: "If a trash can had a bulb, I played it. Strip joints. Places so Mafiosi you were scared to say, 'Stop me if you've heard this.'"[92] Rivers married Edgar Rosenberg, a television producer, in 1965, and the couple would collaborate thereafter until his death in 1987: he often served as her manager, and he produced much of her television work, as well as *Rabbit Test.* The couple moved from New York to Los

Angeles in 1973. By then a known performer with a broadcast presence, including a talk show—*The Joan Rivers Show* for NBC in 1968–1969—Rivers was eager to expand her television career by writing screenplays and acting in movies. That year she wrote the ABC television movie *The Girl Most Likely to . . .* , a revenge comedy starring Stockard Channing as college student who has been bullied and rejected all her life for her looks (over-the-top prosthetic features and a unibrow made her character "homely"). Channing undergoes a plastic surgery makeover and murders everyone who mistreated her as an act of payback. A script Rivers had written, *Roxy Haul*, about two men who kidnap the Radio City Music Hall chorus line and hide the women in the breasts of the Statue of Liberty, was going to be made at Columbia Pictures, but the deal fell through.[93] In 1974 it was announced that the Robert Stigwood Organization would develop the property with Rivers as screenwriter, but again the project went nowhere.[94] In her 1991 autobiography, *Still Talking*, one of several she wrote, Rivers describes her frustration at that time: "I was more and more in demand in Las Vegas—but that increasingly pigeonholed me as a Vegas comic. No acting jobs were being offered. My new scripts were being turned down."[95]

Rivers collaborated on the script for *Rabbit Test* with Jay Redack, a writer-producer on the television game show *Hollywood Squares* on which the comedian was a frequent guest. It was Redack's idea to tell the story of the first pregnant man. "Sounds ridiculous?" Rivers asked her readers in *Still Talking*. "But at the time it stole my creative heart."[96] Lionel is a young and sexually inexperienced man, played by Billy Crystal in his first film, who practices dating with a blowup doll, teaches U.S. citizenship classes at night school, and lives next door to his meddlesome Jewish mother, played by Doris Roberts. Lionel becomes the first pregnant man after being raped and then turns into a miracle figure who is idolized by world leaders and (the voice of) God. The picture's hodge-podge cast was made up of known actors such as Roddy McDowall and established comedians, including Roberts, Imogene Coca, and Alex Rocco. The humor is classic Rivers: coarse and offensive in its use of every kind of cultural, racial, sexual, and religious stereotype and funny in how the writer-comedian-director exploits those stereotypes to make astute social commentary. *Rabbit Test* is her take on the 1970s New Woman film that she refashioned from a man's perspective of experiencing motherhood, literally. It built on her live comedy material, which covered a range of topics, but always with a focus on female-centric themes such as marriage, sex, gynecologists, childbirth, and motherhood, and her 1974 book, *Having a Baby Can Be a Scream*, that lampooned the trials of parenting.

In 1977 Rivers and Rosenberg began to shop around the script for *Rabbit Test*, but were met with rejection by every studio in town. They did have a deal for a few days: Dan Melnick, then the head of MGM, had agreed to make the film for $1.3 million dollars, but the following week he left the studio and the deal died.[97] So Rivers and Rosenberg began to raise money on their own. At one of the comedian's Las Vegas shows, the couple met Thomas Pileggi, a businessman from Philadelphia, who became one of the film's primary investors and eventually a close family friend. Avco Embassy Pictures distributed the picture and put up $500,000; Rivers and Rosenberg gave dinner parties to fundraise, mortgaged their home, and took out loans against her future Las Vegas shows to raise the remaining balance of the picture's initial $1 million budget. The film was made for an estimated $1.2 million.[98]

The production came in one day ahead of its twenty-four-day shooting schedule and $100,000 under budget.[99] Given the limited funds dictated by the small, pieced-together budget, Rivers edited the film in her garage and sometimes even in a space next to her dressing room at the MGM Grand Hotel in Las Vegas where she was performing.[100] The film grossed an estimated $4.7 million at the domestic box office and close to $10 million including Canadian sales.[101]

*Rabbit Test*'s marketing campaign was unique in that it used Rivers's status as a recognizable celebrity to sell the film. In all the film's promotional materials, from ads, to photo shoots, to the sketch done of her and the film's cast by famed illustrator Al Hirschfeld, Rivers wore a t-shirt with the words "Director Person" emblazoned across the front. These words simultaneously dismantled the assumption that directors were always male and thus the power that went with it; by de-gendering "director" they removed the stigma from the female filmmaker category. All the film's posters had an image of Rivers wearing the t-shirt next to the title "Joan Rivers' *Rabbit Test*." In one ad she had a shocked expression as she stood next to a visibly pregnant Crystal. The tagline read, "Where do you buy maternity jockey shorts?"

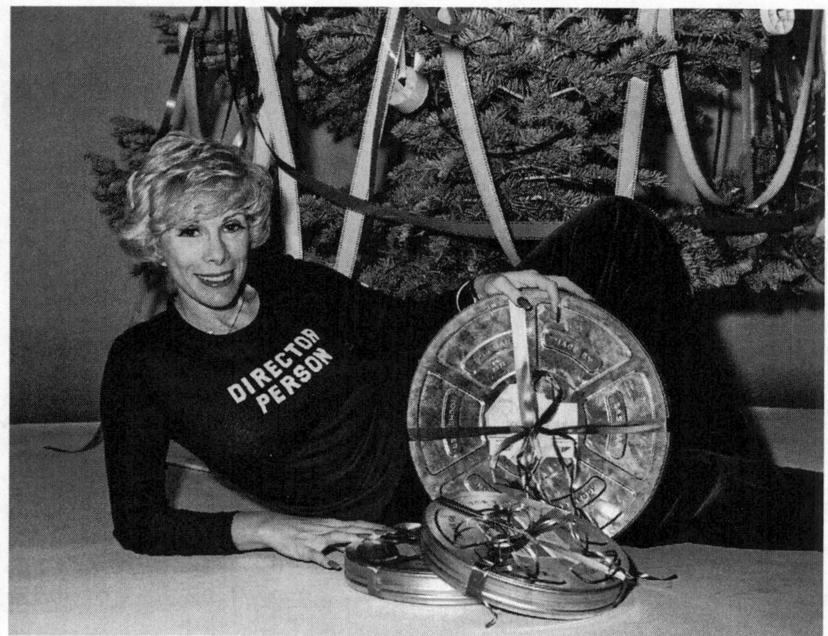


Fig. 18. Joan Rivers in publicity still for *Rabbit Test* (Margaret Herrick Library, Academy of Motion Picture Arts and Sciences)

Rivers's tenacity for self-promotion and skill at creating herself as a brand were exceptional. She promoted the film during her Las Vegas shows and went on the road with the picture, making in-person appearances in theaters and on college campuses.[102] Hers was a family affair: Edgar often joined her for the traveling promotions, as did her ten-year-old daughter, Melissa, whom she joked was the film's associate producer.[103] The team gave away *Rabbit Test* calendars and t-shirts. Film posters parodied famous movies, reimagining them in a *Rabbit* universe: "Paws" for *Jaws*, "Hare Wares" for *Star Wars*, and "King Karrot" for *King Kong* with an illustration of Rivers caught in the paw of a giant King Rabbit. A commercial for the movie featured Rivers wearing the "Director Person" t-shirt, sitting in front of editing equipment working the film reels. "Hi," she faces the camera with a smile. "I'm Joan Rivers and I'm here editing my new film *Rabbit Test*. I just love editing because you can control your film and develop your bust at the same time."[104] Ben Shylen, editor-in-chief and publisher for *Boxoffice* magazine, dedicated a column, titled "Showmanship to the Fore," to her "wildly imaginative showmanship" in the launch of her film and what her publicity team was calling their "think funny" approach. He praised Rivers and Rosenberg's Laugh or Die Productions for its "energy, humor, intelligence and flair . . . remind[ing] us how much that one word—*showmanship* encompasses."[105]

"Joan Rivers" the personality received good reviews in the numerous interviews and profiles of the writer-director and articles describing her experience making the film, but critics were not impressed by the movie itself. Influenced by the tone of her stand-up style, the picture's flimsy plot is dominated by sight gags. *Variety* described it as "an extended Joan Rivers monolog with throwaway pictures." To that reviewer the array of comedian cameos in the film were "occasionally amusing, but make the pic [*sic*] seem slapdash, as if Rivers had to finish their scenes because these performers had something better to do in an hour."[106] The *Independent Film Journal*'s tepid review of the film was still enthusiastic about her directing: "More comic inventiveness and fewer crass scatological jokes would have sharpened the material and made the laughs memorable. As it is, *Rabbit Test* is more good intention than comic invention. But in Rivers' case the seed for movie comedy success is there."[107] During the film's release, the first-time filmmaker defended her work, comparing it to the output of her more experienced male peers: "Sure, it's uneven. But so was *Take the Money and Run*. So were *What's Up, Tiger Lily?* and *The Producers*. Look, this is no *Annie Hall* or *Silent Movie*. I haven't been at it for ten years like Woody Allen and Mel Brooks."[108]

Soon after the film's release Rivers described the anxiety she felt, as a first-time filmmaker and as a woman directing, at the start of production: "I had to prove that I could climb wherever I had to, that I could swear whenever I had to, that I could be tough if I had to. Then I'd go off in a corner and cry a lot, which nobody ever saw. But after that first day or so, I never felt that my being a woman meant anything to the crew. Either they respect you or they don't, they like you or they don't; but whichever it is, it's totally asexual."[109]

Years later Rivers gave a more sobering assessment of her experience making the film. In response to investors' worries about her lack of experience, she had hired veteran cinematographer Lucien Ballard, who had had an extensive career dating back to the 1930s; in the decade before working with Rivers he had filmed John Wayne's *True Grit* (1969) and several pictures for Sam Peckinpah, including *The Wild Bunch* (1969), *The Ballad of Cable Hogue* (1970), and *the Getaway* (1972). The film he had shot just before *Rabbit Test* was Elaine May's *Mikey & Nicky*. As a first-time filmmaker, Rivers had hoped Ballard would be her mentor.[110] Instead he "was a mean son of a bitch, who didn't help me at all. Really mean," she told Allan Neuwirth in an interview with the Television Academy in 2007.[111] Ballard did not watch the dailies, although not surveying the day's work was unconscionable for a cinematographer. When Rivers asked for his expertise on a shot setup he would answer, "Put [the camera] where you want."[112] "He told me things like 'you can't pull a body away from the camera,'" she said with loathing so many years later. "He was not a nice man, so I didn't have a good experience as a director."[113] Ballard's apathy resulted in inadequate coverage and many missing medium shots and close-ups; there were times in postproduction when Rivers and her editor had to blow up frames to re-create the missing footage.[114]

After *Rabbit Test*, Rivers never directed another film. She continued to try to turn her *Roxy Haul* script into a movie; during the summer of 1978 it was about to go into production, but failed to do so.[115] "*Rabbit Test* left me so scarred," she confessed in 2007. "I wanted to do a funny movie . . . but we were too early. We were right before *Airplane* (1980), and we were right before *Animal House* (1978). *We got creamed.*"[116] There were two types of film comedy in the 1970s: the PG-rated, dialogue-heavy, heterosexual-romance-focused style of Woody Allen and Neil Simon and, on the other end of the spectrum, the genre parody and social satire of Mel Brooks who used ample one-liner jokes, sight gags, and slapstick humor. Brooks's work was the closest to that of Rivers, but his onscreen humor, with the exception of *Blazing Saddles* that received an R rating for racial epithets and some swearing, was rated PG; his focus on sexuality was always male centric, and as a male comedian, those jokes were familiar and acceptable. From the onset of her career in stand-up in the mid-1960s, Rivers used herself as source material. This was and still is a common approach for stand-up comedians, and many of her women peers at the time also took a female-centric focus. In 1972, reviewing her current Las Vegas show, *Variety* raved that "her appeal to both sexes keeps her reputation soaring as one of the few really funny distaffers" and described her style as "delightful femme-glam humor."[117]

That humor—in her stand-up material, her books, and her scripts for film and television in the 1970s—had always been brash and vulgar; yet a perceptive social critique was lodged within jokes about female and male vanity, the quest for fame, and gender double standards. This style is what made her comedy distinct *and* popular. *Rabbit Test* was the precursor to the wave of bawdy humor in films like *Animal House*, *Up in Smoke* (1978), and *Porky's* in 1980, a style of cinematic comedy that would turn out to be successful and, for decades, exclusively male. Just as with the other women directors presented in this chapter, Rivers—with better creative support, more reliable financial support, and faith in their own ability and potential—could have achieved much more. Rivers was a star when she took to the director's chair; an investment in her education as a filmmaker would have been worthwhile for any studio. As "Joan Rivers" she might have even been able to successfully move her "femme-glam humor" to the screen in spite of the male dominance of gross-out comedy, a style she was instrumental in popularizing on stage. Years later she reflected on the missed opportunity in her only directorial effort. "Maybe I would have become Woody Allen if someone had said, 'Ok, that's very funny. Let her do another and this time we'll put her with very good people.' We made [*Rabbit Test*] for a dollar so [we did not have] the greatest of anything."[118]

Rivers had a long and dynamic career on television, the stage, and the page, which she redefined again and again by carving out her own, ever-changing niche. She died, unexpectedly, in 2014 at age eighty-one while she was still working full-time. On how directing a feature film affected her, Joan Rivers recalled, "There were two Big Breaks in my life. One was the first time I was on Johnny Carson's show—February 17, 1966—and he said on the air, 'You're going to be a star.' Then there was the second major turning point—actually directing a movie. The first day on the set changed my whole life I mean, they let me do it. When I said, 'Action,' nobody laughed."[119]

## Claudia Weill

INTERVIEWER: Did your personal life suffer during the years it took you to make "Girlfriends"?

CLAUDIA WEILL: As for whether I've lost something while I've been making the film. I just don't know. That's like people asking me

> what it's like to be a woman filmmaker. That's hard for me to judge since I have no idea what it's like to be a man filmmaker."[120]

There is one "happy" story in this chapter on women directing at the end of the decade in the heyday of Hollywood's New Woman films. Whereas Karen Arthur found distribution for her films difficult to come by, Claudia Weill's independently produced feature, *Girlfriends*, was picked up in 1978 by Warner Bros. in what Stephen Klain of *Variety* romanticized as the indie director's "whirlwind Hollywood odyssey."[121] The film is set in contemporary New York City and follows Susan (Melanie Mayron), an aspiring photographer in her twenties, as she struggles with losing her best friend to marriage, her own relationship quandaries, and the missteps of a young adult at the start of her career. Weill, a New York-based filmmaker, whose prior experience was in documentary, often feminist-themed projects, began work on the film in 1975. Four years later she had relocated to the West Coast and was signing a two-year development deal with a major studio.

Born in 1947 in New York City and raised in Westchester County, Claudia Weill did not grow up a cinephile. Weill's mother was a lecturer in the Far Eastern department of the Metropolitan Museum of Art, and her father was the president of the men's fashion boutique, the British American House.[122] As an undergraduate at Radcliffe College, her interest in painting led her to photography, which eventually introduced her to cinematography. In 1967, while still a student at Radcliffe, she worked on the documentary *Revolution* about San Francisco's Haight-Ashbury district; on that project, she learned about film production. Weill continued to make short documentaries while still in school before graduating cum laude from Radcliffe in 1969. After college, Weill worked for PBS, directing several episodes of *Sesame Street*, as well as for New York City's PBS station WNET, where she directed episodes in the series *The 51st State*. As a director-cinematographer, in 1973, she collaborated on the documentary *Joyce at 34*, which profiles filmmaker Joyce Chopra during her pregnancy as she thinks about impending motherhood and its impact on her career. New Day Films, a feminist filmmaking collective that Weill had cofounded in 1971 with a group of filmmakers, including Chopra, Julia Reichert, and Jim Klein, distributed the project. In 1973, Weill collaborated as codirector and cinematographer with Shirley MacLaine on the documentary *The Other Half of the Sky: A China Memoir*. The film was nominated for an Academy Award.

Beginning to tire of documentary filmmaking, Weill and screenwriter Vicki Polon, a colleague from PBS, began conceptualizing the story *Girlfriends* in 1975. Originally imagined as a short film, Weill had some second thoughts, as she was developing it: "The story just seemed to want to go on. It was mostly pretty boring, but I really liked Susan, the main character. . . . I wanted to know what happened to her."[123] At one point, Barbara Schultz, producer for *Visions* (on KCET, Los Angeles's PBS station), offered Weill the opportunity to make the film as part of the program. *Visions* was an independent filmmaker series that funded feature films for broadcast, with budgets of an estimated $200,000. Weill declined the offer: "I turned it down because I was just terrified. I mean the thought of having $200,000 and having to make a 90-minute film was much too scary."[124] Instead, Weill made the movie at her own pace for an estimated $500,000, the budget consisting of $90,000 of grant monies from the AFI Independent Filmmaker's fund, the National Endowment for the Arts, and the New York State Council of the Arts, supplemented by donations from family and friends made along the way. In a 2011 interview, Weill remembered, "When you graduated from college, they used to send you a credit card. So I used that a lot!"[125]

The film was a "labor of love" for the actors and crew. Starring an up-and-coming cast of unknowns (Melanie Mayron, Christopher Guest, and Bob Balaban), and veteran Hollywood actor Eli Wallach, whom Weill cold-called and convinced to join the low-budget production, the project relied on its actors' commitment to the film over the several years it took to complete. Mayron, who at twenty-five years old had appeared in smaller parts in films and television, was particularly invested in the feature, hoping it would be her breakthrough role. The serendipitous timing of the picture's release with Hollywood's recent output of New Woman films gave both cast and crew confidence that their movie had a chance to do well.[126] "I *really* became involved in the completion of the film, for my sake and everybody's," explained Mayron of her hopes, in an interview conducted during the picture's successful release. "When 'Julia' and 'Turning Point' and 'An Unmarried Woman' started to happen, I knew the stage had been set for what we had begun long before those films, and I *prayed* for Claudia to pull it off."[127]

Fig. 19. Melanie Mayron (left) and Claudia Weill (right) during *Girlfriends* (Margaret Herrick Library, Academy of Motion Picture Arts and Sciences)

*Girlfriends* was received well at the Rotterdam Film Festival and was then quickly accepted for screening at Cannes. The movie sparked interest from independent domestic distributors, but buoyed by the positive reviews the film was receiving on the festival circuit, Weill decided to approach the major studios. Never having been to Hollywood, she flew to the West Coast and "checked into a cheap hotel, and started looking up the numbers of the studios in the phone book. Now I could say, 'Hi, you don't know me, but I have a film which I produced and directed and which the Cannes Film Festival has accepted.' And they listened."[128] Within two weeks, she secured a screening of *Girlfriends* with studio executives. Warner Bros. picked it up for distribution in April 1978, and the film was theatrically released in the fall of that year.[129]

*Girlfriends*, a story of two young women entering adulthood and struggling through some uniquely female situations (career vs. marriage, motherhood vs. independence), embodies the feminist spirit of the era while not being politically contentious. The film, while broaching serious topics such as abortion and relationship malaise, both romantic and platonic, also has a sense of humor. (Mayron, Guest, and Balaban would each go on to notable careers in comedy.) Arthur Schlesinger Jr., in his glowing review of the movie, heaved a sigh of relief, describing how "*Girlfriends* is the first fiction film to come easily and spontaneously—i.e., nonpolemically—out of the culture of women's liberation. Feminism operates as an assumption, not as an argument."[130]

While not being overtly feminist, Weill and her collaborators were consciously making a film that spoke to their experiences as twenty-something female New Yorkers in the early 1970s and, in doing so, filled in a gap Weill felt existed in current cinema. Years later, in an interview with filmmaker and television showrunner Lena Dunham, she said she never saw anyone who looked like *her* in a movie: "We wanted to make a movie about someone like us."[131] And as she explained in an interview with Gene Siskel during the film's release, "I'm not interested in stories about superwomen or women as victims. I'm interested in stories about everyday girls, everyday women, everyday people. I like my characters to be flawed a little bit, to have a sense of humor about themselves and not to be too gorgeous."[132] The film was very much a human story, and Weill was as quick to emphasize this in interviews as she was to identify, as a filmmaker, her interest in bringing unseen female characters to the screen. For her the two were not mutually exclusive: *Girlfriends* "is a classical genre picture, a film of initiation.... It's a 'growing up film' ... the difference with my film is that it's about a *woman* doing this. But it's the same story that we've seen all the time about men."[133]

The buzz the film generated at high-profile film festivals was a harbinger of its future commercial appeal. Mayron's insight that the picture's release was well timed to piggyback on the success of Hollywood's New Woman films was not lost on Warner Bros. *Variety* pointed this fact out in its glowing review of the movie: "Without 'Annie Hall,' 'An Unmarried Woman,' 'The Turning Point' and the recent spate of films with strong women characters, there would be no 'Girlfriends,' at least there would be no 'Girlfriends' through Warner Bros. That would've been a shame because this is a warm, emotional and at times wise picture about friendship deserving of a wide audience."[134]

In addition to being in line with popular social trends, *Girlfriends* brought the studio good publicity for its "investing" in new talent outside the establishment. The press glommed onto the young, "rising star, Hollywood outsider" story. Cecile Starr, writing for the *New York Times*, began her profile of Weill by noting how, on the eve of its theatrical release, the film had a "number of unprecedented achievements already to its credit. It's the first independent American dramatic film to be primed with grants . . . in a matter of weeks [Weill] sold it for world distribution to Warner Bros. And even before the release of 'Girlfriends,' Warners signed Miss Weill to develop two more features."[135] Charles Champlin both praised the movie and noted how it came to be made: "One of the small miracles of this year's Cannes Film Festival . . . a candid, intelligent, informed, affectionate, deeply affecting and wryly funny examination of the lives of young career women in Manhattan now. It was, in fact, a double miracle" by being a struggling independent film made on grants and then securing distribution by Warner Bros.[136] Champlin was keen to point out the benefit to Warner Bros. in taking up the small film. "The risk is not high by the standards of 'War and Peace' or 'Sorcerer,'" he explained. "But it is a bet on a little-known film-maker—a woman—and on the kind of film (quite like 'Rocky') which cannot afford to hire stars and so creates them instead."[137] For the studio, distributing the film was an inexpensive investment. With no production costs to cover, the company would be able to reap distribution profits without any financial risk.[138] In 1979 the film made it onto *Variety*'s list of "Big Rental Films of 1978" by earning $1 million at the domestic box office.[139]

Although Weill then signed a two-picture development deal with Warner Bros., she ended up producing no projects with the studio. Her next film, *It's My Turn*, was made by producer Ray Stark's company, Rastar, and distributed by Columbia. The budget was $7 million. Eleanor Bergstein, whom Weill had met years before when she was starting to work on *Girlfriends*; wrote the film. Initially Bergstein and Weill were developing *It's My Turn* for PBS's *Visions*, but encouraged by the film's eventual executive producer, Jay Presson Allen, Weill bought back the rights, and with Jill Clayburgh interested in the lead role, took the project to Ray Stark.[140]

Released in 1980, *It's My Turn* represented to many critics a last tribute to 1970s (cinematic) feminism, in which women fought to be acknowledged as equal to men in both the public and private spheres. These characters, entering the 1980s, had "arrived" and were now struggling to balance their professional and romantic lives. Jill Clayburgh was still a box office draw from her success in *An Unmarried Woman* (1978) and *Starting Over* (1979), both of which garnered Academy Award nominations for her. In *It's My Turn*, Clayburgh plays Kate Gunzinger, a brilliant, bumbling, and beautiful math professor, successful in her career as an academic, but indecisive and disorganized in her personal life. She is torn between her architect boyfriend, played by Charles Grodin, and her new love, Michael Douglas, a professional baseball player. Her character is also very accident-prone throughout the film, tripping and stumbling constantly, a feature that Weill had intended to be funny and endearing.

Weill's interest in the material was rooted in her belief that during the late 1970s women and men were beginning to be consumed by careerist goals at the expense of their personal lives. "I wanted to get into something that I think is happening to a lot of people," she explained in an interview at the time of the film's release. "And that's that they're making significant progress in terms of their work, but they're finding themselves emotionally impoverished—their relationships are negotiated to support their work or they're not involved in any relationships at all."[141] Many reviewers, who liked the film, responded to Weill's theme and found in the movie an honesty in its portrayal of characters faced with the professional versus personal dilemma. Charles Champlin admired Weill's work along with that of screenwriter Bergstein, observing, "Lines and scenes are at their most effective a rewarding combination of wit and poignance, with a real feeling for character and relationships." He was won over by Clayburgh as the archetypical contemporary 1970s woman. "'It's My Turn' is sharply funny and full of well observed characters," complimented the critic. "And Jill Clayburgh is marvelous yet again as the model of the modern woman, torn this time not only between men but between dreams."[142] Writing in the *Village Voice*, Andrew Sarris was effusive in his praise for the filmmaker and the film: "Claudia Weill's *It's My Turn*, with a particularly brilliant script by Eleanor Bergstein, has emerged quite unexpectedly as one of the most affectingly civilized entertainments of the season."[143]

Clayburgh's performance, as the representative of the liberated and successful woman, also displeased some reviewers. In her op-ed column for the *Los Angeles Herald Examiner*, Julia Cameron wrote that *It's My Turn* suffered from the negative impact of Clayburgh's appeal: "In fact, Jill Clayburgh is so non-threatening as to be virtually non-functional. To the men, she says, 'See? The New Woman is really just like the Old Woman—a klutz, no competition, nothing to be worried about.' To the women,

Clayburgh says, 'See? you can keep your new high-powered job *and* your old feminine wiles.' *Feminist* is really just the long form of *feminine*."[144] For that reviewer, Clayburgh's character as a genius mathematician, who stumbled around in high heels unable to make an informed decision about her personal life, did not seem a humorous portrayal of real life, but rather a counterfeit representation of female empowerment. Others, such as Stanley Kauffmann of the *New Republic*, who liked *Girlfriends*, was disappointed in Weill's first studio project, calling it "false and foolish from beginning to end, except when it's trite. . . . Nothing in this film becomes it like the [*sic*] leaving it."[145] Like Cameron, Kauffman also found fault in the film's leading lady, which only worsened what he considered a vapid plot to begin with: Clayburgh fails to meet "the script's basic requirement: to make us wish we were that woman (if you're female) or that we were with her (if you're not)."[146]

Robert Osborne, writing for the *Hollywood Reporter*, found the film "hit-and-miss." For him, something was literally missing from the film itself: "Along the way, one gets the impression there must be something left on the cutting-room floor, or in the typewriter of the scenarist . . . there are so many hazy explanations, unexplained turns and bottomless holes" [in the film].[147] Osborne may have been intuiting problems that occurred in the editing of the movie. During production, rumors had begun to circulate in the press that Weill and Stark had engaged in some disagreements during the editing and that her leads, Clayburgh and Douglas, "walked all over" her during the process.[148] It was reported that Douglas was "so distressed with 'My Turn' [*sic*] . . . he's telling friends he'll do nothing to promote its release." The gossip columnist put all the blame on the screenwriter and director, citing a source from Columbia who claimed, "There was nothing the actors could do to save it. The script was weak, the directing even weaker, and Claudia succeeded in alienating many people who could have helped her."[149] While admitting that the producer and stars had asked for some script changes, Weill's stance in the press was that she welcomed their input: "If their criticism hadn't come I would have searched for it. I never made it a secret that I didn't know all the answers. I like to encourage actors to try things their way. I consider it part of the creative process."[150]

Weill consistently answered in a diplomatic manner all interview questions about rumors of her contentious relationship with Stark and the stars, avoiding any critical statements about her experience. To Gregg Kilday of the *Los Angeles Herald Examiner* she responded in more general terms about what it was like to work for a major motion picture company. "When you're given several million dollars to make a movie, there are all kinds of pressures," she explained. "There's always give-and-take. A producer and a filmmaker often have different ideas. But you work them out." In a final statement of ownership over her film, which expressed her confidence in the experience she had making it, Weill said almost defiantly to Kilday, "If I was unhappy with the film, you'd know it."[151]

In his 1994 biography of Michael Douglas, author John Parker describes the alleged friction as coming from Ray Stark's office. According to Parker, Stark did not like Weill's version of the movie and in an effort to undermine her authority leaked rumors to the press. Douglas was shocked by the reports that he hated the film and immediately called Weill to tell the director they were not true. Executives at Columbia then instructed the cast not to speak to the press about the story. In Parker's account, Stark reedited Weill's version of the movie; the studio preferred hers, but it is unknown which version was released in theaters.[152] Although sources and details about this conflict are vague, what does seem likely is that producer Ray Stark or those in his company were able to exert their power and authority over Weill to some extent. Costar Grodin came to Weill's defense, saying in the press during production that he "resented the way she was treated." The actor explicitly called out the double standard in Hollywood by stating, "If she were a man she wouldn't have been treated that way."[153]

A year after the film's release, Weill, still discussing any disputes in veiled terms, did admit that she and the project were treated differently because she was a woman: "The pressures were the same as on any other Hollywood feature, except (the project) got more attention, more scrutiny because I was a young woman making my first film for a Hollywood studio, which is like being a bit of a freak!'"[154] Stark, a veteran of the Hollywood power structure, may have been threatened by a woman director, a position associated with authority and influence. Furthermore, a female director's rarity in the studio system drew more attention to her and, by association, to the men who hired her. (Weill was the first woman director Columbia had hired since Ida Lupino directed *The Trouble with Angels* for the company in 1966.) As a result, the producer may have wanted to keep in check any power Weill might try to establish as a female director of a major motion picture. Re-cutting her film and releasing negative information about her to the press were ways that Stark could assert his status.

Thirty years later, Weill described the experience at Columbia as neither wholly positive nor negative, but did paint a clear picture of the power dynamic between a young female director on her first studio film and a veteran male producer. While in production on *It's My Turn*, "Stark would come on set and literally run his hand down my back to see if I was wearing a bra or not. That was acceptable at that time. The notion of a woman director was really alien," she told an audience in 2011 during an interview with Lena Dunham at a screening of *Girlfriends*.[155] Even though Weill was a director helming a major studio production with a cast of Hollywood's top stars, her power was limited. In the 1970s there was no recourse for sexual harassment within the industry. This kind of behavior was a normalized part of Hollywood culture, and she was expected to laugh off Stark's conduct as a gesture of good humor to prove that she was not a "difficult" woman and instead was willing to play along as "one of the guys." "It was a very hostile climate," she went on to explain. "And you could not engage in a hostile [battle] because you would lose."[156]

Some press reported *It's My Turn* as a box office failure.[157] What is difficult to determine is whether Ray Stark's dissatisfaction with the film ultimately meant that he withheld in some capacity studio resources during the release of the picture; on a creative level it is also hard to determine how the conflict interfered with the final version of the film. The movie did receive substantial positive reviews from major publications, and box office reports during its opening months reported promising earnings.[158] Ultimately, the movie grossed $5.5 million against an estimated budget of $7 million.[159]

After *It's My Turn*, Weill directed theater and television, including several television movies and multiple episodes of series such as *Chicago Hope*, *thirtysomething*, and *My So-Called Life*. In 2013, she directed an episode of Dunham's HBO series, *Girls*. Weill has yet to make another feature film. Hers was a conscious decision to move out of movies and into television. The episodic schedule was more accommodating for a working parent, and while there was less fame associated with being a television director compared to that of a film director, the work was still exciting and the salary lucrative.[160]

Claudia Weill's formative years making independent, small-budget documentaries and content for public television introduced her to grant-making opportunities to support her first commercial film. Like Karen Arthur, she received an AFI Independent Filmmaker grant that was geared toward supporting women and minority filmmakers. Crucial to Weill's success with her first film was the way in which the domestic and international film festival circuit served as a marketplace for *Girlfriends*, enabling it to find wider distribution, and its fortuitous release during the popularity of Hollywood's New Woman films at the end of the 1970s. Because of this climate, Warner Bros. took notice of Weill and her film, seeing it an inexpensive way to cash in on the popular trend. With the backing of a major studio, the picture reached a large audience, and with it Weill gained access to work as a director in mainstream film and television.

In this way, the film industry's interest in women—on screen and behind the camera—worked in Weill's favor. Yet it also created a burden for the director. Because her first two films were about contemporary women working through the issues of "liberation," the filmmaker was constantly saddled with questions about her identification as a feminist and her work as a *woman* rather than her perspective as a *director*. Demonstrating a similar mix of self-assurance and diplomacy that she had when asked about her working relationship with Ray Stark, Weill responded comfortably to the question of being a feminist filmmaker. "I am a feminist and a film maker [*sic*]. But I don't believe in making didactic or rhetorical films. I believe you move people by making them laugh or cry. To me that is the most political thing you can do," she told the *New York Times* in 1978 during the release of *Girlfriends*. Unafraid to identify as a feminist in an industry that did not welcome such affiliations, Weill was clear that to do so did not mean that she or her work should be pigeonholed: "I feel no pressure to stick with women's films. It seems to me extremely chauvinistic to assume that because you are a woman director you have to make films about women or relationships. Feminism is a point of view you can use on any subject, even a big entertainment film."[161]

## Old Actresses, New Directors: Anne Bancroft, Lee Grant, and Nancy Walker

The first feature films directed by Anne Bancroft, Lee Grant, and Nancy Walker were all released in 1980. By that time, all three had been well-known actresses for decades in theater, film, and television. Bancroft and Grant had won Academy Awards; Grant and Walker had won Emmys. The three had been participants in the American Film Institute's Directing Workshop for Women: Grant and Walker were part of the pilot program in 1974, and Bancroft was accepted in the second year of the program in 1975–1976. The three were selected not only based on their potential talent and ambition to direct but also as part of DWW cofounder Jan Haag's strategy to choose high-profile participants who would bring the program prestige and attention.

The films made by these directors were very different: Grant directed the independent feature, *Tell Me a Riddle*, the story of an older couple coming to terms with aging; Bancroft wrote, directed, and costarred in *Fatso*—a sentimental comedy about a compulsive eater—for 20th Century-Fox; and Walker directed the extravagant musical *Can't Stop the Music* produced by EMI Films. That these women had been actively trying to direct a feature film as early as 1974 and 1975, but had not been able to see that ambition come to fruition until 1980, highlights the fact that even known actresses could not leverage their considerable level of stardom to gain the power needed to advance their careers as filmmakers. Grant said that others even perceived her transition from actress to director as if she had committed a major offense: "The minute I said 'I want to direct something, it was like, 'What is that smell in the room? Who did what here?' It was like I was stepping out of character. I was intruding in a place where it was not attractive. It was not pleasant. Their words were: 'But do you know how to be a captain of the ship?'"[162] In addition, these three directors were, by the end of the 1970s, all accomplished actresses of a certain age—over forty—in an industry that had little room for such a demographic. In different ways Bancroft, Lee, and Walker pursued directing as their second career, having already begun to experience ageism as performers. Being prominent women in Hollywood led each of them to the DWW to participate in a program that addressed industry sexism by explicitly focusing on the *woman* director category. The films they made do not fall under the conventions of the New Woman film, but as actresses building on their years and accomplishments of *female* stardom, their turn toward directing was a strategy influenced by their gender.

## Hollywood Intervention: The Directing Workshop for Women

During the early 1970s, while SAG and the WGA were releasing employment statistics to the press and spurring discussion within the film and television industry regarding sexist hiring policies, the American Film Institute (AFI) made its unique contribution to the feminist reform activism of the time: the Directing Workshop for Women. Founded by Jan Haag with Antonio (Tony) Vellani in 1974, the DWW was a response to the absence of women directors working for the film studios: Elaine May was the sole woman to have directed for a major studio—*A New Leaf* (1971, Paramount) and *Heartbreak Kid* (1972, 20th Century-Fox)—since Ida Lupino made *The Trouble with Angels* in 1966 for Columbia Pictures. The DWW's objective was to train women already established in industry careers for the job of film director. The program, since its early years, selected participants through a competitive application process. Once accepted they were given access to production and editing equipment on the AFI's campus and a small budget to make two short films that they could use as calling cards to demonstrate their directing capabilities and secure future job prospects. The DWW was a practical intervention into Hollywood's sexism. By training more women to be directors, it would increase the pool of skilled potential hires and in doing so challenge the familiar excuse that there were no qualified women for the job.

President Johnson founded the AFI in 1967 with the intent of "bringing together leading artists of the film industry, outstanding educators and young men and women who wish to pursue the 20th-century art form as their life's work."[163] Funded in large part by the federal National Endowment for the Arts and the Ford Foundation, AFI had offices and a theater in Washington, D.C., close to its financial sources, and film school facilities in Los Angeles, close to the industry. Under the leadership of its first president, George Stevens Jr., the nonprofit organization took on film preservation efforts, provided training and educational programs for film students, administered multiple filmmaking grants (some with a focus on independent productions), and hosted an annual, televised Lifetime Achievement Award that honored industry veterans, such as John Ford (1973), James Cagney (1974), and Orson Welles (1975).

In many ways AFI was an appropriate place for the hands-on activism of the DWW. As a conservatory dedicated to training the next generation of filmmakers, with a faculty of seasoned professionals, many of whom were still working in the business, it bridged practical education with industry resources. It occupied a middle ground by supporting upcoming filmmakers not yet working in the system—some who were interested in making Hollywood films and others who were focused on independent productions. At the same time, AFI's ties to Hollywood were strong. In 1974 its board of trustees included several studio and network executives, such as Ted Ashley (Warner Bros.), Barry Diller (ABC), Frank Yablans (Paramount Pictures), and Gordon Stulberg (20th Century-Fox); film producers David Brown, David Picker, and Walter Mirisch; and actors Warren Beatty and board chair Charlton Heston. Of the thirty-eight board members, five were women: actresses Shirley MacLaine and Cicely Tyson, screenwriter Eleanor Perry, journalist Shana Alexander, and Joan Ganz Cooney, president of the Children's Television Network.[164] It bestowed Lifetime Achievement Awards on film industry icons, and the Master's interview seminars spotlighted current performers, screenwriters, producers, directors, editors, and cinematographers as a way to connect students with contemporary Hollywood. AFI's ties to Hollywood bolstered its legitimacy at "bringing together leading artists of the film industry."[165]

However, the organization's affiliations also showed how AFI was an extension of Hollywood's patriarchal system. In December 1970, activists representing the group Women for Equality in the Media (WFEM) protested sexual discrimination and "marched on" the AFI's campus in Hollywood.[166] The press described the incident in confrontational, military terms: "In preparation for a long siege they carried sacks of food and a list of 12 demands 'which must be met before we leave,'" reported Mary B. Murphy for the *Los Angeles Times*.[167] More than fifty feminists participated in the "siege," including documentarian Francine Parker, production assistant Judy Binder, and women's rights lawyer Arlene Colman Schwimmer.[168] The group presented a list of grievances to AFI president Stevens, "who looked uncomfortable squeezed onto a couch with four women, and surrounded on the floor and chairs by the rest."[169] The women made the following demands of the Institute: distribute 51 percent of its awards (grants, scholarships, and internships) to women, including nonwhite women, because women made up 51 percent of the national population; focus recruitment efforts on women in high schools and college with special attention paid to disenfranchised communities of color; ensure that half of the faculty and the organization's board of directors be women; and create a permanent "board of directors," which would serve as a kind of research group, composed of five women who would have office space at AFI where they could "review and combat discrimination and stereotyping of women in the film industry."[170] WFEM's protests were substantiated by statistical evidence of gender discrimination. Of the conservatory's forty "fellows" (students), only two were women; in the apprentice program, there were no female interns assigned to directors; in three years, of nearly sixty-five filmmaking grants, only three of sixty-five had been awarded to women, and none of the twelve television grants had been given to women.[171]

WFEM's protests made Stevens aware that AFI was implicated in the current feminist critique building throughout the film and television industries. One of the outcomes of the confrontation was bringing Jan Haag into the Academy Internship Program, which placed aspiring filmmakers on the sets of major productions. Haag, who was not a member of WFEM or a participant in the group's protests, became the first woman accepted into this program and was assigned to *Harold and Maude* (1971) and director Hal Ashby.[172] Then the director of educational films for the John Tracy Clinic and the Department of Health, Education and Welfare in Los Angeles, Haag had been experimenting with early video technology. She had applied and been rejected for an AFI grant, but was known to Kay Loveland, who oversaw the internship program and who "pounded" on Stevens's desk demanding that he accept Haag as AFI's first female intern.[173]

After completing the internship, Haag was hired by Tony Vellani, director of AFI's Center for Advanced Film and Television Studies, for the position that would eventually become AFI's admissions and awards administrator, responsible for overseeing the Academy Internship

Program, the Independent Filmmaker Program, and the Center for Advanced Film Studies Admissions. A few years later, in 1974, Vellani and Haag were given a letter from feminist and social activist Dr. Matilda Krim expressing her interest in assisting AFI in the support of women working in the film industry. Krim, a research scientist, who in the 1980s would become an influential AIDS activist, was married to Arthur Krim, at the time the chair of United Artists. She was also on the board of the Rockefeller Foundation. Haag met with Krim, Eleanor Perry (screenwriter and active Hollywood feminist), and Michael Novak, a program officer from the Rockefeller Foundation, to brainstorm what would soon become the Directing Workshop for Women. Securing $35,000 in start-up funds, Haag and Vellani finalized the pilot program's details. As Haag called around looking for possible candidates, she was surprised by the overwhelming response they received from established women: the "Big Ladies."[174]

Haag never imagined the DWW to be a film school, describing how "these top Industry Women, didn't so much need repeated experiences as they needed tapes to use as demos. They didn't need, nor were they given, instruction. The DWW was designed for quick accomplishment, not talk. It was *not* a workshop for students."[175] She and Vellani agreed that, during its early years, the participants should be high-profile women who were already experiencing success in their current industry jobs. A program of unknowns would not generate any attention, but a roster of Oscar- and Emmy-winning actresses and producers, studio executives and guild presidents, prolific editors and writers would catch Hollywood's attention. The first year's group included producer Julia Phillips, who had just won an Academy Award for Best Picture for *The Sting* (1973); actresses Ellen Burstyn, Lee Grant, Margot Kidder, Susan Oliver, Lily Tomlin, and Nancy Walker; SAG president Kathleen Nolan; television writer-producer-director Joanna Lee; casting executive and vice president of creative affairs at Columbia Pictures Nessa Hyams; writer and actress Maya Angelou; producer-editor Susan Martin; script supervisor Marjorie Mullen; network news writer-producer-director Giovanna Nigro-Chacon; novelist and television writer Gail Parent; feature film editor Marion Rothman; and independent filmmakers Karen Arthur and Juleen Compton.

Haag and the DWW were criticized in the press by women in the industry for selecting participants who seemed to already have access to Hollywood resources. Mary Murphy, writing for the *Los Angeles Times*, quoted an unnamed female producer who was "shocked and offended that the AFI, which was supposed to help people break into the industry, would choose so many women who were already established and . . . had enough money to make their own films." Elly Graf, an assistant director and Directors Guild member, was annoyed by the secretive selection process: "We didn't' know anything about it until [it] was over," objected Graf. "It was done very quietly."[176] Aware of the immense obstacles facing women who wanted to direct, Haag, five years into the program, continued to be a stout defender of the Workshop's "celebrity" factor: "If you had started the workshop with completely unknown women," she explained, "you could not have had nearly that kind of bombshell effect on the whole Hollywood scene. When [we had] Julia Phillips and Lee Grant, Kathleen Nolan, Ellen Burstyn participating in it, that really shook the studio heads awake." To support her point, she cited the following comment made to her by a studio head: "Oh, they must be *serious*—to lay their career on the line for a budget of $360 [per student tape] and say 'I'm going to take a chance.'"[177]

Participants in the DWW were expected to make two shorts shot on video (the equipment available then was early videotape) for a budget of $300 each; their length could range from twenty minutes to an hour, as determined by the director. AFI provided them with a crew made up of the conservatory's student body, and they could bring in any additional professional help at their own discretion and expense. Many of the participants excelled in this environment. "I shot my tape as if I were shooting film," explained Lee Grant. "It was like having scratch paper. It was wonderful for someone who is learning. . . . The AFI crew was wonderful! Such concerns, such tastes. I am very grateful for my workshop experience."[178] Grant, an established Emmy Award- and Academy Award-winning actress who still had an active career as a performer during her year in the DWW, did have the means and contacts to augment AFI's considerably small contributions. "Many of the women in the first [DWW] cycle could have bought and sold AFI," said Karen Arthur, describing the access to monetary and filmmaking connections enjoyed by some of her more established colleagues. "But that's missing the point. The women needed the workshop for camaraderie and courage."[179]

Yet some of the harshest critics of the early DWW were the participants themselves. Joanna Lee, one of the more experienced members, ended up leaving the program when her expectations were not met. "All the program offers is one little half-inch videotape camera and a couple of kids from AFI as crew," she said, disappointed. "We are getting no advice from professional directors."[180] Contrary to Haag's belief that the participants neither needed nor were looking for instruction, Lee, who was a seasoned television writer-producer and had already directed an independent feature, was seeking expert guidance in how to enhance her talents as a filmmaker.

Working out DWW's kinks would be an ongoing process. The DWW may have attracted many high-profile and accomplished women in Hollywood, but funding did not come as easily or in such large quantities. The AFI, despite its industry associations, was a nonprofit organization, and the Directing Workshop for Women was just one of many programs competing for a piece of its budget. Haag had planned the pilot year based on a program budget in the $200,000–300,000 range, but the funders could only provide AFI with $30,000. The second year, the budget increased to $100,000 with support from the Rockefeller Foundation and $10,000 from alum Julia Phillips. In its third cycle, it grew to $150,000 with the support of a grant from the John and Mary Markle Foundation. In addition, philanthropist Anna Bing Arnold contributed to the DWW in each of its first three years.[181]

Jan Haag and Tony Vellani's strategy during the pilot years to use the participants' celebrity status and recognition as criteria for qualifying a woman in Hollywood as capable of directing a studio film was bold, practical, and a little desperate. But desperation over the bleak number of women directors was what spurred DWW's founding in the first place. "Fame legitimized not only the Workshop, but also the director potential of the women in it," recalled Haag thirty years after the founding of the DWW.[182] By stacking DWW with notable Hollywood women, the hope was that their reputations would not only boost the profile of the program—drawing the attention of studio executives and producers—but also that those men in positions of power would be more likely to hire a woman whose reputation was already well founded and familiar to them.

This was a practical approach to tackling a difficult problem. Haag and Valleni had assessed the resources they could tap into: feminist funders not affiliated with Hollywood, AFI's industry connections to offer legitimacy, and a pool of participants who had a degree of insider status and knowledge that they could apply to the job forbidden to women, directing. Finally, the short films or "tapes" produced as part of the DWW would provide tangible proof of these women's potential talent. Forty years later, the Directing Workshop for Women is still active. Challenges of equipment and crew continue to be met, and a cap on the amount each participant can receive to make her film is in place to equalize participant spending. In 1980, when Jean Picker Firstenberg replaced George Stevens Jr. as AFI's president and began to oversee the program more directly, the emphasis on high-profile, celebrity participants decreased in favor of recruiting women who were extremely accomplished industry employees—screenwriters, producers, editors, cinematographers—but who did not have the "visibility" of the first generation.[183]

In the 1970s, the program had an impact in a way that was proportional to its resources and the number of its participants (an average of twelve women participated in each cohort). Several of the women from those years did go on to make features, although most not until the following decade: they included Karen Arthur (*Mafu Cage*, 1978, and *Lady Beware*, 1987), Anne Bancroft (*Fatso*, 1980, a feature-length version of her DWW short), Lee Grant (*Tell Me a Riddle*, 1980), Nancy Walker (*You Can't Stop the Music*, 1980), Lynne Littman (*Testament*, 1983), Juleen Compton (*Buckeye and Blue*, 1988), and Nessa Hyams (*Leader of the Band*, 1988). Some made their theatrical debuts as late as the 1990s, as in the case of Maya Angelou with her film *Down on the Delta* (1998). Other participants from the 1970s started careers as television directors: Marjorie Mullen and Joanne Woodward directed a few episodes, while Karen Arthur, Lee Grant, Joanne Lee, and Nancy Malone embarked on long and prolific careers in broadcasting. Unlike its contemporaries, the Women's Committees of the guilds, the DWW was not created to go down the path of negotiations by meeting with studios or networks. Instead, in concert with the discourse taking place during the era, the DWW contributed to feminist reform efforts by focusing on a functional solution: training industry women as directors.

## Anne Bancroft

> I don't want to direct a Mel Brooks film. I want to direct
> an Anne Bancroft film! This is a matter of identity!
> And Mel agrees with this!
> —Anne Bancroft[184]

Anne Bancroft, originally Anna Maria Louisa Italiano, was born in the Bronx on September 17, 1931. She studied at the New York Academy of Dramatic Arts and in 1951 signed a contract with 20th Century-Fox, appearing in small roles in inconsequential films. Bancroft described this early period of her as career as unremarkable: "Twentieth Century Fox told me what to do and I did it. I learned nothing."[185] In 1958 Bancroft won her first Tony Award for her performance in the Broadway production of *Two for the Seesaw*, in which she costarred with Henry Fonda; the next year she earned her second Tony Award for her role as Annie Sullivan, teacher to Helen Keller in *The Miracle Worker*. She reprised this role in the film adaptation of the play, for which she won an Academy Award for Best Actress in 1963. In 1967 she played Mrs. Robinson, a stylish and dissatisfied Southern California housewife in the movie *The Graduate*, a role in which she received an Oscar nomination for Best Actress. In 1971 Bancroft turned forty—which, by Hollywood's standards, was "old." The interesting characters that she had previously been cast as became difficult to come by. It was fortuitous then that she joined the Directing Workshop for Women in 1976 and began to develop her creative skills in a new way as a writer-director *and* performer.[186]

Bancroft made *Fatso* as a short film while in the DWW. It starred Dom DeLuise, Ron Carey, and Estelle Reiner—principal cast members who would appear again in the feature version.[187] Three years later, in May 1979, she was preparing to direct the film as a feature for 20th Century-Fox to be produced by her husband Mel Brooks's company, Brooksfilms.[188] In 1980 she was one of six women between 1971 and 1980 to have directed for a major studio. *Fatso,* a romantic comedy set in an Italian-American neighborhood in New York City, starred Dom DeLuise as Dominick DiNapoli, an overweight man in his early forties who decides to improve his eating habits when he falls in love with Lydia, played by Candice Azzara. Bancroft costarred as Antoinette, Dominick's overbearing sister who is concerned for her brother's health to the point of near-hysteria. The film follows, with a mix of humor and sensitivity, the challenges Dominick faces in changing his eating habits in the pursuit of true love.

In its press material, 20th Century-Fox did not draw attention to the fact that a woman directed the film. (In 1980 this was still a rarity, as Fox's last woman director was Elaine May and *The Heartbreak Kid* in 1972.) It, however, did note that Brianne Murphy, the film's cinematographer, was the first female director of photography for a studio picture.[189] Bancroft was adamant in wanting to hire women on her film. "When I started I wanted as many women as possible in the crew," explained Bancroft in a 1979 interview. "I said isn't there a woman director of photography and they finally found Bri."[190] Murphy had come to Hollywood in the 1950s in hopes of becoming a director of photography (DP). As discussed in chapter 1, being a member of a technical union was required for below-the-line craftspeople to get hired on studio pictures, and those unions were some of the most discriminatory sites for women in Hollywood. It was not until 1973 that Murphy was able to join the Local 659 of International Photographers of the International Alliance of Theatrical Stage Employees, becoming the first woman to do so; in 1979, when she was hired to shoot *Fatso*, Murphy was still the union's only female member.[191] "Anne was *very, very, very* specific about what she wanted," Jonathan Sanger, who was the production manager and associate producer on *Fatso*, described Bancroft's rigorous pursuit of a female-populated crew: "She wanted a lot of women. And there weren't a lot of women in traditional roles in Hollywood, except as script supervisors. She wanted a female cinematographer. Female art director, set decorator. In any category we could find—we couldn't find a gaffer, but we had a woman electrician."[192]

It is not known whether Bancroft had been actively trying to make a film during those years between her participating in the DWW in 1974 and her deal with 20th Century-Fox. During that time, she focused on her work as an actress: she appeared as Mary Magdalene in the television miniseries *Jesus of Nazareth* in 1977, and she received an Oscar nomination in 1978 for Best Actress alongside her costar Shirley MacLaine in the film *The Turning Point*.

For Bancroft, collaborating with her established performer-director-producer husband was a strategic decision in getting her film made. During this time Brooks made three of his own films at 20th Century-Fox:

Fig. 20. Anne Bancroft directing *Fatso* (Margaret Herrick Library, Academy of Motion Picture Arts and Sciences)

*Silent Movie* (1976), *High Anxiety* (1977), and *History of the World: Part I* (1981). His relationship with Fox gave Bancroft access to a studio deal that she most likely would not have been offered otherwise. The opportunity for her to direct coincided with Brooks' interest in producing projects with new directors, that is, those other than himself.[193] According to Brooks, "I began lending a lot of free advice to a lot of young film makers [*sic*] who couldn't get in the studio doors without my validation. So I decided to put them under my own banner."[194] Sanger, who had first worked with Brooks as an assistant director on the film *High Anxiety*, had optioned the script to *The Elephant Man* and had brought the project to the veteran filmmaker.[195] In 1980, *Fatso* and *The Elephant Man*, which Sanger produced and Bancroft was cast in a small role, were Brooksfilms' first projects—two films that were made possible by the success and status of Mel Brooks, but stood apart from the comedian's distinct brand in their dramatic narratives. Bancroft could be considered a viable investment for the studio as a first-time director based on her status as an accomplished actress and her participation in the DWW years before, and her husband's involvement made her and her film even more attractive, but she still had to pitch the film to studio executives. Noted Sanger, who would go on to work with Brooks over the years and maintained a close relationship with the couple, "She had the unique opportunity to be able to direct because of who she was. But I also don't think the studio was in the business of making movies for people just because of who they were. They weren't going to make it a big budget movie, but the level of the budget was reasonable and the movie was something that they were proud of, so they were happy to do it."[196]

Critical response to the film was mixed. Michael Sragow, writing for the *Los Angeles Herald Examiner*, delivered a particularly harsh critique of what he thought was Bancroft's poor direction and lack of comedic timing, describing how the writer-director "appears to believe that by *not* directing the film consistently toward comedy, pathos or romance, she can achieve them all. But her characters aren't full enough to contain those three dimensions, so what she gets is *failed* comedy, *failed* pathos, *failed* romance." Sragow also focused his attack on Bancroft's inability to be original: "It's impossible to tell whether she has any literary or directorial personality, so derivative is her work. Her idea of comedy derives as surely from the excesses of her husband, Mel Brooks, as her sense of drama does from the little-people sappiness of Paddy Chayefsky and her notion of romance from Chaplin—'Young Marty Goes to Weight-Watchers Under City Lights.'"[197] For Sragow, Bancroft was unsuccessful in writing, directing, and starring in her own work, which he considered a poor imitation of her husband's humor.

Tom Cullen, reviewing *Fatso* for the *Village Voice*, also panned the film, calling it as "bumbling and sluggish as its title would suggest, a lamentable affair which ricochets uncontrollably between attempts at hilarity and pathos."[198] Like Sragow, Cullen was relentless in accusing Bancroft of drawing heavily on her famed comedian husband with no success: "Writer-director Bancroft, wife of Mel Brooks, is the latest of [Brooks'] disciples, following Gene Wilder and Marty Feldman, in grooving on pain and on comic protagonists with arbitrarily exaggerated physical disabilities. . . . Unfortunately, Bancroft has about as much instinct for comedy as Michelangelo Antonioni has for farce."[199]

Writing about the film for the *Hollywood Reporter*, critic Arthur Knight was much more forgiving of what other reviewers were insistent in pointing out: Bancroft's uneven directing and what many considered her own "dreadful" performance as the overbearing Antoinette. As he had done in his review of Joan Darling's *First Love*, Knight emphasized the efforts of a first-time director most pointedly by considering Bancroft as equal to male first-time directors. "For all [Woody Allen's] humor, his first efforts had far more bumbles than 'Fatso,'" compared Knight. "As a director on her first major outing . . . she still has a long way to go before she achieves the technical security and artistic maturity of an 'Annie Hall' or 'Manhattan.' Nevertheless, she's well on her way, and I can only say that I'll have no reticence about viewing the next Anne Bancroft movie, whatever it may be called, whoever may be its star. Maybe she'll become the Italian Woody Allen."[200] Knight was also acutely aware of how the film made history by having Murphy as its cinematographer, pointing out that "it's important to note also that, however the miracle was accomplished, 'Fatso' was photographed by a woman—Brianne Murphy—and very well."[201]

Kevin Thomas, for the *Los Angeles Times*, gave the film a favorable review, and also recognized the importance of Murphy's achievement. Thomas ended his article with an emphatic praise of the female DP that simultaneously shamed the industry for taking so long: "'Fatso' (PG) also marks a fine theatrical feature debut for cinematographer Brianne Murphy, who as far as anyone knows is the first woman director of photography ever to work for a major Hollywood studio. To say it's about time is to indulge in reckless understatement."[202]

Bancroft never directed again after *Fatso*. "I think to be a director you have to have a certain kind of personality which I don't have," she explained. "I do not like manipulating people. My greatest philosophy is to let everybody just be who they want to be, but it isn't workable. Somebody has to have a very dominating hand, and I just don't have that kind of hand."[203] In interviews during the years following the movie's release, it was common for the actress-director not to mention the project, her experience making the picture, or any follow-up thoughts on directing. Having worked closely with Bancroft during the making of *Fatso* and was privy to her insights in subsequent years, Sanger speculated that it was her own decision not to direct again. "The experience was a complete experience for her," he reflected. "I don't think her not directing again was because nobody would let her direct. It was mainly her choice. After that she said, 'I'm not so sure I want to direct again. I might write again, but I'm not sure I want to direct again.'" Sanger was confident about Bancroft's skills, but he understood how difficult it was for her as a director to make the transition from being behind the camera to being onscreen as a performer: "She saw herself as an actor first."[204] A consummate actress, Bancroft was in tune with her casts' needs, but it was that profound understanding as a fellow performer, and the struggle to strike a balance between the two, that made it difficult for her as a director.

Brianne Murphy, interviewed by Mollie Gregory in her book, *Women Who Run the Show*, suggests another reason for Bancroft's difficulties: there was a power dynamic between Bancroft and Brooks that might have made directing challenging for the first-time filmmaker. According to Murphy, "Word had gotten around that [Brooks] was very controlling."[205] For one thing, Bancroft and Brooks watched dailies—the footage shot that day—alone. Industry custom was for a director and the cinematographer to watch together, so that they could discuss what footage the director liked; often other members of the cast and crew would watch the dailies at the director's discretion. Yet Murphy would view the footage alone in the film lab, and then Bancroft and Brooks would watch it together. "I guess he told her what he liked," surmised Murphy from the odd behavior.[206]

As told by Murphy, Brooks would pick up his wife from the set every day. "We never knew when he'd arrive, and it seemed to be at his convenience rather than hers because whenever he did appear, she'd start wanting to complete a shot," remembered Murphy. One such day he came while she was still shooting. Without saying hello or introducing himself to anyone, Brooks went to the video assist—a monitor attached to the camera that shows what is being filmed—and in the middle of the shot said, "Cut, cut, that's no good, that won't work, cut it." Nobody on a set says "cut" except the director. Bob Lavar, the camera operator, responding to this breach, looked at Brooks and said, "Who the fuck is that little guy?" Describing the scene, Murphy recalled, "All hell broke loose. Very upset, Anne picked up her stuff and left."[207]

The following day Bancroft was very late to the set. Finally she arrived and asked Murphy to come see her in her dressing room. Visibly distressed and red-eyed from crying, Bancroft said to her DP, "I hate to tell you this, but Mel says you have to fire Bob. . . . Mel says he's potentially dangerous." Murphy defended her camera operator, explaining to Bancroft that Lavar was defending and protecting *her* power as the director.

Still not convinced, Bancroft brought Murphy back into her dressing room later that day. "I guess Mel had gotten to her," Murphy said. "She and I went through it again. I said I wouldn't fire the operator, there was no reason to, and he should get a medal. It was a standoff. We got no shots all day."[208] Eventually, the production resumed and Lavar kept his job. "On the set everybody loved Anne and we had a wonderful camaraderie," emphasized Murphy. "Anne Bancroft is a very talented person [and] I always thought she could have been a great director."[209]

From their marriage in 1964 until her death in 2005, Bancroft and Brooks presented a harmonious relationship.[210] That Bancroft's interest in writing, directing, and acting in a film was possibly inspired and encouraged by Brooks does not seem a surprise; nor that Brooks, as a successful writer, director, producer, and performer in turn would help his wife pursue her filmmaking goals. Sanger later described the pair as "one of the best Hollywood marriages you ever heard of. They were a tremendous couple. They didn't often work together. It was usually because they both did their own things. He was tremendously supportive of her. She was very supportive of him. In many, many ways she was funnier than him. She was one of the funniest human beings I've ever met. And loveable and strong, and *very, very* strong willed."[211] Murphy's memory of Brooks treading on his wife's authority and the difficulty she had asserting herself adds complexity to the reasons why Bancroft did not want to direct more. Perhaps the "dominating hand," which she found counterintuitive to her own approach to behind the camera (of letting "everybody just be who they want to be"), was intertwined with the challenges of having to negotiate power with her husband when she was in the position of ultimate creative authority.

After her single foray into directing, Bancroft continued to act in film, television, and theater until her death from uterine cancer in 2005 at age seventy-three.[212] Although she did not seem to speak much about her experience as a Hollywood director or as a woman director, she was candid about the age discrimination that actresses experienced in the industry. In an interview in the *New York Times* in 1984 promoting her role in the film *Garbo Talks*, Bancroft explained her predicament in Hollywood as a fifty-something-year-old woman: "I have a good life, and it's very hard to find something you really want to go to work in. People don't write wonderful parts for women, because women have not been given a chance to live wonderful lives that people would want to write about, and because most of the writers are men."[213] Her understanding of the exclusion of women's creative agency and representation within the film industry could apply to the role of director as well. Bancroft came to directing from a privileged position compared to the majority of her peers. With her husband's access and support she was given an opportunity to explore her talent. In what seemed to be her decision not to pursue directing again, Bancroft enjoyed the freedom of making that choice to say no. In a rare mention of her experience directing *Fatso*, Bancroft confessed to Patt Morrison in *More* magazine her aversion to directing. "I didn't like it, not at *all*," she admitted. "The script was very funny, but there are lots of people with needs in this business. I find directing extremely exhausting, meeting the needs of all those people. My husband thinks it's good to be the king. I do not. I think it's very good to be the king's wife."[214] As an actress beginning to encounter the obstacles of aging in 1979, directing, with the encouragement of her family, may have seemed the next career trajectory to explore. But for Bancroft it was not the pedestal she felt most comfortable standing on.

## Nancy Walker

> To tell you the truth, disco isn't anything I'd want to live with forever, but I think we can make a terrific movie out of it.
>
> —Nancy Walker[215]

Born Anna Myrtle Swoyer in 1922 in Philadelphia, Nancy Walker started her career on the stage primarily performing musical theater, with an emphasis on comedy, before moving into television as an actress. In 1970 she became popular as Ida Morgenstern, the overbearing mother of Rhoda (Valerie Harper), best friend to Mary Tyler Moore on the *Mary Tyler Moore Show*. Walker's Ida became a recurring role on Harper's spinoff series, *Rhoda*. She was not only a guest character on both these sitcoms but she also directed episodes of both series. According to the *Hollywood Reporter*, in 1973, Walker was not only the first woman to direct for *The Mary Tyler Moore Show*, but also possibly the first woman to direct a sitcom.[216] In fact, Ida Lupino was the first woman to direct sitcoms (and a range of episodic television shows, beginning in the 1950s), but Walker, along with Joan Darling, was one of the very few to be doing so during the early 1970s. Walker was nominated for a total of eight Emmys for supporting actress on *Rhoda* and the series *McMillan & Wife*, in which she also had a recurring role. During these years she also appeared on television as the spokesperson for Bounty paper towels. Her famed tagline was "Bounty, it's the quicker picker-upper."

Allan Carr became her manager in the 1970s. Carr, whose other clients during that era included Ann-Margaret and Olivia Newton-John, was known for his elaborate showmanship. "Allan has changed our lives," said Walker in a 1977 interview with *TV Guide*. Carr renegotiated her contracts with *Rhoda* and *McMillan & Wife*, "quadrupling [her] price."[217] He negotiated the deal for her program, *The Nancy Walker Show*, on ABC in 1976, which was canceled after one season. Carr was a manager turned producer and promoter. Carr was also known for his decadent parties where there were ample amounts of drugs, sex acts (every sexual orientation was welcomed and represented) took place openly, and every rank of celebrity was invited, along with the press so they would be sure to report on the festivities in the next day's paper.

After the success of *Grease* (starring Newton-John and John Travolta), which he cowrote and produced, *Can't Stop the Music*, originally titled *Discoland*, was to be Carr's follow-up—contemporary disco—musical extravaganza. The film featured the popular disco group, the Village People, whose costumed performances played on cultural stereotypes and coded lyrics that appealed to a large gay fan base. A supermodel played by Valerie Perrine and her roommate, an aspiring music producer, played by Steve Guttenberg, "discover" and make famous the musical group. Olympic gold medalist Bruce Jenner makes his screen début as a straight-laced lawyer who becomes Perrine's love interest. The plot of the film was of little importance, because the lavish musical scenes were the crux of the movie's appeal. The British company EMI Films produced the picture for a reported budget of $20 million: an estimated $13.8 million was spent on production and an additional $5 million on promotion.[218]

Walker seemed an odd choice for directing *Can't Stop the Music*. In 1979, when she was signed to the project, she was fifty-seven years old. She had been married to acting coach David Craig since 1951 (and would remain married to him until her death in 1992). The couple had one child. Profiles of her in the press emphasized her professionalism, busy work schedule, and dedication to her family. Nowhere did those articles mention weekend binges at Carr's parties. In fact, the press delighted in painting a picture of Walker and Craig as celebrity homebodies. "I don't like to be up later than 10 o'clock—well, 10:30 at the latest," she bragged to *The Advocate* in 1979. "When we arrive at a dinner party, somebody always shouts, 'Get the food on. It's eight o'clock and the Craigs go home at nine.' It's true—we do!"[219]

In addition, although Walker had extensive stage experience as a performer in musical theater in the 1940s and 1950s, as well as an understanding of actors, having been one for so many years, her directing experience was in three-camera sitcoms. Tom Buckley of the *New York Times* wondered why she was chosen as director of *Can't Stop the Music*: "If you were Allan Carr and you were looking for a director for 'Discoland' starring the Village People, whom would you be likely to choose? A young fellow, 30 years old tops, right, who had grown up in the rock world and then . . . segued into the even more fervid world of Studio 54 . . . Wrong. You pick Nancy Walker, whose career in show business dates back approximately to 'Blossom Time.'" Buckley's comments were snarky and ageist, but not entirely off the mark. In the same article, Walker confirmed her miscasting on the production when she admitted, "Rock [music], I've got to tell you, I don't get. I kind of shy away from it, in fact. I never understood the words, and from what I've read it's probably just as well."[220]

Indeed Walker was surprised by Carr's offer to direct her first feature. When he asked her, "Are you ready for a change of life?" she responded, "What do you mean, professionally or menopausally?"[221] To compensate for Walker's lack of experience directing musicals, choreographer Arlene Philips was asked to direct the musical-dance sections of the film, a codirecting strategy that was common in this genre.[222] Carr's biographer, Robert Hofler, suggests that the producer-promoter chose Walker to direct his elaborate production, which he wrote, produced, and created the publicity campaign for, because he needed someone he could, in turn, direct. At the time, the star and her manager were close, as was the nature of that business relationship. And the mature Walker brought professional experience and personal stability to an outlandish production, both of which Carr could benefit from: he required a director who would be both responsible and compliant.

For her part, Walker was well aware of the difficulties facing women who were nearing sixty years old in the business. Never considered a typical "beauty" by industry standards, the actress, who was four foot, eleven inches tall and had bright-red hair, was a comedic success on Broadway in the 1950s. During the 1960s she had experienced a career low point when she "couldn't get arrested. They had begun not writing vehicle shows, and I'm one of those ladies that if you give me a small part, it becomes a large part."[223] It was then that she got the idea to do television commercials; she excelled as the paper towel spokesperson, conveying trustworthiness with a quirky touch. Pressed by John Gruen of the *New York Times* as to whether she felt "bad doing commercials," she chirped, "Not at all. One minute's work done well is just as important as one hour. . . . I'm not cheating anybody. I mean, an artist is an artist no matter what he does."[224] The success of the commercial spots brought her to the attention of *The Mary Tyler Moore Show* and *McMillan & Wife*. Walker's ability and willingness to evolve as an entertainer, through reinvention across media content and platforms, kept her working. The chance to direct a feature film, even one whose subject was foreign and on which her creative authority would be controlled, was an opportunity not to be missed.

In the press, Walker was enthusiastic about making the year's most publicized musical dance film. She credited Carr with being the one to offer her a feature to direct. "Everyone said, 'why don't you do it' but nobody said 'on my time!' [referring to directing a movie]. 'Only Allan Carr said, 'let's do it,' and I can't believe how smoothly everything is going." She gushed about the dynamics on the set to the *Hollywood Reporter* in the fall of 1979. "We're all having a gorgeous love affair making the film," she said and then listed all the cast members to make sure her interview read like a press release.[225] Several months later after the movie was completed, in front of an audience at the AFI, Walker continued to describe the making of the film in her breezy manner: "It was offered to me as a first film. . . . I liked a lot of the script, and thought I could do something with it. It's an old-fashioned musical. In a sense, that it's kind of like, 'Hey, let's put on a show.' But it's done with some very attractive people who were fun to work with. Some I'd met before we started, some I hadn't. But it all turned out (whistles) very well, thank God."[226] For his biography of Carr, Hofler interviewed several principal cast and crew members who

Fig. 21. Nancy Walker directing *Can't Stop the Music* (Margaret Herrick Library, Academy of Motion Picture Arts and Sciences)

described a different situation on the set of *Can't Stop the Music*. Perrine recalled how by day four of the film shoot she and Walker were fighting. David Hodo, a member of the Village People, remembered Carr pulling the two women off the set and into his limousine where he threatened, "If you two cunts don't start getting along, I'm going to publish it in every magazine and newspaper in America."[227] Eventually, Carr had to separate the women: during Perrine's scenes, Walker could be seen off set watching *All My Children*.[228] The press sheets released by the film's distributor, Associated Film Distribution, covered up any sort of discontent by literally silencing the director. Instead, the material described how "Allan Carr was delighted with the fact that his director also knew how to get a film in the can on time. The diminutive Nancy worked so quietly on the set of 'Can't Stop the Music' that visitors were not certain who the director actually was. She speaks in a low-key voice and allowed her assistants to call out the orders to cast and crew." Perrine was quoted saying, "Being an actress herself, Nancy knew how to communicate with the minimum of confusion. She never wastes words."[229] Not being on set, Walker never had to.

By the time the film was released in 1980, disco had fallen out of fashion, and audience response to the movie was tepid. Fortunately, for Walker, reviewers did not seem to hold the director responsible for the flaws of the film. *Motion Picture Product Digest* offered support by suggesting that "Nancy Walker, the director, is the veteran performer of many a Broadway musical and she worked hard to cover up the weaknesses of 'Can't Stop the Music' by having all the actors and singers conduct themselves with unflagging energy."[230] It was clear to critics that this over-the-top film was Carr's creation and, subsequently, his responsibility. "Obviously Allan Carr is a genius, right?" exclaimed David Ansen of *Newsweek*. "Who else would have had the insight to put the Village People in the same movie? Who else would have hired comedienne Nancy Walker to direct 'the movie musical event of the '80s!'? Who else would have gotten Baskin-Robbins to name an ice-cream flavor after his movie?" Ansen's sarcasm was unconcealed when he declared, *Can't Stop the Music* "is the first all-singing, all-dancing horror film, the 'Dawn of the Dead' of the disco generation. If this movie doesn't scare you, you're already dead."[231]

After *Can't Stop the Music* had completed production, *Variety* reported that Allan Carr and EMI Films had signed Walker to a three-film, non-exclusive deal to direct future pictures. The "open-ended pact will have the femme director, one of the few active in the film arena, doing one pic for Carr, one for EMI, and one which Carr will produce for EMI," with Carr "culling through his numerous pix in various stages of development, looking for at least one musical and one comedy as possible projects for Walker" and gushing that "EMI wants her as badly as I do."[232] Yet Walker never directed another feature, and it is unclear what other projects she and Carr attempted to collaborate on after the poor reception of *Can't Stop the Music.*

In 1983, Walker was diagnosed with lung cancer and then had a hip replacement.[233] Once her health stabilized, she returned to television, where she directed a few episodes of the sitcom *Alice,* but mostly focused on her acting. At the time of her death from cancer in 1992, she was working on the Fox series *True Colors.* In interviews conducted some time after the film came out, Walker did not talk much about her experience on *Can't Stop the Music,* and it is unclear what relationship she and Carr had after the project was completed. However, at one of the movie's premieres, she appeared to have strong feelings, telling film critic Robert Osborne, "You think I'm sitting through this piece of shit again," before leaving the theater when the film started.[234]

## Lee Grant

> I don't think Elaine [May] and Barbara [Loden] are Women's Lib types. They're extraordinarily talented directors.
>
> —Lee Grant[235]

During the 1970s, Lee Grant claimed to have had no awareness of women directors' struggles to be hired or even that she might be interested in becoming a filmmaker: "It never entered my consciousness, because all I was was an actress and that's all I wanted to be."[236] Born in Manhattan in 1927 as Lyova Haskell Rosenthal, Lee Grant began her career as a child actress performing in the theater. As a young adult, she began appearing in films; in 1951 she was nominated for her first Academy Award for Best Supporting Actress in *Detective Story.* During the 1950s, she and her first husband Arnold Manoff were targeted by the House Un-American Activities Committee, and the couple was blacklisted from working in Hollywood. By the mid-1960s, Grant was able to clear her name, and her career began to flourish again in both television and film, with her performances earning many award nominations. In 1966 she won an Emmy for Best Supporting Actress in *Peyton Place,* and she received another for her performance in *The Neon Ceiling* in 1971. She was awarded an Oscar for Best Supporting Actress in 1976 for her role in *Shampoo.*

Grant's first directing job was in 1968 for the Actors Studio West in Los Angeles; she helmed the stage production *The Adventures of Jack and Max*. In 1972, while appearing on Broadway in Neil Simon's *The Prisoner of Second Avenue* opposite Peter Falk, Grant began making plans to direct the film *I'm Waiting*, written by Sam Reese and produced by her second husband Joe Feury. She told the *New York Times* that she was not giving up acting for directing, but "I'd be an idiot not to try to exercise the talent others think I have."[237] The project was never completed. In 1973 George Schlatter, known for creating *Laugh-In*, asked her to codirect the one-hour television special *The Shape of Things*, a comedy revue made for CBS that played on contemporary topics related to the women's movement. The offer came out of the blue. "George!" she exclaimed. "Get a hold of yourself! I've never directed anything. And a comedy show? Where are you coming from?"[238] It turned out to be a positive experience for her. Grant codirected the program with Carolyn Raskin, a producer for *Laugh-In*, who took care of the camera positions while she did the staging and worked with the actors. The show starred Phyllis Diller, Valerie Harper, Lynn Redgrave, Joan Rivers, and Brenda Vaccaro. Grant also appeared in the cast and was nominated for an Emmy for her performance. The *Los Angeles Times* noted that it was the first time two women codirected a major television special.[239] Journalist Mary Murphy joked that Grant "became the first woman to direct a prime-time entertainment special with hot rollers in her hair."[240]

In 1974 Jan Haag, from the AFI's Directing Workshop for Women, called the actress, asking her for recommendations of possible candidates for the program's pilot year.[241] Grant thought, "Why not me?"[242] The DWW turned out to be an important experience for her. Although the program's first year was disparaged by critics who disagreed with Haag's decision to choose only high-profile women in the industry as a way to generate press and instill confidence in potential employers familiar with their "celebrity" reputations, Grant benefited from the chance to practice the craft of filmmaking. "I love this workshop," she said in an interview in 1974, "even if we are being given equipment that is one step above Mickey Mouse."[243] Grant's short film *The Stronger*, based on August Strindberg's one-act play, screened at festivals and won an award at the Chicago Film Festival.[244]

The years 1977 and 1978 were pivotal for Grant. Beginning to think more seriously about directing, Grant had developed a screenplay based on another play by Strindberg. She started raising money for the film in which she cast Max Schell, Anjelica Huston, Carol Kane, and Richard Jordon. During rehearsals she received a call that the financing had fallen through.[245] Needing to work, Grant took roles in a series of big-budget exploitation films: *Airport '77*, *The Swarm*, and *Damien: Omen II* (1978). These movies had action or horror plots and large casts filled with a range of older Hollywood luminaries; for example, in *The Swarm* Grant appeared with José Ferrer, Henry Fonda, and Olivia de Havilland. In her autobiography, *I Said Yes to Everything*, she explained, "To keep making a living, you have to say yes to second-rate films but try your best to do first-rate work, and it's possible."[246] While this kind of work paid the bills, Grant realized that her desirability—and bankability—as an actress was diminishing by industry standards. "I could no longer get away with looking young and beautiful," she wrote. "The train was coming. I was on the tracks. My age was showing. . . . I either had to move to older character parts or concentrate on a new career."[247] Directing was her lifeboat.

*Tell Me a Riddle* was a Godmother Production, a San Francisco Bay Area producing team made up of the "Godmothers," three women in their late twenties: Mindy Affrime, Rachel Lyon, and Susan O'Connell. *Riddle*, based on a story by Tillie Olsen, was their first feature film. Melvyn Douglas and Lila Kedrova starred as an older couple grappling with their almost fifty-year marriage and the realities of aging. Independently financed, the project took two years to put together while the producers raised money from several individual investors. Eventually, Saul Zaentz and Michael Rosenberg of Fantasy Films also became producers on the film, and the movie was made for an estimated $1.5 million.[248] A male director under consideration for the film had recommended Grant to the "Godmothers." She was interested in the film for personal reasons: the husband and wife were Russian Jewish immigrants, similar to Grant's family. "It was about people I cared about. It was about my roots . . . and it had all the intimations of the politics which interested me."[249]

Janet Maslin of the *New York Times* described the film as "a slow, restrained, dignified effort." The critic noted both the movie's touching qualities and its persuasive sentimentality, advising, "If you bring the right sad baggage to it, you may be deeply moved; if you resent being

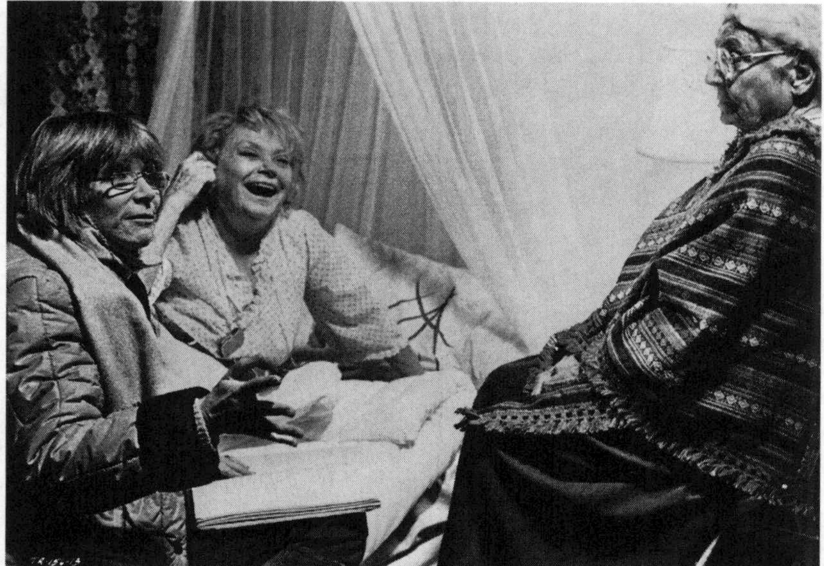

Fig. 22. Lee Grant, Lila Kedrova, and Lili Valenty on the set of *Tell Me a Riddle* (Margaret Herrick Library, Academy of Motion Picture Arts and Sciences)

manipulated, you may be moved in quite another direction."[250] In contrast, Kevin Thomas of the *Los Angeles Times* was impressed by the film's honest depiction of old age and death, particularly in "this era of mega-million hardware and special effects movies." Thomas was moved not only by the performances of veteran actors Douglas and Kedrova but also the film's effective visual sensibility. "It's not a surprise that a fine actress can elicit extraordinary portrayals from her cast," acknowledging Grant's capabilities, "but 'Tell Me a Riddle's' power is not only in its performances but in its images. . . . Grant and [cinematographer] Fred Murphy dare to hold an image long enough to establish a sense of place and mood." For Thomas the movie was powerful in its ability to tell "the truth about what it is like to grow old in America."[251]

Grant enjoyed working with the actors and her cinematographer on *Riddle,* but ultimately what she realized on her first feature was that she only wanted to make movies about things she really cared about: "I tell you, it was a lot of work. When you're acting you do your thing and go home. As director your day never seems to end. I was permanently exhausted" [on *Riddle*].[252] In a 2008 interview, Grant recalled that during the editing stage of the film she and the producers were battling each other over the final product: "Here were these three young women, so passionate that they raised the money to do *Tell Me Riddle* and the only chance they got to put in their two cents was after filming. So they wanted to fight for *their thing*, but by this time this was something I had given birth to."[253] She laughed while reminiscing, but the experience seemed to have given her clarity about how to choose future projects. In 1980 she told Rodrick Mann of the *Los Angeles Times*, "Understand, I'm not gung-ho on directing. I could only do something that really interested me."[254]

While waiting for the "Godmothers" to raise money for *Riddle*, Grant made her first documentary, *The Wilmar 8* (1981), about a group of women in Minnesota protesting job discrimination at the bank they worked for; in 1984 Grant would direct the television movie adaptation of the documentary that aired on NBC. It was this experience that informed the majority of the director's subsequent work. After *Riddle*, her career as a director was primarily of documentaries (for television) and television movies with strong social themes. In these formats she was prolific and successful. In 1986 her HBO documentary, *Down and Out in America*, won an Academy Award for Best Documentary Feature. Grant also continued to act in film and television through the early years of the twenty-first century. She was hired to direct two feature films, *Staying Together* in 1989 and an unfinished Bruce Willis movie called *Broadway Brawler* in 1997, but was fired from both. In her defense she claimed to have had difficulties with the male actors, in particular Willis, who was a big star at the time. "I have such an antipathy to star stuff," she explained. "He was taking his jet out every weekend to fuck somebody . . . and something in me turned off."[255]

In his book, *The Gross: The Hits, the Flops—the Summer That Ate Hollywood*, former editor-in-chief of *Variety* and former studio executive Peter Bart describes the production's problems in a similar way. Compared to the blockbuster action films Willis was known for, *Broadway Brawler* was a small independent movie. Three weeks into the filming the star was displeased with the footage and wanted to pull out of the project: because he was Bruce Willis, the production closed down.[256] Again, in 2008, Grant was candid and introspective about her experiences on both projects and what she saw as her weakness in directing stars, particularly male movie stars:

> I think I saw that I wasn't meant to be there [on a Hollywood feature film], I couldn't deal with stars and I could not deal with production companies. As an actress I was a diva. I am. As an actress you have everything going your way—everyone wants you to feel comfortable and happy in order for you to do your job. And you're spoiled. I carry that with me as a director. When I feel that I can't work with somebody, when their work is so off-putting to me, all the things that are not good director qualities come up in me.[257]

Lee's assessment that her "diva" qualities as an actress got in the way of her directing the two features she was fired from may be correct. However, her prolific career making documentaries and television movies suggests that she was capable of maintaining her "good director qualities" in the many varied situations that arise during production. Thus, her "failure" on those projects may have been due to their particular circumstances rather than her inability to make feature films. After the disappointing experience on the Willis project, Grant continued directing movies and documentaries for television with much success. This actress's realization that directing was her next career—and that she could find a place for herself not only in television but also with programming that reflected her interest in sociopolitical topics—was, as Grant put it, "another rock in the rapids I could jump to. Not only could, but wanted to. Needed to. A director was born."[258]

In an interview with *Playgirl* magazine in 1977, Joan Rivers, in her devil-may-care way, pontificated on the status of women's liberation. "I never ever thought that I couldn't get where I wanted to get being a woman," she said with cheeky confidence. "And I realize, of course, that in the past there were tremendous limitations. But now, I think, it's a great advantage to be a woman. Four years ago you were hot to be Black, two years ago you were hot to be Puerto Rican—in 1977 it's got to be the obligatory woman."[259] Rivers's speculation on the advantages of being a woman, in Hollywood at least, might have been more crass than they were accurate, but the comedian was perceptive of the slight changes taking place. As the decade waned, the film industry could no longer explain away the existence of women directors as a novelty or a fluke. Their numbers were small but growing; their ranks included industry newcomers and veteran stars. Feminism was an established political movement, and

Gloria Steinem was a household name. Hollywood responded by emphasizing gender as an opportunity *and* a form of containment, and women directors worked hard to make the best of complicated options. Where had the Directors Guild of America, the most powerful labor union in the industry, been during these years? A small group of women wanted to know, and before the 1970s could close there would be one more revolution.

# 4

# Radicalizing the Directors Guild of America

The Directors Guild of America sat out the social activism of the 1960s and would have come close to doing the same during the 1970s if it had not been for the efforts of six of its women members: Susan Bay, Nell Cox, Joelle Dobrow, Dolores Ferraro, Victoria Hochberg, and Lynne Littman. In 1979 this small group of women established the DGA's Women's Steering Committee (WSC)[1] and spearheaded an effort not only to change the sexist hiring practices rampant throughout the film and television industries but also to confront the patriarchal culture of the Directors Guild itself.

According to its website, the mission of the Directors Guild is to protect the "economic and creative rights of directors and members of the directorial team"—including unit production managers, first and second assistant directors, associate directors, stage managers, and production assistants—working in all formats of film, television, and, in the contemporary landscape, new media.[2] To realize this mission, the Directors Guild—also known as a labor organization and labor union—performs two main functions: it negotiates industry-wide collective bargaining contracts and enforces its Basic Agreement (BA) that protects its members when working for companies that are signatories of the union's labor contract (production companies, television networks, and motion picture studios).[3] Under the terms of the BA, Guild members, according to their job categories, are afforded certain rights and benefits regarding screen credits, working conditions, creative control of the filmmaking process, pay scale, residuals, and pensions.[4] In the final years of the 1970s and into the early 1980s, feminist activism internal to the union radicalized the Directors Guild, the most prestigious labor organization in the entertainment industry whose power, status, and domination by its white male members had previously allowed it to exist outside of societal politics and employment justice issues. Continuing the investigation of workplace inclusion instigated by the EEOC in 1969, and completing the trajectory of hard-line activism begun by the women of the Writers and Screen Actors Guilds during the early 1970s, for a brief moment the DGA was the leading advocate for antidiscrimination labor policies in Hollywood. Positioned at the forefront of this fight, the Directors Guild experienced its own paradox of progress: it was arguably the only institution in the industry during this period with the stature to fight sexism and racism experienced by directors and yet simultaneously was a body of power built on those very systems of workplace exclusion.

The Screen Directors Guild, which later became the Directors Guild of America, was founded in 1936 by thirteen men who had banded together with the goal of protecting their financial worth and creative authority in Hollywood during a time when their status felt increasingly vulnerable. Threatened by the growing power of studio executives to control directors' salaries and creative output, the founding members followed the model of the Screen Actors Guild and the Screen Writers Guild—both established in 1933—and organized their own union. Among the founders were Hollywood's top directors, including Howard Hawks, Henry King, Lewis Milestone, Rouben Mamoulian, King Vidor, and William A. Wellman.[5] In an interview conducted in 1985, Mamoulian, then one of the last surviving founders, explained that the Guild was created not just to protect the salaries of the wealthiest filmmakers but also to safeguard those who were not as powerful, both financially and creatively, within the studio system. Mamoulian emphasized that the founders were motivated by more than just money: "The ultimate purpose was better films. We were thinking about the quality of films. The director who has no authority and gets a very miserable little salary cannot do what his idea of film is. Therefore, we felt that it was elevating the quality of films."[6]

As discussed in the introduction, by the early 1930s, the number of women directors had diminished significantly since the silent era when a considerable number were making films. In 1938 Dorothy Arzner, as the only woman director then working in Hollywood, became the Directors Guild's first female member in the director category; in 1950 Ida Lupino became its second.[7] The year 1960 saw the Guild's largest influx of female membership: one production assistant, nine associate directors, and eight television directors became members then.[8] In 1967 Shirley Clarke joined, becoming the DGA's third female feature film director. She had never directed a union film and must have joined when her aspirations turned toward Hollywood.[9] Elaine May, as the first woman to direct a studio film since Lupino in 1966, became the fourth woman in the feature film category, joining in 1969.[10] As this short list of women feature directors demonstrates, the Directors Guild was a "boys club" of the most exclusive kind. Its founding *fathers* were many of the industry's wealthiest and most powerful employees, and they established the organization to protect their creative and financial dominance. Key to sustaining their power was maintaining the patriarchy in which it originated and flourished. This mode of operation continued to thrive unchecked for more than forty years.

Between 1971 and 1973, the SAG and the WGA both established Women's Committees through which each guild's female membership found a platform to voice their criticism of the industry's imbalanced employment practices. Both committees collected employment statistics, on a regular basis, that they released to the press, exposing which production companies, studios, networks, and individual television shows failed to hire women writers and, in the case of actresses, pigeonholed performers into demeaning or secondary roles. These guilds mobilized across venues in their attempt to build an industry-wide feminist reform movement that would affect above- and below-the-line female employees. Present at many of these meetings were women members of the Directors Guild.[11]

In 1974 *Variety* reported that the DGA had formed a "women's committee," "a special wing . . . to draw public attention to their creative presence in the film and tv [*sic*] fields."[12] At this time, organizing efforts within the Directors Guild against sexist hiring practices were still in their nascent stages. Giovanna Nigro-Chacon was one of a small group of women speaking up about the difficulties they were encountering getting work that they were qualified for and questioning what role their Guild—one of the most powerful and prestigious unions in the industry—played in their professional lives. Originally from New Jersey, Nigro-Chacon had been one of three women out of a class of sixty-three to graduate from New York University's film department in the early 1960s. Working then in New York, she joined the DGA on the East Coast in 1971 as a director of news for NBC. Nigro-Chacon moved to Los Angeles in 1974, feeling confident that, as an accomplished writer-producer-director of nonfiction television with extensive technical training, she would have no difficulty getting work after relocating to the West Coast. Nigro-Chacon, however, found that the men in charge of hiring held a strong degree of animosity toward the small yet slowly growing influx of women who were making inroads into the industry. She also learned how the DGA reinforced those sexist attitudes by imposing its own set of obstacles on its female members.

The New York and Los Angeles branches of the Directors Guild were part of the same national union, but they had only merged in 1960, and the transition to a united Guild was not always smooth.[13] Historically the New York-based Radio & Television Directors Guild represented those working in television, and the Los Angeles-based Screen Directors Guild, those in film. By the 1970s, in regard to television, New York-DGA represented more television news members, while Los Angeles-DGA represented those working in sitcom and episodic series. Geographical separation created a cultural divide that reinforced an already existing gender prejudice. The Los Angeles-DGA told Nigro-Chacon that she would have to join the union as an assistant director (AD), and not in the director category she was in as a member of the New York-DGA. But she could only join the union in that category if she already had a job as an AD. The catch was that, to be hired as an AD, she needed to be a member of the union in that category and to have worked a certain amount of hours. "You can't get in," the Los Angeles-DGA told her. "You have to be an assistant director." She recalled, "They made me wait six months." Nigro-Chacon described the exchange: "'If you have a job [you can get in].' I said: 'Why don't I get into the [DGA Assistant Director Training Program].' 'No. You can't do that. You don't have the background.' That's when it started; *then* I knew there was something not right."[14]

In 1974 the 163 female Guild members made up 3.9 percent of its total membership of 4,127.[15] This low percentage was evidence of a twofold problem facing women working in DGA categories. Because the union made it difficult for women to become members of the Guild, there was only a small pool of eligible female employees among union crews to hire from. By keeping the numbers low, the Guild helped maintain a primarily male workforce and in doing so perpetuated sexist attitudes that women should not work in film and television production because they lacked the skills or were biologically unsuited for such employment. Nigro-Chacon was vocal about the DGA's role in preventing its female members from getting jobs. "I was always an agitator," she said in a 2012 interview, describing herself in the 1970s. "I said [to a small group of women]: 'We've got to sue the Guild. That's the only way it's going to happen for us. *We have to sue the Guild*. It's a class action suit.'"[16] But her peers, already finding it difficult to obtain work, were worried about being seen as troublemakers, so no aggressive organizing took place.

In 1974 the scarcity of female members at the Los Angeles-DGA meetings was notable. "You'd go to those Directors Guild meetings there's like sprinklings of [women]," remembered Nigro-Chacon. "I said, 'We've got to get together.'"[17] On behalf of a small group of women, she presented to the all-male Directors Council (a council of elected members representing the Guild's director category) and to Robert Wise, who at the time was DGA president, the idea of a Women's Steering Committee to "explore ways of getting work." Nigro-Chacon remembers Wise and film director Richard Donner being supportive of the women's concerns, but many of the other men in the meeting "just sat back." After telling her to leave the room while they voted, this group of voting members approved a Women's Committee. However, its original mandate was only to organize a tribute event for seventy-four-year-old veteran director Dorothy Arzner.[18] Nevertheless it was through this focus on history, on early Hollywood, that the first glimmer of a contemporary feminist consciousness began to manifest at the Directors Guild.

## The Directors Guild Gets a History Lesson

Between 1973 and 1975 women DGA members were initiating conversations about their status within the Guild and the industry. In 1973 the

July–August issue of the DGA magazine *Action*, which was available both to the public *and* Guild members, was dedicated to a "Special Report: The Woman Director." The issue used historical subject matter—women directors of the past and the exclusion of their accomplishments from film studies—to imply a correlation with the working conditions of contemporary directors. Documentarian and Guild member Francine Parker wrote lengthy profiles on the DGA's most accomplished female directors to date—Dorothy Arzner and Ida Lupino. Nancy Dowd, who would go on to become an Academy Award-winning screenwriter and at the time was not a member of the DGA, authored a comprehensive overview of women directors during the silent era.[19] Alongside attention paid to the past, the details of the present were accounted for in brief, innocuous statements.

The quarter-page introduction (written by an uncredited author, but presumably Dowd or Parker) to the special issue reminded readers that the role of director has been male dominated for most of film history, but in 1973 "that is changing."[20] It also included a quote from Alice Guy, made in the early twentieth century, declaring that directing is "more natural to a woman than to a man."[21] Noting that the Guild's female membership was growing in all positions—especially in television in the roles of director and first and second assistant director—the introduction did not provide any details that would quantify this "change," such as statistical breakdowns or names of contemporary DGA members, nor did it provide a broader analysis of Hollywood's inherently patriarchal system.

In 1973 the Directors Guild, and even its most outspoken feminist constituents, found the relationship between the Guild and its women members to be uncharted territory. Parker and Dowd, two politically outspoken filmmakers (having just completed the antiwar documentary *F.T.A*, which Parker directed and for which Dowd was one of its several screenwriters), strategically embedded in their study of the past a commentary on the status of contemporary women directors. As a "history lesson" the special issue of *Action* provided an education for the majority of members who were unaware of the legacy of women directors. In her overview, Dowd wrote, "Hopefully, future histories will deal more accurately with the contributions of women to the art of the motion picture. Their work has been substantial and significant, and, with the growing awareness that the female point of view is worthy of attention, women film makers will be proving their art more and more."[22] She thus used the inequities of the past to highlight how the future would demand something different.

Influenced by the feminist buzz within the industry that was beginning to surface among its own members in 1974, DGA president Robert Wise, in his editorial "Directors Guild Broadens Scope," in *Variety's 41st Anniversary Issue*, asserted that "in 'The New Hollywood' . . . , the Directors Guild of America has grown and diversified."[23] The article foregrounded the union's growing female presence in the Guild: Wise cited the low figure of 163 women of a total membership of 4,127 as an indication of progress, marking it as an improvement from recent history when Arzner and Lupino had been the only working women directors in Hollywood. "Now with Liberation, women are steadily acquiring membership in the DGA, not just as directors but also as assistants and associates," he reported. Yet six more years would pass before the DGA, a latecomer to feminism, would be positioned as the movement's loudest advocate in Hollywood.

## Directors Guild Membership: Professional Legitimacy and Industry Backlash

As the Guild representing holders of the most powerful and revered position on a film set—and by extension the film industry—membership in the Directors Guild was proof not only of an individual's professional excellence but also of his or her acceptance to a privileged sector of Hollywood. To become a member of the DGA meant a director was validated through his or her representation by such an esteemed organization. "It was the most thrilling thing that ever happened. I wanted to be a member of the Directors Guild. I remember taking the papers in my hand [to the Guild]. It was an honor," recalled Lynne Littman. "It was about legitimacy."[24] Littman joined the DGA as a director in 1974–1975 while working as a director-producer for a weekly news series on KCET, Los Angeles. She would go on to win an Academy Award in 1977 for her documentary *Number Our Days*, and in 1983 she directed the feature film *Testament* for Paramount Pictures.

Similar to Littman, Joelle Dobrow considered becoming a member of the DGA a measure of professional "legitimacy," an acknowledgment by the establishment that she had officially become part of the industry elite: "When I joined the DGA, it was a thrill for me. It was like the pantheon of Hollywood." Dobrow became a member of the Guild in 1973–1974, first in the stage manager category and then as an associate director (AD), while working at KABC's morning show *AM Los Angeles* as KABC's first female AD/stage manager. In 1977 Dobrow would begin to direct Rona Barrett's West Coast segments of *Good Morning America*.[25]

Becoming a member of the DGA "meant you were not a man's assistant anymore," explained Victoria Hochberg, who had joined the Guild in 1971 while working as an editor for the PBS series *American Playhouse* at WNET in New York. "We had become real professionals."[26] To compensate for the inexperience of the male theater director hired by the series to adapt live productions for broadcast, Hochberg was asked by her supervisor to rewrite the play's script into a screenplay format while also creating a shot list under the guise of "helping" herself in the edit room—both tasks were the responsibility of a show's director, not the editor. When it came time to assign credits, her boss Jac Venza acknowledged her work as a "codirector." PBS, which had recently become a signatory of the DGA, attempted to follow through by giving Hochberg the appropriate screen recognition, but the Directors Guild, which balked at codirecting credits, rejected that title. Instead she initially joined the union in the Assistant Director category.

Women directors during the early 1970s were acutely aware of the gender inequities within the industry and how joining the DGA meant an elevation in their professional status that would presumably offer protection from the sexism they experienced as females employees. Once they joined, however, female members of Hollywood's most prestigious Guild began to understand that the organization's elitism was based not only on the craft it represented but also on the gender exclusion it perpetuated. For example, as Dobrow recalled, "I was scared to go alone. I had my roommate go with me. When I walked in [to attend a screening] I would be the only woman who had my own card. All the other women there were wives, girlfriends, mistresses."[27] In 1967–1968, only 0.99 percent of female DGA members were directors (twenty women).[28] In 1974–1975, that figure had increased to 1.54 percent (forty-six women), but only three of them—Clarke, Lupino, and May—were feature film directors.[29] The others were directors of television—not only of episodic programs but also of news (many in local news), live shows, and special televised events—and directors of educational and industrial films. The feminist movement produced for Hollywood a first generation of young women who were ascending the employment ranks and breaking out of jobs traditionally coded as female (assistants, secretaries, script supervisors), all the while Hollywood continued to maintain its patriarchal hierarchy. Resistant to and incredulous at the very idea of a woman director, the membership office initially listed *Victoria Hochberg* as *Victor A. Hochberg* when she joined.

Nell Cox, a New York-based documentary and independent filmmaker, had moved to Los Angeles in 1976–1977 to pursue a career in feature films and episodic television only to realize that there were hardly any women directors in Hollywood. In New York, being a woman had never overtly harmed Cox's career. She had moved there in 1959 while in her early twenties and was soon hired as an assistant editor for Drew Associates, then a subsidiary of Time Life Broadcast. Working with D. A. Pennebaker and Richard (Ricky) Leacock throughout the 1960s, she became part of the New York City cinema verité and direct cinema community. In this style of filmmaking, the division of labor on a crew was not rigidly defined within the traditional film production hierarchy. Like her colleagues, Cox held multiple positions on any one project, including editor and soundperson. "That was the theory," explained Cox of her formative years. "You go out in the field and then come back and edit. There was none of this divide and conquer; you go out and make your whole film, you weren't just the cameraperson."[30] The combination of positive professional relationships with male mentors and the fluidity between the crew positions created a work environment that was only occasionally sexist. Putting into a wider context her experience working with these men, in particular Leacock with whom she collaborated on several projects, Cox explained, "I think the glass ceiling doesn't kick in until you get to the ceiling. Or higher up. So as long as I was working to help them make movies, I didn't experience [the glass ceiling]. They were always hiring me, that's the main thing."[31]

After Cox moved to Los Angeles, her work experience changed drastically from that in New York, in which she enjoyed steady employment on an egalitarian production team. In 1969, with Leacock's encouragement, Cox applied for and received a $10,000 American Film Institute

Independent Filmmakers grant (similar to the grants received by Karen Arthur and Claudia Weill) to make *A to B*, a half-hour fictional film that she wrote and directed. Filmed in her home state of Kentucky with a skeleton crew—she was joined by Robert Leacock (Ricky's son) as soundperson, Peter Powell as cinematographer, and her sister, Mary Nash Cox—the short served as her Hollywood calling card for fictional content. The strategy was successful. In 1976 Cox was chosen to be part of the KCET series *Visions*, at the time led by executive producer Barbara Schultz, whose mission was to enlarge the pool of potential directors in Hollywood by giving them opportunities to produce feature films for broadcast on Los Angeles's local PBS station. Cox wrote, produced, and directed the feminist-themed Western *Liza's Pioneer Diary* (1977), a ninety-minute period piece shot on location in New Mexico for a total budget of $191,000. Nominated for Best Writing by the Television Critics' Circle, the film lost out to the epic television miniseries *Roots*.[32] Yet encouraged by the recognition given her feature film and armed with an extensive resume in documentary film, Cox was hopeful that her entry into Hollywood would be smooth. She recalled, "I took out a full page ad with a photo of me and the glowing reviews in the *Hollywood Reporter* and *Variety*. 'Here I am, call my agent!' No one responded."[33]

Sometime in 1977, Women in Film, an organization dedicated to creating networking opportunities for a membership comprised of accomplished above-the-line women working in the industry, asked Cox to set up a group for directors. Susan Bay, Dolores Ferraro, Joelle Dobrow, Lynne Littman, and Victoria Hochberg became part of this informal group. All of them were highly qualified, with ample professional experience that had received the highest industry accolades, but none could get hired for the job they were trained to do: direct commercial film and television. "It was awful," recalled Cox of their meetings. "We would sit around and someone would say: 'I went to CBS and they were so rude to me and this guy said, yeah, if you sit here for a year as an intern without pay we *might* think of hiring you.' And everyone would come in with these distressing stories and we would just sit and cluck at each other about how horrible it was." Cox remembered standing up at one of those meetings and saying, "We are all doomed to stunted careers if we don't get our act together."[34]

Initially, no one in the group wanted to admit to a room full of their peers that she was not working. Eventually, prompted by the outpouring of shared horror stories about not getting hired, they confessed. "We all looked at each other," recalled Hochberg. "*I'll never forget that.* Somehow it happened that night, maybe it was Nell who started asking: 'Are you working? No. Are you working? No.' And it was like: 'What? Unbelievable. We have to get together and talk about this.'"[35]

This group of women had come of age during the civil rights, antiwar, and feminist movements. Some had participated in consciousness-raising groups, and others had been involved in the feminist reform efforts that took place in the entertainment industry earlier in the decade. Dobrow, who came from a family of union organizers, was a member and on the board of Women in Film "when they were still an organization that was happening out of someone's garage"[36]; she had also been a leader in KABC's internal group, ABC Women, which was organized "to make the industry more responsible to women in the areas of programming and job opportunities."[37] Several had worked on projects that reflected these social values. Cox had made the critically acclaimed female Western *Liza's Pioneer Diary*; Hochberg had directed the documentary *A Simple Matter of Justice* (1978) about the Equal Rights Amendment and had been nominated for an Emmy for her work as director for the segment "The Right to Die" (1974) on the ABC News program *Close Up* about patient rights; and Littman's documentary, *Number Our Days*, a portrait of Eastern European Jewish senior citizens living in Venice, California, won an Academy Award in 1976. By 1979, as they shared the epiphany of themselves as Hollywood pariahs, embedded in their personal and professional lives were a commitment to social justice and the fortitude required to fight for their civil rights in the workplace. Key to their mobilizing was the realization that they were members of the Directors Guild. Entrance into the organization they each held with such esteem had validated what they understood to be their place among the highest echelon of industry employees. As their union, what responsibility did the DGA have in helping rectify the groups' unemployment status? As members of the most prestigious guild in the industry, why were these women even in this situation?

The women then approached DGA national executive secretary, Michael Franklin—who would become the group's most important ally—with their concerns and a proposal to conduct research on the employment patterns of women directors. In April 1979, the Guild approved this research plan, and in May 1979 a letter sent to the entire membership from the Directors Guild's national office and signed by "the DGA Women's Committee" announced, "We are reactivating the DGA Women's Committee. We are concerned that women members are underemployed. We are equally convinced that we can help each other do something about this."[38]

This small group of DGA women then undertook a similar course of action to that of the Writers Guild Women's Committee in the early 1970s. The group's initial "Chores and Statistics to Collect" to-do list ranged from the basic task of finding out how many women were DGA members and gathering their contact information, to calculating how many women were hired to direct each type of format for television networks and film studios.[39] While it was clear to them that their inability to get hired was due to discrimination, to construct an argument in their defense—to whom they did not yet know—the group needed to track the patterns and sources of bias. Statistics would not only provide hard evidence of the imbalance but would also identify the offenders.

A key supporter in this effort was Harry Evans, who at the time was the DGA's assistant executive secretary after having served as its "field representative, charged with enforcing the new film contract provisions."[40] Evans had close to twenty years' experience as a union organizer and contract negotiator, having previously worked for the United Auto Workers and the AFL-CIO State, County and Municipal Workers. Described by the women as an "old time labor guy," Evans saw their situation as a labor issue, rather than just gender discrimination: they were qualified members of the union and the industry and were being denied the right to work. For him it was an obvious choice to help them build their case by giving the group access to the necessary documents. And so he provided Dobrow and Hochberg the deal memos each production company was required to submit to the DGA: these short-term contracts were mandatory for every television episode and feature film and listed the director's fee and residual payments. Having just recently computerized its record system, at the time the Guild was still filing these memos in paper format.[41]

For close to a year, Bay, Cox, Dobrow, Ferraro, Hochberg, and Littman delegated research assignments. This effort was part of the new Women's Steering Committee, but they operated on a "do-it-yourself basis," with no official budget provided by the Directors Guild except for a small stipend and limited access to office supplies and meeting spaces. Dobrow noted that "all writing, planning, research, evaluation, coordination and typing [was] done by the committee."[42] Their synchronicity with one another was superb. Thirty-three years later, she described the group as "some of the most brilliant women I've ever met in my entire life. After my contact with [them], nothing—*nothing*—compared. And it meant so much to me. We had a shared vision and a shared goal." Hochberg remembered how compatible each of their skill sets were: "There was *never* an argument. Everybody understood what each person was good at, and we were each good at different things." "And there was no ego," echoed Littman.[43] What is important to emphasize in Dobrow, Hochberg, and Littman's descriptions of their experience as part of this group in the late 1970s is that the camaraderie described by them dispels the common stereotype that women cannot work together because they are too competitive with one another—and, specifically, that in the entertainment industry during this period there were so few opportunities for women that everyone was out for herself. Many individuals interviewed for this project did describe encountering other women in their field who did not extend common professional courtesy to them because they were threatened by having a female coworker. In contrast, these six women, as a disenfranchised group, knew that one of their most powerful assets was to join together as women, to represent women. Their success in working together came from a shared and profound level of commitment and compatibility in their skills and worldview.

The group's ability to rotate leadership and delegate responsibilities, making adjustments when somebody got too busy with other obligations, enabled the team to plan and execute a massive research project: the first of its kind that both focused on women directors and was completed under the auspices of the Directors Guild. It tracked the employment history of women directors working in feature films and prime-time dramatic television over thirty years, from 1949–1979. Some combed through the deal memos attempting to confirm the gender of directors hired on more recent productions. To find comparable information on older shows and movies, others fanned out to the Margaret Herrick Library at the Academy of Motion Picture Arts and Sciences, where they scoured industry trade papers for any mention of a woman director. In a memo summarizing the early work of the WSC and its approach to finding evidence of employment bias, Dobrow wrote, "Eight months, several hundred woman-hours later the DGA statistical packet on hiring trends in the industry was finished. The data unequivocally proved discrimination."[44]

The group found that between 1949 and July 1979 the major distribution companies released 7,332 films, of which seven women directed 14, or 0.19 percent.[45] The comparable statistics for television were that twenty-two women directed 115 of approximately 65,500 hours of prime-time dramatic broadcasting. Of that 115, an estimated 35 hours were directed by Ida Lupino; of the eighteen women who directed episodic programs, six were also the producer and/or star of the series (e.g., Lucille Ball, Penny Marshall, Mary Tyler Moore, and Meta Rosenberg).[46] Largely unaccounted for were those women (and men) who directed live television such as sports shows, talk shows, political conventions, telethons, because deal memos for this kind of programming did not yet exist.

The statistical data confirmed the reality that the group was experiencing: women, specifically female DGA members, were not being hired to direct feature films or work in network television. However, it was still unclear who was responsible for the severe employment inequalities. Was it the Guild specifically or the industry as a whole? Undecided as to what their next move should be, the women consulted with lawyers A. Thomas Hunt and Walter Cochran-Bond, attorneys accomplished in class action and antidiscrimination suits, who at the time were working at the Center for Law and the Public Interest. These attorneys urged the group to ally themselves with the DGA. On their own they would have no muscle against the industry, but represented by one of the most powerful unions in Hollywood, their struggle would become the Directors Guild's fight on behalf of its female members.

While convinced that asking the DGA to be their advocate was the best tactic, the women still had reservations about their union's willingness to campaign on their behalf. Echoing the earlier experience cited by Dobrow, Hochberg remembered the realization she had had at the first DGA meeting she attended in 1977 at the Beverly Hills Hilton: "There were me and three other women. I'll never forget this. And I went into the lobby and called a friend and said, 'I'm never going to be able to do this here. They'll never let me in. They'll *never let me in*.' It was not because of the producers it was because of the *D—G—A*."[47] While

Joan Tewkesbury had encountered sexism during this time as something "you could never quite address because it was never overt, but there was this Chinese Wall," Hochberg, at the DGA meeting in 1977, was struck by the clear evidence of gender discrimination as she entered a crowded DGA meeting room with only three women in attendance. White men dominated the Directors Guild membership, executive staff, and board of directors. What made the experience of the six women organizing within their union during the late 1970s different from that of the sixteen women making feature films throughout this decade was their membership in a Guild that had this mission: to protect its constituencies' employment rights (contractually enforced by the DGA's Basic Agreement). If its female members were experiencing discrimination in the workplace it was the Directors Guild's responsibility to advocate on their behalf. If the Directors Guild itself appeared to have a gender imbalance, by these same guidelines, it was obligated to take seriously its members' needs and concerns. In contrast, outside of the DGA, Barbara Peeters and Stephanie Rothman, working on non-union productions, had no choice but to comply with the demands of the exploitation market. Joan Darling, celebrated as a "woman director," was exploited by the studio because of her minority status and as a first-time director was unaware of her rights as a DGA member. Claudia Weill had to choose between enduring sexual harassment on set or losing a "hostile battle," a situation that had no precedent yet established of confrontation or recourse, and therefore it was too risky for the filmmaker to ask the Directors Guild to mediate on her behalf.

## Hollywood Feminist: Michael Franklin

A year later, in 1980, the women were armed with statistics and had formulated a plan of action based on guidance from their lawyers. However, they needed someone in a position of power at the DGA who would partner with them not only internally within the Guild but also publicly as their industry representative. That partner would be Michael Franklin. It "struck me, the amount of research [the group] had done. They laid it out very clearly that women were discriminated against," remembered Michael Franklin.[48] He quickly understood the importance of making the women's struggle the DGA's fight.

A Los Angeles native, Michael Franklin had graduated from UCLA in 1948 and received his law degree from USC in 1951, after which he worked as an attorney for CBS-TV and Paramount Pictures. From 1958–1977, Franklin was the national director of the Writers Guild before becoming the national executive secretary of the Directors Guild in 1978.[49] This was a surprising career move considering the adversarial relationship between the two guilds. Franklin had been at the forefront of a particularly heated clash between writers and directors over the "possessory" credit in 1967–1968 and again in 1977 shortly before he left the WGA to assume his post at the DGA. The dispute centered on screenwriters' argument that credits such as "A Film by . . ." suggested the director was sole author of a film, failing to acknowledge the essential role of the writer in creating the source material. In response, directors asserted that they were entitled to top billing because ultimately they were responsible for all aspects of a film required to transform the script into its final product. The DGA accused the writers of "eroding the role of the director." "When I go on the stage, for better or worse I am the boss," explained Directors Guild member Ronald Neame. "If I say I want a door to go up there, the door goes up there."[50] Responding to such claims from his position at the WGA, Franklin was adamant about the need for fairness in what he deemed a collaborative profession, pointing out, "What about the cinematographer, the costumes, the set designer, etc.? No one deserves single possessory credit."[51]

In January 1977, he and Robert Aldrich, then president of the DGA, traded insults in the press. Aldrich described the screenwriters' demands as "ludicrous," "egomaniacal," and "pompous." Justifying the directors' position, the Directors Guild president disparaged what he perceived as the weak pool of talented writers: "The reason the WGA wants to take that right away from us is that we have many prominent directors who can get that credit billing, but after [Gore] Vidal and [Patty] Chayefsky the WGA runs dry."[52] Franklin was unwavering in his defense of filmmaking's collective process, responding to Aldrich's attacks by accusing the DGA of "spouting utter nonsense. Nothing could be further from the truth when they accuse us of infringing on their jurisdiction . . . we're standing firm on no possessory credits where a collaborative work is involved."[53] This dispute both illustrated the mutual animosity between the two crafts over issues of creative authorship and how the Directors Guild saw its members as the pinnacle of the film industry's professional and artistic hierarchy. The DGA members did not take well to having their status questioned by colleagues they considered to be in subordinate professions or, as the women of the DGA would soon find out, by peers within their own Guild.

A fierce union leader, Franklin was an ardent advocate for labor justice, never swayed or intimidated by artistic or corporate elitism. The friction between the two guilds and the fearlessness of the less "prominent" union's leader, who frequently charged the directors with acts of "pure unadulterated hogwash," were well known within the industry.[54] Aldrich was quick to see that Franklin's assertiveness would better serve the DGA as an asset within the organization than as a quality to reckon with in a rival. In 1977, during the battle over screen credits, Aldrich contacted Franklin with a proposal. "One day I got a call from him," remembered Franklin. "He was very flattering. . . . He wanted me to do for the Directors Guild what I had done for the Writers Guild. He used the reference: 'We want the bastard, but he'll be our bastard.' I had put in twenty years with the writers and enjoyed it, thoroughly, and he felt that the directors needed a little bit of a push and refreshing."[55] Franklin accepted Aldrich's offer in September 1977, and the following January, he assumed his new position as one of the leaders—and reformers—of the DGA.[56]

The role of a male mentor or advocate has surfaced in different ways in this study of 1970s women directors. In a patriarchal film industry, both in independent film communities and in Hollywood, it could be assumed that a successful man—most likely a producer, director, or studio executive—would be able to use his power to create opportunities for a woman filmmaker. As detailed in chapters 2 and 3, however, that did not always occur. Joan Tewkesbury was unable to leverage her achievements as a screenwriter working with a successful male producer, Robert Altman, to become a director, which so many of her male screenwriting peers were able to do. Barbara Peeters and Stephanie Rothman were prolific exploitation filmmakers when employed by Roger Corman, but the low-budget films they made with him did not hold the same currency as they did for their male peers when the women tried to move into mainstream pictures. In contrast, Anne Bancroft was able to leverage the success of her husband Mel Brooks's films at 20th Century-Fox to secure a deal at the same studio for her movie *Fatso.* Joan Darling got her first break directing sitcoms for prominent television showrunner Norman Lear, which drew the attention of Paramount Pictures; the studio then hired her to direct a feature, on which she encountered obstacles presented by a male producer and male studio executives.

As demonstrated by these examples powerful industry men could be a crucial asset to a woman director, but just as often they could be of no help. Given the Directors Guild's mission—to protect its members' employment rights—the six women should have been able to approach its executive staff or board of directors with their concerns. Yet, in 1978 and 1979, the DGA represented Hollywood male-centric hierarchy. Whether the six women's feminist reform agenda could have moved forward without Michael Franklin is difficult to determine. What is undisputed is that his position as national executive secretary of the Directors Guild and his personal beliefs in employment equality made him an influential ally.

## Consciousness Raising and Industry Backlash

The DGA leadership reacted carefully to the women's research findings. The Directors Guild's long-standing position as Hollywood's most prestigious professional union had allowed the organization to comfortably maintain a cautious and seemingly apolitical position without much criticism—internally from the majority of its members or externally from its industry peers. "The Guild in 1978 was really going through an institutional change . . . it was very informal, everyone knew everybody, and the leadership of the Guild felt that it needed to modernize," recalled Warren Adler, DGA associate national executive director since 1998. Hired by Franklin in 1978 as a "junior" associate general counsel, Adler, who retired in 2011, would be a key figure in establishing and directing DGA's evolving diversity programs for the following three decades. "For example, the Guild didn't have a legal department. It didn't have a department that tracked and policed residual [reports]. [The Guild] said, 'We've got to change.' That was when Mike Franklin was hired. . . . In every respect the Guild needed to be a more forward thinking institution. In a sense this was just the right time: the women had done this work, you had a Board that was just open minded to the idea that there were things the Guild should be doing. It was time."[57]

Before the women came forward, there had never been such an organized effort to address job discrimination from the bottom up, nor had the National Board and the Directors Councils (Eastern and Western Councils representing the two different regions where directors worked) acted on their own accord. Although the women would meet with detractors within their union, the harmony and cohesiveness the cohort had generated during the past year spent researching would continue to strengthen as they prepared to go public with their case—first to the Directors Guild and then to the industry. In collecting the extensive data, their process had been meticulous and relentless. They were equally fastidious in preparing for the different stages of presenting their findings: the group created detailed reports bound in plastic sleeves, and they practiced their presentations over and over again with each other, role-playing every possible response from the DGA board members. No detail went unaddressed, and no possible scenario was left to chance. As an institution governed by white, affluent men, who had successful and lengthy careers, and established to protect their professional success within the industry, the Directors Guild had never had its status challenged by its own membership. "There were some [men]—two or three—that were supportive in the sense that yes, we would talk about this and what was on the agenda for the National Board," remembered Franklin. "But there weren't any that I can recall were gung ho and would say, 'By God, we should do something about this!' It just wasn't in their makeup."[58]

The women did find some support in what would become the "Co-ed Committee." Male DGA members such as Gil Cates, Jack Haley, Jay Sandrich, and Boris Sagal came together to act as the women's "buddies." Initially, the women's expectations were that these older, established male directors would operate as their advocates, and to a certain extent they did. Hochberg explained the relationship between these veteran men and the upstart women in the context of 1979: "You have to understand. We were the first rash of women who said, 'Excuse me, you're not better than I am. We're your equal.' We were functioning like guys. We were challenging them, and we were smart and we were really well organized. There was no flirtation at all. They were running the Guild. And they were smart enough to see that we were on to something. They had to be on the right side of progress."[59] Cates in particular, who in 1979 was one of the five DGA vice presidents and would be elected Guild president from 1983–1987, served as a representative to the industry and press as the WSC, with the support of the DGA, took its demands public.

Some of these men must have seen something of themselves in their younger, female peers. Both groups were members of the same exclusive professional union, sharing the same drive and focus necessary to succeed at their craft. Susan Smitman, who became a member of the DGA around 1980 as a director of television commercials and would later join the lawsuit as a plaintiff, sensed that many of the men at the Directors Guild were empathetic toward the women's situation. "You have to be a certain kind of person to be a director," concluded Smitman in a 2013 interview. "And anybody with any sensitivities to the realities of the situation said that it was not right. It was not fair. And some of these guys probably had daughters and wives and girlfriends who were in the business or trying to be in the business. So I think for the most part the smarter people got it." Smitman noted the connection between union values and a larger commitment to employment justice. "The reality is, if you are in a union, there is some part of you that feels that that is a representation of who you are in the world that you are to the left of center and you believe that people have a right to organize to get what they want."[60]

Yet the women also encountered varying degrees of disapproval from their male colleagues at the Guild. Their cause ignited debates between the men themselves. Sometime in 1979, after the group had presented its findings to Michael Franklin and then to the National Board, which granted them committee status, the women went back to the board to request the formation of an Affirmative Action Committee. This committee would present industry representatives from the major film studios, television networks, and leading production companies with proof of their sexist hiring patterns, per the numerical data, and demand adherence to quota and timetable programs in order to remedy the situation. Failure to do so would be negligent and would result in the Directors Guild taking legal action against those companies.

Hiring quotas and timetables were a highly controversial topic, and debate over whether to support the women's next—public—step in addressing discrimination ensued. Nell Cox remembers a heated argument between board members Mel Brooks and Elia Kazan in response to the women's request. "There was one electrifying moment. . . . Kazan got up and said, 'My wife, Barbara Loden, directed a feature film. 'She won the grand prize at Venice and then she came back to Hollywood and no one would speak to her . . . that's just crazy—that's just terrible, but I can't support this." Thus, even while acknowledging that industry sexism hurt his wife's career, Kazan, a controversial yet highly esteemed filmmaker, could not support the DGA's taking a role in enforcing quotas as a way to equalize employment opportunities. In response, Brooks stood up and declared that his wife, Anne Bancroft, had just written, directed, and starred in her first feature and that the Guild should support the women's position. Drawing an historical parallel, Brooks accused Kazan of "sending these women back to the shit house just like you did at the House Un-American Activities Committee!"—invoking the time when Kazan infamously "named names" during the McCarthy period almost thirty years earlier.[61]

Victoria Hochberg remembered not only Brooks's fervent advocacy on behalf of the women's proposal that day but also opposition from an unexpected source. African American director Ivan Dixon stood up to argue against the proposal because the Directors Guild, a decade earlier, had vetoed a similar request made by a group of African American male DGA members. His position was that the DGA should first support its minority members, primarily men, before helping women, who were primarily white. Hochberg explained what happened next:

> I remember, Jud Taylor was the president at the time, and the Board was sort of going towards Ivan's point of view, which was "you can't do it for them when you didn't do it for us." And Mel Brooks stood up and started walking back and forth—filled with energy, like a lightning bolt was coming off his body, and he said, "You are nitpicking and pettifogging these women into the shit house! This is their time! This is their time!" at which point Jud banged his gavel and called for a vote. Right after Mel did that and they were all so stunned by what Mel Brooks had said that they voted in our favor. It was unbelievable.[62]

On March 1, 1980, the National Board accepted the proposal from the WSC to establish an official Affirmative Action Committee that would be part of the negotiating process for the 1981 Basic Agreement. Although the Directors Guild had gradually become more receptive to the women's demands, at that time the National Board was not eager to get involved in an industry-wide civil rights battle, whether in support of its minority or of its female members: it "feared the idea of 'quotas'" and wanted to avoid having to threaten legal action against companies that did not comply.[63] For the women the only way to systematically intervene and alter employment patterns was to implement an affirmative action model with goals and timetables that would require networks, production companies, and film studios to hire a certain amount of women by a set deadline. However, because the WSC felt that the board's support was essential at that time, the group compromised and "modified [its initial proposal of] goals and timetables and stated them in the form of a 'suggested number of women to be hired.' No specific timetable was mentioned."[64]

By holding the women off, the board would also appease Dixon: postponing the WSC's plan to more aggressively negotiate with industry representatives regarding strategies to employ women until the following year could be justified as giving the proposed Ethnic Minority Committee time to organize and officially become part of the DGA's antidiscrimination effort initiated by the women. What would become the Ethnic Minority Committee, which during this time was not as structured and focused as the WSC, had tried, years earlier, to organize on behalf of the DGA's members of color, but were met with extreme resistance from the Guild's executive administration. In an interviewed in 1990, Michael Franklin remembered how several African American men, who were members of the DGA in different job categories, had told him, "'Look we have been trying to do something within the Guild for a long, long time' . . . [they] had told me that they had over a period of years come to my predecessor and/or had come to the Directors Council, the [Assistant Director/Unit Production Manager Council] on the West Coast and tried to get them to do something about the employment of minorities and their answer was 'that is not a Guild function, that is not a Guild objective' and so on."[65] During the summer of 1979, four months after the WSC was officially established, Wendell Franklin (the DGA's first African American member, male or female, who had joined the Guild in 1960 as an assistant director and later became a feature film director) sent a letter to the National Board stating, "We as members of this Guild, request you address yourselves to promulgating the advancement of its Black members, as well as other minorities."[66] A year later, on August 16, 1980, the National Board approved the formation of the Ethnic Minority Committee; Dixon was its first chairman, and the organizing members were Wendell Franklin, Reuben Watt, and William Crain.[67]

## Confronting the Industry: The Honcho Meeting

On June 18, 1980, the Directors Guild called a meeting at which the Women's Committee, joined by DGA vice president Gil Cates and Michael Franklin, presented their statistics and affirmative action demands to the leading producers, showrunners, and executives of all the major studios, production companies, and networks. Despite the National Board's March decision to postpone presentation of the women's completed research and ready-to-implement hiring strategy so the Ethnic Minority Committee could organize and develop its data, the DGA allowed this meeting to go forward.

By then the Women's Committee had expanded to include assistant directors Janet Davidson, Cheryl Downey, and Nancy Heydorn, and East Coast representatives Paula Marcus and Carol Smetana.[68] As per their usual preparedness, for weeks before the meeting the women went over their plan for what they and the Guild nicknamed the "Honcho Meeting." According to the committee's meeting minutes, the "Honcho" agenda was as follows:

- To ensure commitment to an on-going affirmative action on voluntary basis. Inform [industry representatives] that the DGA will monitor their efforts for full production year (reporting their hiring practices for women to Guild).
- Discuss what the law of the land is regarding discrimination and employment. Discuss the federal state union and industry obligation to equal employment in non-threatening terms. Indicate to honchos they are, according to statistics we have gathered, *very* vulnerable to serious legal attack.
- Decision to inform honchos that employment statistics will be released to press the day after this meeting.
- Consciousness Raising: describe how discrimination works against women in the industry. Statements will be made to the press about

> honcho meeting. We will meet with them and *we will wait and see* if there are any evident changes.[69]

The women and the Directors Guild had decided to approach the industry directly in a spirit of peaceable negotiations and potential partnership, rather than taking an antagonistic approach and filing complaints with the labor representatives or legal departments at the studios or production companies. Of significance was that the DGA decided to go straight to the companies with their grievances, instead of appealing to federal antidiscrimination laws through the EEOC under the jurisdiction of Title VII of the Civil Rights Act.[70] At the same time, as could be gleaned from the minutes of the meeting, the Guild representatives did not shy away from invoking the law in an attempt to impress on the industry the severity of the situation and executives' and producers' possible role in both causing and resolving the inequities.

Thirty-two industry representatives attended the meeting. They included Steven Bochco, executive producer, *Hill Street Blues*, MTM; James Brooks, executive producer, John Charles Walters Productions; Marcia Carsey, senior vice president, Primetime Series, ABC; Barry Diller, chairman Paramount Pictures; Norman Lear, T.A.T. Communications; Alan Shayne, president, Warner Bros. Television; Ned Tanen, president, Universal Pictures; Grant Tinker, president, MTM; Claire Townsend, vice president, Production, 20th Century-Fox; and Ethel Winant, vice president, NBC.[71] The proposed plan focused on episodic television where the majority of directorial hiring took place. Episodic programming was considered a good training ground for directors who wanted to work on features; for those who had "proven themselves" in other formats such as news, documentary, commercials, and public television and wanted to cross over; and for those in DGA categories such as assistant and associate directors, production, and stage managers who were interested in moving into directing. Cox, who presented the statistics to the room, remembered how "it was daunting, my knees were shaking."[72] The WSC recommended that for every thirteen television episodes contracted, producers hire at least one woman director. At the meeting Hochberg emphasized that what they were suggesting was not quotas, "which were meant to keep people out," but instead "affirmative action which is meant to let people in."[73] Reporter Lee Grant (not to be confused with *film director* Lee Grant), writing about the "Honcho" meeting for the *Los Angeles Times*, had to convince the committee members, who were concerned about possible industry backlash, to let her run a photo of them in the paper. Grant argued that putting names and faces to their fight would help emphasize the seriousness of the situation. The women agreed, and a photo of Nell Cox, Lynne Littman, Susan Bay, Dolores Ferraro, and Gil Cates appeared in the paper with the caption, "Where Are the Women Directors?"[74]

A news conference was held the next day at the DGA offices, at which Michael Franklin explained that, while the meeting focused on "equity and fairness" regarding women, "in the very near future" the Guild would be addressing the discrimination against its ethnic employees.[75] The Directors Guild's press release, released at the press conference, described how "the atmosphere of the meeting was receptive and positive. Support for affirmative action efforts was voiced by some of the attendees."[76] The press similarly described the meeting in friendly terms as a get-together whose intention was to provide "information-gathering" and "consciousness-raising," and not to be "adversarial."[77] Yet the coverage noted the conviction of the union in seeking equity for its female members and that it did not skirt the serious implications of the employment statistics. The *New York Times* quoted Franklin stressing how "this is a voluntary program of affirmative action"; however, "if the networks and the studios don't comply, then we move to Title VII and that is not voluntary."[78] For the Directors Guild, engaging in negotiations was the ideal way to address inequity, but legal recourse could still be an option.

In the actual meeting, the reaction, as had become a typical experience for the women when presenting their case, was mixed. The gathering was held in a big room at the Guild's main offices. Seven rows of industry representatives faced a large wooden table where the women sat with Franklin and Cates. Norman Lear, a television producer known for his socially conscious programs, experienced a cathartic moment after their presentation when he told the women that he "had always been sexist until this meeting." Lear told a story about how several women had been outside his office talking about something in the hall. Cox recalled Lear's story: "He came out and said, 'Can you go somewhere else because you're laughing and making noise and I can't work.' And one of the women turned to him and said, 'Norman, this is the sound that women make.'

And it was like—and he teared up when he told this story! He confessed that there was something so deeply ingrained in men—'we don't like the sounds, we don't like [women] laughing; it's like a bunch of hens cackling. We have all these negative ideas about it.'"[79]

Not all the attendees were as reflective as Lear, who attempted to turn sexism into a moment of introspection. Several men, angry at the women for challenging their approach to hiring, confronted them directly. Director and showrunner James L. Brooks was particularly hostile toward the group. Littman remembered Brooks saying out loud at the meeting to her, "'You've got a lot of nerve. You're clearly going to be successful. Why are you standing up here whining?' Now that's what you call damning me with praise. I was devastated. This was the man who created *Mary Tyler Moore*. This is the man who put, presumably, the first 'liberated' female on TV and this was his response."[80]

Yet the dominant reaction was one of apathy. Franklin remembered that even though the meeting "was very well attended, by and large the reaction of the upper echelon of the major studios was really nothing. They were not moved other than the regular [reaction] 'Oh, yes. Right. We'll see what we can do.' That kind of attitude. But they did nothing that was a positive thing, as I recall and they weren't moved. They didn't care."[81] Their silence hinted at what eventually would be a lack of enthusiasm for the women's proposal.

On June 20, two days after the gathering, Franklin sent a packet to all DGA signatories, including those present at the "Honcho" meeting, that gave a detailed breakdown of the gender employment percentages for film and television by format (features, television movies, episodic, miniseries) from 1949–1979, as well as the worksheets that tallied the hiring ratio of women to men—directors, first and second assistant directors, and unit production managers—on popular television by specific series and production companies.[82] The accompanying letter was almost identical to that sent by Franklin to the WGA signatories in 1973 accompanying the Writers Guild's Women's Committee statistics. Also included was a questionnaire asking producers about their potentially sexist hiring policies. The questions referenced current civil rights legislation, reinforcing the DGA's message during the "Honcho" meeting that legal recourse was not off the table if the companies did not actively try to increase the number of women hires. The letter attempted to preempt familiar industry justifications for company hiring patterns by reminding the members that "existing state and federal legislation regarding [sex] discrimination . . . do not accept 'lack of intent' to discriminate as an excuse for the practice of discrimination." Franklin's questions included the following:

- Have you done anything subtly or directly to discourage women from seeking employment in any Directors Guild category on your projects?
- Have you ever communicated to an agent a preference for male directors over female directors?
- When interviewing DGA members do you include women before making a hiring decision? If not, why not?
- Is it possible that you have not hired a woman in any DGA category for an action or adventure film because you think women don't know how to work on "men's" stories? Do you feel the same way about hiring men to work on "women's" stories?
- Numerous federal and state laws have been enacted prohibiting employment based on sex. Do you believe that you conform to the spirit of these laws? Would your hiring statistics bear this out?

In his letter, Franklin also outlined the Directors Guild's Affirmative Action Program that required, in no uncertain terms, the producers' participation. The program's goal was to increase job opportunities for women directors who were DGA members, with an emphasis on providing experience in episodic television for those trained in other formats. The objective was to ensure that a woman would direct at least one of every thirteen episodes of a series. To help facilitate this hiring, the Guild would establish a Resource Committee made up of members from the WSC, DGA Director Volunteers, and representatives from the networks and production companies. The WSC had created a directory of qualified female directors so no company could claim that it did not know how to contact eligible employees, and the Director Volunteers, who were experienced male DGA members, would provide support to women preparing for a job. To ensure that these guidelines were being adhered to, the Directors Guild requested that companies file reports with the DGA that tracked the number of female members interviewed and hired.

Attempting to act as an enforcer of civil rights law, the union originally intended to run its Affirmative Action Program from July 1, 1980, through June 1, 1981, assessing its progress throughout the year.[83] However, not having involved a federal agency such as the EEOC, and having no legal authority of its own, the Directors Guild could only function in an unofficial and therefore an ultimately ineffective capacity. For the next few months, women met with production company representatives, but eventually the envoys sent were from human resource departments—areas that had no knowledge of or authority to hire directors. When companies started sending their secretaries to meet prospective female hires, the DGA understood that its Affirmative Action Program, as it had initially realized it, was being treated by the industry as a farce.

In October 1980, just four months into the plan, Franklin hosted a breakfast meeting at the Directors Guild's office, inviting industry executives to discuss employment progress. Not only did no one attend but no one even paid attention to the formalities of canceling and call to say they were not coming. Ten years later in a special edition of *DGA News* dedicated to the political activism of the Women's Steering Committee, Joelle Dobrow interviewed Franklin about what would be called the "Danish Crisis" or "debacle," after the uneaten food ordered for a meeting that no one attended. "As I remember," said Franklin, "the executives' excuse [for not attending the meeting]—which they would deny—was that their legal people told them there was a problem for them to be participating in this ongoing program. This was their way of extricating themselves and leaving it in the laps of their labor people. Once that was done, they figured it was going to die a natural death."[84] Yet by this time, as an organization, the Directors Guild had a great deal invested in the effort to combat employment discrimination. Not only had it taken a very public position on the issue in June by calling the "Honcho" meeting and press conference but also, if it did not hold the industry accountable, the possibility that its female membership would look toward the DGA as liable was a serious threat. The industry's response to the DGA's demands—not showing up to meetings, sending secretaries as production representatives to the Affirmative Action Program to discuss hiring prospects—illustrated how those companies felt about being told that they were behaving in discriminatory ways. Perhaps more offensive to the industry representatives was what Warner Bros. would later describe in a court document as an infringement on its (and by association the entire industry's) constitutional right to free speech. In what the studio labeled as a "First

Affirmative Defense," the ability of a production company to hire at its own discretion without having to meet quotas was "part of the creative process of making a motion picture or television production and thus represents a form of speech protected by the first amendment to the United States Constitution."[85] This echoed the industry's defense in 1969 and 1970 when the EEOC conducted hearings on the same problem of job discrimination, but at that time against below-the-line male minority employees: production is dependent on the unpredictable nature of the "creative process."

## Legal Action Part I: Filing with the EEOC

Frustrated with the industry's response to the Directors Guild's various attempts to negotiate affirmative action policies and programs since it had announced the initiative the previous June, the DGA filed discrimination complaints with the EEOC and the state Fair Employment Practices Commission on February 25, 1981. These complaints did not warrant a lawsuit, yet, filing with the EEOC would allow the Directors Guild to take legal action against any of the companies under the jurisdiction of Title VII of the Civil Rights Act if it ever decided to do so, which two years later it would. By involving the EEOC, the federal agency established to enforce the Civil Rights Act, the Directors Guild conveyed the seriousness of its agenda—having the film and television industries address, in a meaningful way, their sexist and racist hiring patterns. Filing those complaints placed the responsibility on the government—not the DGA—to ensure that the studios, production companies, and networks would address their low numbers of minority and female hires.

The complaints were submitted by the DGA on behalf of its female and minority membership against twenty companies, including the ABC, CBS, and NBC networks and these studios: Columbia Pictures, Paramount Pictures, 20th Century-Fox, Universal Studios, Warner Bros., and Walt Disney Productions. Also named were leading independent production companies such as Aaron Spelling Productions (*Vegas*); T.A.T. Communications, including Tandem, Norman Lear's company (*Archie Bunker's Place*, *The Jeffersons*); MTM Enterprises, Mary Tyler Moore's company with her husband Grant Tinker (*Lou Grant*, *WKRP in Cincinnati*);

Lorimar Productions (*Dallas*); and Nicholl-Ross-West Enterprises (*Three's Company*).[86]

The industry responded defensively to the Directors Guild's accusations that they were responsible for a "'pattern of discrimination' in all DGA categories" and were being uncooperative in working together to improve job numbers by "[u]nilaterally withdrawing . . . and terminating [their] involvement in the affirmative action program."[87] Alan Horn, president of T.A.T. Communications, was surprised by the Directors Guild's decision to issue a formal complaint, confessing that "we freely admit not using women in a representative sense according to their numbers in the Directors Guild. We have been doing everything in our powers consistent with our existing commitments to hire more women." Of T.A.T.'s twenty-four directing jobs, however, only two women were hired to fill seven positions.[88] Grant Tinker, president of MTM Enterprises, was also taken aback by the legal action, saying, "To my knowledge, there was a dialogue occurring." However, he admitted that his company did not have a history of hiring women directors: "The record has been dismal and something should be done about it. We're going to use some ladies."[89] Quoted in the *New York Times* as "questioning how many women were really qualified to direct a $10 million movie," Jack Valenti, president of the Motion Picture Association of America, inadvertently boosted the Women's Steering Committee and DGA's argument by stating "that women [should] serve an apprenticeship in television first." Victoria Hochberg responded to Valenti's proposal with this analogy: "I'm at school and there's a big exam at the end of the year that will be graded fairly. The only problem is that only men are allowed into the library to study. Getting into the library is the equivalent of being allowed to direct episodes on television."[90]

In December 1982, the EEOC notified the Directors Guild that, in the more than nine months since the DGA had filed discrimination complaints with it, "not a single production company had complied with the EEOC's Request for Information."[91] With the government unable to make any progress, in May 1983, the DGA received a "right-to-sue" letter from EEOC, which formally granted the union permission to proceed with litigation.[92] The Directors Guild then sent letters to the networks and the major and independent studios threatening a lawsuit if these companies did not agree to meet and negotiate some kind of policy to address the discriminatory hiring practices through the implementation of numerical goals and timetables. The press reported that within the next month all seven major studios and three of the leading independent production companies—Lorimar Productions, MTM, and Aaron Spelling Productions—had agreed to meet with the DGA, but not to follow the affirmative action guidelines insisted on by the Guild.[93] The DGA stood by the implementation of affirmative action plans, while the studios and companies continued to reject goals and timetables.[94] On June 15, *Variety* reported that the DGA had dropped the networks from its action and was focusing only on the studios.

In retaliation, the studios filed their own grievances with the EEOC against the Directors Guild, claiming that, if there were instances of discrimination, it was the DGA Basic Agreement contract that was partially at fault.[95] By July, talks between Warner Bros. and the DGA had completely broken down as the studio continued to refuse to "accept 'goals and timetables' as a condition of bargaining."[96] The core of the studio's defense continued to be that it could "not allow our right to express ourselves creatively [to] be controlled by a numbers game."[97] For more than a decade, the studios had been adamant that affirmative action limited their creative rights, a freedom that was key to the functioning of the film business.

## Legal Action Part II: Filing the Lawsuit

On July 25, 1983, the Directors Guild filed a class action suit against Warner Bros. and, on December 21, against Columbia Pictures: *Directors Guild of America, Inc. v. Warner Brothers, Inc. and Columbia Pictures Industries, Inc.* (hereafter *DGA v. WB/CPI*).[98] The DGA charged both studios with employment discrimination in violation of Title VII of the Civil Rights Act of 1964 and Section 1981 of the Civil Rights Act of 1866 (nineteenth century). The following individual plaintiffs, who represented the DGA, were named in the cases: (Warner Bros.) Joelle Dobrow, Luther James, Lorraine Raglin, and Cesar Torres; (Columbia) Bill Crain, Dick Look, Sharon Mann, Susan Smitman, and Frank Zuniga.[99] At the time of the first filing in July, the DGA supported its claim against Warner Bros. by citing its poor hiring record: between January 1978 and June 1980 the studio had 233 directing jobs, of which women filled only

9, or 3.9 percent.[100] From April 1, 1982, to March 31, 1983, none of the 177 directing jobs went to women, and 2.8 percent went to minority men.[101] Several months later, in November, talks between the Guild and Columbia fell apart. Columbia, like Warner Bros., balked at the DGA's affirmative action demands, considering them an infringement on its creative rights and freedom. In a statement to the press, the studio explained that "despite Columbia's expressed willingness to continue negotiations aimed at achieving increased levels of employment opportunities for women and minorities . . . the Guild's position with respect to quotas essentially was that Columbia's only choice was either to accept quotas or to reject quotas and be sued."[102] Michael Franklin responded, "In our judgment, Columbia's hiring practices are in violation of Title 7 [sic] of the Civil Rights Act of 1964. In our judgment, their hiring practices are discriminatory and unlawful."[103] Between January 1978 and June 1980, of the 264 directors hired by Columbia Pictures, only 4 were women; from April 1982 to March 1983, of 83 directors hired by the studio, only 3 were men of color.[104]

The lawsuit was filed in federal court in Los Angeles, and the randomly selected judge appointed to the case was U.S. District Judge Pamela Ann Rymer. A graduate of Stanford University, Judge Rymer was known for her strong conservative connections. In 1964 she served as the director of political research and analysis for the Goldwater for President Committee. Ronald Reagan had appointed her to the federal bench in February 1983, and DGA's suit was one of her first major cases.[105]

The law firm of Taylor, Roth & Hunt represented the plaintiffs in the case, both the DGA and the individuals. A. Thomas Hunt and Walter Cochran-Bond were the lawyers that the women originally met at the Center for Law and the Public Interest when they first began to organize. The third partner at the firm was Jay Roth, who would serve as the DGA's national executive director from 1995 until 2017. Hunt, had acquired a reputation as a successful antidiscrimination lawyer, especially regarding the employment of women and minorities.[106] An allegation was made by the defendants that Hunt had participated in the collective bargaining negotiations between the Directors Guild and its signatories (studios, production companies, networks) in the DGA's 1981 Basic Agreement (BA) and thus had a conflict of interest. This claim, which appeared in the cross-complaint and the decision, was later found to be false: the attorney's area of expertise was in class action suits and not labor issues, and therefore he had not participated in the BA talks.[107]

Negotiated every three years the BA protected Guild members in all categories (director, UPM, first and second AD, stage managers) with regard to such issues as pay scales, creative rights during production and postproduction, and residuals. The BA also included provisions covering the DGA's maintenance and administering of its qualification lists that included all Guild categories *except* that of director. Qualification lists, also known as roster lists (as discussed in chapter 1), are a type of directory of union members organized by seniority. For example, when a production company is looking for a first AD to hire, it could contact the Directors Guild and ask for the qualifications list of eligible candidates. Those with the most experience would be at the top of the list and would be the first considered for the job.

Hunt's reputation was earned during the administrations of President Jimmy Carter and California governor Jerry Brown and the liberal days of the EEOC. After assuming office, President Ronald Reagan and Governor George Deukmejian of California began appointing more conservative judges to the state and federal judiciaries, who presumably were not as sympathetic to traditional labor union issues. As attorney Hunt remarked of this period, "We started losing civil rights cases that shouldn't have been lost. We also found it harder and harder to get decent settlements."[108] The implication of Hunt's comment is that a less conservative, more pro-labor judge than Rymer would have ruled in favor of the DGA and the individual plaintiffs in their class action suit. Joelle Dobrow, Victoria Hochberg, and Lynne Littman came to agree with Hunt's sentiment. They felt strongly that in 1980, when the National Board, under the guise of waiting for the Ethnic Minority Committee to organize, delayed the Women's Steering Committee's first proposal to confront the industry, it missed a window of opportunity in the last year of the Carter administration when affirmative action plans were more widely accepted and enforced by the government.[109]

On March 5, 1985, nearly fifteen months since the two cases were joined, Judge Rymer made a "tentative" ruling against the Directors Guild and in favor of Columbia Pictures and Warner Bros.[110] The final ruling was then handed down on August 30.[111] The judge's decision was based on two findings. First, the Directors Guild could not be the "class representative" of the women and minorities involved in the case because it created a "conflict of interest" in that the DGA might, as a union, be guilty of discrimination, while also claiming to be victimized by the same prejudice. Second, Judge Rymer found that the DGA's lawyers, Taylor, Roth & Hunt, could not represent the plaintiffs in the case because the firm also represented the Directors Guild, thus creating another conflict of interest.[112] Furthermore, she ruled that the nine DGA plaintiffs could not act as representatives of a class for other women or minorities, as in a class action suit, but could, as individuals, sue the film studios for discrimination.[113]

## Results of the Court's Decision

In filing its first legal challenge to discrimination in the hiring practices of the film industry, the DGA made a number of legal missteps and encountered some political misfortune. As discussed earlier, the increasingly conservative political climate in California and the random assignment of a conservative judge were unfortunate developments that could not have been anticipated and were out of the Guild's control. But the DGA did make strategic legal decisions, which at the time had proven to be reliable tactics in winning—or settling—class action suits regarding gender and racial discrimination, but that in hindsight were devastating to the outcome of the case. As the judge's ruling made especially clear, it was a mistake for the DGA to serve as the plaintiff representative in the case and for the law firm of Taylor, Roth & Hunt to represent both the DGA and the individual plaintiffs. As the defendants were quick to point out, it was the DGA and not the studios that had devised and participated in the assembly of a discriminatory system, primarily through the qualification lists.[114] To get on the list an employee in one of the categories would have had to work a certain amount of hours to "qualify." The amount of hours worked then determined one's seniority on the list.[115] The defendants' cross-complaint alerted the judge that the attorneys for the plaintiffs were instrumental in negotiating the Basic Agreement, which the studios argued was the cause of many discriminatory practices.[116] As a result, attorney Hunt was—incorrectly—singled out for the alleged potential of having an adverse relationship to the plaintiffs who were appearing as individuals.

Shortly after the filing of the complaint, the defendants filed a cross-complaint against the Directors Guild "which assert[s] that [the DGA] is wholly or partially responsible for whatever discrimination may exist against women and minorities as a result of its role as bargaining representative and acquiescence in discriminatory practices, if any."[117] The attorneys at Warner Bros. and Columbia anticipated the conflict of interest inherent in the Basic Agreement and planned their defense and attack accordingly. Reflecting back to 1979, the women's original hunch—that the Guild itself was a guilty party—was, according to the defendants and eventually the court, correct.

On March 5, 1985, before there had been any significant legal activity or any substantive courtroom proceedings, Judge Rymer brought the entire action to a halt and pronounced a "death knell to the suit." She announced to a very "glum" audience of plaintiffs that the case could not proceed until the DGA was removed as the class representative and the attorneys, especially Hunt, could prove that they in fact represented the best interests of the individual plaintiffs.[118] The case never recovered from this decision. It was subsequently abandoned by the DGA and never successfully revived by any of the individual plaintiffs.

The use of statistics—versus a focus on an individual plaintiff's account of bias—was a common approach to class action discrimination cases during this time. The rationale for using data was that an individual's testimony could be vulnerable to a range of unpredictable criticism, whereas such large numbers would point toward a pattern that demanded attention. The firm of Taylor, Roth & Hunt's strategy was to obtain the class certification from the court and then to negotiate with the studios, as a settlement, an affirmative action solution of goals and timetables that would begin to alter the industry's hiring practices.[119] The firm had ample experience and success settling similar disputes using data, but had not yet waged any suits in the film industry. Other business sectors have a more clearly defined route toward employment (i.e., becoming a firefighter involves passing a test) and therefore offer a more transparent process through which to expose flaws. In contrast, within the studios' long-standing custom of decentralized, word-of-mouth hiring, it was more difficult to identify the actual hiring decisions and whether they were discriminatory, because they were not standardized and could change with every film. The distinction between industries—that Hollywood was an entirely *different* kind of business—and therefore the legal team's inability to adjust its strategy accordingly, may have been an unanticipated weakness in the DGA's argument.

The relevant rules on proceeding with a class action in federal court are very clear. In order to maintain a lawsuit as a class action, the plaintiffs must satisfy each of the four conjunctive criteria set forth in the Federal Rules of Civil Procedure as follows:

> Section 23 (a): Prerequisites to a Class Action. One or more members of a class may sue or be sued as representative parties on behalf of all only if (1) the class is so numerous that joinder of all members is impracticable, (2) there are questions of law or fact common to the class, (3) the claims or defenses of the representative parties are typical of the claims or defenses of the class, and (4) the representative parties will fairly and adequately protect the interests of the class.[120]

Judge Rymer in her decision established additional legal requirements: "Before ordering that a lawsuit may proceed as a class action, the trial court must rigorously analyze whether the prerequisites of Rule 23 have been met. The class plaintiff bears the burden of establishing that the action may be maintained as a class action. Thus, the failure of plaintiffs to carry their burden as to any one of the requirements of Rule 23 precludes the maintenance of the lawsuit as a class action."[121] Thus, as the class representative, the DGA had the burden of proving the existence of each of the four identified criteria. On this basis, Judge Rymer gave her decision: "Having considered the papers and oral argument, I conclude that the class cannot be determined at this time."[122]

As to the first requirement, often referred to as "numerosity" (the number of individuals representing the class—in this case, the total number of DGA members being discriminated against based on their gender and/or race), there was no disagreement between the parties as to whether the plaintiff's numerosity requirements would be adequate, and the issue did not play a part in the final decision.[123] To satisfy the second condition known as "commonality," the Directors Guild had to allege that there was a class of women and minorities who shared a "question of law or fact common to the class" related to the discrimination they experienced in pursuing employment opportunities. To meet the "commonality" requirement, the judge stated that the law expects the DGA to "present significant evidence from which it may be inferred that there is an identifiable pattern or practice affecting a definable class in common ways."[124] The purpose of this requirement is to guarantee judicial economy, so that the court can focus on an identifiable unlawful practice that is experienced in a similar way by every member of the class and can be attributed to the similar actions of any number of different defendants.[125] The defendants argued that hiring in the film industry, especially in the director and assistant director categories, was essentially "decentralized," meaning that no one person had the responsibility of selecting applicants because everyone responsible for hiring a director—whether they were studio executive or producers—used a different hiring procedure.[126] Moreover, there was not one specific place a director could go to see a posted list of job opportunities with an exact list of qualifications to be met. In addition, the artistic nature of the subject matter made employment decisions a "highly subjective" process often dependent on word of mouth, personal chemistry, and unique technical competence.[127]

The Directors Guild responded to the "commonality" arguments by emphasizing the discriminatory nature of the hiring system, as expressed in the raw numbers contained in the defendants' own reports that had been provided in accordance with Section 15-301 and 15-401 of the DGA's Basic Agreement. The addition of "Non-Discrimination" Article 15 and its sections 15-101 to 15-604 was a major accomplishment for the Women and Ethnic Minority Committees during the negotiation process for the 1981 Basic Agreement. Using language from Title VII of the Civil Rights Act, Article 15 plainly states the Directors Guild's nondiscrimination policy: "The parties [the DGA and its signatories] mutually reaffirm their policy of non-discrimination in the employment or treatment of any Employee because of race, creed, age, religion, color, sex or national origin, in accordance with applicable State or Federal laws."[128] Including the words "State or Federal laws" made clear that the DGA would defer to the government's authority over employment rights.[129]

A direct outcome of the activism that had been taking place over the previous three years, Article 15 is a landmark addition to the DGA's Basic Agreement, formalizing within the union's contract a method for making signatory companies accountable for how many woman and monitories they did—or did not—hire. Section 15-300, "Reports," requires companies to submit to the Directors Guild quarterly reports of the "sex and ethnicity of persons employed."[130] These reports are then aggregated to create the employment statistics that the DGA collects and circulates through the present day. Article 15 also institutionalizes as part of the Basic Agreement many of the affirmative action efforts the Directors Guild had attempted to establish with the studios and production companies, but to no avail. Negotiating the 1981 Basic Agreement had not been much easier. Initially the DGA was hoping to include in the contract an affirmative action policy, but not surprisingly the industry representatives refused to accept it. Instead Section 15-200 specifies that signatories "shall make good faith efforts to increase the number of working ethnic minority and women" in the different Guild categories.[131] During the contract talks, Michael Franklin reflected on this language: "It's the kind of compromise that I'm not altogether thrilled about, and I'm sure some of our members won't be [either]."[132]

To make its case that unfair hiring was taking place, on November 20, 1984, the DGA included in a memorandum to the court statistics collected as a result of the provisions in Article 15. The data showed that Columbia Pictures had hired 0 percent and Warner Bros. only 3.9 percent women directors.[133] The Directors Guild argued that, on the basis of these numbers, it was obvious that something improper was going on within the industry, which was characteristic of a system of unlawful discrimination.

Judge Rymer was not persuaded by the DGA's arguments, however. She unequivocally concluded that "due to the decentralization of the industry and the subjective nature of the hiring process, plaintiffs have not demonstrated that this action is susceptible to class treatment."[134] In practical terms the court determined that "in the motion picture industry . . . hiring decisions are vested in numerous individuals who act independently of each other. . . . Hiring decisions are made project-by-project by a variety of persons . . . who utilize different criteria which varies depending on the type of project involved . . . and under a variety of conditions."[135] Based on this "diversity" of factors the court found that "the existence of common questions of law or fact has not been demonstrated."[136] However, despite the judge's detailed explanation for the plaintiff's failure to prove "commonality," it is unclear from the decision whether this failure *alone* would have been fatal to the success of the case.[137]

What was more devastating to the case was the court's analysis of the fourth criterion for "fair and adequate protection." As stated in the decision, "this prerequisite has been called the most crucial requirement because of the preclusive effect a judgment will have on the rights of absent members."[138] Specifically, the judge ruled that the plaintiffs had to show that their interests in the case were not antagonistic to those of the remainder of the class and, more specifically, that the interests of the DGA, the named representative of the class, did not conflict with the interests of the named (and unnamed) individuals in the class. In short, the court was asking the Directors Guild, Whose side are you on in this dispute? The women and minority members of the union or the union as a whole, which was made up of a majority of white men?

This was not an unusual relationship, and the court noted that in such situations the issue of whether a union can adequately represent a class made up of its members was a question of fact to be determined on a case-by-case basis. The court described several factors relevant to making that decision: whether there was a majority of women members, the union's history of fighting discrimination in collective bargaining efforts, the number of complaints filed with the EEOC, and whether there was a cross-complaint against the union's own hiring practices.[139] This last factor was especially critical because the filing of a cross-complaint by the defendants would enable them to raise the issue that the DGA as a class representative actually was responsible for the very discrimination about which it complained.[140]

Unfortunately, the Directors Guild was hardly in a position to meet these criterion of adequately representing the class of women since 80 percent of its membership, as well as its officers and National Board, were white men. Furthermore, it did not have a history of consistently seeking equal employment rights for its members.[141] Since much of this information was not known to the public, it became the purpose of the defendants' cross-complaint to bring these allegations of the DGA's own misdeeds to the attention of the court in a powerful and convincing manner. Through the cross-complaint, the defendants argued that the DGA was not a victim of discrimination, but in fact had contributed to producing the kinds of disturbing statistics that formed the basis for their case. More importantly, the defendants claimed that the DGA's negotiating tactics—demanding an unrepresentative qualifying list of candidates and refusing to institute an affirmative action program suggested by the production companies—had contributed to the discriminatory impact of hiring practices in the motion picture industry.[142]

By the time the court ruled on the question of whether there was a class of individuals with a common complaint worthy of class certification, it appeared to have accepted the defendants' point of view, with very little analysis or critique. It made the following ruling: "The conflict of interest raised by the DGA's role is sufficiently concrete and immediate to preclude the DGA's representation of the class comprised of females and minorities. Accordingly, the DGA is dismissed as a plaintiff."[143] This dramatic outcome had the effect not only of eliminating the Directors Guild's financial support for the individual plaintiffs in the case but also of leaving in place the defendants' cross-complaint. This was the worst possible result for both the DGA and the individual plaintiffs. The court in effect decided that the case could go forward for the individual plaintiffs without financial backing from the DGA to cover legal fees and that the defendant studios could pursue their cross-complaint alleging that the DGA was guilty of discrimination. As a result, if the case continued to proceed, the DGA could conceivably find itself liable to *both* the plaintiffs *and* the defendants for any alleged discriminatory activity.

The final blow to the plaintiffs was Judge Rymer's explicit reminder to the DGA attorneys of the obvious rule that they could not represent clients with conflicting interests: "It is equally clear that the attorneys representing the individual plaintiffs, the law firm of Hunt & Cochran-Bond, may not represent both the plaintiffs and the DGA."[144] Using many of the arguments raised by the defendants in their cross-complaint, the court admonished the DGA's attorneys for "potentially" violating their duty of undivided loyalty. For example, there could possibly have been a point in the trial where the individual plaintiffs would find themselves on the side of the production companies complaining about restrictive DGA membership policies, specifically the qualification list, and then in a sudden turn of events, these same individual plaintiffs would be siding with the DGA against the hiring practices of the production companies.

## Case Legacy: The Refashioning of Failure

The loss was so shocking that the DGA did not attempt again to bring a suit to rectify the employment discrimination issue. Yet the failure was consequently reframed as being part of a legacy of honorable efforts by the Directors Guild. The lawsuit was the first time that the DGA, an influential and reputable guild, had taken legal action on behalf of its female and minority membership; never before had such attention been drawn to women and minority directors. It was an uncharacteristic action taken by an industry organization that was not known for having overt political positions informed by potentially controversial issues such as feminism, sexism, and racism.[145] The suit was a landmark case, something historic attempted by the Directors Guild. As Lynne Littman said in the press before the case was lost, "The important thing about the action the guild is taking now is that it is being taken by the whole guild, not by the women's committee. The guild is not a notoriously radical organization, and their support for us is a major advance."[146]

Although implicated by the court's decision in the employment discrimination experienced by its minority and female members, the DGA soon began to refashion its guilty verdict as a sign of the organization's progressive transformation. A decade after the filing of the suit, the Directors Guild published a special "women's" issue of its newsletter, *DGA News,* that celebrated the ten-year anniversary of the Women's Steering Committee and highlighted the accomplishments of its female membership. In the newsletter, film director Arthur Hiller, then DGA president, wrote, "It's hard to believe, but some people question whether women are people too! But not at the DGA; we are one Guild and we are there for *all* of our members." He went on: "We set up plans and recommendations for raising the number of working women. We even filed lawsuits."[147] By not mentioning the outcome of the "lawsuits," Hiller avoided a difficult part of the Directors Guild's history: that the DGA played a significant role in perpetuating Hollywood's white-male-dominated directors' pool, as stated by Judge Rymer in her decision and was suspected by the women early on in their organizing effort.

The union has absorbed this chapter of its history by focusing on the legal case as a noble effort in its commitment to "diversity," rather than on the suit's loss. Prominent on the homepage of the DGA website is a link to

"Diversity," which highlights the Guild's continually evolving mission to "support diversity in the entertainment community through membership committees, networking opportunities and job training and mentoring programs."[148] Whereas in the spring of 1979 six women presented their statistical findings on the status of female directors to a series of elected DGA officials, arguing for the necessity of a formal Women's Steering Committee, in 2017 the Directors Guild promotes as part of its public and internal persona multiple diversity committees: the African American Steering Committee (formerly the Ethnic Minority Committee), the Asian American Committee, the Eastern Diversity Steering Committee (representing African American, Asian, Native American, Latino, and Arab-Middle Eastern Guild members located on the East Coast), the Latino Committee, and the Women's Steering Committee.

The statistical model of the 1970s used to collect employment data has also been absorbed into the Directors Guild's diversity persona. On its website, annual reports on employment numbers—focused on episodic television where the majority of directing jobs can be found—are broken down by gender and race. As did the 1979 Women's Steering Committee, the DGA continues to provide statistics on hiring by gender and race for individual networks, studios, production companies, including streaming platforms, and television series.

In the "Diversity" section of the DGA's website there is also a link to a 2011 article with the headline "The Good Fight" on the history of women's activism in the DGA; it includes the 1980 photograph that accompanied Lee Grant's *Los Angeles Times* article on the "Honcho" meeting, showing Bay, Cates, Cox, Ferraro, and Littman. "The Good Fight," just like this study, begins with Kathryn Bigelow's Oscar win, citing it as an achievement made possible by the feminist activism of the 1970s. Now, over thirty-five years later, that tense and hostile "Honcho" meeting is framed within the historical journey of progress, with an emphasis on the Directors Guild's commitment to inclusion over time. The article acknowledges the Women's Steering Committee's groundbreaking research and brushes over the intricacies of why the case was lost by quoting Victoria Hochberg's assessment: "It was tossed out of court, that's true, but it was a game changer nonetheless."[149]

In actuality, the game changers were the six women and not the failed lawsuit. Without the support of the men from the DGA, such as Michael

Franklin, Gil Cates, and Harry Evans, the women would have had a more difficult time pleading their cause, but they would have still found a way—through the press and working with civil rights' attorneys—to generate attention to the statistics they had compiled. In 1979 and 1980 the feminist movement and the last vestiges of a liberal administration before the election of Ronald Reagan continued to have a powerful influence on discussions of workplace equality, and the then-strong interest in affirmative action policies would have generated high-profile support for the group's fight. In contrast, *without the women* the Directors Guild would never have examined discrimination with such detail nor fought it with such aggressive action. Until the women approached Franklin, the DGA had ignored the social politics of the 1960s and 1970s.

Despite losing the case, the Directors Guild's involvement in fighting discriminatory hiring patterns had a positive impact on the organization. After retiring from the DGA in 1988, Michael Franklin reflected on the consequences of the political activism in which he had been so instrumental in an interview conducted by Joelle Dobrow and included in the *DGA News* anniversary tribute to the Women's Steering Committee: "Prior to 1978, the Guild had an image of a gentlemen's club. It didn't make waves. The lawsuit improved the Guild's status because the industry recognized that not only did the DGA represent important creative elements within the industry, but it was a strong force for the positive improvement of society as well!"[150]

*DGA v. WB/CPI* represented the culmination of the activism the Directors Guild had taken part in since the spring of 1979 when the nascent Women's Steering Committee first shared its employment data with Franklin. Although the case was a failure in that it indicted the DGA for the discriminatory behavior the union was itself trying to fight, the mere fact that it was making that effort indicated that a major shift was taking place within the organization. The addition of Article 15 to the DGA Basic Agreement in 1981 was another demonstration of significant change. The inclusion of a "nondiscrimination" section in its contract—a document that defined the Directors Guild—made the union's position on employment equity and equality official.

During the early and mid-1980s the DGA experienced a newfound activism within the organization. Nevertheless, it continued to be difficult to change the way directors were hired throughout the industry. As in the early 1970s, industry reformers encountered impasses in the early 1980s that made it impossible to implement any official policy (i.e., one that was legally enforced) to monitor discrimination across the industry. As discussed in chapter 1 the EEOC's efforts in 1969 and 1970 to address the well-documented disparity in the hiring of minorities were neutered by other factions of the government that privileged the economic benefits of Hollywood as an industry over protecting the civil rights of the workers who made the industry possible. Mirroring the difficult and contentious dialogue between the DGA and industry representatives between 1980 and 1983 was a similar cycle of blame: the unions blamed the studios, the studios blamed the unions, and the employees blamed both. Unions upheld their use of qualification and roster lists as a way of facilitating work for their members and claimed the studios could choose minority and women members from those lists in a conscious effort to ensure a diverse workplace. In turn studios accused the unions of perpetuating the dominance of white male employees by organizing their lists based on seniority. And they claimed that the creative process of making a film could not be beholden to affirmative action quotas and timetables; it was an unpredictable process contingent on many unique and uncontrollable variables such as individual relationships, personalities, and timing.

All of these issues that arose early in the 1970s reappeared during the DGA lawsuit. What was also consistent during this time span was the use of "good faith" agreements as a "compromise" for the disagreements between each party. In 1970 after the EEOC hearings a "good faith" agreement was issued by the Justice Department that the unions and studios would essentially promise to try harder to hire more women and minorities. But as the California Advisory Committee to the Commission on Civil Rights showed in its follow-up investigation published in 1978, not only had the unions and film studios failed to increase the diversity of their membership in any significant way but also the government agency designated to enforce the 1970 agreement, the EEOC, had failed to monitor their actions with any thoroughness.[151]

The addition in 1981 of Article 15 to the Basic Agreement was an important step forward in increasing the low number of women and minority directors, assistant directors, unit production managers, and stage mangers. But as Franklin had said in the press during the contract negotiations, it was a disappointing concession to a more binding and regulated hiring system that the DGA had tried to propose to the industry. For studios, production companies, and networks to agree to "make good faith efforts to increase the number of working ethnic minority and women" was to leave wide open the definition of what those "efforts" might entail. As a result companies could fall back on their justification that the hiring process—and the creative process on the whole—was unpredictable and therefore could not be regulated.

Measured by the tepid and borderline hostile response at the "Honcho" meeting in 1980, the superficial impact of Article 15 in the 1981 Basic Agreement, and the crushing of the lawsuit that took place between 1983 and 1985, this period of feminist reform generated by the Directors Guild, both by its members and executive staff, is complex. The DGA spent the years after the case's dismissal creating a diversity persona, but the data showed that the number of working women and minority directors had not increased in significant ways. During the mid- to late 1990s, filmmaker Jamaa Fanaka (1943–2012) filed multiple lawsuits against many of the studios, networks, and the Directors Guild for job discrimination based on race. Fanaka, who had written, directed, and produced several low-budget independent films in the 1970s such as *Welcome Home Brother* (1975) and the successful *Penitentiary* trilogy (*Penitentiary* [1979], *Penitentiary II* [1982], and *Penitentiary III* [1987]) in the 1980s, joined the DGA in 1990; in 1993 he was one of the founding members of its African American Steering Committee. His dispute with the studios, television networks, and the DGA was similar to that in the 1983 case, which he cited frequently in the construction of his own legal approach. Unable to secure an attorney to represent himself in the suits—presumably because this kind of case had failed so significantly a decade earlier that no law firm or potential fellow plaintiffs were willing to take on the cause in a similar legal manner—Fanaka spent years pursuing the cases while representing himself, but with no success. Although he was unable to gain traction within the court system, the DGA did take his accusations seriously as measured by the amount of correspondence the organization's legal department conducted with him. There is even some speculation that Jay Roth was hired as the DGA's national executive director in 1995 to "expel Fanaka from the DGA"—suggesting that not only did Fanaka's accusations pose a real threat to the Directors Guild but also that the DGA would do everything in its power to not be implicated in another discrimination suit.[152]

Today Article 15, which is still part of the DGA's Basic Agreement, seems far less powerful than it did when it was first added. After almost four decades of "good faith" agreements, the number of working women directors is still low: in 2017, 11 percent of the top 250 films made in Hollywood were directed by women, and that figure has never climbed higher, mostly staying between 7 and 9 percent.[153] The legacy of the Women's Steering Committee is most apparent in a resurgence of political action within the Directors Guild. Current members of the DGA Women's Steering Committee are asking similar questions to those posed by their predecessors in 1979 about the role played by their Guild, still one of the most powerful in the industry, in changing these dire employment conditions for its female members and in perpetuating them. In 2015, the American Civil Liberties Union requested that state and federal officials investigate discrimination against women directors. In its letter to the EEOC the ACLU cited the DGA as culpable in perpetuating discriminatory employment practices against its women and members of color for the way that it uses "short lists to recommend directors for particular projects, but the lists are not transparent or publicly available" and the questionable enforcement of the Guild's "diversity agreements" that are also not made public.[154]

The activism during those historically crucial years during the 1970s and early 1980s was less about policies and official means of enforcement, which to the disappointment of those involved were not achieved, and more about the slow, painstaking process of changing the prejudicial attitudes embedded within the entertainment industry. Because of the feminist reform efforts that took place throughout the 1970s—the work done by the Women's Committees at the DGA, SAG, and the WGA, the establishment of AFI's Directing Workshop for Women, the coverage in the press, and the presence of a variety of individuals who were outspoken about industry sexism—things did begin to change for women and for women film directors. In turn, the small, but increasing cadre of working women directors continue to alter perceptions of women's creative and economic power throughout the entertainment industry.

# Epilogue

## *Desperately Seeking the Eighties*

Looking at 1980—as the end of a "breakthrough" decade—the five films made by women directors that were released that year seem like a testament to the dire straits of the 1970s generation. All five were the last features those women filmmakers would make. Two were the first *and* last features made by Anne Bancroft (*Fatso*) and Nancy Walker (*Can't Stop the Music*); Barbara Peeters, who had hoped to make the transition from exploitation films to one-hour television dramas to Hollywood features, released her last movie then, *Humanoids from the Deep*. Both Claudia Weill (*It's My Turn*) and Lee Grant (*Tell Me a Riddle*) made their last pictures, although, at the time, both filmmakers commented that it was more of a choice on their part not to continue to pursue feature film work than the result of an obstacle imposed on them. Weill moved into television exclusively to better balance her personal and professional lives, and Grant found her niche in documentaries and movies made for television that provided the opportunity to express creatively her interest in certain sociopolitical topics.

While it is reassuring to hear a director say that on her own volition she chose to take her career in another direction, that "choice" might have been one of self-preservation and protection. A career as a television director, which so many of the sixteen filmmakers had settled into during the 1980s, was certainly a professional and economic achievement. Yet, if some measure of progress had occurred over the last ten years, these women should have been able to make more films of their choosing. In 1980 the 5 named movies constituted only 4 percent of the 125 studio and independently produced films made in the United States, and served as a reminder of the major obstacles faced by the women of the 1970s as that decade came to a close.[1]

Fortunately, women directors did fare better in the 1980s. During that decade an estimated forty women made close to ninety commercially distributed films: a 150 percent increase in the number of women directors from the previous decade (see the appendix). The work accomplished by the sixteen women during the 1970s, the films they made, and the way their presence within the industry, incrementally, made real the existence of women directors in Hollywood opened the door a little wider for the next generation. From this perspective, looking at the year 1980 as a starting point—the start of a *new* decade—the release of five films by five filmmakers was an encouraging sign of what the next ten years would produce. Five movies by five directors was a 150 percent increase from the two films made in 1970, one directed by Barbara Peeters and one by Stephanie Rothman. During the 1970s, with the exception of Joan Micklin Silver, Beverly Sebastian, and to a certain extent Elaine May, women had an impossible time sustaining a career in feature films. Arthur, Darling, and Grant were hired to make features in the 1990s, but all three women had bad experiences. Arthur clashed with the producer, who changed the content of the movie against her wishes; Darling had disputes with her producer over his effectiveness in running the production; and Grant's conflict with her leading actors resulted in her being fired.

Producer Lili Fini Zanuck, who would win an Academy Award for Best Picture (as producer) in 1989 for *Driving Miss Daisy* and would direct one feature film, *Rush,* in 1991, described a discernible change—for the better—in the 1980s. "The need for changes was being brought to everybody's attention. When the DGA statistics came out [in 1980] . . . all of a sudden the reality that women were taking such a backseat was so clear. . . . Men were very open to helping you. It was a good time."[2] One noticeable change during the 1980s was the increase in the number of female executives in positions of power to green light films. In 1980 Sherry Lansing became the first woman to head production for a studio when she was hired as president of 20th Century-Fox Productions; in 1981 Paula Weinstein was the president of the motion picture division at

United Artists; Lucy Fisher was named vice president of production for Warner Bros. in 1982; Barbara Boyle was senior vice president of worldwide production for Orion Pictures in 1982; and in 1987 Dawn Steel was the first woman to head a studio when she became president of Columbia Pictures.[3]

The growing number of female executives helped normalize the idea of women working in the upper echelons of male-dominated Hollywood. During the 1980s, male executives became acquainted with their female peers and, as a result, became more familiar with the concept of women in power. Consider this quote in chapter 1 from Dan Melnick, vice president of production at MGM, which captured the alienation experienced by the Hollywood patriarchy during the 1970s before this change: "We don't have many women in management positions. Here you have what is symptomatic of the whole industry, which is a tradition that takes a long time to overcome. To be honest about it, there are many of us in this business who have unconscious areas of being threatened by women executives."[4] Melnick would serve as an important mentor to Lansing during the 1970s, although his reputation as a supporter of women was mixed. As described in Rachel Abramowitz's book, *Is That a Gun in Your Pocket?*, one woman who worked for him said, "Melnick was one of those guys who learned early that women were great and undervalued resources. He gave us all jobs. He wouldn't even read the script, just go into the meetings with the notes I had given him, and he would take credit for it."[5]

In an industry that ostracized women for not being men—or rather, for being women—some male executives saw value in what they perceived as a gendered difference. Interviewed for a 2005 *New York Times* story about the prominence of women studio executives, Peter Guber, an executive at Columbia Pictures in the 1970s and an independent producer associated with films such as *Flashdance* (1983) and *The Color Purple* (1985) in the 1980s, reflected on the rise of female studio executives during those years: "Most men at the time, including me, just roughed people up, they had no governor on their testosterone. These women used their power elegantly. And it turned out they were right. That's why they're on top now [in 2005]."[6]

Whether it was women's "elegance" in using power as admired by their male peers or, more likely, the cumulative pressure of a decade's worth of feminist reform within Hollywood that had begun to change attitudes throughout the film industry, the increase of women in positions of authority became noticeable in the 1980s. But the increase in female executives did not automatically translate into the hiring of more women directors. In a 1981 article on the "struggle" of women directors, Barbara Peeters observed that women executives were careful not to seem as if they were playing gender favorites. "They'll bring up a woman director's name a couple of times," explained Peeters, "then they simply have to let it drop. Otherwise, they might be asked, 'What's the matter with you, can't you work with a man?'"[7] A DGA Women's Steering Committee member, who in 1980 preferred to remain anonymous for an interview about the status of women directors, was adamant about the misperceived state of "progress" in Hollywood: "Suddenly there's the impression that discrimination against women has vanished in Hollywood. Well, it's a lie. For every Sherry Lansing there are 500 others who are being blacklisted—in every area from directing to costume design—simply because they aren't men."[8]

While the increased number of women executives helped shift Hollywood's perception of gender—in different ways—what had the greatest impact on the hiring of women directors was the growing number of ways in which movies could be produced and distributed. Commercial filmmaking in the United States during the 1980s was characterized by two kinds of filmic outputs. On one end of the spectrum were the studio-made blockbuster franchises (e.g., *Star Wars: The Empire Strikes Back* [1980] and *Return of the Jedi* [1983], *Raiders of the Lost Ark* [1981], *Beverly Hills Cop* [1984], and *Back to the Future* [1985]). On the other end were a broad range of commercial independent films identified with small but profitable distribution companies like Cinecom Pictures, First Run Features, Miramax, New Line Cinema and with the prominent Sundance Film Festival and Independent Film Market, domestic marketplaces in which independent filmmakers could attract critical and financial interest.[9]

During the 1980s, no woman directed any of the big-budgeted franchises, but a few did direct studio-financed pictures, including Amy Heckerling, *Fast Times at Ridgemont High* (1982, Universal), Barbra Streisand, *Yentl* (1983, United Artists), Lynne Littman, *Testament* (1983, Paramount), Randa Haines, *Children of a Lesser God* (1986, Paramount), Elaine May, *Ishtar* (1987, Columbia), and Penny Marshall, *Big* (1988, 20th Century Fox). Some of these films were box office successes; for example, Heckerling's high school teen comedy, made for $9 million, earned an estimated $17 million upon its initial release,[10] and Streisand's period-piece musical—in which she starred and also wrote, directed, and produced—had an estimated budget of $14 million, and earned approximately $36.5 million domestically.[11]

As independent filmmakers during the 1970s, Penny Allen, Karen Arthur, Barbara Loden, Joan Micklin Silver, and Claudia Weill struggled to secure funding from private investors and the limited monies that were available through nonprofit grants; distribution options were narrow, and securing worthwhile deals was a grueling and unpredictable process. Ten years later the marketplace for "specialty" films—what independent producer John Pierson called "independent features" during the 1980s to separate them from the elitist stigma of being labeled "art films"—had expanded. There was an increase in the number of companies vying for products, and buying those properties had become a lucrative and competitive business. The interest in these kinds of movies was so high that several major studios—United Artists, 20th Century Fox, Universal—established "classics" divisions where they could pick up for distribution small and cheaply made films, as was done by Warner Bros. with Weill's *Girlfriends* in 1978.[12]

With a market that was more accessible to a range of films—in terms of content, filmmaker background, and financial resources—independent women directors of the 1980s had more opportunities to make a profit selling their work to a distributor and securing a theatrical release. The dominance of the home video market as an exhibition site ensured a second life for independent films and enlarged the profit margin, creating additional incentive for distributors and more exposure for filmmakers. Some of the notable independent filmmakers during this time were Kathryn Bigelow, *The Loveless* (1981, Atlantic Releasing), Susan Seidelman, *Smithereens* (1982, New Line Cinema), Penelope Spheeris, *Suburbia* (1983, New World Pictures), Joyce Chopra, *Smooth Talk* (1985, American Playhouse), Donna Deitch, *Desert Hearts* (1985, Samuel Goldwyn Company), Lizzie Borden, *Working Girls* (1986, Miramax Films), Allison Anders, *Border Radio* (1987, International Film Marketing), Mira Nair, *Salaam Bombay!* (1988, Cinecom Pictures), and Nancy Savoca, *True Love* (1989, New Line Cinema).

"I found you were either offered women's movies or projects that were not terribly interesting," reflected Joan Tewkesbury in 2011 on the tendency of producers to pigeonhole women directors during the 1970s. "The ones that really broke that paradigm—Susan Seidelman's *Desperately Seeking Susan*—and Amy Heckerling with *Fast Times*, that group, they were probably ten years younger or maybe even a little bit more; they came with terrific movies that had a really strong tone and sensibility that was definitely their own." Tewkesbury saw in the examples of Seidelman and Heckerling what she had tried so hard to accomplish near the start of her career when attempting to direct her script *After Ever After*: even with her success with *Nashville* and the endorsement of a successful male director, she was unable to make any progress toward directing her own film.

*Desperately Seeking Susan* was Susan Seidelman's second film after the success of her independently produced comedy *Smithereens* (1982), which is about an ambitious punk rock girl trying to make a name for herself in the downtown New York music scene. Seidelman, who received her master's degree from New York University Film School in 1977, began filming *Smithereens* in 1980. As with Weill and *Girlfriends*, the film took Seidelman a few years to complete, and she had to raise the $80,000 budget along the way. *Smithereens* was the first independent American film accepted into competition at the Cannes Film Festival, where it premiered in 1982.[13] The independent distributor New Line Cinema released the film that same year.

Soon after the successful release of Seidelman's first film, Barbara Boyle, senior vice president of worldwide production of Orion Pictures, who—atypical of female executives at the time—was actively trying to hire women directors, signed her to a three-picture deal.[14] Not a screenwriter, Seidelman was particular about picking the script for her first project. "Since I don't write my own material, it takes me a while to find a script that even has a kernel of an idea that would be something that I'd want to spend the next two years of my life working on. When I got the script for *Desperately Seeking Susan*, the central idea was something that really appealed to me right from the start."[15] *Desperately Seeking Susan*, a female buddy, screwball caper costarring Rosanna Arquette and Madonna, charmed both critics and audiences. The film's 1985 theatrical release coincided with Madonna's hugely successful second album, *Like a Virgin*.

Bolstered by the singer's fame, the film, reportedly made for under $5 million, earned almost $26 million within four months of its release.[16] In a 1985 interview Seidelman attributed part of her success to the directors of the previous decade: "I'm 32 years old. I've reaped a lot of benefits that women 10 years older worked hard for. I'm not saying I take feminism for granted—I'm a feminist, glad to be a woman and have a female sensibility—but it was easier for me. I tend to think of myself as being a woman the same way I think of myself as a New Yorker and short."[17]

Amy Heckerling also attended NYU film school in the early 1970s and then graduated from the AFI Conservatory's directing program in 1974. Her first feature, made for Universal, was *Fast Times at Ridgemont High*, an R-rated teen picture that centers around a female protagonist. The film starred a cast of young actors including Jennifer Jason Leigh, Phoebe Cates, Sean Penn, and Judge Reinhold. The script was based on a book about teenagers in Southern California written by future film director Cameron Crowe, who at the time was a music critic. Heckerling took her time choosing her first project and settled on Crowe's script on her own accord, without being coerced by producers or studio executives. Although she had to make concessions to meet the ratings board's objections to depictions of male nudity, Crowe vouched for her creative control over the project: "Amy made the film she wanted to make," said the writer. "There were a lot of people willing to tell her their way to do it, but she certainly had her own vision." Of the experience, Heckerling said, "I tried to make a movie that was realistic, not some cartoon version of high school."[18] The studio was unsure how to market the film, an R-rated comedy about teens with a considerable amount of onscreen sex and drug use. Opened without much fanfare in Southern California, the film soon drew long lines of teenagers.

Heckerling's and Seidelman's experiences of selecting their material and maintaining creative authorship of the project while bringing it to the screen were starting to become common occurrences during the 1980s, distinguishing that decade from the previous one. A considerable number of women filmmakers were directing their own scripts or working on projects that they had chosen. Marisa Silver, daughter of Joan Micklin Silver, wrote and directed her first film, *Old Enough*, in 1984 at age twenty-three; she made her second picture, *Permanent Record*, in 1988. "I had complete autonomy making the movie. I really made the film I wanted to make rather than a compromise," she said at the time of her second movie's release. Unsurprisingly, history was not lost on Marisa: "It's better than when my mother started working 15 years ago. Having seen the struggles she went through in her early films because she's a woman and seeing my career taking shape with fewer walls, I feel that she and the generation of the 1970s paved the way for us."[19]

What made the 1980s significantly different from the previous era was the ability for women directors to sustain a career and create a body of work over the course of several years and, in many instances, decades (see the appendix). The majority of the directors in the 1970s did not have this experience: although almost all of them pursued projects after their last directing job, most had no success. For example, Stephanie Rothman had never intended to be an exploitation filmmaker. In a 2002 interview, she reflected on her career: "I didn't even realize that what I was making was exploitation films until a reviewer described *Student Nurses* as an exploitation film. I thought I was just making low budget pictures, because that's what I had always heard people referring to them as being." She had seen directing B-films as a training ground and jumping-off point to Hollywood. This was not a fantasy: so many of her male peers in exploitation had accomplished just that. "I had hoped that I might make art films or commercial films. I would have liked to have been another Ingmar Bergman. So would many other people, obviously," she recalled with a laugh.[20] A woman's status in the industry had little impact on lessening these challenges. In the late 1970s, when accomplished veteran actress Lee Grant tried to generate interest in a project she was planning to direct with A-list Hollywood star Jill Clayburgh attached, she was met with disdain: "It was as if I had *betrayed* all these people who had loved me and had given me so many accolades and so many awards. 'But you're an actress.' It was like I turned on them. I never got to do that movie. Well—there were a lot of movies I didn't get to do."[21]

During these years many women filmmakers never got to do *their* movie. These women were prepared to direct, having signed development deals with studios or were attached to projects scheduled to go into production. Yet none of these ventures were ultimately realized. In 1971 journalist Estelle Changas, writing for the *Los Angeles Times*, reported that screenwriter Carole Eastman, who used the pseudonym Adrien Joyce, was scheduled to direct her own script for Warner Bros. starring French actress Jeanne Moreau. Eastman, whose screenplays included the films *Puzzle of a Downfall Child* (1970) and *The Shooting* (1971), had also received an Oscar nomination for Best Original Screenplay for the movie *Five Easy Pieces* (1970). Changas praised Eastman as a screenwriter for writing "one of the most arresting American films of the decade [*Five Easy Pieces*]" and acknowledged her feat in doing so as a woman in Hollywood:

> But she's even more rare than this: She's about to direct a film, and you can count on the fingers of one hand women who do such things—Elaine May, Barbara Loden, Susan Sontag, Shirley Clarke. The fact that Adrien Joyce and the bare handful of articulate women writers in existence (notably Eleanor Perry, Harriet Ravetch and Edna O'Brien) have escaped being trapped in lightweight entertainment, "women's films," and bland, G-rated family fare, and have managed to deal with a wide range of serious contemporary issues may be a sign that sexual barriers are crumbling.[22]

Like many journalists during the decade, Changas was aware of the sexism in the industry and took the opportunity to call out Hollywood's tradition of inequality while championing the few women who were directing. Six months later, when Eastman's first project had not materialized, the *Los Angeles Times* reported that she was "rumored to be directing a Jack Nicholson film in the future."[23] It seemed that Changas's hope that the "sexual barriers are crumbling" was too optimistic: none of these titles Eastman was rumored to direct were ever made.

Producer Julia Phillips, who was the first woman to win an Academy Award for Best Picture in 1973 for *The Sting*, had tried for several years to direct the screen adaptation of Erica Jong's best-selling novel, *Fear of Flying*. After participating in the Directing Workshop for Women's pilot year in 1974, she had bought the rights that same year to *Fear*. In 1975 Columbia Pictures signed Phillips to direct the film, and principal photography was set to start in February 1976. However, a legal battle between Phillips and Jong ensued over what the author claimed was contract violation on the part of the producer-director.[24] The lawsuit and problems in developing the script, combined with Columbia's hesitation to use Phillips as a first-time director, stalled the project indefinitely.[25]

In 1977 actress Dyan Cannon was reported to have signed a development deal with 20th Century-Fox to produce and direct a film "dealing with relationships" between a woman and two brothers.[26] Cannon had participated in the second cohort of DWW in 1976. The short film that she had made as part of the workshop, *Number One*, was described by journalist Gregg Kilday in the *Los Angeles Times* as a "painful if humorous parable about childhood innocence encountering adult inhibitions." In 1977 it received an Academy Award nomination for Best Short Film. Cannon told Kilday, "To me, films should be about the subtleties of life. I enjoy big adventure productions. But I want to do movies about the little things we all deal with, the things that drive us crazy."[27] Cannon never directed the "relationships" film for Universal. In 1990 she did write, direct, and star in her first, and to date only, directorial effort, the independently produced *The End of Innocence.*

Some women were offered the opportunity to direct by men in significant positions of power under conditions that seemed ideal. In her autobiography, *Then Again*, actress Diane Keaton describes how at the end of the 1970s Warren Beatty had encouraged her to start directing films. By the time Keaton and Beatty had begun dating in 1978, Keaton had won an Oscar for Best Actress in *Annie Hall* (1977), and he was one of the most powerful writers, directors, producers, and actors of the decade. In 1980 she costarred with Beatty in his historical epic *Reds*, for which they received Oscar nominations for Best Actor and Best Actress. The film was also nominated for Best Screenplay and Best Picture, and Beatty won an Oscar for Best Director. In a letter Beatty wrote Keaton around this time, he advised her to take advantage of her position in the industry:

> You've made a lot of money for the movie business and your percentages for the profits haven't been so huge that you should feel guilty about taking some of the industry's money and making your own film. I think they'd be happy to do it. Stop messing around and do it. You'd do it better than anybody. You know more than anybody. Its rough edges would be fascinating. I can set it up early. And either produce or get completely out of the way.[28]

Beatty was comfortable with his movie star status—as a performer and filmmaker—and as a deal maker. In her autobiography Keaton describes him affectionately at "The Pro," always brokering a deal: "It was impossible to drag him away from a phone, a restaurant, a meeting, a club, you name it."[29] In contrast, Keaton was insecure and unsure about how she felt as a prominent Hollywood actress and at that time did not feel she was ready to pursue directing, even with the support of Beatty whom she "loved." "I had a few healthy instincts," she writes, "but I didn't have the fortitude to prolong my moment in the sun. I preferred retreating."[30] Keaton would eventually go on to direct two feature films fifteen and twenty years later, *Unstrung Heroes* (1995) and *Hanging Up* (2000). Beatty was not involved with either one.

It is common in Hollywood for development deals to never be realized. Similarly, many of the difficulties that women directors experienced while their movies were in production—conflicts with producers and stars, going over budget, and even problems caused by their own idiosyncratic creative visions—occurred often in the 1970s: in fact the decade was defined by such episodes. Yet even though male directors experienced such problems frequently, their careers did not end because of them. Clearly, women directors faced an additional risk factor—their gender—that made their professional lives more difficult. As has been reiterated throughout this study, these filmmakers were so often forced to experience their professional lives both as women in a sexist industry *and* as directors in a highly competitive one.

In the mid-1990s I started counting the number of new releases by American women directors. At that time the numbers were still small enough that it was easy to keep track both of what was in production and what titles would be released theatrically. What was noticeable during these years was how many new filmmakers were making their first features. In 1998 an estimated twenty feature films directed by women were produced and distributed in the United States. They included first-time independent directors Maya Angelou (*Down on the Delta*), Lisa Cholodenko (*High Art*), Tamara Jenkins (*Slums of Beverly Hills*), and Cauleen Smith (*Drysolong*), as well as studio filmmakers such as Nora Ephron (*You've Got Mail*), Betty Thomas (*Doctor Doolittle*), and Penelope Spheeris (*Senseless*). This progress was possible *and* remarkable.

In 2000, I participated in Allison Anders's Miramar Summit at which more than one hundred women (and some men) gathered to talk about the current status of female filmmakers. Well known was the importance of buying tickets for films on their opening weekends. This was especially important for films directed by women, who, even with the increase in their numbers, were under pressure to perform at the box office. To generate audience interest in films ahead of their theatrical release, many of us who attended the summit worked together to create a weekly email newsletter—before the convenience of emerging social media platforms—initially titled "Features Directed by Women." This weekly email blast included film titles, filmmakers, and theater listings in major cities and we hoped that this increased level of awareness could have a positive impact on box office revenues.[31]

Today there are so many women directors that it is nearly impossible to keep track of them. In 2015 Maureen Dowd's profile, "The Women of Hollywood Speak Out," for the *New York Times Magazine* featured more than fifty women filmmakers—ranging from those directing independents to those helming bigger budgets for established companies—working in narrative features. Even with a disclaimer that read, "This is not every woman working in Hollywood today," still readers complained and wrote Dowd with the names of those women left out of the article.[32] Grassroots organizations like Film Fatales boast an affiliation of more than 500 women directors in the United States and hundreds more internationally "who have directed at least one feature film, documentary or television episode."[33] Journalists such as Melissa Silverstein and her website "Women and Hollywood" profile countless women filmmakers, female-centric films, and opening weekend details. Parity has not yet been achieved, but an abundance of women filmmakers is now being experienced.

In the 1970s, in contrast, there were so few women directors that their film releases each year could be counted on one hand: their small numbers and recent emergence placed them under extreme scrutiny. "What we need right now is a huge box-office success," remarked Karen Arthur in 1978. "Unfortunately, at this moment, every woman who goes out is a test case. We are very visible because there are so few of us."[34] In that decade the studio system and different commercial independent production communities overlapped in terms of filmic content, distribution, exhibition resources, and the hiring of cast and crew. The era's social movements not only influenced film subject matter and audience demographics but also the culture in which movies were made. For all its potential, this era was particularly difficult for women filmmakers. Male studio executives and producers who had never had female colleagues and the powerful fraternity-like unions that had never shared their ranks with female members resisted the changes taking place. For women directors in the 1970s the coinciding of the feminist movement with a film industry experiencing major economic and cultural shifts allowed for a very small opening in which they began to squeeze through, something they did with equal parts determination and trepidation.

One of the challenges of writing a history of women directors in Hollywood is balancing the push and pull between stark discrimination and progress, often of the smallest kind. Both must be acknowledged: to call out inequality and, in the same breath, acknowledge filmmakers' accomplishments, sometimes measured by their mere presence and resolve. To quantify progress means not only to look at the way statistics change or stay the same, but to study who composes those numbers, however small. Joan Rivers whose singular experience directing a film was a disappointment, years later still found satisfaction in the project. In her autobiography, *Still Talking* in 1991, Rivers admitted that "the movie does look amateurish—bad photography, bad sound, bad lighting—everything unfocused and ugly—but there are fifteen hysterical minutes I am extremely proud of. . . . Failure is devastating, but . . . *Rabbit Test* was one of the most successful experiences I have ever had. It is part of my education, part of my consciousness."[35] Maya Angelou, who tried several times to direct film and television in the 1970s and eventually made a feature in 1998, saw failure not as an end all, but rather part of the process. In 1976 she explained to the *Los Angeles Times*, "It's not that I have confidence but I believe that if I fail, so what? So what'cha gonna do—stop liking me? I mean, really if you're going to stop liking me because I tried to direct a film and I fell on my face or tried to love somebody and had a divorce, I mean, I tried."[36] Joan Micklin Silver relayed an inspirational mantra to an audience at the AFI in 1991 that echoes throughout the experiences detailed in this book. She rallied the group of aspiring filmmakers: "Be tenacious. Be strong. Be courageous. What can I say? Keep it up. You have to learn to take rejection. You have to learn to believe in yourself."[37]

These filmmakers faced difficulties in a hostile industry with grit and gusto in pursuit of professional aspirations; they persevered despite disappointments and especially their failures. Determined to make films in an industry defined in so many ways by sexism, gender clearly played a key role in shaping their experiences during this decade. But what is of equal historical importance is how these women, as *individual* filmmakers, contributed to a mythic and monumental era of American cinema.

# APPENDIX

## Women Directors' Filmography: 1960s and 1970s

This list accounts only for the feature films made by these directors; it does not include their documentary and television work. The dates correspond with the title's initial release in a festival or theater.

### *1960s*

*The Connection* (1961) **Shirley Clarke**
*The Cool World* (1963) **Shirley Clarke**
*Stranded* (1964) **Juleen Compton**
*Blood Bath* (1966, aka *Track of the Vampire*) **Stephanie Rothman, codirected with Jack Hill**
*The Plastic Dome of Norma Jean* (1966) **Juleen Compton**
*The Trouble with Angels* (1966) **Ida Lupino**
*I Need a Man* (1967, aka *I Need*) **Beverly and Ferd Sebastian**
*It's a Bikini World* (1967) **Stephanie Rothman**
*The Love Clinic* (1969) **Beverly and Ferd Sebastian**

### *1970s*

*The Dark Side of Tomorrow* (1970, aka *Just the Two of Us*) **Barbara Peeters**
*The Student Nurses* (1970) **Stephanie Rothman**
*Bury Me an Angel* (1971) **Barbara Peeters**
*A New Leaf* (1971) **Elaine May**
*The Velvet Vampire* (1971) **Stephanie Rothman**
*Wanda* (1971) **Barbara Loden**
*Group Marriage* (1972) **Stephanie Rothman**

*The Heartbreak Kid* (1972) **Elaine May**
*The Hitchhikers* (1972) **Beverly and Ferd Sebastian**
*Bloody Friday* (1973, aka *Single Girls*) **Beverly and Ferd Sebastian**
*Terminal Island* (1973) **Stephanie Rothman**
*'Gator Bait* (1974) **Beverly and Ferd Sebastian**
*Legacy* (1974) **Karen Arthur**
*Summer School Teachers* (1974) **Barbara Peeters**
*The Working Girls* (1974) **Stephanie Rothman**
*Hester Street* (1975) **Joan Micklin Silver**
*Flash and the Firecat* (1976) **Beverly and Ferd Sebastian**
*Mikey & Nicky* (1976) **Elaine May**
*Between the Lines* (1977) **Joan Micklin Silver**
*First Love* (1977) **Joan Darling**
*Girlfriends* (1978) **Claudia Weill**
*Mafu Cage* (1978) **Karen Arthur**
*Moment by Moment* (1978) **Jane Wagner**
*Property* (1978) **Penny Allen**
*Rabbit Test* (1978) **Joan Rivers**
*Starhops* (1978) **Barbara Peeters**
*Chilly Scenes of Winter* (1979 aka *Head Over Heels*) **Joan Micklin Silver**
*Delta Fox* (1979) **Beverly and Ferd Sebastian**
*Old Boyfriends* (1979) **Joan Tewkesbury**
*On the Air Live with Captain Midnight* (1979) **Beverly and Ferd Sebastian**
*Can't Stop the Music* (1980) **Nancy Walker**
*Fatso* (1980) **Anne Bancroft**
*Humanoids from the Deep* (1980) **Barbara Peeters**
*It's My Turn* (1980) **Claudia Weill**
*Tell Me a Riddle* (1980) **Lee Grant**

## Women Directors: 1980s

The following is a list of directors who made their first narrative feature—produced and released in the United States—in the 1980s: this list represents both studio and independent films. It is organized chronologically according to the year of their first film, as a way to visualize the increase in the number of women making feature films in the American film industry throughout the decade; the number of features that the filmmakers have directed to date is in the parentheses. This list only reflects their film work and not episodic television, television movies, or documentaries they may have also directed, formats in which many of them have excelled. These calculations are an *estimation* of the number of films directed by women in the 1980s and are not intended to be complete. The following names and numbers have been identified over the course of much research so there is no one authoritative source, but rather the information is gathered from multiple places.

1. Jessie Maple: 1981 (2)
2. Kathryn Bigelow: 1982 (10)
3. Patricia Birch: 1982 (1)
4. Kathleen Collins: 1982 (1)
5. Amy Jones: 1982 (4)
6. Susan Seidelman: 1982 (10)
7. Lizzie Borden: 1983 (4)
8. Martha Coolidge: 1983 (12)
9. Bette Gordon: 1983 (3)
10. Jackie Kong: 1983 (4)
11. Lynne Littman: 1983 (1)
12. Euzhan Palcy: 1983 (3)
13. Barbra Streisand: 1983 (3)
14. Gillian Armstrong: 1984 (7)
15. Amy Heckerling: 1984 (9)
16. Marisa Silver: 1984 (4)
17. Penelope Spheeris: 1984 (12)
18. Joyce Chopra: 1985 (2)
19. Donna Deitch: 1985 (2)
20. Joan Freeman: 1985 (2)
21. Lisa Gottlieb: 1985 (4)
22. Randa Haines: 1986 (4)
23. Connie Kaiserman: 1986 (1)
24. Sondra Locke: 1986 (3)
25. Michelle Manning: 1986 (1)
26. Penny Marshall: 1986 (7)
27. Evelyn Purcell: 1986 (1)
28. Allison Anders: 1987 (8)

29. Mary Lambert: 1987 (6)
30. Katt Shea: 1987 (6)
31. Sandra Weintraub: 1987 (1)
32. Catlin Adams: 1988 (1)
33. Janet Greek: 1988 (1)
34. Fran Rubel Kuzui: 1988 (2)
35. Mira Nair: 1988 (10)
36. Tina Rathborne: 1988 (1)
37. Geneviève Robert: 1988 (1)
38. Zelda Barron: 1989 (2)
39. Julia Cameron: 1989 (1)
40. Nancy Savoca: 1989 (6)

## Directors from the 1970s Who Also Made Films in the 1980s

41. Penny Allen (1)
42. Karen Arthur (1)
43. Joan Darling (1)
44. Elaine May (1)
45. Beverly Sebastian (3)
46. Joan Micklin Silver (2)

# ACKNOWLEDGMENTS

I was first introduced to the study of American women feature film directors as an undergraduate at Boston University (BU) when I saw Barbara Loden's *Wanda* (1971) and Claudia Weill's *Girlfriends* (1978) in Ray Carney's illuminating class on American independent cinema. Gerald Peary, another of my BU instructors, introduced me to Dorothy Arzner, Ida Lupino, and Stephanie Rothman. His book, *Women and the Cinema: A Critical Anthology* (1977), coedited with Karyn Kay, has been a tremendous influence on me and one that set me on my course. For well over a decade before entering academia, I was able to combine my interest in female filmmakers with a professional career working in production with women directors and being employed at organizations dedicated to those media makers, such as the American Film Institute's Directing Workshop for Women, under the guidance of Joe Petricca, and Women Make Movies. These experiences laid the foundation for *Liberating Hollywood*.

The most exciting and rewarding aspects of writing about American cinema during the 1970s is hearing firsthand accounts of this important era from those who were part of it. I had the opportunity to interview many of the individuals who are featured in *Liberating Hollywood*. These interviewees give depth to my study, and my appreciation and gratitude for their generosity, time, candor, insights, and humor is enormous. I cannot thank each of them enough for their contributions to this book and to film history. Thank you, Leslie Mitchner of Rutgers University Press, for ushering in this history.

Over the years I have benefited greatly from the mentorship of Janet Bergstrom, John Caldwell, and Allyson Nadia Field. Their enthusiasm and encouragement have been key to the success of this project at every phase. Many thanks to Jan-Christopher Horak, director of the UCLA Film and Television Archive, and Mark Quigley, manager of the Archive

Research and Study Center, for their ongoing support of my research and their dedication to representing women filmmakers in the archive. Teresa Barnett, director of the UCLA Center for Oral History Research, and Jane Collings, the UCLA Center's principal editor, provided invaluable advice to me over the years. So much of the research for this book depended on the expertise of librarians and archivists who pointed me in the right direction. I want to thank the staff of the Margaret Herrick Library, especially Jenny Romero, Faye Thompson, and Louise Hilton; Diana King, UCLA Arts Library; Hilary Swett and Joanne Lammers, Writers Guild Foundation, Shavelson-Webb Library; Valerie Yaros, SAG-AFTRA; and Mike Pepin, Louis B. Mayer Library at the American Film Institute. I would also like to acknowledge the AFI's Harold Lloyd Master Seminars ©1971, ©1975, ©1977, ©1978, ©1979, ©1980, ©1988, ©1991, courtesy of the American Film Institute. Teague Schneiter and Mae Woods of the Academy of Motion Picture Arts and Sciences, Preservation and Foundation Programs have given me a unique opportunity to build my research skills while contributing to their invaluable archive. Since 2002, I have been a lecturer in the School of Media Studies at the New School and during those years I was fortunate to have the opportunity to workshop many of the ideas presented here in the classroom: my gratitude goes to this department for the opportunity to teach and to my students for their excellent thinking.

My fellow comrades in academia have made the grueling aspects of research and writing worth it: Jennifer Porst has been with me since this project's incubator stage; Erin Hill and Benjamin Raphael Sher read, problem solved, and rescued so much of this book; and Alexandra Seros never tired of the topic. I am especially grateful to Maria San Filippo for being a good friend and mentor and for understanding the importance of *Shampoo.*

I am so lucky to have such good friends: Kasja Alger, Kristin Carey, John Donovan, John Gilmore, Lori A. Hersey, Michael Jones, Janice Linhares, Kristen Meehan, Marilyn Pappert, Sandi Perlmutter, Galeen Roe, Mara S. Rose, Jason Tomasian, and Christopher Trudeau. Samuel Flores, thank you for showing me what it is to work hard. Thank you, Tom Giesler and Heidi Van Heel, for your ongoing technical support. Thank you to my great mentors: Allison Anders, for teaching me the art of the fan letter, and Carolyn Jacobs, for hiring me to write them. Thank you,

Gina Marie Helms Donovan, for being the perfect muse. And Alanya Snyder, my best reader since age fifteen, thank you for making writing such a pleasure.

I am grateful for my adorable family and their endless generosity, love, and constant interest in who I am: for my grandparents, Blanca and Eli Montañez; my stepparents, Claudia Dawn Smukler, Vincent Aviles, William Flounders, and Vardit Kindler; my brother, Eli Corey Smukler; and my parents, Wilma Montañez and Howard Smukler, who have always believed in the rights of children and let me see R-rated movies at a very young age.

# NOTES

## Introduction

1 Including Bigelow, five women have been nominated for an Academy Award for Best Director: Lina Wertmüller, *Seven Beauties* (1977, Italy), Jane Campion, *The Piano* (1994, Australia), Sofia Coppola, *Lost in Translation* (2004, United States), Kathryn Bigelow (2010, United States), and Greta Gerwig, *Lady Bird* (2018, United States).

2 For a discussion of Streisand's ambition to direct starting in the 1970s, see Rachel Abramowitz, *Is That a Gun in Your Pocket? Women's Experience of Power in Hollywood* (New York: Random House, 2000).

3 Ironically, Streisand is a frequent presenter at the Academy Awards for its most prestigious honors, including Best Director (Clint Eastwood, *Unforgiven*, 1993), Best Picture (Clint Eastwood, *Million Dollar Baby*, 2005), and the Academy Honorary Award (Robert Redford, 2002).

4 This number is calculated from the Women Film Pioneers Project. Because the early film industry was configured differently from the classical Hollywood studio system, the studio system, and the independent commercial film communities of 1970s, it is difficult to compare the body of work from filmmakers of different eras. For my purposes, this number demonstrates the larger presence of women filmmakers in the United States during the silent era compared to later decades. Jane Gaines, Radha Vatsal, and Monica Dall'Asta, eds., Women Film Pioneers Project, Center for Digital Research and Scholarship, Columbia University Libraries, 2013, https://wfpp.cdrs.columbia.edu/.

5 See the following authors who speak to this statistic: Ally Acker, *Reel Women: Pioneers of the Cinema, 1896 to the Present* (New York: Continuum, 1991); Amelie Hastie, *The Bigamist* (London: British Film Institute, 2009); Louise Heck-Rabi, *Women Filmmakers: A Critical Reception* (Metuchen, N.J.: Scarecrow Press, 1974); Karyn Kay and Gerald Peary, eds., *Women and the Cinema: A Critical Anthology* (New York: E. P. Dutton, 1977); Annette Kuhn, ed., *Queen of the 'B's: Ida Lupino Behind the Camera* (Westport, Conn.: Praeger, 1995); Judith Mayne, *Directed by Dorothy Arzner* (Bloomington: Indiana University Press, 1994); Lauren Rabinovitz, *Points of Resistance: Women, Power & Politics in the New York Avant-Garde Cinema,*

*1943–1971* (Urbana: University of Illinois Press, 1991); and Sharon Smith, *Women Who Make Movies* (New York: Hopkinson and Blake, 1975).

6 Directors Guild of America, et al. v. Warner Brothers Inc. and Columbia Pictures Industries, Inc., 1985 U.S. Dist. LEXIS 16325; 2 Fed. R. Serv. 3d (Callaghan) 1429, 30 Aug. 1985.

7 For histories of "feminist filmmaking" during the 1970s see Robin Blaetz, ed., *Women's Experimental Cinema: Critical Frameworks* (Durham, N.C.: Duke University Press, 2007); Jean Petrolle and Virginia Wright Wexman, eds., *Women & Experimental Filmmaking* (Urbana: University of Illinois Press, 2005); and B. Ruby Rich, *Chick Flicks: Theories and Memories of the Feminist Film Movement* (Durham, N.C.: Duke University Press, 1998).

8 For a discussion of these filmmakers see Tania Modleski, "Women's Cinema as Counterphobic Cinema: Doris Wishman as the Last Auteur," in *Sleaze Artists*, ed. Jeffrey Sconce (Durham, N.C.: Duke University Press, 2007), 47–70; Alexandra Heller-Nicholas, "What's Inside a Girl? Porn, Horror and the Films of Roberta Findlay," *Senses of Cinema* 80 (September 2016), http://sensesofcinema.com /2016/american-extreme/porn-horror-roberta-findlay/; and Elena Gorfinkel, *Lewd Looks: American Sexploitation Cinema in the 1960s* (Minneapolis: University of Minnesota Press, 2017).

9 Molly Haskell, "How an Independent Filmmaker Beat the System (with Her Husband's Help)," *Village Voice*, September 22, 1975, 83; Leticia Kent, "They Were behind the Scenes of 'Between the Lines,'" *New York Times*, June 12, 1977, 83.

10 Kevin Thomas, "Tomlin and Travolta in 'Moment,'" *Los Angeles Times*, December 22, 1978, G28.

11 Dan Rottenberg, "Elaine May . . . or She May Not," *Chicago Tribune*, October 21,1973, 55–58; Andrew Tobias, "For Elaine May, a New Film—but Not a New Leaf," *New West*, December 6, 1976, 57–65.

12 Barbara Peeters, interview by author, April 11, 2010.

13 African American male directors in the 1970s who made a range of feature films, some of which were independent, include Charles Burnett, Larry Clark, William Crain, Ossie Davis, Ivan Dixon, Jamaa Fanaka, Wendell Franklin, Haile Gerima, Berry Gordon, Gordon Parks, Gordon Parks Jr., Bill Gunn, Stan Lathan, Sidney Poitier, Michael Schultz, and Melvin Van Peebles. See Allyson Nadia Field, Jan-Christopher Horak, and Jacqueline Najuma Stewart, eds., *L.A. Rebellion: Creating a New Black Cinema* (Berkeley: University of California Press, 2015); and Keith Corson, *Trying to Get Over: African American Directors after Blaxploitation, 1977–1986* (Austin: University of Texas Press, 2016).

14 For a discussion of the cultural trends and economic changes that shaped Hollywood's modes of production, distribution, and exhibition during the late 1960s and 1970s, see Douglas Gomery, "The American Film Industry of the 1970s," *Wide Angle* 5, no. 4 (1983): 53–59; and Thomas Schatz, "The New Hollywood," in *Film Theory Goes to the Movies*, ed. Jim Collins, Hilary Radner, and Ava Preacher

Collins (New York: Routledge, 1993), 8–36. For production histories of the 1970s that include an examination of the era in terms of genre, individual filmmakers, and independent commercial film communities that existed outside of the dominant cinema but frequently shared with it audiences, production staff (above- and below-the-line), and exhibition spaces (i.e., exploitation and cult or "midnight movies"), see David A. Cook, *Lost Illusions: American Cinema in the Shadow of Watergate and Vietnam 1970–1979* (Berkeley: University of California Press, 2000); J. Hoberman and Jonathan Rosenbaum, *Midnight Movies* (New York: Harper & Row, 1983); David E. James, "'Movies Are a Revolution': Film and Counterculture," in *Imagine Nation: The American Counterculture of the 1960s & 70s,* ed. Peter Braunstein and Michael William Doyle (New York: Routledge, 2002), 275–303; and James Monaco, *American Film Now* (New York: Oxford University Press, 1979).

15 For histories of the MPAA and CARA rating system see Jon Lewis, *Hollywood v. Hard Core: How the Struggle over Censorship Saved the Modern Film Industry* (New York: New York University Press, 2000); and Justin Wyatt, "The Stigma of X: Adult Cinema and the Institution of the MPAA Ratings System," in *Controlling Hollywood: Censorship and Regulation in the Studio Era,* ed. Matthew Bernstein (New Brunswick, N.J.: Rutgers University Press, 1999), 238–263.

16 Mel Gussow, "Movies Leaving 'Hollywood' Behind," *New York Times,* May 27, 1970, 36.

17 Cook, *Lost Illusions,* 98.

18 Letter to signatories from Michael Franklin regarding employment statistics, June 20, 1980, DGA Clipping File, Margaret Herrick Library, Los Angeles.

19 For a history of the establishment of Women in Film, see Mollie Gregory, *Women Who Run the Show: How a Brilliant and Creative New Generation of Women Stormed Hollywood* (New York: St. Martin's Press, 2002).

20 Alison McMahan, "Alice Guy Blaché," Women Film Pioneers Project, https://wfpp.cdrs.columbia.edu/pioneer/ccp-alice-guy-blache/. For additional scholarship on Guy Blaché see Alison McMahan, *Alice Guy Blaché: Lost Visionary of the Cinema* (New York: Continuum, 2002); Anthony Slide, ed., *The Memoirs of Alice Guy Blaché,* trans. Roberta and Simone Blaché (Metuchen, N.J.: Scarecrow Press, 1986); and Gerald Peary, "Alice Guy Blache: Czarina of the Silent Screen," in *Women and the Cinema: A Critical Anthology,* ed. Karyn Kay and Gerald Peary (New York: E. P. Dutton, 1977), 139–145.

21 For discussion of "double in brass" see Karen Ward Mahar, *Women Filmmakers in Early Hollywood* (Baltimore: Johns Hopkins University Press, 2006), 39–42.

22 For general studies of Weber and her status as a director during these years, see Anthony Slide, *Lois Weber: The Director Who Lost Her Way in History* (Westport, Conn.: Greenwood Press, 1996), 110; and Shelley Stamp, *Lois Weber in Early Hollywood* (Berkeley: University of California Press, 2015), 67.

23 For additional sources on women in early Hollywood, see Kay Armatage, *The*

*Girl from God's Country: Nell Shipman and the Silent Screen* (Toronto: University of Toronto Press, 2003); Cari Beauchamp, *Without Lying Down: Frances Marion and the Powerful Women of Early Hollywood* (Berkeley: University of California Press, 1997); Mark Garrett Cooper, *Universal Women: Filmmaking and Institutional Change in Early Hollywood* (Urbana: University of Illinois Press, 2010); Gaines et al., Women Film Pioneers Project; Anthony Slide, *The Silent Feminists: America's First Woman Directors* (Lanham, Md.: Scarecrow Press, 1996).

24 For discussion of how the early film industry adopted a business model that excluded women, see Karen Ward Mahar, "'A Business Pure & Simple': The End of Uplift and the Masculinization of Hollywood 1916–1928," in *Women Filmmakers in Early Hollywood*, 133–203.

25 Here I am using Mary Ann Doane's definition of the "woman's film": a Hollywood genre popular particularly during the 1930s and 1940s that focused on a female protagonist's point of view, with a narrative that revolved around "female problems" (domestic life, children, self-sacrifice), and was geared toward a female audience. In the 1970s the New Woman film, discussed in chapter 3, updated the classical Hollywood genre for a second-wave feminist generation. Mary Ann Doane, *The Desire to Desire: The Woman's Film of the 1940s* (Bloomington: Indiana University Press, 1987), 3.

26 For example, see Todd Berliner, *Hollywood Incoherent: Narration in Seventies Cinema* (Austin: University of Texas Press, 2010); Thomas Elsaesser, Alexander Horwath, and Noel King, eds., *The Last Great American Picture Show* (Amsterdam: Amsterdam University Press, 2004)—with the exception of Bérénice Reynaud's essay "For Wanda," on Barbara Loden; and Robert Kolker, *A Cinema of Loneliness: Penn, Stone, Kubrick, Scorsese, Spielberg, Altman* (Oxford: Oxford University Press, 2000).

27 Barbara Koenig Quart, *Women Directors: The Emergence of a New Cinema* (New York: Praeger, 1988); and Mary G. Hurd, *Women Directors & Their Films* (New York: Praeger, 2006).

28 For example, Charlotte Brunsdon ed., *Films for Women* (London: British Film Institute, 1986); Patricia Erens, ed. *Sexual Stratagems: The World of Women in Film* (New York: Horizon, 1979); Lucy Fisher, *Shot/Countershot: Film Tradition and Women's Cinema* (Princeton: Princeton University Press, 1989); and E. Ann Kaplan, *Women & Film: Both Sides of the Camera* (London: Methuen, 1983). For histories of "feminist filmmaking" during the 1970s, see Blaetz, *Women's Experimental Cinema*; Petrolle and Wexman, *Women & Experimental Filmmaking*; and Rich, *Chick Flicks*.

29 Martha M. Lauzen, *The Celluloid Ceiling: Behind-the-Scenes Employment of Women on the Top 100, 250, and 500 Films of 2017* (San Diego: Center for the Study of Women in Television and Film, San Diego State University, 2018).

30 Joan Tewkesbury, interview by author, January 27, 2011.

### Prologue

1 Lauren Rabinovitz, *Points of Resistance* (Urbana: University of Illinois Press, 1991), 110, 119.

2 Eugene Archer, "Woman Director Makes the Scene," *New York Times Magazine*, August 26, 1962.

3 For a discussion of *The Connection*'s struggle with censorship and related legal battles see Rabinovitz, *Points of Resistance*, 120–122.

4 "Prize Winners at Cannes Fest," *Variety*, May 24, 1961, 5.

5 Gene Moskowitz, "The Cannes Film Fest Pictures: The Connection," *Variety*, May 10, 1961, 7.

6 Sharon Smith, *Women Who Make Movies* (New York: Hopkinson and Blake, 1975), 45.

7 Sandra Shevey, "Pic-Maker Shirley Clarke Says Second Class Status of Women in Films Is Result of Viewers' Standards," *Variety*, January 28, 1975. For the complete AFI interview, see Shirley Clarke, interview at the American Film Institute, 1975, Harold Lloyd Master Seminars, Louis B. Mayer Library, Los Angeles.

8 Linda Gross, "Rebel Film-Maker: An Out-of-the System Person," *Los Angeles Times*, June 21, 1978, H1.

9 Nell Cox, interview by author, April 8, 2011.

10 Barbara Peeters, interview by author, April 11, 2010.

11 Gross, "Rebel Film-Maker," H1.

12 Lawrence Van Gelder, "Shirley Clarke Is Dead at 77; Maker of Oscar-Winning Film," *New York Times*, September 26, 1997.

13 Juleen Compton, interview by author, July 9, 2013.

14 Compton, interview by author, July 9, 2013.

15 Compton interview by author, September 7, 2013.

16 Compton's performance in Little Red Riding Hood for the Children's World Theatre was described to the author in an interview with Compton conducted on September 7, 2013. Also see Harold Clurman, *All People Are Famous (Instead of an Autobiography)* (New York: Harcourt Brace Jovanovich, 1974), 280; and "Fun for Children," *New York Times*, March 25, 1950, 13. For *The Cherry Orchard* see Sidney Fields, "Only Human," *New York Mirror*, 1955; and Juleen Compton Clipping File, New York Public Library for the Performing Arts. For *Good as Gold* see Sam Zolotow, "Run of 'Candide' May Close Feb. 2," *New York Times*, January 18, 1957, 16; and "Sad and Happy Yuletide Faces in a Comedy Opening This Week," *New York Times*, March 3, 1957, 107.

17 A discussion of her work as a colorist on these military bases was told to the author in interviews conducted with Compton on July 9, 2013, and September 7, 2013; also see Fields, "Only Human;" and Juleen Compton Clipping File.

18 Clurman had been married to Stella Adler, the renowned acting teacher, since 1943; the couple divorced in 1960 so that Clurman and Compton could wed. Compton, interview by author, July 9, 2013; Clurman, *All People Are Famous*, 280.

19 Compton, interview by author, September 7, 2013.

20 Thomas Lask, "Little Woman with Big Ideas about Her New Theater," *New York Times*, April 30, 1961. See also "Five New Off-Broadway Theatres to Cost a Half-Million Dollars," *Back Stage*, April 21, 1961.

21 "Women Directors Multiply," *Variety*, May 19, 1965; Corinne Crawford, "Petite Miss Compton Is Bigger than Life," *Los Angeles Times*, December 23, 1966.

22 Gene Moskowitz, "More Femmes Directing Films," *Variety*, March 11, 1964. Ironically this article on Compton and contemporary women directors working in Europe includes a note from the editors that the "National Board of Review has just rediscovered Alice Guy-Blache, now 91 and living in Brussels."

23 Compton, interview by author, September 7, 2013.

24 For a description of the San Francisco screening see Crawford, "Petite Miss Compton Is Bigger than Life"; for the award at Cannes see "See Distaff Pic Fest in Int'l Female Week," *Variety*, March 13, 1968.

25 "$1 Top Policy," *Variety*, December 11, 1974, 3.

26 Virginia Lee Warren, "She Throws out All the Furniture and Moves Every Few Years," *New York Times*, January 5, 1970.

27 Jan Haag, "Women Directors in Hollywood," accessed July 13, 2012, http://janhaag.com/ESTheDWW.html.

28 Kevin Thomas, "Virginia Hill Given an Extra Dimension," *Los Angeles Times*, November 19, 1974.

29 Mary Murphy, "Movie Call Sheet: Film Forecast for the New Year," *Los Angeles Times*, December 31, 1975.

30 Compton, interview by author, September 7, 2013.

31 Compton, interview by author, September 7, 2013.

32 Compton, interview by author, September 7, 2013.

33 Compton, interview by author, September 7, 2013.

34 Compton, interview by author, September 7, 2013.

## Chapter 1

1 Marjorie Rosen, "From the Folks Who Are Taking over Hollywood," *Ms.*, December 1977, 1.

2 The figure for the total number of films released during these years accounts for those titles made by major, minor, and independent companies that received a letter rating from the MPAA. "Rated Major Pix Up 21% from Last Yr, per MPAA," *Variety*, November 7, 1979, 24.

3 Kirk Honeycutt, "Women Film Directors: Will They, too, Be Allowed to Bomb?," *Los Angeles Times*, August 6, 1978, 1.

4 For a discussion of male directors as "movie brats" during the 19070s, see Michael Pye and Lynda Myles, *The Movie Brats: How the Film Generation Took over Hollywood* (New York: Holt, Rinehart and Winston, 1979). For an example of male director excess and studio executives' compliance, see Steven Bach, *Final Cut: Dreams and Disaster in the Making of Heaven's Gate* (New York: William Morrow,

1985); and Peter Biskind, *Easy Riders, Raging Bulls: How the Sex-Drugs-and-Rock 'n' Roll Generation Saved Hollywood* (New York: Simon & Schuster, 1998).

5 Honeycutt, "Women Film Directors."

6 Sally Ogle, "The Struggle of Women Directors," *New York Times*, January 11 1981, SM9.

7 Joan Micklin Silver, interview at the American Film Institute, 1979, Harold Lloyd Master Seminars, Louis B. Mayer Library, Los Angeles.

8 Rosen, "From the Folks."

9 Rosen, "From the Folks."

10 Joanna Lee, *A Difficult Woman in Hollywood* (New York: Vantage Press, 1999), 71.

11 Mary Murphy, "Movie Call Sheet: Michael Caine to Join 'Limey' Cast," *Los Angeles Times*, December 9, 1972; "Los Angeles," *Boxoffice*, May 19, 1975; "Joanna Lee Film Will Be Shown at Aghape Benefit," *Los Angeles Times*, August 17, 1976.

12 Mary Murphy and Cheryl Bensten, "Women in Hollywood: Part III, Coming to Grips with the Issue of Power," *Los Angeles Times*, August 16, 1973, 19.

13 "DGA Statement on the Passing of Maya Angelou," Directors Guild of America, May 28, 2014, https://www.dga.org/News/PressReleases/2014/140528a-DGA-Statement-on-the-Passing-of-Maya-Angelou.aspx; "Maya Angelou," *Directory of Members 1976–77* (Los Angeles: Directors Guild of America, Inc., 1976), 15.

14 "'L. S. Fields' ('Derby') Really Quentin Kelly; Quits Group W For Pix," *Variety*, July 28, 1971, 31;"Kelly-Jordan Own Distrib (Hendel); Black Pix Only," *Variety*, November 8, 1972, 5; Frank Segers, "Quent Kelly Enterprises Succeeds Two-Tone Producing Partnership; No 'Head-Busting' of Whites," *Variety*, November 20, 1974, 3, 22.

15 "Poet Goes to Battle With TV Wizards," *Los Angeles Times*, November 10, 1978, H36.

16 Charles Champlin, "Movie Review: Insights into Black Experience," *Los Angeles Times*, April 5, 1972, F1.

17 Gordon R. Watkins, "Women in Film: Maya Angelou, Writer," *Millimeter*, July–August 1974, 49.

18 "Georgia, Georgia," *Variety*, March 8, 1972, 24.

19 Howard Rosenberg, "NBC Delays Showing 2 Black Productions," *Los Angeles Times*, April 24, 1981, G1.

20 David Galligan, "Maya Angelou: Joyous? Yes. Happy? Very Rarely," *Drama-Logue*, January 7–13, 1982.

21 Honeycutt, "Women Film Directors."

22 Mary Murphy and Cheryl Bensten, "Women in Hollywood: Part I, Fighting to Enter the 'White Male Club,'" *Los Angeles Times*, August 14, 1973, 9.

23 Alice Kessler-Harris, *Gendering Labor History* (Urbana: University of Illinois Press, 2006), 259. For further discussion, see Kessler-Harris, *In Pursuit of Equity: Women, Men, and the Quest for Economic Citizenship in 20th-Century America* (Oxford: Oxford University Press, 2001).

24 Erin Hill, *Never Done: A History of Women's Work in Media Production* (New Brunswick, N.J.: Rutgers University Press, 2016), 55.

25 Hill, *Never Done*, 128.

26 The use of paradox to understand the push and pull of progress that these filmmakers experienced is informed by Chon A. Noriega's *Shot in America: Television, the State, and the Rise of Chicano Cinema* (Minneapolis: University of Minneapolis, 2000). Noriega identifies the constant contradictions that Chicano media makers faced during the 1960s and 1970s in attempting to appeal to government regulators of the television industry as a means to fight racial and ethnic discrimination. For these activists, the paradox was that the state, which was meant to represent the public, simultaneously protected the marketplace, a contradiction that created sets of stumbling blocks in the way of progress. Increasing the number of women directors and their ability to build bodies of work during the 1970s, on the one hand, appeared possible considering the social and industrial shifts taking place, but change of this kind posed a threat to Hollywood's patriarchal foundations and progress was met with resistance.

27 For a discussion of studio losses at the end of the 1960s and attempts by Hollywood to find the next "hit," see Thomas Schatz, "The New Hollywood," in *Film Theory Goes to the Movies*, ed. Jim Collins, Hilary Radner, and Ava Preacher Collins (New York: Routledge, 1993), 8–36; Paul E. Steiger, "Movie Makers No Longer Sure What Sparkle Is," *Los Angeles Times*, November 17, 1969, 1; Mel Gussow, "Movies Leaving 'Hollywood' Behind," *New York Times*, May 27, 1970, 36: and Aljean Harmetz, "How Do You Pick a Winner in Hollywood? You Don't," *New York Times*, April 29, 1973, 35.

28 In 1968, Jack Valenti, president of the MPAA, spearheaded, with the financial support of the major studios, a survey tracking moviegoing demographics. Daniel Yankelovich, Inc. reported that 58 percent of film audiences were between the ages of 16 and 29; 30 percent of those were between the ages of 16 and 20. Wayne Warga, "Facts of Life about Movie Audiences," *Los Angeles Times*, December 29, 1968, O1.

29 Stanley Penn, "Focusing on Youth: A New Breed of Movie Attracts the Young, Shakes up Hollywood," *Wall Street Journal*, November 4, 1969.

30 Gussow, "Movies Leaving 'Hollywood' Behind."

31 Robert Windeler, "Study of Film Soaring on College Campuses," *New York Times*, April 18, 1968, 58.

32 Charles Champlin, "Can Film-Maker Find Happiness in New Hollywood?," *Los Angeles Times*, June 4, 1967, C11; and Vincent Canby, "Zanuck Discusses Films with Youth," *New York Times*, May 1, 1967, 44.

33 See Robert E. Dallos, "20th Century-Fox Earnings Decline in First Quarter," *Los Angeles Times*, May 21, 1969, C9; Wayne Warga, "It's Nail-Biting Time at 20th Century-Fox," *Los Angeles Times*, June 15, 1969, O1; and Alexander Auerbach, "20th Century Omits Dividends as It Posts $4.6 Million Loss," *Los Angeles Times*, August 29, 1969, C12.

34 Rochelle Reed, "No Lib Yet for Women in the Entertainment Industry," *Hollywood Report*, October 16, 1970, 1.

35 Reed, "No Lib Yet."

36 Joan Tewkesbury, interview by author, January 27, 2011.

37 Roe v. Wade, 410 U.S. 113, 93 S. Ct. 705, 35 L. Ed. 2d 147 (1973).

38 For histories of the 1970s feminist movement and its impact on American society, see Susan Brownmiller, *In Our Time: Memoir of a Revolution* (New York: Dial Press, 1999); and Ruth Rosen, *The World Split Open: How the Modern Women's Movement Changed America* (New York: Penguin Group, 2000).

39 The preliminary observations made in this chapter on the EEOC's 1969 hearing are similar to Quinn's assessments of the same event. However, Quinn then concentrates exclusively on race and on Hollywood management's perpetuation of "'color-blind' conservatism," whereas the argument here focuses on gender, using the testimonies as a jumping-off point for the feminist reform efforts that would define the entertainment industry during the 1970s. Eithne Quinn, "Closing Doors: Hollywood, Affirmative Action, and the Revitalization of Conservative Racial Politics," *Journal of American History* 2, no. 1 (2012): 466–491.

40 United States v. Paramount Pictures, Inc., 334 U.S. 131 (1948).

41 Equal Employment Opportunity Commission, *Hearings before the United States Equal Employment Opportunity Commission on Utilization of Minority and Women Workers in Certain Major Industries, Los Angeles March 12–14, 1969* (Washington, D.C.: U.S. Government Printing Office, 1969), 2–3. Hereafter, EEOC Hearings March 1969.

42 EEOC Hearings March 1969, 341.

43 EEOC Hearings March 1969, 189.

44 EEOC Hearings March 1969, 532–533.

45 EEOC Hearings March 1969, 227.

46 EEOC Hearings March 1969, 228.

47 IATSE membership forms included in EEOC Hearings March 1969, 501–508.

48 The testimony refers to the memberships of two craft unions. One union had approximately 4,000 members, of whom 8 were black and 51 Latino. The second union had an estimated 1,000 total members that included 1 black and 50 Latino members. These members were presumably all male. EEOC Hearings March 1969, 153.

49 EEOC Hearings March 1969, 158.

50 For an explanation of union membership and roster lists as they functioned in 1969, see EEOC Hearings March 1969, 116–126, 149–164.

51 Robert Kistler, "Film Executive Blames Hiring Bias on Unions," *Los Angeles Times*, October 19, 1969, 14.

52 Paul Delaney, "Major Moviemakers Agree to a Fair-Hiring Plan," *New York Times*, April 1, 1970.

53 Vincent J. Burke, "Film and TV Minority Job Plan in Effect," *Los Angeles Times*, April 1, 1970.

54 Delaney, "Major Moviemakers Agree." It appears that Universal Studios was excused from signing the agreement based on the company's better track record in hiring minorities.

55 Delaney, "Major Moviemakers Agree."

56 In 1967, the city's labor force was 10.1 percent Latino and 7.4 percent African American. "Executives Participating in 3-Day Public Hearing," *Los Angeles Sentinel*, March 13, 1969.

57 California Advisory Committee to the United States Commission on Civil Rights, *Behind the Scenes: Equal Employment Opportunity in the Motion Picture Industry* (Washington, D.C.: U.S. Government Printing Office, 1978), 13–14.

58 This percentage was calculated from the number of employees—broken down by gender—submitted individually by the studios (MGM, 20th Century-Fox, Universal, Walt Disney, Warner Bros.) as part of the 1969 hearing. Columbia and Paramount did not attend the hearing; therefore their employee numbers from 1969 are unknown. EEOC Hearings March 1969, 498–549.

59 EEOC Hearings March 1969, 165.

60 EEOC Hearings March 1969, 165, 168.

61 "Executives Participating in 3-Day Public Hearing"; Ethel L. Payne, "EEOC Slates Discrimination Hearings," *Chicago Daily Defender*, March 11, 1969.

62 For a discussion of women's "economic citizenship" and the debates over the enforcement of sex as a protected category under Title VII, see Kessler-Harris, *In Pursuit of Equity*, 239–289; and Hugh Davis Graham, *The Civil Rights Era: Origins and Development of National Policy 1960–1972* (Oxford: Oxford University Press, 1990), 205–232.

63 Graham, *The Civil Rights Era*, 228.

64 "Founding: Setting the Stage," National Organization of Women, July 2011, http://now.org/about/history/founding-2/; Graham, *The Civil Rights Era*, 225–228.

65 Marjorie Hunter, "Dirksen Upbraids U.S. Rights Official," *New York Times*, March 28, 1969, 1.

66 Hunter, "Dirksen Upbraids U.S. Rights Official."

67 Marjorie Hunter, "President to Replace Chairman of Job Opportunity Commission," *New York Times*, March 29, 1969.

68 David A. Cook, *Lost Illusions: American Cinema in the Shadow of Watergate and Vietnam 1970–1979* (Berkeley: University of California Press, 2000), 9.

69 Cook, *Lost Illusions*, 12; Quinn, "Closing Doors," 486.

70 Harry Bernstein, "U.S. Ready to Settle Bias Case against Movie, TV Industries," *Los Angeles Times*, February 5, 1970.

71 Tichi Wilkerson Miles, "Sock it to 'Em," *Hollywood Reporter*, March 17, 1969.

72 "Negro Film Roles Show Sharp Increase," *Hollywood Citizen News*, April 22, 1969. Originally cited in Quinn, "Closing Doors," 477.

73 Quinn, "Closing Doors," 477.

74 For Valenti's concern regarding "special treatment," see Will Tusher, "Valenti Calls

Black's Bluff; Rejects 'Special' Treatment," *Hollywood Reporter*, September 29, 1972. Originally cited in Quinn, "Closing Doors," 484.

75 Aljean Harmetz, "Suit to Allege Sex Bias By TV and Film Makers," *New York Times*, February 25, 1981.

76 "Mission," womeninfilm.org, accessed June 1, 2017, https://womeninfilm.org/about-wif/.

77 California Advisory Committee, *Behind the Scenes*, 24–25.

78 California Advisory Committee, *Behind the Scenes*, 22–23.

79 For a discussion of the EEOC's failure to enforce the 1970 antidiscrimination agreement see California Advisory Committee, *Behind the Scenes*, 36–38.

80 For examples of sex discrimination and technical unions, see Bill Edwards, "Femme Lenser Sues to Join IA," *Variety*, October 12, 1971; "Bri Murphy First Woman Accepted by IATSE Photogs," *Hollywood Reporter*, March 14, 1973; "Lady Film Cutter Sues MGM over 'Discrimination,'" *Variety*, April 9, 1973; Ron Pennington, "Woman Takes Grip on Universal Assignment, Breaks Male Hold," *Hollywood Reporter*, August 14, 1973; "First Female Grip Checks into TBS," *Hollywood Reporter*, September 5, 1973; "Projectionists Get 1st Femme Member," *Variety*, June 28, 1974; "Barbara Robinson Named IATSE Representative," *Variety*, July 22, 1974; "And a Woman Shall Lead Pub Labor Talks," *Variety*, December 13, 1974; and "Sound Local 695 Stingy with the Money for Gals, Madery Claims," *Variety*, December 31, 1976. Filmmaker Jessie Maple was the first African American woman to join Local 644, International Photographers of the Motion Picture Industries, as a camerawoman in 1974; she filed a complaint with the City of New York Commission on Human Rights against ABC and CBS Local News on the basis of racial and sex discrimination in 1976. See Jessie Maple, *How to Become a Union Camerawoman Film-Videotape* (New York: LJ Film Productions, 1977).

81 Steve Toy, "Femme Showbiz Movement Broadens," *Daily Variety*, November 29, 1972.

82 "Femme Showbiz Movement Broadens."

83 "Femme Showbiz Movement Broadens." Also see Steve Toy, "Creative Women of America Formed by Union Talent to Plug Femmes," *Daily Variety*, April 27, 1973; and "Women's Report," *Screen Actor* 15, no. 1 (January 1973), 9.

84 Diana Gould, "Women Writers," *WGAw Newsletter*, June 1972, 16. Writers Guild Foundation Shavelson-Webb Library. For an organizational context in which this feminist activism took place within the history of the Writers Guild of America see Miranda J. Banks, *The Writers: A History of the American Screenwriters and Their Guild* (New Brunswick, N.J.: Rutgers University Press, 2015).

85 "Do Agents Push Women Writers for the Job?," *WGAw Newsletter*, November 1971, 11. Writers Guild Foundation Shavelson-Webb Library, Los Angeles.

86 Maggie Weisberg, "A Council Profile: Diana Gould," *WGAw Newsletter*, February 1972, 6–7. Writers Guild Foundation Shavelson-Webb Library.

87 Gould, "Women Writers."
88 Gould, "Women Writers."
89 Diana Gould, author interview, June 20, 2016.
90 *I Lost It At the Movies* (1968) is available at the UCLA Film and Television Archive, Los Angeles.
91 Gould, interview by author.
92 Gould, interview by author.
93 Gould, interview by author.
94 Betty Ulius, interview for the Guild History Committee, April 12, 1978, 1. Writers Guild Foundation Shavelson-Webb Library.
95 Mollie Gregory, *Women Who Run the Show* (New York: St. Martin's Press, 2002), 7.
96 Gregory, *Women Who Run the Show*, 8.
97 Jean Butler, interview by the Guild History Committee, July 31, 1978, 21. Writers Guild Foundation Shavelson-Webb Library.
98 Gregory, *Women Who Run the Show*, 9.
99 Gregory, *Women Who Run the Show*.
100 Sue Cameron, "Coast to Coast," *Hollywood Reporter*, November 27, 1973. For a breakdown of the still meager number of women writers hired during the 1974 television season, see "Women's Committee Statistics Report," November 7, 1974, Internal WGA document. Writers Guild Foundation Shavelson-Webb Library.
101 Bill Greeley, "Ladies Demand Their Writes on TV," *Daily Variety*, October 31, 1973.
102 Michael H. Franklin, "Letter to All Signatories to the 1973 WGA MBA," April 8, 1974; reprinted as Michael H. Franklin, "Underemployed Women," *WGAw Newsletter*, June 1974, 6–7. Writers Guild Foundation Shavelson-Webb Library.
103 Franklin, "Underemployed Women."
104 Betty Ulius, interview by the Guild History Committee, 9.
105 Dennis Weaver, "In the Matter of the Investigation of the Image of Women in the Media." Speech to the Status of Women Commission of the State of California, Los Angeles, 1974, 2. SAG-AFTRA Archive, Los Angeles.
106 Weaver, "In the Matter of the Investigation." Also see "Tackling the Problem of Bias," *Screen Actor* (July) 1973: 6–9; "Webs, SAG in 'Historic' Pow on Minority Topics," *Variety*, August 15, 1973.
107 David F. Prindle, *The Politics of Glamour: Ideology and Democracy in the Screen Actors Guild* (Madison: University of Wisconsin Press, 1988), 114.
108 Prindle, *The Politics of Glamour*, 93; "SAG Opens Campaign to Improve Image, Status of Gals in Industry," *Variety*, June 1, 1976, 1.
109 Prindle, *The Politics of Glamour*, 113.
110 Steve Toy, "First Femme to Hold Top Post Vows Militant Action," *Variety*, November 4, 1975, 11.
111 Bob Thomas, "Actress Organizes Industry's Women," *Los Angeles Times*, October 20, 1972, D25.
112 "SAG Survey Reveals Public Attitudes Preference in TV," press release, October 31, 1974, 2. SAG-AFTRA Archive, Los Angeles.

113 "SAG Survey Reveals Public Attitudes Preference in TV," 3.
114 "SAG Survey Reveals Public Attitudes Preference in TV," 4.
115 "Webs, SAG in 'Historic' Pow on Minority Topics."
116 "What the Viewers Want on TV," *Screen Actor* (Fall 1974): 1–2. Also see Kathleen Nolan, first vice president, SAG, "In the Matter of the Investigation of the Image of Women in the Media," remarks to the Status of Women Commission of the State of California, Los Angeles, 1974, 3, 6–7. SAG-AFTRA Archive, Los Angeles.
117 "Webs, SAG in 'Historic' Pow on Minority Topics."
118 Will Tusher, "Femme Kissoff on TV Charged at SAG Seminar," *Hollywood Reporter*, August 8, 1973; Steve Toy, "'Historic' Meet as SG, Top Net Exex Discuss Minorities," *Daily Variety*, August 8, 1973, 11.
119 Steve Toy, "SAG Wants to Meet with U on Hiring of Women," *Variety*, October 16, 1975.
120 "Actors Guild Cheers Universal's Welcome on Sex Slant Casting," *Variety*, December 28, 1976; "Hollywood: Where Have All the Women Gone?," *Screen Actor* (October/November 1976): 13.
121 Will Tusher, "GSA Report Alleges Serious Underutilization of Femmes, Minorities in Film Industry," *Daily Variety*, October 27, 1976.
122 Will Tusher, "SAG Will Take Its Case for Affirmative Action in Hiring of Performers to the Public," *Variety*, May 25, 1979.

## Chapter 2

1 "Paramount Pictures Starts Program to Give Film Writers Star Status," *Boxoffice*, May 6, 1968.
2 "Ambitious Product Slate Revealed at Paramount," *Boxoffice*, January 30, 1967.
3 "Ambitious Product Slate Revealed at Paramount."
4 Elaine May, interview with Haden Guest, Harvard Film Archive, November 13, 2011.
5 A. H. Weiler, "Elaine May Director," *New York Times*, May 12, 1968.
6 Gordon Cotler, "For the Love of Mike—and Elaine," *New York Times*, May 24, 1959.
7 Thomas Thompson, "Whatever Happened to Elaine May," *Life*, July 28, 1967.
8 Thompson, "Whatever Happened to Elaine May."
9 Jeffrey Sweet, *Something Wonderful Right Away* (New York: Limelight Editions, 1986), 83.
10 Rachel Abramowitz, *Is That a Gun in Your Pocket? Women's Experience of Power in Hollywood* (New York: Random House, 2000), 61.
11 "Inter-Office Communication from Bernard Donnenfeld to Charles Bluhdorn and Martin Davis, Re: *A New Leaf*," February 26, 1968. *A New Leaf*, Paramount Pictures Special Collection, Margaret Herrick Library, 1–2.
12 "Inter-Office Communication from Bernard Donnenfeld," 2.
13 Abramowitz, *Is That a Gun in Your Pocket?*, 61.
14 Michael Rivlin, "Elaine May: Too Tough for Hollywood?," *Millimeter* 3, no. 10 (1975): 16.

15 Elaine May, interview with Mike Nichols, Film Society of Lincoln Center, February 26, 2006, accessed April 1, 2008, www.filmcomment.com/article/elaine-may-in-conversation-with-mike-nichols.

16 "Inter-Office Communication from A.N. Ryan to Eugene H. Frank, Re: *A New Leaf*," April 3, 1968. *A New Leaf*, Paramount Pictures Special Collection, Margaret Herrick Library, 1–3.

17 Abramowitz, *Is That a Gun in Your Pocket?*, 61.

18 "Paramount Pictures Corporation: Production Notes, *A New Leaf*," August 20, 1970. *New Leaf* Production Files, Margaret Herrick Library, 10.

19 For *A New Leaf*'s production start date, see "Hollywood Production Pulse," *Variety*, August 27, 1969, 30. For a discussion of the film's budget, see "Inter-Communication to Charles Bluhdorn and Martin Davis, from Bernard Donnenfeld, Re: *A New Leaf*," May 16, 1969. *A New Leaf*, Production Files, Margaret Herrick Library, 2.

20 "Inter-Communication from Peter Bart to Robert Evans, Subject: *A New Leaf*," February 7, 1969. *A New Leaf*, Production Files, Margaret Herrick Library, 1.

21 "Inter-Communication to Charles Bluhdorn and Martin Davis, from Bernard Donnenfeld, Re: *A New Leaf*," May 16, 1969. *A New Leaf*, Production Files, Margaret Herrick Library, 1–2.

22 "Letter from Howard W. Koch to Elaine May, Re: *A New Leaf*," July 22, 1969. *A New Leaf*, Production Files, Margaret Herrick Library.

23 Stanley Jaffe, interview by Mae Woods, Academy of Motion Picture Arts and Sciences, Visual History, April 21, 2015.

24 "Letter from Stanley Jaffe to Charles Bluhdorn, Martin Davis, Robert Evans, Bernard Donnenfeld," October 7, 1970. *A New Leaf*, Production Files, Margaret Herrick Library.

25 "Letter from Norman Flicker to Stanley Jaffe, Subject: *A New Leaf*," February 16, 1970. *A New Leaf*, Production Files, Margaret Herrick Library, 1.

26 Abramowitz, *Is That a Gun in Your Pocket?*, 63.

27 "Evans May Have Been Thinking of Her," *Variety*, February 10, 1971, 13.

28 "Elaine May Sues Par," *Variety*, January 20, 1971, 7.

29 Abramowitz, *Is That a Gun in Your Pocket?*, 63.

30 "Deny Elaine May's Plea," *Variety*, March 10, 1971, 4.

31 Jaffe, interview with Mae Woods.

32 "'Leaf' Is Radio City 250G Easter Egg; 'Love 65G 17th; 'Ginger' Hot 32G; 'Andromeda' \$34,045; 'Claire's' 15G," *Variety*, April 14, 1971, 9.

33 Gene Siskel, "Elaine May Turns over 'A New Leaf' Just for Laughs," *Chicago Tribune*, March 28, 1971, E1.

34 Larry Cohen, "New Leaf," *Hollywood Reporter*, March 10, 1971, 4.

35 Vincent Canby, "W.C. Fields and Elaine May—Two of a Kind?," *New York Times*, March 14, 1971, D1.

36 "Big Rental Films of 1971," *Variety*, January 5, 1972, 9.

37 Rivlin, "Elaine May: Too Tough for Hollywood?," 17.

38 "Hollywood Production Pulse," *Variety*, March 22, 1972, 34.

39 Abramowitz, *Is That a Gun in Your Pocket?*, 64.
40 Vincent Canby, "Film: 'Heartbreak Kid,'" *New York Times*, December 18, 1972, 56.
41 Stephen Farber, "You See Yourself in 'Heartbreak,'" *New York Times*, February 18, 1973, 165.
42 Joan Mellon, *Women and Their Sexuality in the New Film* (New York: Horizon Press, 1973), 42.
43 Molly Haskell, *From Reverence to Rape: The Treatment of Women in the Movies* (London: Penguin Books, 1973), 353.
44 Marjorie Rose, *Popcorn Venus: Women, Movies and the American Dream* (New York: Coward, McCann & Geoghegan, 1973), 363–364.
45 Gregg Kilday, "The Dreams of Jeannie," *New York Times*, February 19, 1973, 1, 11.
46 John Gruen, "More than Elaine May's Daughter," *New York Times*, January 7, 1973, 13, 16.
47 A. B. Weiler, "Now It's Simon and May," *New York Times*, November 21, 1971, 15.
48 "Dialogue on Film: Neil Simon," *American Film*, March 1, 1978, 38.
49 "Elaine May's 'Bumpy Ride' on 'Leaf': Manduke Sticks on 'Mickey (sic) & Nicky,'" *Variety*, August 27, 1969, 6.
50 Lee Beaupre, "Elaine May's 'Mikey' to Paramount; Palomar in Scratch when Budget Rises," *Variety*, March 21, 1973, 3.
51 Andrew Tobias, "For Elaine May, a New Film—but Not a New Leaf," *New West*, December 6, 1976, 59.
52 Tobias, "For Elaine May, a New Film—but Not a New Leaf," 62.
53 Dan Rottenberg, "Elaine May . . . or She May Not," *Chicago Tribune*, October 21, 1973, 55.
54 Rottenberg, "Elaine May . . . or She May Not."
55 Tobias, "For Elaine May, a New Film—but Not a New Leaf," 65.
56 Abramowitz, *Is That a Gun in Your Pocket?*, 66.
57 For the phone call between Diller and May see Tobias, "For Elaine May, a New Film—but Not a New Leaf," 66. For details of the lawsuit and the disappeared film reels also see "Par, Elaine May Sue Each Other; Film Over-Budget and Incomplete," *Variety*, October 29, 1975, 5; and "Par Charges Criminal Conduct In 'Mikey' Suit vs. Elaine May," *Variety*, September 15, 1976, 5.
58 Elaine May, interview by Haden Guest.
59 Elaine May, interview by Haden Guest.
60 Charles Champlin, "'Mikey, Nicky' Play Cat and Mouse," *Los Angeles Times*, December 25, 1976, D1.
61 "Buying & Booking Guide: Mikey & Nicky," *Independent Film Journal*, December 24, 1976, 30–31.
62 May, interview by Haden Guest.
63 Thomas Thompson, "Whatever Happened to Elaine May?," *Life*, July 28, 1967, 59.
64 Thompson, "Whatever Happened to Elaine May?," 54B.
65 Janet Coleman, *The Compass: The Improvisational Theatre That Revolutionized American Comedy* (Chicago: University of Chicago Press, 1990), 167.

66 Elaine May, interview by Mike Nichols.
67 Stanley Jaffe, interview by Mae Woods.
68 May, interview by Mike Nichols.
69 Abramowitz, *Is That a Gun in Your Pocket?*, 68.
70 It is an ironic example of sexism that Beatty is also often described as an "obsessive" filmmaker for the prolonged time he spends as a "perfectionist" on the films he makes as actor, writer, director. For a discussion of Beatty's difficult behavior see: Peter Biskind, *Star: How Warren Beatty Seduced America* (New York: Simon & Shuster, 2010), 232.
71 The original budget and ultimate cost of *Ishtar* have long been in dispute. May claimed that the studio sabotaged the film and leaked incorrect information about how much the production was going over budget. May, interview by Haden Guest. In his biography of Warren Beatty, Peter Biskind describes the varying budget figures given for the film, citing sources that said the picture was made for $26 million, $34 million, or $51 million. The film's box office gross was $12.7 million. Biskind, *Star*, 336, 382.
72 May, interview by Mike Nichols.
73 Gene Arneel, "Cut Directors down to Size, Bob Evans: 'We Keep Control,'" *Variety*, February 3, 1971, 1, 22.
74 For a definition of exploitation films in terms of sensationalized style and promotional strategies see Eric Schaefer, *Bold! Daring! Shocking! True! A History of Exploitation Films, 1919–1959* (Durham, N.C.: Duke University Press, 1999), 1–16. For an overview of Roger Corman's "generation" of exploitation filmmakers in the 1970s, see Maitland McDonagh, "The Exploitation Generation or: How Marginal Movies Came in from the Cold," in *The Last Great American Picture Show*, ed. Thomas Elsaesser, Alexander Horwath, and Noel King (Amsterdam: Amsterdam University Press, 2004), 107–130. For an historical study of exploitation films' exhibition patterns see David Church, "From Exhibition to Genre: The Case of Grind-House Films," *Cinema Journal* 50, no. 4 (2011): 1–25. For a discussion of exploitation films' production schedule, see "The American Film Institute Seminar with Roger Corman, March 11, 1970," in *Roger Corman Interviews*, ed. Constantine Nasr (Jackson: University of Mississippi Press, 2011), 44–61.
75 Schaefer, *Bold! Daring! Shocking! True!*, 8.
76 For the history of art house, commercial independent films of the 1970s see Annette Insdorf, "Ordinary People, European-style: Or How to Spot an Independent Feature," in *Contemporary American Independent Film: From the Margins to the Mainstream*, ed. Chris Holmlund and Justin Wyatt (London: Routledge, 2005), 27–33; and John Pierson, *Spike Mike Slackers & Dykes* (New York: Miramax Books, 1995). For a discussion of independent commercial film distribution in the late 1970s and early 1980s see Gerald Peary, "Getting It on or How to Make Deals and Influence Exhibitors," *American Film*, September 1, 1981, 60–64.
77 Kevin Thomas, "Miss Loden's 'Wanda'—'It's Very Much Me': Barbara Loden and 'Wanda,'" *Los Angeles Times*, April 8, 1971, G1.

78 Marion Meade, "Lights! Camera! Women!," *New York Times*, April 25, 1971, D11.
79 Burt A. Folkart, "'Dumb Blonde' Made One Brilliant Film," *Los Angeles Times*, September 8, 1980, B21.
80 McCandlish Phillips, "Barbara Loden Speaks of the World of 'Wanda,'" *New York Times*, March 11, 1971, 32.
81 Barbara Loden, interview at the American Film Institute, April 2, 1971, Harold Lloyd Master Seminars, Louis B. Mayer Library, Los Angeles, 10–11.
82 Dick Kleiner, "Is There also a Barbara Loden?," *La Crosse Tribune* (La Crosse, Wisconsin), March 9, 1964, www.newspapers.com/newspage/83852596/. Kleiner's interview is mentioned in Kate McCourt, "Who was Barbara Loden?," *Propeller Magazine* (Fall 2012), www.propellermag.com/Fall2012/McCourtLodenFall12.html.
83 Thomas, "Miss Loden's 'Wanda.'"
84 Rex Reed, "Watch out for Barbara's 'Wanda,'" *Los Angeles Times*, February 1971, 52.
85 In her essay on *Wanda*, Bérénice Reynaud draws attention to the different accounts of the film's budget: Loden, when asked in multiple interviews, said the film cost an estimated $115,000, whereas in his autobiography, Kazan gives a figure of $200,000. Elia Kazan, *A Life* (New York: Alfred A. Knopf, 1988), 793. Nicholas Proferes claimed the budget was $75,000 (interview with Reynaud) in Bérénice Reynaud, "For Wanda," in *The Last Great American Picture Show*, 245. Shuster owned one-third of the film, while the rest was owned by the Foundation for Filmmakers, a nonprofit established by Loden, Kazan, and their attorney Milton Wessel. Any profits from *Wanda* would go to the foundation for future films. Army Archerd, *Variety*, April 2, 1971.
86 Reynaud, "For Wanda," 230.
87 On Loden cooking for her crew see Reynaud, "For Wanda," 231; on her as a babysitter, see Reed, "Watch out for Barbara's 'Wanda,'" 52.
88 Reed, "Watch out for Barbara's 'Wanda.'"
89 Phillips, "Barbara Loden Speaks of the World of 'Wanda,'" 32.
90 "Dallas," *Boxoffice*, March 15, 1971, SW2.
91 Thomas, "Miss Loden's 'Wanda.'"
92 Roger Greenspun, "Young Wife Fulfills Herself as a Robber: Barbara Loden's Film Opens at Cinema II," *New York Times*, March 1, 1971, 22.
93 George Moskowitz, "At Venice Film Fest: Wanda," *Variety*, September 2, 1970, 32.
94 Thomas, "Miss Loden's 'Wanda.'"
95 "Barbara Loden's Own Film Project: On Set, Hubby Elia Kazan Raps Television as 'Mutilators' of Celluloid," *Variety*, September 3, 1969, 17.
96 Vincent Canby, "Wanda's a Wow, so's THX," *New York Times*, March 21, 1971, D1.
97 Kazan described Leo as his and Loden's "love child" in Kazan, *A Life*, 616. On her writing the script while pregnant, see Reed, "Watch out for Barbara's 'Wanda.'"
98 For a discussion of Loden and Kazan's breakup while she was pregnant see Kazan, *A Life*, 616–620.
99 Loden, interview at the American Film Institute.

100 "Shuster, Loden Confer on 'Wanda' Opening," *Hollywood Reporter*, January 28, 1971; "Bardene 'Wanda' Distrib," *Variety*, February 18, 1971; *Wanda* display ad, *Los Angeles Times*, April 11, 1971, C17.

101 Reynaud, "For Wanda," 230.

102 "She's 'Sorry' Now," *New York Times*, January 31, 1971.

103 Army Archerd, *Variety*, April 2, 1971.

104 "Form HHH Rainbow for Filming; Goal: 'Low Budgets from Names'; Zuker, Jaglom, Lange out Front," *Variety*, May 1, 1974, 7.

105 Mel Gussow, "The Stage: Ing's 'Love Death Plays,'" *New York Times*, July 10, 1975, 19; Carol Lawson, "Broadway," *New York Times*, March 28, 1980, C2.

106 Reed, "Watch out for Barbara's 'Wanda.'"

107 Lawson "Broadway," C2.

108 Linda Gross, "Karen Arthur Dares to Do It All," *Los Angeles Times*, April 16, 1978, N54.

109 Karen Arthur, interview by Antonio Vellani, American Film Institute, 1978, Harold Lloyd Master Seminars, Louis B. Mayer Library, Los Angeles.

110 Karen Arthur, interview, DVD extra, *Legacy*, dir. Karen Arthur, Scorpio Releasing, 2011. DVD.

111 Arthur, interview, DVD extra, *Legacy*.

112 Karen Arthur, interview by author, February 16, 2017.

113 "Ten Share $80,000 of Film Institute; 424 Disappointed," *Variety*, July 10, 1975, 22.

114 Arthur, interview by author.

115 *Legacy* screened at the San Francisco and Chicago film festivals in 1975 (*Hollywood Reporter*, October 8, 1975; at the Los Angeles International Film Exposition, also known as Filmex (*Variety*, October 20, 1975); and at the London Film Festival (*Variety*, October 8, 1975).

116 Vincent Canby, "Day in the Life of Bissie Hapgood: Karen Arthur 'Legacy' at Cinema Studio," *New York Times*, May 3, 1976, 41.

117 Marjorie Rosen, "Suffer Much, Learn Much?," *Ms.*, November 1975, 46.

118 Rosen, "Suffer Much, Learn Much?"

119 George Moskowitz, "Legacy," *Variety*, August 27, 1975.

120 Canby, "Day in the Life of Bissie Hapgood."

121 Arthur, interview by author.

122 Rosen, "Suffer Much, Learn Much?"

123 Karen Arthur, interview, DVD extra, *Legacy*.

124 "Broadway," *Boxoffice*, April 26, 1976, E2.

125 Arthur, interview by author.

126 Jean M. White, "Depicting a Woman's 'Legacy,'" *Washington Post*, April 12, 1975, C3.

127 Arthur, interview by author.

128 Arthur, interview, DVD extra, *Mafu Cage*, dir. Karen Arthur, Scorpio Releasing, 2011. DVD.

129 Arthur, interview by Antonio Vellani.

130 Karen Arthur, interview, DVD extra, *Mafu Cage*.

131 Nancy Mills, "'Lady Beware' Warning Never Intimidated Her," *Los Angeles Times*, May 29, 1986, J1.

132 Marjorie Worcester, "On Location," *Hollywood Reporter*, September 6, 1977.

133 Arthur, interview by author.

134 Arthur, interview by author.

135 Charles Champlin, "Movie Review: Madness, Horror in 'The Mafu Cage,'" *Los Angeles Times*, December 1, 1978, I26.

136 Arthur Knight, "On Film," *Westways*, May 1970, 60.

137 For the *Legacy* and *Mafu Cage* budgets see Gross, "Karen Arthur Dares to Do It All," N54. During the 1970s the seven major studios controlled worldwide film distribution, making it extremely difficult for outside companies to compete or for independent filmmakers to release their films without major distribution deals. The costs for theatrical films were in the multimillions of dollars: in 1972 the average budget was $2 million; in 1976, $4 million; and in 1980, $10 million. According to Douglas Gomery, "An independent entrepreneur would need to raise so much money to create and distribute theatrical films as to make most such ventures unprofitable." Douglas Gomery, "The American Film Industry of the 1970s," *Wide Angle* 5, no. 4 (1983): 53.

138 Mills, "'Lady Beware' Warning Never Intimidated Her," J1.

139 Mills, "'Lady Beware' Warning Never Intimidated Her," J1.

140 Nancy Mills, "'Lady Beware'—or Director Beware?," *Los Angeles Times*, September 13, 1987, 24.

141 Arthur, interview by Antonio Vellani.

142 Leticia Kent, "They Were behind the Scenes of 'Between the Lines,'" *New York Times*, June 12, 1977, 83.

143 Joan Micklin Silver, interview by Michael Pressman, Directors Guild Visual History Project, September 19, 2005, New York City.

144 Joan Micklin Silver, interview at the American Film Institute, November 1, 1988, Harold Lloyd Master Seminars, Louis B. Mayer Library, Los Angeles.

145 Sharon Rosenthal, "Two on an Island," *Daily News*, March 23, 1981, M8.

146 Kent, "They Were behind the Scenes of 'Between the Lines.'"

147 Molly Haskell, "How an Independent Filmmaker Beat the System (with Her Husband's Help)," *Village Voice*, September 22, 1975, 83.

148 Joseph McBride, "Overcome Exhibs Fear of Yiddish, 1896," *Variety*, February 25, 1976, 7.

149 Micklin Silver, interview by Michael Pressman.

150 Joan Micklin Silver, "Letter to the Editor: Pic Not 'Too Jewish' for Dallas Festival," *Variety*, May 28, 1975, 7.

151 Gene Moskowitz, "Film Reviews: Critic Week–Cannes, Hester Street," *Variety*, May 14, 1975, 27.

152 Addison Verrill, "So They Distributed Film Themselves," *Variety*, February 18, 1976, 5.

153 A. D. Murphy, "'The Deep' Pulls $8,124,316 in 800," *Variety*, June 22, 1977, 3; Justin

Wyatt, *High Concept: Movies and Marketing in Hollywood* (Austin: University of Texas Press, 1994), 109–112.

154 Peary, "Getting It on or How to Make Deals and Influence Exhibitors," 61.

155 Vincent Canby, "Film: Good Reading 'Between the Lines,'" *New York Times*, April 28, 1977, 76.

156 "Film Reviews: Between the Lines," *Variety*, April 20, 1977, 73.

157 "Three Actors Unite as UA Producers," *Variety*, May 30, 1979, 39.

158 For a detailed history of United Artists during the time *Head Over Heels* was made—although no mention of the film is included in the book—see Tino Balio, *United Artists The Company That Changed the Film Industry* (Madison: University of Wisconsin Press, 1987).

159 Micklin Silver, interview at the American Film Institute, November 1. 1988.

160 Micklin Silver, interview at the American Film Institute, November 1. 1988.

161 James Atlas, "How 'Chilly Scenes' Was Rescued," *New York Times*, October 10, 1982.

162 Vincent Canby, "Screen: 'Head Over Heels,' Drama, Open," *New York Times*, October 19, 1979, C12.

163 Micklin Silver, interview by Michael Pressman.

164 Sheila Benson, "Obsessive Love in 'Chilly Scenes,'" *Los Angeles Times*, October 21, 1982, J4.

165 Joan Micklin Silver, interview at the American Film Institute, October 26, 1979, Harold Lloyd Master Seminars, Louis B. Mayer Library, Los Angeles.

166 Kent, "They Were behind the Scenes of 'Between the Lines.'"

167 Penny Allen, interview by author, July 2, 2017.

168 Allen, interview by author.

169 Steve Macfarlane, "Activist Resistance and Organization in Portland and Elsewhere: Penny Allen and Her Career," *Filmmaker.com*, January 6, 2017, https://filmmakermagazine.com/100963-activist-resistance-and-organization-in-portland-and-elsewhere-penny-allen-on-her-career/#.W2Yc-34h3YJ.

170 "U.S. Briefing," *Screen International*, September 30, 1978.

171 "Entermedia Screens Obscure Indie Pix," *Variety*, January 19, 1979, 48, 64; "Broadway," *Boxoffice*, January 22,1979, E2.

172 Vincent Canby, "'Property,' at the American Mavericks Film Festival," *New York Times*, February 3, 1979, 14.

173 David Harris, "Film" Portland's Counterculture," *New Age*, n.d., accessed July 17, 2017, http://allen.penny.pagesperso-orange.fr/pennyallen/frfilms.htm.

174 Allen, interview by author.

175 Allen, interview by author.

176 Allen, interview by author; "New York Sound Track," *Variety*, February 7, 1979, 38.

177 Jack Goodman, "Festival Report: Salt Lake City," *American Film*, December 1, 1978.

178 Allen, interview by author.

179 Will Tusher, "Dimension Pictures Opens up Opportunities for Women," *Hollywood Reporter*, June 1, 1972.

180 Stephanie Rothman, interview by Jane Collings, UCLA Center for the Study of Oral History, January 29, 2002, 75.
181 Roger Corman and Jim Jerome, *How I made a Hundred Movies in Hollywood and Never Lost a Dime* (New York: Da Capo, 1990), 124. Rothman confirms this same story in her interview with Collings, 75.
182 Rothman, interview by Jane Collings, 13.
183 Rothman, interview by Jane Collings, 28.
184 Rothman, interview by Jane Collings, 47.
185 Rothman, interview by Jane Collings, 47.
186 Rothman, interview by Jane Collings, 49.
187 Rothman, interview by Jane Collings, 62.
188 Rothman, interview by Jane Collings, 66.
189 Rothman, interview by Jane Collings, 76–77.
190 Rothman, interview by Jane Collings, 90–91.
191 Rothman, interview by Jane Collings, 85.
192 Stephanie Rothman, interview by author, Academy of Motion Picture Arts and Sciences, Visual History, August 10, 2015, 25.
193 Tusher, "Dimension Pictures Opens up Opportunities for Women."
194 Kit Snedaker, "Movies," *Los Angeles Herald Examiner*, September 20, 1970.
195 "The Student Nurses," *Variety*, September 17, 1970.
196 "Rothman Helmed Exploitationer." *The Student Nurses* Clipping File, Margaret Herrick Library.
197 Corman and Jerome, *How I made a Hundred Movies*, 181.
198 Tony Williams, "Feminism, Fantasy and Violence: An Interview with Stephanie Rothman," *Journal of Popular Film & Television* 9, no. 2 (1981): 85.
199 Ben Sher, "Q & A with Stephanie Rothman," *Center for the Study of Women Update Newsletter*, April 1, 2008.
200 Williams, "Feminism, Fantasy and Violence," 86.
201 Rothman, interview with Jane Collings, 150.
202 Tusher, "Dimension Pictures Opens up Opportunities for Women."
203 Stephanie Rothman, interview with author, 43.
204 For an additional discussion of Rothman's use of feminist themes in *Terminal Island* see Henry Jenkins, *The Wow Climax: Tracing the Emotional Impact of Pop Culture* (New York: New York University Press, 2007).
205 Rothman, interview by Jane Collings, 103.
206 Rothman, interview by Jane Collings, 157. In its first year, Dimension invested $1.5 million in five films and grossed an estimated $8–10 million; *The Hollywood Reporter*, February 16, 1972. Although the company maintained profitability throughout the 1970s, the stakes for independent film companies—producers and distributors, in Dimension's case, both—were extreme. As a small company selling low-budget films its fate rested to a great extent in the hands of regional distribution exchanges, where as a newcomer it had little clout. By the end of the decade the company was named in several lawsuits regarding disputes over distribution deals.

See Ed Lowry, "Dimension Pictures: Portrait of a 1970s' Independent," in *Contemporary American Independent Film: From the Margins to the Mainstream,* ed. Chris Holmlund and Justin Wyatt (London: Routledge, 2005), 41–52. On January 30, 1981, Dimension Pictures filed for Chapter 7 bankruptcy; "21st Century Acquires 28 Films from Dimension," *Boxoffice*, September 1, 1981.

207 Rothman, interview by Jane Collings, March 18, 2002, 231; Academy of Motion Picture Arts and Sciences, Visual History Interview, August 10, 2015, 74.

208 Rothman, interview by Jane Collings, 229.

209 Sher, "Q & A with Stephanie Rothman."

210 Sher, "Q & A with Stephanie Rothman."

211 Carolyn Giardina, "Led USC Showbiz Tech Unit," *Hollywood Reporter*, February 14, 2007, accessed November 12, 2013, www.hollywoodreporter.com/news/led-usc-showbiz-tech-unit-130201.

212 Director-wife, producer-husband teams were not unusual during the silent era, although job categories tended to be more fluid then. At her New Jersey studio, Alice Guy-Blaché directed films, some of which were produced by her husband Herbert Blaché; spouses Lois Weber and Philip Smalley did the same. In the late 1940s, Ida Lupino and her second husband, Collier Young, worked together in the director-producer capacity on *Never Fear* (1949). After the two were divorced in 1950, they continued a successful professional collaboration. Young produced four of the subsequent films directed by his ex-wife and was the creator/executive producer for the CBS sitcom *Mr. Adam and Eve* (1957–1958) starring Lupino and her third husband, Howard Duff. In 1967, married couple Tom Laughlin and Delores Taylor collaborated on their "Billy Jack" series (*Born Loser* [1967], *Billy Jack* [1971], *The Trail of Billy Jack* [1974], and *Billy Jack Goes to Washington* [1977]). The films' original directing credits were T. C. Frank or Frank Laughlin, pseudonyms representing the couple's collaboration. When the DVDs were released in 2005, the directing credits on the packaging were parenthetically amended with only Laughlin's name.

213 Snedaker, "Movies."

214 "When Lightning Strikes Thunder Rolls . . . The Making of *Running Cool!*," DVD extra, *Running Cool*, dir. Beverly and Ferd Sebastian, Panama Films, 2012.

215 Ralph Kaminsky, "Sebastians Rely on 'Common Folks' as Key to Filmmaking, Distributing," *Boxoffice*, April 28, 1975, W-1; Keith Makenas, "Five Quick Questions with Beverly and Ferd Sebastian, *B Movie Nation,* April 22, 2013, accessed August 10, 2015, www.bmovienation.com/?p=6849.

216 *The Love Clinic* might also be known as *Oral Hygiene for the Handicapped*. "Marital Fulfillment," *Variety,* May 13, 1970, 14.

217 *I Need a Man*, aka *I Need* (1967), and *The Love Clinic* (1968) are currently unavailable in any screening format. According to an interview with Ferd in 1999, the lab where the negatives were held went bankrupt, and all the materials were stolen. Andrew Leavold, "Interview with Gator Bait's [*sic*] Ferd Sebastian," *Mondo Stumpo!*, November 25, 2007, accessed December 10, 2013. http://mondostumpo.blogspot

.com/2007/11/ferd-sebastian-interview-1999.html. The description of the film's plot and the credits are from Richard Krafsur, ed., *American Film Institute Catalog of Motion Pictures in the United States: Feature Films 1961–1970* (Los Angeles: Hollywood Film Archive, 1996), 517.

218 Terry and Tiffany DuFoe, "Interview with Ferd and Beverly Sebastian," *CRAGG LIVE*, February 18, 2017, https://archive.org/details/CRAGGLIVEFerdBeverlySebastian2ndAppearanceInterviewOnly.

219 An image of *The Love Clinic* poster is on Emovieposter.com, accessed October 1, 2015, www.bmovienation.com/?p=6849.

220 Terry and Tiffany DuFoe, "Interview with Ferd and Beverly Sebastian."

221 "Marital Fulfillment," 14.

222 Addison Verrill, "Cable-TV Might Be Home-Opener for Sex Manual Theatrical Films?," *Variety*, May 13, 1970, 38.

223 "Marital Fulfillment," 14.

224 "Marital Fulfillment," 14.

225 "Film Reviews: Red, White and Blue," *Variety*, March 3, 1971, 22.

226 "Film Reviews: Red, White and Blue," 22.

227 The budget for *The Hitchhikers* was an estimated $45,000. Terry and Tiffany DuFoe, "Interview with Ferd and Beverly Sebastian." The film earned $1.425 million and was ranked 92 out of 104 movies in *Variety*'s "Big Rental Films of 1975," January 7, 1976, 52.

228 The exception here is *Running Cool* (1993), which could be read as an anticorporation land-rights narrative in which a community of bikers fights the local developer who is trying to take over the wetlands owned by a fellow rider.

229 Gregg Kilday, "The Emergence of the Minimogul," *Los Angeles Times*, May 18, 1975, R37.

230 Kaminsky, "Sebastians Rely on 'Common Folks,'" W-1.

231 Kilday, "The Emergence of the Minimogul."

232 *Variety*, October 18, 1978, 146.

233 "Distributors of Theatrical Films," *Boxoffice*, September 1, 1987, 40.

234 "When Lightning Strikes Thunder Rolls . . . The Making of *Running Cool*!"

235 Kilday, "The Emergence of the Minimogul." According to the website for Panama Films Distribution, LLC, the Sebastians' most recent film company, *'Gator Bait* was made for a total of $90,000 and grossed $15 million. Accessed November 2, 2013, http://panamafilms.com/.

236 "When Lightning Strikes Thunder Rolls . . . The Making of *Running Cool*!"

237 Kevin Thomas, "Take of a Backwoods Runaway," *Los Angeles Times*, June 3, 1972, B6.

238 Marjorie Bilbow, "The New Films: Flash and the Firecat," *Screen International*, August 6, 1977, 16.

239 Ferd Sebastian, "This Is Why I Know God's Word Is True," 2Jesus Testimonies, August 1998, accessed November 2, 2013, www.2jesus.org/testimony/wordistrue.html.

240 "When Lightning Strikes Thunder Rolls . . . The Making of *Running Cool*!"
241 Ferd Sebastian, "This Is Why I Know God's Word Is True."
242 The National Greyhound Foundation, Inc., Sebastian Int. Marketing, 2003, accessed November 2, 2013, www.4greyhounds.org/about.html.
243 Panama Films Distribution. Accessed Nov. 2, 2013, http://panamafilms.com/.
244 "When Lightning Strikes Thunder Rolls . . . The Making of *Running Cool*!"
245 Linda Gross, "A Woman's Place Is in . . . Exploitation Films?," *Los Angeles Times*, February 12, 1978, 35.
246 Barbara Peeters, interview by author, April 10, 2010.
247 Alan Rosenberg, "Barbara Peeters—Don't Ask Her about 'Humanoids from the Deep,'" April 19, 2012, accessed June 20, 2012, http://ashlandplayreviews.com/barbara-peeters-dont-ask-her-about-humanoids-from-the-deep/. This story was also told to the author in a conversation during 2010.
248 "Film Reviews: The Fabulous Bastard from Chicago," *Variety*, July 2, 1969, 26.
249 Peeters, interview by author.
250 John Goff, "'Dark Side of Tomorrow' Dim Any Day at Boxoffice," *The Hollywood Reporter*, July 2, 1970.
251 "Film Review: The Dark Side of Tomorrow," *Daily Variety*, July 2, 1970.
252 Peeters, interview by author. Peeters was the sole author on *Bury Me an Angel*'s script.
253 Dixie Peabody's real brother, Dennis Peabody, played her brother in the film. In an eerie turn of events, he was killed in a motorcycle accident in Nebraska soon after the film was made.
254 Peeters, interview by author.
255 Peeters, interview by author.
256 "Film Reviews: "Eat My Dust," *Variety*, April 28, 1976, 30.
257 "Film Reviews: Moving Violation," *Variety*, July 28, 1976, 24.
258 Peeters, interview by author.
259 "Summer School Teachers," *Boxoffice*, August 19, 1975.
260 Linda Gross, "A Parlay of ERA, Sex and Football," *Los Angeles Times*, April 29, 1977, G19.
261 Gross, "A Parlay of ERA, Sex and Football."
262 *Variety* reported that Peeters replaced Stephanie Rothman as director on *Starhops;* "creative differences" with Rothman were blamed for the change; "Bar Replaces Stephanie," *Variety*, July 13, 1977, 21. On some of the film's promotional material, Rothman is given a credit as screenwriter; Cover, *Boxoffice*, October 3, 1977. In separate interviews with the author, neither Peeters nor Rothman recalled knowing anything about the reports of "creative differences." Rothman did not complete any work on the film.
263 Linda Gross, "'Starhops': Female Horatio Alger Tale," *Los Angeles Times*, March 10, 1978, F33.
264 Peeters, interview by author.
265 "Film Review: Starhops," *Variety*, March 22, 1978, 26.

266 Peeters, interview by author.

267 Peeters, interview by author.

268 Peeters, interview by author.

269 Peeters, interview by author.

270 "Barbara Peters," *Directory of Members 1977–78* (Los Angeles: Directors Guild of America, Inc., 1979), 266. The Directors Guild made Peeters change her name to "Peters." Peeters, interview by author.

271 Andrew Epstein, "'Humanoids' Haywire, Women Say," *Los Angeles Times*, May 8, 1980, 5.

272 Epstein, "'Humanoids' Haywire, Women Say."

273 "Humanoids from the Deep," *Variety*, April 23, 1980, 22.

274 "Humanoids from the Deep."

275 Epstein, "'Humanoids' Haywire, Women Say."

276 Roger Corman, letter, "Corman on Women in Power," *Los Angeles Times*, May 25, 1980, 25. In this letter, Corman attempted to distance himself from the film by saying that he did not produce the picture (Martin Cohen, producer, and Hunt Lowry, coproducer), even though his company released it and he was the one who hired Peeters and consulted on the added footage. In 1996, he reclaimed authorship when the film was re-released on home video as part of "Roger Corman Classics" for his company New Horizons. The VHS included an on-camera introduction by Corman where he made no mention of the public dispute and praised Peeters's work on the film: "Barbara Peeters was a young woman director whose work I'd admired very much. If I have any distinguishing thoughts on hiring directors is I try to go on ability—I don't care if it's a man, woman—whoever is the best at that time. And it was a little unusual to have a woman do this type of bloody horror film, but I felt Barbara was the best."

277 Peeters, interview by author.

278 Peeters, interview by author.

279 Peeters, interview by author.

## Chapter 3

1 Jane Wilson, "Hollywood Flirts with the New Woman," *New York Times*, May 29, 1977, 1.

2 Joan Mellen, "Hollywood Rediscovers the American Woman," *New York Times*, April 23, 1978, 2.

3 Jane Wilson, "Hollywood Flirts with the New Woman."

4 Molly Haskell, *From Reverence to Rape* (New York: Penguin Books, 1973), 323.

5 Joan Mellen, *Women and Their Sexuality in the New Film* (New York: Horizon Press, 1973), 55.

6 Jane Ross, "Box-Score on Distaff Roles in Films," *Daily Variety 41st Anniversary Issue*, October 29, 1974.

7 Eleanor Perry, "If You Wanna Make a Film about Women, Better Forget It," *Variety*, January 7, 1975.

8 Mary Murphy and Cheryl Bensten, "Women in Hollywood: Part I, Fighting to Enter the 'White Male Club,'" *Los Angeles Times*, August 14, 1973, 9.

9 Janet Maslin, "A Turning Point in the Career of Shirley MacLaine," *New York Times*, January 22, 1978.

10 Mellen, "Hollywood Rediscovers the American Woman." During the 1970s, there were four women senators: Elaine S. Edwards (D-Louisiana), 1972, Muriel Humphrey (D-Minnesota), 1978, and Maryon Allen (D-Alabama), 1978, who were each appointed to replace their husband after his death and served for just part of the year that each took office; and Nancy Landon Kassebaum (R-Kansas), the first elected woman senator, who served from 1978 to 1997. See www.senate.gov /artandhistory/history/common/briefing/women_senators.htm.

11 Carol MacGuineas, "Portrait of the Filmmaker as a Young Woman," *Cultural Post*, National Endowment for the Arts, July/August 1979.

12 Joan Darling, author interview, August 13, 2012.

13 "To All the Friedas of the World," *TV Guide*, March 17, 1973, 15.

14 The details of Darling's early career were told to the author in an interview on August 13, 2012. Also see "To All the Friedas of the World"; Louise Farr, "Hollywood's Newest Darling: In the Director's Chair," *New West*, October 10, 1977, 56.

15 Darling, interview by author.

16 Darling, interview by author.

17 Farr, "Hollywood's Newest Darling."

18 Darling, interview by author. Lear was well known for the socially progressive content of his 1970s sitcoms, such as *All in the Family*, *Good Times*, *Maude*, and *One Day at a Time*, but he had a poor track record of hiring women directors during the 1970s. *Mary Hartman, Mary Hartman* had several female writers on staff, including Ann Marcus and Gail Parent; the series also stood out as the only one of his shows with several women directors, three in all: Darling, Kim Friedman, and Nessa Hyams. This information was culled from the credits of *Mary Hartman, Mary Hartman*.

19 Darling, interview by author.

20 Darling, interview by author.

21 Darling interview by author.

22 Robert Sklar, "A Woman Directs in Hollywood!" *American Film*, July–August 1977, 12.

23 Joan Darling, interview at the American Film Institute, November 16, 1977, Harold Lloyd Master Seminars, Louis B. Mayer Library, Los Angeles.

24 The details of Darling's conflict with Turman were told to the author in an interview on August 13, 2012; also see Darling, interview at American Film Institute.

25 Darling, interview at the American Film Institute.

26 Darling, interview by author.

27 Art Murphy, "Film Review: First Love," *Variety*, November 2, 1977, 17

28 Molly Haskell, "'First Love' and Other Mixed Blessings," *New York Magazine*, November 14, 1977, 132.

29 Arthur Knight, "Movie Review: First Love," *Hollywood Reporter*, November 2 1977.

30 *First Love*, press release 1: "Joan Darling Likes Her Test as Woman Director of a Major Film as Former Actress Brings Her Talents to 'First Love' Project," Paramount Pictures, 1977. *First Love* Clipping File, Margaret Herrick Library.

31 *First Love*, press release 1.

32 *First Love*, press release 1.

33 *First Love*, press release 2: "With 'First Love' Direction Now under Her Belt, Joan Darling Begins Building a New Tradition for Women in Motion Pictures," Paramount Pictures, 1977. *First Love* Clipping File, Margaret Herrick Library.

34 Darling, interview by author.

35 Lawrence Christon, "Someone's Listening to Jane Wagner Again," *Los Angeles Times*, April 16, 1978, 60.

36 Details of Wagner's biography were told to the author in an interview on May 27, 2011. Also see David Halberstam, "The Brightest Lights on Broadway," *Parade-Daily News*, May 18, 1986.

37 Nigel Andrews, *Travolta: The Life* (New York: Bloomsbury, 1998), 96–97.

38 Kevin Thomas, "Travolta's Best Foot Forward for Disco Role," *Los Angeles Times*, December 16, 1977, 31.

39 Andrews, *Travolta*, 97.

40 Gregg Kilday, "Tomlin Signs Two-Picture Pact," *Los Angeles Times*, January 25, 1977, F8.

41 As a first-timer it was not unusual for Wagner to be hired by Universal, which was noted in the press for hiring several "newcomers." What was unique was the fact that she was Universal's only woman director. Charles Schreger, "Pictures: Universal Mostest on Firstest," *Variety*, April 26, 1978, 4, 42.

42 Christon, "Someone's Listening to Jane Wagner Again," 55.

43 Bruce Vilanch, "The Entertainer Lily Tomlin," *Advocate.com*, November 10, 2009, www.advocate.com/comedy/2009/11/10/entertainer-lily-tomlin.

44 Ann Hornaday, "Lily Tomlin Has Led a Singular Comedic Life. And That's the Truth," *Washington Post*, December 3, 2014, www.washingtonpost.com/lifestyle/style/lily-tomlin-has-led-a-singular-comedic-life-and-thats-the-truth/2014/12/03/595daa88-7187-11e4-8808-afaa1e3a33ef_story.html?utm_term=.2ef418dd8e77.

45 Doug Edwards, "T 'n' Fizzles Brinks Job Sizzles," *The Advocate*, January 25, 1979.

46 Frank Rich, "Cinema: Winter Camp," *Time*, December 25, 1978.

47 "Film Reviews: Moment by Moment, *Variety*, December 20, 1978, 30.

48 Edwards, "T 'n' Fizzles Brinks Job Sizzles."

49 Kevin Thomas, "Tomlin and Travolta in 'Moment,'" *Los Angeles Times*, December 22, 1978, G28.

50 "Big Rental Films of 1979," *Variety*, January 1, 1980, 70. In the last few years the film has streamed on Netflix and HBO, but still has not been officially released on DVD.

51 Jane Wagner, interview by author, May 27, 2011.

52 Judson Klinger, "Playboy Interview: John Travolta," *Playboy*, December 1978, 124.

53 Andrews, *Travolta*, 99.
54 Klinger, "Playboy Interview: John Travolta," 115.
55 Andrews, *Travolta*, 106.
56 Gene Siskel, "'Urban Cowboy': Will Travolta Fever Rise Again?," *Chicago Tribune*, June 1, 1980, 21.
57 Wagner, interview by author.
58 Wagner, interview by author.
59 P. H. B., "'Moment by Moment' Seemed like Hour by Hour," *Los Angeles Times*, December 23, 1979, 14.
60 Siskel, "'Urban Cowboy,'" D3.
61 Janet Maslin, "Lily Tomlin: 'Shrinking Woman' Stands Tall," *New York Times*, January 29, 1981.
62 Erica Abeel, "She Wrote the Book," *Newsday*, November 18, 1985, 10.
63 Leslie Bennetts, "Behind Lily Tomlin, Another Star," *New York Times*, October 4, 1985.
64 Klinger, "Playboy Interview: John Travolta."
65 Joan Tewkesbury, interview by author, April 16, 2010.
66 "'Maiden' to Omnipotent," *Variety*, January 19, 1972, 32.
67 Wagner, interview by author.
68 The details of Tewkesbury's biography were told to the author in an interview on April 16, 2010. Also see Jan Stuart, *The Nashville Chronicles* (New York: Limelight Edition, 2000), 48, 52–53.
69 Stuart, *The Nashville Chronicles*, 54.
70 Stuart, *The Nashville Chronicles*, 49.
71 Joan Tewkesbury, interview by Katt Shea, Directors Guild Visual History Project, Los Angeles, December 2, 2006.
72 Tewkesbury, interview by Katt Shea.
73 Tewkesbury, interview by author, April 16, 2010.
74 Tewkesbury, interview by Katt Shea.
75 Hedy Kleyweg, "'Old Boyfriends,' 'Conan' on Pressman's Schedule," *Hollywood Reporter*, February 24, 1978.
76 Tewkesbury, interview by Katt Shea.
77 Tewkesbury, interview by Katt Shea.
78 Kevin Jackson, ed., *Schrader on Schrader* (London: Faber and Faber, 2004), 122.
79 Tewkesbury, interview by author, April 16, 2010.
80 Tewkesbury, interview by Katt Shea.
81 Tewkesbury, interview by author, January 27, 2011.
82 Tewkesbury, interview by author, April 16, 2010.
83 David Denby, "Old Boyfriends," *New Yorker*, April 9, 1979, 91.
84 Robert Osborne, "Movie Review: Old Boyfriends," *Hollywood Reporter*, March 26, 1979.
85 Tewkesbury, interview by author, April 16, 2010.

86 Tewkesbury, interview by author, January 27, 2011.

87 Tewkesbury, interview by author, January 27, 2011.

88 Tewkesbury, interview by author, April 16, 2010.

89 Arthur Knight, "Joan Rivers: Director Person," *Hollywood Reporter*, March 3, 1978, 42.

90 Richard Meryman, "Directing Her First Movie or Cracking up Carson, Joan Rivers Has Angst in Her Pants," *People*, January 9, 1978, 46.

91 Meryman, "Directing Her First Movie or Cracking up Carson," 45.

92 Meryman, "Directing Her First Movie or Cracking up Carson," 46.

93 Bruce Williamson, "Movies," *Playboy*, May 1978, 24.

94 "RSO, Stigwood Arm, Is Readying Four Features; One, 'Roxy Music Haul,'" *Variety*, July 3, 1974, 6.

95 Joan Rivers and Richard Meryman, *Still Talking* (New York: Random House, 1991), 90.

96 Rivers and Meryman, *Still Talking*, 103.

97 Rivers and Meryman, *Still Talking*, 103.

98 Rivers and Meryman, *Still Talking*, 105; Bobby Shriver, "At Last, Joan Rivers Made Her Own Movie," *Los Angeles Herald Examiner*, April 7, 1978, B1.

99 Shriver, "At Last, Joan Rivers Made Her Own Movie."

100 Bridget Byrne, "Joan Rivers at the Controls—Zany 'Rabbit Test,'" *Los Angeles Herald Examiner*, September 20, 1977, B1.

101 "All-Time Film Rental Champs," *Variety*, January 9, 1980, 52. *Variety*'s totals are calculated from U.S. box office numbers only. The *Hollywood Reporter* reported that the film earned more than $10 million in the United States and Canada. "Rivers Destroys Note That Pledged House for 'Test,'" *Hollywood Reporter*, May 25, 1978, 13.

102 "Joan Rivers Even Risked Family Fortune to Direct 'Rabbit Test,'" *Variety*, January 18, 1978.

103 "Promotional Tour for 'Rabbit Test' Tests Director Joan Rivers' Stamina," *Boxoffice*, March 27, 1978, W1. Comment about Melissa Rivers is found in Bruce Williamson, "Movies," *Playboy*, May 1978, 24.

104 Joan Rivers, *Rabbit Test* trailer, YouTube.com, accessed May 11, 2017, www.youtube.com/watch?v=tEDp8M3gSQk.

105 Ben Shlyen, "Showmanship to the Fore," *Boxoffice*, April 3, 1978, 2.

106 "Film Reviews: Rabbit Test," *Variety*, February 22, 1978, 19.

107 "Buying & Booking Guide: Rabbit Test," *Independent Film Journal*, April 14, 1978, 8.

108 Williamson, "Movies," 24.

109 Arthur Knight, "Knight at the Movies: Joan Rivers: Director Person," *Hollywood Reporter*, March 3, 1978, 8.

110 Rivers and Meryman, *Still Talking*, 106.

111 Joan Rivers, interview by Allan Neuwirth for Archive of American Television, Part 1 and Part 2, emmytvlegends.org, October 3, 2007, http://emmytvlegends.org/interviews/people/joan-rivers#.

112 Rivers and Meryman, *Still Talking*, 106.
113 Rivers, interview by Allan Neuwirth.
114 Rivers and Meryman, *Still Talking*, 107.
115 Williamson, "Movies," *Playboy*, May 1978, 24.
116 Rivers, interview by Allan Neuwirth.
117 "Caesars Palace, L.V.," *Variety*, March 1, 1972, 61.
118 Rivers, interview by Allan Neuwirth.
119 "Joan Rivers," *Los Angeles*, January 1978, 124. Joan Rivers Clipping File, Margaret Herrick Library.
120 Cecile Starr, "Claudia Weill Discusses 'Girlfriends,'" *Filmmakers Newsletter*, October 1978, 28.
121 Stephen Klain, "'Girlfriends' Release Puts Claudia Weills [*sic*] into Majors," *Variety*, August 11, 1978, 3.
122 "W. S. Teller Wed Claudia Weill," *New York Times*, July 15, 1985, A9.
123 Carol MacGuineas, "Portrait of the Filmmaker as a Young Woman," *Cultural Post*, National Endowment for the Arts, July–August 1978, 5.
124 Carey Winfrey, "Claudia Weill: It's Her Turn Now," *New York Times*, December 7, 1980, D1.
125 Claudia Weill, interview by Lena Dunham, Human Resources, Los Angeles, October 14, 2011. Author in attendance.
126 Paul Mazursky, writer-director of *An Unmarried Woman*, credited Weill, a friend, with suggesting New York City locations for his studio picture. Both *Girlfriends*, which went into production years before *An Unmarried Woman*, and Mazursky's film have many scenes that take place in SoHo. Cecile Starr, "Claudia Weill: From Shoestring to Studio," *Los Angeles Times*, August 6, 1978, D11.
127 "Melanie Mayron: A Dream of the First Starring Role," *Los Angeles Times*, August 20, 1978, P43.
128 MacGuineas, "Portrait of the Filmmaker as a Young Woman," 5.
129 Winfrey, "Claudia Weill: It's Her Turn Now," D1. For the Warner Bros. pickup date, see "GIRLFRIENDS, Production Information," Warner Bros., Girlfriends, 1978 Production File. Margaret Herrick Library.
130 Arthur Schlesinger Jr., "The Movies: One Feminist Film That Works," *Saturday Review*, September 2, 1978, 28.
131 Weill, interview by Lena Dunham.
132 Gene Siskel, "Directors' Ranks Gain a New Winner," *Chicago Tribune*, October 15, 1978, F4.
133 Siskel, "Directors' Ranks Gain a New Winner."
134 "Girlfriends," *Variety*, May 5, 1978.
135 Starr, "Claudia Weill: From Shoestring to Studio."
136 Charles Champlin, "'Girl Friends': On 'Rocky's' Road," *Los Angeles Times*, August 20, 1978, P1.
137 Champlin, "'Girl Friends.'"
138 For a discussion of Warner Bros.' interest during the 1970s in distributing

independent films see James Monaco, *American Film Now* (New York: Oxford University Press, 1979), 400–401.

139 "Big Rental Films of 1978," *Variety*, January 3, 1979, 50.

140 Gregg Kilday, "It's Her Turn in the Big Time," *Los Angeles Herald Examiner*, October 22, 1980, D6.

141 Kilday, "It's Her Turn in the Big Time."

142 Charles Champlin, "Good 'Turn' Deserves a 'Loving' Companion," *Los Angeles Times*, October 24, 1980, G1.

143 Andrew Sarris, "Films in Focus: Energy Isn't Everything," *Village Voice*, October 22–28, 1980, 180.

144 Julia Cameron, "You Mean Jill Clayburgh Is the '80s Woman? That Means None of Us Will Get *Anything* Done," *Los Angeles Herald Examiner*, November 13, 1980, A17.

145 Stanley Kauffmann, "Stanley Kauffmann on Films: Mod and Victorian," *New Republic*, October 18, 1980, 24.

146 Kauffmann, "Stanley Kauffmann on Films."

147 Robert Osborne, "It's My Turn," *Hollywood Reporter*, October 22, 1980.

148 For mentions of conflict see Kilday, "It's Her Turn in the Big Time"; Richard K. Rein, "Claudia Weill Steps up to the Big Leagues of Hollywood Directing with Hit Aptly Titled 'It's My Turn,'" *People*, December 1, 1980.

149 "The Douglas Syndrome," *Los Angeles Herald Examiner*, August 1, 1980.

150 Marilyn Beck, "Marilyn Beck's Hollywood: 'It's My Turn' Director Is Ready to Sound Off," *Milwaukee Journal*, October 8, 1980, 3.

151 Kilday, "It's Her Turn in the Big Time."

152 John Parker, *Michael Douglas Acting on Instinct* (London: Headline Publishing Group, 1994), 170–171.

153 Rein, "Claudia Weill Steps Up."

154 Clarke Taylor, "Weill: She Did It Her Way and Their Way, Too," *Los Angeles Times*, June 6, 1981, B8.

155 Weill, interview by Lena Dunham.

156 Weill, interview by Lena Dunham.

157 Taylor, "Weill: She Did It Her Way."

158 *It's My Turn* earned $2,232,290 during its first three days playing at 636 theaters. Teri Ritzer, "'It's My Turn's' 1st Week B.O. Tally Exceeds $2.7 Million," *Hollywood Reporter*, November 5, 1980. The film's domestic rental earnings for its first two months were estimated at $5 million, and it had been presold to television (ABC) for $4.5 million; "Col Presold 'Crazy' 'My Turn,' to ABC," *Variety*, December 31, 1980, 5.

159 For *It's My Turn* box office earnings, see "Big Rental Films of 1980," *Variety*, January 14, 1981, 29. For the estimated budget for *It's My Turn* see "Weill Takes Her Turn at Directing Big-Budget Pic," *Variety*, November 5, 1980, 6.

160 Weill, interview by Lena Dunham.

161 Judy Klemesrud, "'Girlfriends' Director on Female Friendship," *New York Times*, August 4, 1978, A12.

162 Lee Grant, interview by Barbara Kopple, Directors Guild Visual History Project, Los Angeles, June 25, 2008.
163 John H. Averill, "Stevens Heads New U.S. Film Institute," *Los Angeles Times*, June 6, 1967, C9.
164 Press release for first year of Directing Workshop for Women, "Women to Direct," AFI, September 26, 1974. Directing Workshop for Women Clipping File, New York Public Library for the Performing Arts.
165 Averill, "Stevens Heads New U.S. Film Institute."
166 Mary B. Murphy, "Women on March, Give AFI Demands," *Los Angeles Times*, December 11, 1970.
167 Murphy, "Women on March, Give AFI Demands."
168 "Women's Libs March on AFI; Want 51% All Scholarships," *Hollywood Reporter*, December 10, 1970.
169 Murphy, "Women on March, Give AFI Demands."
170 Murphy, "Women on March, Give AFI Demands." Also see "Women's Libs March on AFI"; "Film Institute Hears Women's Equality Demands," *Daily Variety*, December 11, 1970; and "Women's Lib Group Presents Formal Demands to Stevens," *Hollywood Reporter*, December 11, 1970.
171 Murphy, "Women on March, Give AFI Demands."
172 Jan Haag's nonparticipation in the WFEM meeting confirmed in an email from Haag to the author. Jan Haag, "Directing Workshop for Women," email message to author, August 20, 2012.
173 "Pounding" story is in an email from Haag to the author. Jan Haag, "Directing Workshop for Women," email message to author, August 20, 2012.
174 Jan Haag, "Women Directors in Hollywood," janhaag.com, 2007, July 13, 2012, http://janhaag.com/ESTheDWW.html.
175 Haag, "Women Directors in Hollywood."
176 Mary Murphy, "A Camera Is Not Enough," *Los Angeles Times*, October 27, 1974, 92.
177 Louise Sweeney, "Lights! Camera! Affirmative Action!," *Christian Science Monitor*, August 14, 1979.
178 Sweeney, "Lights! Camera! Affirmative Action!"
179 Mary Mizell, "AFI Women Directors' Workshop," *Premiere* 11, no. 5 (1981): 19.
180 Murphy, "A Camera Is Not Enough."
181 For funding sources see Jan Haag, "Women Directors in Hollywood," and Mary Mizell, "AFI Women Directors' Workshop." Future AFI president Jean Picker Firstenberg was a program officer at the Markle Foundation when it first funded the DWW, and she continues to financially contribute to the program through the Jean Picker Firstenberg Endowment.
182 Jan Haag, "Women Directors in Hollywood."
183 DWW graduates who have directed features films include Neema Barnette, Lesli Linka Glatter, Randa Haines, Victoria Hochberg, and Matia Karrell.
184 James Robert Parish, *It's Good to Be the King: The Seriously Funny Life of Mel Brooks* (Hoboken, N.J.: John Wiley & Sons, 2007), 228.

185 Robert Berkevist, "Anne Bancroft, Stage and Film Star in Voracious and Vulnerable Roles, Dies at 73," *New York Times on the Web*, June 7, 2005, www.nytimes.com /2005/06/07/movies/07cnd-bancroft.html.

186 Judith Martin, "Toward More Women Directors: Doubling the Odds for Success," *Washington Post*, July 21, 1976, B7.

187 Parish, *It's Good to Be the King*, 228.

188 For Bancroft preparing *Fatso* in 1979 see Aljean Harmetz, "Mel Brooks to Film Own Version of 'Elephant Man,'" *New York Times*, May 1, 1979, C20. Harmetz's article names Brooks's company as "Crossbow Productions," but the credits on the film poster say "Brooksfilms Ltd," which was the name of his new company set up for his turn at more dramatic work. Parish, *It's Good to Be the King*, 227.

189 "Anne Bancroft: Lady with Three Hats," 1980, press release in *Fatso* press kit. Dom DeLuise Special Collection, Margaret Herrick Library, 2.

190 Susan Smith, "Bri Murphy: Eye of the Camera," *New York Times*, May 27, 1979, M34.

191 Smith, "Bri Murphy: Eye of the Camera"; "Bri Murphy First Woman Accepted by IATSE Photogs," *Hollywood Reporter*, March 14, 1973

192 Jonathan Sanger, interview with author, July 14, 2016.

193 Brooks's company, Crossbow Productions, had produced his films *The Producers* (1967), *Blazing Saddles* (1974), *Young Frankenstein* (1974), *Silent Movie* (1976), and *High Anxiety* (1977). According to his biographer James Robert Parish, Brooks was starting to be interested in more serious work: in 1979 his company was developing *The Elephant Man* (1980); it was directed by David Lynch as his first studio-released picture.

194 Harmetz, "Mel Brooks to Film Own Version of 'Elephant Man,'" C20.

195 Jonathan Sanger, *Making the Elephant Many: A Producer's Memoir* (Jefferson, N.C.: McFarland & Company, 2016).

196 Sanger, interview with author.

197 Michael Sragow, "'Fatso': Looking for Mr. Cholesterol," *Los Angeles Herald Examiner*, February 1, 1980.

198 Tom Cullen, untitled article, *Village Voice*, February 11, 1980.

199 Cullen, untitled article, *Village Voice*.

200 Arthur Knight, "Fatso," *Hollywood Reporter*, February 1, 1980, 24.

201 Knight, "Fatso," 24.

202 Kevin Thomas, "Fat, 40 and Fed up in Bancroft's 'Fatso,'" *Los Angeles Times*, February 1, 1980, F1.

203 Parish, *It's Good to Be the King*, 229.

204 Sanger, interview with author.

205 Mollie Gregory, *Women Who Run the Show: How a Brilliant & Creative New Generation of Women Stormed Hollywood* (New York: St. Martin's Press, 2002), 138.

206 Gregory, *Women Who Run the Show*, 138.

207 Gregory, *Women Who Run the Show*, 138–139.

208 Gregory, *Women Who Run the Show*, 139.

209 Gregory, *Women Who Run the Show*, 138–139.

210 Rebecca Traister, "A Fine Romance," *Salon.com,* June 8, 2005, www.salon.com/2005/06/08/bancroft_brooks/; Mel Brooks, interview with Judd Apatow, Town Hall, *SiriusXM*, April 27, 2013, accessed July 17, 2013, www.youtube.com/watch?v=wP8WRS36m1U.

211 Sanger, interview by author.

212 Berkevist, "Anne Bancroft, Stage and Film Star."

213 Leslie Bennetts, "Bancroft Portrays a Feisty Frump," *New York Times*, October 15, 1984. C13.

214 Patt Morrison, "And Here's to You, Mrs. Robinson: As Seductive as Ever, the Incomparable Anne Bancroft," *More*, May/June 2000, 144.

215 Tom Buckley, "At the Movies: Nancy Walker to Direct 'Discoland,'" *New York Times*, June 22, 1979, C8.

216 "Nancy Walker Set to Direct MTM," *Hollywood Reporter*, August 28, 1973.

217 Arnold Hano, "Funny Lady?," *TV Guide*, February 19, 1977, 25.

218 "Carr, EMI Sign Nancy Walker to Directing Pact," *Variety*, November 13, 1979, 21; for *Can't Stop the Music* box office grosses see *Hollywood Reporter*, July 8, 1980.

219 Gregg Hunter, "Nancy Walker 'Can't Stop' Directing," *The Advocate*, December 13, 1979.

220 Buckley, "At the Movies: Nancy Walker to Direct 'Discoland,'" C8.

221 Buckley, "At the Movies: Nancy Walker to Direct 'Discoland,'" C8.

222 "Nancy Walker Helms 'Discoland;' Arlene Phillips Will Choreograph," *Variety*, May 16, 1979.

223 John Gruen, "Her Face Is Her Fortune," *New York Times*, October 14, 1973, 1, 23.

224 Gruen, "Her Face Is Her Fortune."

225 George Christy, "The Great Life," *Hollywood Reporter*, November 9,1979.

226 Nancy Walker, interview by Janna Dettmer, American Film Institute, March 12, 1980, Harold Lloyd Master Seminars, Louis B. Mayer Library, Los Angeles.

227 Robert Hofler, *Party Animals: A Hollywood Tale of Sex, Drugs, and Rock 'n' Roll Starring the Fabulous Allan Carr* (New York: De Capo Press, 2010), 107.

228 Hofler, *Party Animals*, 113.

229 "Film Directing Bow for Nancy Walker on 'Can't Stop the Music,'" press materials, n/d. *Can't Stop the Music* Clipping File, Margaret Herrick Library.

230 "Reviews: "Can't Stop the Music," *Motion Picture Product Digest*, July 9, 1980.

231 David Ansen, "Can't Stop the Music," *Newsweek*, July 7, 1980, 68.

232 "Sign Nancy Walker for More Directing," *Variety*, November 21, 1979.

233 Elaine Warren, "Nancy Walker and Her Gift of Courage," *Los Angeles Herald Examiner*, October 13, 1983, B1.

234 Hofler, *Party Animals*, 123.

235 A. H. Weiler, "Lee Grant Directs: Who's Directing? A Lady Named Lee Grant," *New York Times*, January 23, 1972, D11.

236 Lee Grant, interview by Henry Colman for Archive of American Television, Part 6 and Part 7, May 10, 2000, www.emmytvlegends.org/interviews/people/lee-grant.

237 Weiler, "Lee Grant Directs," D11.
238 Grant, interview by Henry Colman.
239 "Women to Codirect CBS Comedy Special," *Los Angeles Times*, August 3, 1973, E19.
240 Mary Murphy, "TV Comedy Revue for Women Making Man the Fall Guy," *Los Angeles Times*, October 9, 1973, D1.
241 In interviews, Grant remembers getting a call from the Directing Workshop for Women after she had won her Oscar for *Shampoo* in 1976, but actually it was at least two years before that that she was enrolled in the workshop's pilot program, which launched in 1974.
242 Grant, interview by Henry Colman.
243 Murphy, "A Camera Is Not Enough," 92.
244 Susan Smith, "'It Changed My Life,'" *Los Angeles Times*, September 13, 1979, 30.
245 Lee Grant, *I Said Yes to Everything* (New York: Blue Rider Press, 2014), 315.
246 Grant, *I Said Yes to Everything*, 315.
247 Grant, *I Said Yes to Everything*, 320.
248 "Godmothers Bow with a 'Riddle,'" *Screen International*, July 9, 1989, 6.
249 Judy Stone, "How the 'Godmothers' Brought 'Tell Me a Riddle' to the Screen," *New York Times*, December 14, 1980, 32.
250 Janet Maslin, "Film: 'Tell Me a Riddle,' Aged Pair's Love Story," *New York Times*, December 15, 1980, C13.
251 Kevin Thomas, "Simple 'Riddle': Death and Old Age," *Los Angeles Times*, December 13, 1980, 11.
252 Roderick Mann, "Welcome Praise for Director Lee Grant," *Los Angeles Times*, December 16, 1980, G1.
253 Lee Grant, interview by Barbara Kopple, Directors Guild Visual History Project, Los Angeles, June 25, 2008.
254 Mann, "Welcome Praise for Director Lee Grant."
255 Grant, interview by Barbara Kopple.
256 Peter Bart, *The Gross: The Hits, the Flops—the Summer That Ate Hollywood* (New York: St. Martin's Press, 1999), 85–86.
257 Grant, interview by Barbara Kopple.
258 Grant, *I Said Yes to Everything*, 320.
259 Barbara Cady, "Playgirl Interview: Joan Rivers," *Playgirl*, November 1977, 34.

## Chapter 4

1 The "Women's Steering Committee" is this group's official name, although at times in the press and in various archival documents it is listed as the "Women's Committee."
2 "History: About the DGA," dga.org, 2011–2017, accessed September 1, 2017, www.dga.org/The-Guild/History.aspx.
3 The DGA's Basic Agreement is negotiated every three years. The current BA is available from the DGA website as a downloadable PDF. In 1981 the contract, which is relevant to this chapter, was published in a booklet put out by the DGA:

"Definition of Employees Recognized," *Basic Agreement of 1981* (Los Angeles, Directors Guild of America, Inc., 1981), 4–7.

4 "History: About the DGA," 2011–2014.

5 For histories of the DGA see Douglas Gomery, *The Hollywood Studio System: A History* (London: British Film Institute, 2005), 191–193; David Robb, "Directors Guild Born out of Fear 50 Years Ago," *Variety 50th Anniversary Issue*, October 29, 1985, 21.

6 Robb, "Directors Guild Born out of Fear 50 Years Ago," 21.

7 "Legends: Dorothy Arzner and "Ida Lupino," *DGA Quarterly*, 2006, accessed March 1, 2013, www.dga.org/Craft/DGAQ/Categories/Legends.aspx.

8 "First 25 Women to Join the DGA," *DGA News* 15, December 1990–January 1991, 33.

9 *Directory of Members 1967–68* (Los Angeles: Directors Guild of America, Inc., 1967), 54.

10 *Directory of Members 1969–70* (Los Angeles: Directors Guild of America, Inc., 1969), 199.

11 "Ten Groups of Media Women Combine for Actions Improving Status of Women," *Media Report to Women*, July 1, 1975, 1.

12 "Femme DGA Members Form Special Wing," *Variety*, October 17, 1974; Beverly Walker, "Fem Breakthrough Mostly Symbolic," *Variety*, October 29, 1974.

13 Amy Dawes, "A More Perfect Union," *DGA Quarterly*, Spring 2011, www.dga.org/Craft/DGAQ/All-Articles/1101-Spring-2011/Feature-RTDG-SDG-Merger.aspx.

14 Giovanna Nigro-Chacon, interview by author, August 27, 2012.

15 Robert Wise, "Directors Guild Broadens Scope," *Variety 41st Anniversary Issue*, October 29, 1974.

16 Nigro-Chacon, interview by author.

17 Nigro-Chacon, interview by author.

18 Confirmed by Nigro-Chacon and by Dobrow, who was part of the 1974 Women's Committee. Joelle Dobrow, interview by author, November 11, 2012.

19 Dowd had received an MFA from UCLA's Film Department where she studied directing and made a couple of short films while a student. She was a screenwriter and assistant editor on the documentary *F.T.A.* (1972), directed by Francine Parker.

20 Special Report: The Woman Director," *Action Directors Guild of America* 8, no. 4 (July–August 1973), 8.

21 "Special Report: The Woman Director," 8. "Guy is quoted in "Woman's Place in Photoplay Production," *Moving Picture World*, July 11, 1914.

22 Nancy Dowd, "The Woman Director through the Years," *Action Directors Guild of America* 8, no. 4 (July–August 1973), 18.

23 Wise, "Directors Guild Broadens Scope."

24 Lynne Littman, interview by author, August 27, 2012.

25 Joelle Dobrow, interview by author, August 27, 2012.

26 Victoria Hochberg, interview by author, August 27, 2012.

27 Dobrow, interview by author.

28 *Directory of Members 1967–68.*

29 *Directory of Members 1974–75* (Los Angeles: Directors Guild of America, Inc., 1974).

30 Nell Cox, interview by author, April 8, 2011.

31 Cox, interview by author.

32 Cecil Smith, "TV Critics Name 'Eleanor,' Visions, 'Roots,'" *Los Angeles Times*, March 18, 1977, G1.

33 Cox, interview by author.

34 Cox, interview by author.

35 Hochberg, interview by author.

36 Dobrow, interview by author.

37 "ABC Women Organize in Los Angeles, Begin a Newsletter," *Media Report to Women* 3, no. 4 (April 1, 1975), 7. This information also confirmed by Dobrow, interview by author, November 11, 2012.

38 Letter to DGA Members from Women's Committee regarding reactivating committee, May 25, 1979. Joelle Dobrow, personal papers.

39 "Chores and Statistics to Collect (sample)," notes from the DGA Women's Committee, 1979. Joelle Dobrow, personal papers.

40 "New Faces of '1978' at DGA Hollywood Office," *Directors Guild of America News* 2, no. 2 (February 1978), 2.

41 In May 1978 the DGA members' newsletter reported, "Within the next few months the Directors Guild will redesign and convert many of its office systems to computerization. . . . This step was approved by the National Board at its meeting on March 4, 1978." "Computers to Streamline Guild," *Directors Guild of America News* 2, no. 5 (May 1978), 1.

42 "History, DGA Women's Committee," September 7, 1980. Joelle Dobrow, personal papers, 6.

43 Dobrow, Hochberg, and Littman, interview by author, August 27, 2012.

44 "History, DGA Women's Committee," 7.

45 These seven directors and the number of features they made between 1949 and 1979 were Ida Lupino (7), Elaine May (3), Joan Micklin Silver (1), Joan Darling (1), Jane Wagner (1), and either Joan Rivers (1) or Claudia Weill (1), who directed independently produced features that had wide distribution. This number accounts for films produced and/or distributed in some part by a major studio, production, or distribution company; it does not include low-budget independent or exploitation films (see chapters 2 and 3).

46 Letter to signatories from Michael Franklin regarding employment statistics, June 20, 1980. DGA Clipping File, Margaret Herrick Library. The original worksheets that the group created to tally their statistical findings are available in this letter to the DGA signatories.

47 Hochberg, interview by author.

48 Michael Franklin interview by author, May 10, 2012.

49 "A Talk with Michael Franklin," *Newsletter Directors Guild of America* 12, no. 11 (December 1987), 1.

50 Joseph McBride, "DGA Hyphenated Get Work Orders—Even if WG Strikes," *Daily Variety*, February 28, 1977.
51 Gerry Levin, "DGA Threatens to Strike if Producers Accede to WGA's Contract Proposals," *Hollywood Reporter*, January 20, 1977.
52 Levin, "DGA Threatens to Strike."
53 Levin, "DGA Threatens to Strike."
54 Jim Harwood, "Franklin Switching from WGA to Become Chief of the DGA," *Variety*, September 8, 1977.
55 Franklin, interview by author.
56 Dates confirmed by Franklin in interview by author. Also see Hardwood, "Michael Franklin Switching over to Become DGA Chief."
57 Warren Adler, interview by author, May 10, 2012.
58 Franklin, interview by author.
59 Hochberg and Littman, interview by author.
60 Susan Smitman, interview by author, September 26, 2013.
61 Cox, interview by author.
62 Hochberg, interview by author.
63 "History, DGA Women's Committee," 2.
64 "History, DGA Women's Committee," 2.
65 Joelle Dubrow, interview with Michael Franklin, 1990. Joelle Dobrow, Personal Papers, 10. (Complete transcript of Joelle Dobrow, "Interview: The Man behind the Women's Movement at the Guild," *DGA News*, December 1990–January 1991.)
66 Wendell James Franklin, letter to Directors Guild of America, National Board of Directors, July 29, 1979. See also Warren Adler, letter to Jamaa Fanaka, September 7, 1995. Jamaa Fanaka Papers, Performing Arts Special Collections, UCLA, Los Angeles.
67 Zeinabu Davis, *Wendell Franklin* (Los Angeles: Directors Guild of America, Inc., 1995), 126. Crain, Franklin, and Watt all joined the DGA as ADs; Crain went on to direct episodic television and the feature films *Blacula* (1972) and *Dr. Black, Mr. Hyde* (1976); and Franklin directed one feature film, *The Bus is Coming* (1971). Dixon began his film and television career as an actor in the late 1950s before becoming a prolific television director in the 1970s; he also directed two features during this time, *Trouble Man* (1972) and *The Spook Who Sat by the Door* (1973).
68 Eunice Post Field, "DGA Committee Wants More Women Directing for TV," *Hollywood Reporter*, June 20, 1980; Morrie Gelman, "DGA Wants More Work for Women: Asks One Femme Director for Every 13 Television Segs," *Variety*, June 20, 1980; Victoria Hochberg, "History of DGA Women's Committee," May 13, 2014, email to author.
69 Hochberg, interview by author. Hochberg read from the minutes of the meeting during this interview, no date available.
70 Gelman, "DGA Wants More Work For Women"; Post Field, "DGA Committee Wants More Women Directing for TV."
71 Gelman, "DGA Wants More Work for Women"; DGA press release, "Directors

Guild Study Reveals Dramatic Underemployment of Women Members," June 18, 1980. DGA Clipping File, Margaret Herrick Library.

72 Cox, interview by author.

73 Gelman, "DGA Wants More Work for Women"; DGA press release, "Directors Guild Study Reveals Dramatic Underemployment of Women Members."

74 Lee Grant, "Where Are the Women Directors?," *Los Angeles Times*, June 20, 1980, G1.

75 Gelman, "DGA Wants More Work for Women."

76 Gelman, "DGA Wants More Work for Women."

77 Gelman, "DGA Wants More Work for Women."

78 Aljean Harmetz, "Suit to Allege Sex Bias by TV and Film Makers," *New York Times*, February 25, 1981.

79 Cox, interview by author. Reiterated by Dobrow, Hochberg, Littman, interviews by author, August 27, 2012.

80 In her study of the *Mary Tyler Moore Show* author Jennifer Keishin Armstrong details how the series' creators, James L. Brooks and Allan Burns, did put "the first 'liberated' female on TV" and to do so hired a significant number of women writers to make sure their series conveyed a genuine contemporary female perspective. In the seven years the program was on the air, it appeared, however, to have had only two women directors, Joan Darling and Mary Tyler Moore. Jennifer Keishin Armstrong, *Mary and Lou and Rhoda and Ted: And All the Brilliant Minds Who Made the Mary Tyler Moore Show a Classic* (New York: Simon & Schuster, 2013).

81 Franklin, interview by author.

82 Letter to signatories from Michael Franklin regarding employment statistics.

83 Letter to signatories from Michael Franklin regarding employment statistics.

84 Dobrow, "Interview: The Man behind the Women's Movement at the Guild," 20–21.

85 Answer to Complaint and Counterclaim against Plaintiff, 5, DGA v. WB/CPI, (C.D. Cal. Oct. 6, 1983), originally accessed at the Federal Records Center, National Archives, Perris, CA. Case files destroyed by archive in 2011.

86 "DGA Law Suits Attack Sex Discrimination," *Directors Guild of America News* 5, no. 3 (March 1981), 1, 5. For television production companies and their show titles also see Lee Grant, "Directors File Charges of Sex Discrimination," *Los Angeles Times*, February 25, 1981.

87 Gail Williams, "DGA Files Sex Discrimination Suit vs. Networks, Prod'n Co's," *Hollywood Reporter*, February 25, 1981.

88 Elaine Woo, "DGA Files Sex-Bias Grievances," *Los Angeles Herald Examiner*, February 25, 1981.

89 Grant, "Directors File Charges of Sex Discrimination."

90 Harmetz, "Suit to Allege Sex Bias by TV and Film Makers."

91 Declaration of Michael Franklin in Support of Motion for Class Certification, 8, DGA v. WB/CPI (C.D. Cal. Nov. 14, 1984), originally accessed at the Federal Records Center, National Archives, Perris, Calif. Case files destroyed by archive in 2011.

92 David Robb, "DGA Poised to Sue Industry over Alleged Discrimination against Femmes, Minorities," *Variety*, June 15, 1983.

93 Ray Loynd, "Threatened Suits Cue Production Firms to Begin DGA Minority Talks," *Variety*, May 31, 1983; David Robb, "DGA-Industry Minority Talks," *Variety*, June 10, 1983.

94 David Robb, "DGA & Columbia Lock Horns over Affirmative Action," *Variety*, November 9, 1983.

95 David Robb, "7 Majors and Larger Indies Agree to Talk with Directors over Femme, Minority Hiring," *Variety*, June 15, 1983.

96 David Robb, "DGA Will Sue WB over Minorities Talks Turndown," *Variety*, July 13, 1983.

97 David Robb, "Warner Bros. Says It'll Turn Tables in DGA Minorities Suit," *Variety*, September 30, 1983, 38.

98 Directors Guild of America, Inc. v. Warner Brothers, Inc. and Columbia Pictures Industries, Inc., CV 83-4764-PAR, CV 83-8311-PAR, 1985 U.S. Dist. LEXIS 16325; 2 Fed. R. Serv. 3d (Callaghan) 1429 (C.D. Cal. Aug. 30, 1985). Hereafter the case is referred to as DGA v. WB/CPI. Judge Rymer in her decision ruled on these cases together in one opinion; the press also began describing the suits as one case. *DGA v. WB/CPI* was a nonpublished case; therefore it has an unusual case citation. As an unpublished case the decision can be difficult to locate. It is accessible through the online catalog LexisNexis, which assigned the lawsuit this case citation: 1985 U.S. Dist. LEXIS 16325. It is also available in the *Federal Reporter*, a print source that lists the case title, date of decision, and outcome. Because of these two ways to locate information on this case it has a "parallel citation": both its LexisNexis and *Federal Reporter* locations.

99 Published decision for case DGA v. WB/CPI, 1. Hereafter "Decision." The page numbers cited from the Decision correspond to the pagination found in the document when accessed through LexiNexis, not from the original court document originally available at the National Archives in Perris, Calif.

100 Henry Schipper, "DGA Files Suit against Warners; Charges Race, Sex Discrimination" *Hollywood Reporter*, July 26, 1983.

101 David Robb, "DGA Sues Warner Bros.," *Variety*, July 26, 1983.

102 David Robb, "Col Pix Blames DGA for End to Minority Talks," *Variety*, November 9, 1983.

103 Henry Schipper, "Guild Points to Hiring Data as Discriminatory, Unlawful," *Hollywood Reporter*, November 9, 1983.

104 Michael London, "Film Clips," *Los Angeles Times*, December 23, 1983.

105 Shortly after her decision in the case on August 30, 1985, Judge Rymer was appointed by President Reagan to the Ninth Circuit Court of Appeals. Her nomination was initially rejected by the Democratically controlled Senate, and it was only in 1989 that she was renominated by President George H. W. Bush and subsequently approved as an appellate justice. Rymer died in 2011. Dennis McLellan, "Pamela Ann Rymer Dies at 70; Judge on U.S. 9th Circuit Court of Appeals," *Los*

*Angeles Times*, September 24, 2011, www.latimes.com/news/obituaries/la-me-pamela-rymer-20110924,0,702607.story.

106 For example, Hunt's legal work was instrumental in the integration of the fire and police departments in Los Angeles: police department suit, County of Los Angeles, v. Van Davis, 440 U.S. 625, (1979); fire department suit, Craig v. County of Los Angeles, 626 F.2d 659 (9th Cir. 1980). For a description of Hunt's legal work on antidiscrimination cases prior to the 1983 DGA lawsuits see A. Thomas Hunt, "Fit to Practice," *California Lawyer*, February 2005, 2.

107 For mention of Hunt's participation in the BA negotiations see Decision 11–12. Verification of Hunt's inability to participate in the Directors Guild's BA negotiations came from Chris Knowlton, who was a partner in the law firm of Taylor, Roth & Hunt and was involved in the DGA lawsuit. Chris Knowlton, interview by author, February 12, 2013.

108 Hunt, "Fit to Practice," 3.

109 Dobrow, Hochberg, and Littman, interviews by author.

110 David Robb, "DGA Hiring Suit against WB, Col Dealt a Setback," *Variety*, March 6, 1985, 1.

111 See the Decision.

112 David Robb, "Rule against DGA as Minority Rep in Class Action Suits," *Variety*, March 13, 1985, 2.

113 David Robb, "DGA Dropped from Hiring Suit," *Variety*, September 23, 1985, 1. Also see Decision for all of these points.

114 Robb, "DGA Hiring Suit against WB, Col Dealt a Setback"; "Fed. Judge Finds DGA Interest Clash," *Hollywood Reporter*, March 6, 1985; Judith Michaelson, "Key Decision Withheld in DGA Suit," *Los Angeles Times*, March 6, 1985; Robb, "Rule against DGA as Minority Rep in Class Action Suits"; Robb, "DGA Dropped from Hiring Suit."

115 For further details of DGA qualification lists see Section 14-200 Qualification Lists, Basic Agreement of 1981, 109–117.

116 Answer to Complaint and Counterclaim Against Plaintiff, 10–12, DGA v. WB/CPI, (C.D. Cal. Oct. 6, 1983), originally accessed at the Federal Records Center, National Archives, Perris, Calif. Case files destroyed by archive in 2011.

117 Decision, 9–10.

118 Judith Michelson, "Key Decision Withheld in DGA Suit," *Los Angeles Times*, March 6, 1985.

119 Knowlton, interview by author.

120 Steven S. Gensler, *Federal Rules of Civil Procedure, Rules and Commentary*, vol. 1 (Eagan, MN: Clark Boardman Callaghan, 2013), 429.

121 Decision, 2.

122 Decision, 4.

123 Decision, 4.

124 Decision, 4.

125 For example, an environmental class action settlement like the 2010 British

Petroleum Deepwater Horizon oil spill may claim that a specific act of negligence on the drilling rig caused the contamination of the Gulf shrimp population, which in turn damaged all the individuals in the Louisiana fishing industry. The famous Brown v. Board of Education, 347 U.S. 483 (1954) decision claimed that the state of Kansas denied the civil rights of all African American students who were required to go to specific schools determined by race. In each instance, there was an identifiable act that affected a specific group in a common way.

126 Decision, 5.

127 See Decision, 5, for discussion of "decentralized manner"; see Decision, 5–7, on Judge Rymer's summary of the defense's description of hiring process.

128 "Article 15: Section 15-101 Policy," Basic Agreement of 1981, 118.

129 Title VII of the Civil Rights Act of 1964 states that "it [is] illegal to discriminate against someone on the basis of race, color, religion, national origin, or sex." "Laws Enforced by EEOC," U.S. Equal Employment Opportunity Commission, accessed February 3, 2014, eeoc.gov.

130 "Article 15: Section 15-300 Reports," Basic Agreement of 1981, 118.

131 "Article 15: Section 15-200 Employment of Minorities and Women," Basic Agreement of 1981, 118.

132 Ray Loynd, "Directors, Majors on the Verge of Complete Contract Settlement," *Hollywood Reporter*, June 29, 1981, 1.

133 Memorandum of Decision and Order Denying Summary Judgment, 8, DGA v. WB/CPI, (C.D. Cal. Nov. 20, 1984), originally accessed at the Federal Records Center, National Archives, Perris, Calif. Case files destroyed by archive in 2011. This Memorandum does not specify which years the studio employment statistics were taken from. Cross-referenced against the following sources, the statistics indicated here represent different calculations made at various times between 1978 and 1983. See Schipper, "DGA Files Suit against Warners"; "Directors Guild Sues Columbia Charges Illegal Hiring Practices," *Variety*, December 28, 1983.

134 Decision, 8.

135 Decision, 7.

136 Decision, 7.

137 Although the commonality hurdle is often difficult for a class action suit to clear, up until the mid-1980s the courts did provide some flexibility to plaintiffs who resubmitted their cases with either a more focused cause of action or an individual lawsuit. Melissa Hart, "Will Employment Discrimination Cases Survive," *Akron Law Review*, 37 (2004). Today, as a result of the Supreme Court decision in the well-publicized Dukes v. Wal-Mart Stores, Inc., 131 S. Ct. 2541 (2011) case, it would be virtually impossible for a lawsuit involving an employer with a decentralized hiring system to receive class certification, the Court having effectively made an informal hiring system a complete barrier to a class action suit. Robert Barnes, "Supreme Court Blocks Massive Sex-Discrimination Suit against Wal-Mart," *Washington Post*, June 20, 2010.

138 Decision, 8.

139 Decision, 7–8.

140 In an ironic twist, before its Supreme Court victory (Dukes v. Wal-Mart Stores, Inc., 131 S. Ct. 2541 [2011]), Wal-Mart had lost its "commonality" argument before the Ninth Circuit Court of Appeals on a 6–5 vote; the deciding justice who agreed that the 1.6 million female workers at 3,500 Wal-Mart stores over a fifteen-year period *all* had a commonality of interests was Judge Pamela Ann Rymer. It would seem that the judicial philosophy of Judge Rymer, which was not inclined to find commonality in hiring in the film industry, was more inclined to find it in the discount department store market.

141 Decision, 8.

142 Defendants' Cross-Complaint at First Counterclaim, 10–13, DGA v. WB/CPI, (C.D. Cal. Oct. 6, 1984), originally accessed at the Federal Records Center, National Archives, Perris, Calif. Case files destroyed by archive in 2011.

143 Decision, 9.

144 Decision, 10.

145 Douglas Gomery establishes the nonpolitical position the DGA (originally the Screen Directors Guild) had taken since its inception by describing how, in 1936 when the Guild was first organized, the directors decided to not ally with the Screen Actors and Screen Writers' Guilds, both of which had been founded a few years earlier. "The decision was made that no such alliance should be formed. This decision was attributed to the fact that both of the other guilds had gained radical reputations, and the directors did not wish to commit themselves to such a stand. It is important to realize that the directors who formed the SDG were not interested in a revolution against the studio system." Gomery, *The Hollywood Studio System*, 191.

146 Harmetz, "Suit Allege Sex Bias by TV and Film Makers."

147 Arthur Hiller, "From the President," *DGA News*, December 1990–January 1991, 3.

148 "Diversity," dga.com, 2011–2017, accessed November 1, 2017, www.dga.org/The-Guild/Diversity.aspx. The DGA's statement on diversity has been updated over the years, presumably as a reflection of changes taking place in the industry and in the organization's membership in terms of employment trends and discourse regarding those trends.

149 Lyndon Stambler, "The Good Fight," Fall 2011, Directors Guild of America, accessed March 1, 2013, www.dga.org.

150 Joelle Dobrow, "Interview: The Man behind the Women's Movement at the Guild," 21.

151 *Behind the Scenes: Equal Employment Opportunity in the Motion Picture Industry* (Washington, D.C.: U.S. Government Printing Office, 1978), 36–38.

152 For information on Fanaka and his legal efforts see Jamaa Fanaka Papers, Performing Arts Special Collections, UCLA. For Jay Roth see Maria Giese, "After the Summit—Halfway There," *Women Directors: Navigating the Hollywood Boy's Club*, March 4, 2014, www.womendirectorsinhollywood.com/about/.

153 Martha M. Lauzen, *The Celluloid Ceiling: Behind-the Scenes Employment of Women*

*on the Top 100, 250, and 500 Films of 2017* (San Diego: Center for the Study of Women in Television and Film, San Diego State University, 2018).

154 Melissa Goodman and Ariela Migdal, American Civil Liberties Union, letter to Anna Y. Park and Rosa Viramontes, EEOC Los Angeles District Office, May 12, 2015, 9, 11. See also Cara Buckley, "A.C.L.U., Citing Bias against Women, Wants Inquiry into Hollywood's Hiring Practices," *New York Times*, May 12, 2015; Rebecca Keegan, "The Hollywood Gender Discrimination Investigation Is On: EEOC Contacts Women Directors," *Los Angeles Times*, October 2, 2015; Marian Evans, "Director Activist Maria Giese: Update on Women Directors, the ACLU & the Feds," *Medium*, January 11, 2017, https://medium.com/women-s-film-activists/director-activist-maria-giese-update-on-women-directors-the-aclu-the-feds-bdb6a8fcb115.

## Epilogue

1 Joel W. Finler, *The Hollywood Story* (New York: Crown Publishers, 1988), 280.

2 Mollie Gregory, *Women Who Run the Show* (New York: St. Martin's Press, 2002), 157. For a detailed discussion of the generation of female executives that emerged in the 1970s and their relationships to their male mentors, see Rachel Abramowitz, *Is That a Gun in Your Pocket? Women's Experience of Power in Hollywood* (New York: Random House, 2000).

3 Gregory, *Women Who Run the Show*, 157.

4 Mary Murphy and Cheryl Bensten, "Women in Hollywood: Part I, Fighting to Enter the 'White Male Club,'" *Los Angeles Times*, August 14, 1973.

5 Abramowitz, *Is That a Gun in Your Pocket?*, 93.

6 Nancy Hass, "Hollywood's New Old Girls' Network," *New York Times*, April 24, 2005, 13.

7 Sally Ogle Davis, "The Struggle of Women Directors," *New York Times*, January 11, 1981, 72.

8 Marilyn Beck, "Where Are the Women Filmmakers?," *Chicago Tribune*, March 2, 1980, K1.

9 For histories of U.S. commercial independent filmmaking that include a discussion of the 1980s see Jon Jost, "End of the Indies: Death of the Sayles Men," in *Contemporary American Independent Film: From the Margins to the Mainstream*, ed. Chris Holmlund and Justin Wyatt (London: Routledge, 2005), 53–58; Geoff King, *American Independent Cinema* (Bloomington: Indiana University Press, 2005); and John Pierson, *Spike Mike Slackers & Dykes* (New York: Miramax Books, 1995).

10 Dale Pollack, "The Life and Times of 'Fast Times,'" *Los Angeles Times*, August 15, 1982; "Box-Office Tallies—As of September 15," *The Film Journal*, October 8, 1982, 8.

11 James Spada, "Streisand's 15-Year Quest to Make 'Yentl,'" *Billboard*, December 10, 1983, BS8; "Box-Office Tallies—As of February 29," *The Film Journal*, April 1, 1984, 32.

12 Pierson, *Spike Mike Slackers & Dykes*, 17.

13 Richard Patterson, "An Interview with Susan Seidelman on the Making of Smithereens," *American Cinematographer*, May 1983, 68.

14 Janis Cole and Holly Dale, *Calling the Shots: Profiles of Women Filmmakers* (Kingston, ON: Quarry Press, 1993), 194.

15 Cole and Dale, *Calling the Shots*, 192.

16 For budget figures see Richard Miller, "Susan Seidelman Directs 'Desperately Seeking Susan,'" *Backstage*, November 30, 1984, 1. For film grosses, see "U.S. Box Office: June 30," *Screen International*, July 6, 1985, 30.

17 Julia Cameron, "Women in Film: It's 'Better'—It's Just Not Better Enough," *Chicago Tribune*, November 24, 1985, 8.

18 Pollack, "The Life and Times of 'Fast Times,'" 20, 22.

19 Annette Insdorf, "Women Film Directors Make a Strong Comeback," *New York Times*, April 24, 1988, 20.

20 Stephanie Rothman, interview by Jane Collings, UCLA Center for the Study of Oral History, January 29, 2002, 236.

21 Lee Grant, interview by Henry Colman for Archive of American Television, May 10, 2000, accessed March 11, 2014, emmytvlegends.org.

22 Estelle Changas, "'Easy' Author on Cutting Edge of Lib in Films," *Los Angeles Times*, May 12, 971, S1.

23 "Credit Sheet for Women in Film, TV," *Los Angeles Times*, November 7, 1971, H14.

24 "Erica 'Fear of Flying' Jong Sues a Filmmaker Friend for Stealing Her Steaming Tale," *People*, August 11, 1975, 12–13; "Filmmaker Phillips Talks to NATO in New Orleans," *Boxoffice*, October 13, 1975; Doug Mirell, "Defense Responds to Jong Litigation," *Hollywood Reporter*, July 11, 1975, 1, 12.

25 Phillips, who coproduced *Taxi Driver* (1976) and *Close Encounters of the Third Kind* (1977), discusses these factors in her autobiography, particularly the way in which she felt out of place as a successful (i.e., aggressive) woman producer in 1970s Hollywood. Julia Phillips, *You'll Never Eat Lunch in This Town Again* (New York: Signet, 1992).

26 Gregg Kilday, "Film Clips: Dyan Cannon's Shooting Star," *Los Angeles Times*, November 16, 1977, G19.

27 Kilday, "Film Clips: Dyan Cannon's Shooting Star."

28 Diane Keaton, *Then Again* (New York: Random House, 2011), 132.

29 Keaton, *Then Again*, 133.

30 Keaton, *Then Again*, 134.

31 Tara Veneruso, filmmaker and advocate based in Los Angeles, and Katie Lanegran, publicist for the Sundance Channel in New York, oversaw the initial efforts with the "Features Directed by Women" newsletter beginning in 2000. Eventually, the First Weekenders Group, specifically for women filmmakers, was established as a website and run by Veneruso for several years.

32 Maureen Dowd, "The Women of Hollywood Speak Out," *Sunday New York Times Magazine*, November 20, 2015, MM40.

33 "Film Fatales Press Notes," www.filmfatales.org, accessed October 1, 2017, www

.dropbox.com/sh/h51wmha7vdbm751/AAACSDejmg49wJORD7sSnDQRa?dl=0&preview=2017FilmFatalesPressNotes.pdf.

34 Linda Gross, "Karen Arthur Dares to Do It All," *Los Angeles Times*, April 16, 978, 59.

35 Joan Rivers and Richard Meryman, *Still Talking* (New York: Random House, 1991), 108.

36 Beth Ann Krier, "Maya Angelou: No Longer a 'Caged Bird,'" *Los Angeles Times*, September 24, 1976.

37 Joan Micklin Silver, interview at the American Film Institute, October 23, 1991, Harold Lloyd Master Seminars, Louis B. Mayer Library, Los Angeles.

# INDEX

## ABOUT THE AUTHOR

MAYA MONTAÑEZ SMUKLER heads the research and study center at the UCLA Film & Television Archive and is a part-time associate teaching professor in the School of Media Studies at the New School.